THE RULES OF THE GAME

Kenneth W. Dam

THE
RULES
OF THE
GAME

Reform and Evolution in the International Monetary System

THE UNIVERSITY OF CHICAGO PRESS
CHICAGO & LONDON

The University of Chicago Press, Chicago 60637
The University of Chicago Press, Ltd., London

© 1982 by The University of Chicago
All rights reserved. Published 1982
Paperback edition 1983
Printed in the United States of America
90 89 88 87 86 85 84 83   2 3 4 5 6

Library of Congress Cataloging in Publication Data

Dam, Kenneth W.
The rules of the game.

"Joseph Gold, a select bibliography": p.
Bibliography: p.
Includes index.
I. International finance.   I. Title.
HG3881.D326   332'.042   81-10416
ISBN 0-226-13499-7 (cloth)   AACR2
0-226-13500-4 (paper)

"Experience is the name we give to past mistakes,
reform that which we give to future ones."

Henry C. Wallich,
"The Monetary Crisis of 1971—The Lessons to be Learned"
(Per Jacobsson Lecture, 1972).

CONTENTS

FIVE

The International Monetary Fund as a Legal Institution

SIX

The Collapse of Bretton Woods and Its Legal Aftermath

TABLES

PREFACE

Although this book addresses the lively and urgent issue of the proper design of the international monetary system, it reflects a long-standing interest in the intersection of two academic disciplines, law and economics, and in the accommodation of two fields of practical endeavor, law and diplomacy. In neither economic affairs nor diplomacy would law seem a priori to have much of a role to play. When they are combined, the role for law becomes even smaller. Yet if understood not as a sovereign statement of the legal and the illegal but rather as a set of substantive and procedural rules influencing behavior and embodying understandings of the moment, law turns out to be of central importance. The subject is, then, the role of these rules in international monetary affairs.

In this book I have continued an inquiry that I commenced in the allied field of international trade in a book that appeared just over a decade ago, *The GATT: Law and International Economic Organization*. A decade is a long time, and in that period my perspective has changed radically. In *The GATT* the perspective was prescriptive. I sought there a set of international rules that would lead naturally, if not ineluctably, toward a goal of freer trade.

Since *The GATT* was written, I have changed and so has the trend of events. Practical experience in the U.S. decision-making process, especially in the arena of international affairs, has convinced me that scholarship has little to offer by way of direct advice to those who would restructure the international economic system. The value of scholarly research to the policymaker lies rather in providing a perspective against which contemporary events can be understood and the likely consequences of particular policy initiatives assessed. In any case, the 1970s has been a time of lowered horizons in international economic affairs as much as in U.S. domestic affairs. In trade, it is a close question whether liberal or protectionist influences had the edge in the 1970s. And in money, the only assessment that gains widespread acceptance is that the current international monetary system is the worst conceivable with the possible exception of the one that preceded it.

The perspective that I have adopted in this book is therefore historical and detached. It is historical because the most interesting and perhaps even the most important question is how the international monetary system changes and adapts to underlying conditions. Change has been the order of the day. Even the international gold standard, as a universal institution, lasted only a few decades. And the 1970s was a period of constant, sometimes headlong, change.

The contrast between evolution, in the sense of unplanned change, and reform, in the sense of consciously planned change, provides a useful theme for much of the discussion. The well-informed reader will note that I use the term "evolution" somewhat differently from the way in which it is used in current International Monetary Fund discussions. Today all officials are evolutionists and readily declare their opposition to reform. But by reform they mean comprehensive reform of the entire monetary system. Hence, in the Fund's corridors it is common to describe, for example, plans for adopting new international rules changing the attributes of the Special Drawing Rights as a step in the evolution of the system. As used in this book such conscious and deliberate attempts to alter the system by the adoption of new rules are the very essence of reform.

The perspective in this book, unlike *The GATT*, is detached, in part because there is no goal in monetary affairs that commands the intellectual and official assent that freer trade commands even today. To be sure, nearly everyone agrees that national monetary measures, such as exchange restrictions, can be as significant in distorting the allocation of world resources as tariffs and quotas, and therefore warrant international efforts to regulate them. But when one turns to the more central issues of the exchange rate and reserve asset regimes, one is more likely to find agreement on means than on ends. Even the notion that the international monetary system should be neutral with respect to its impact on domestic economic policy, a proposition that has a considerable intellectual appeal and that dominated U.S. official thinking during the early 1970s, is not widely accepted in central banking circles. Moreover, neutrality as a goal is losing support in the United States as outside constraints on domestic economic policymaking are sought to limit the inflationary biases found in almost every country.[1] Therein lie the roots of the current nostalgia for the gold standard as well as the much more practical striving toward fixed rates among central bankers and many European statesmen. A detached, nonprescriptive perspective therefore affords a better understanding of how, for example, the alternate striving for autonomy and for external constraint in domestic economic policymaking shapes the international monetary system.

A word about the audience I envision for this book may be helpful to readers. On the one hand, I have sought to write about law in a way that will make it understandable to those readers whose primary interests lie in economic and political fields. On the other hand, I have also sought to write for lawyers who shy away from international monetary matters under the impression that the economics is too difficult or the institutions too mysterious to be approachable by lawyers. In short, this book will, I hope, expose to general view—for lawyers, economists, political scientists, and governmental officials alike—the legal foundations of the international monetary system as it has evolved from the gold standard period before World War I to the present day and will do so in a way that emphasizes the interrelationship of legal, economic, and political factors.

I should like to acknowledge a large number of debts. Perhaps the main one is to the ambiance at the University of Chicago. It led me to undertake a book that does not fit within any single discipline and that cannot be said to contribute to any narrowly defined body of existing scholarly literature. Although I have been a professional lawyer teaching in a law school, I very quickly became acquainted, not just by reading their works but also through personal conversation, with the thinking on international monetary affairs of my economist colleagues Milton Friedman and Harry Johnson, whose intellectual influence in converting world opinion on international monetary policy has been profound. In the Law School I have had the benefit of working within the Law and Economics group, a subset of the Law School faculty composed of both lawyers and economists who are devoted to bridging the gap that separates the two disciplines. The ideas in this book have been gradually developed over more than a decade and one-half of teaching law students a course most recently entitled International Economic Institutions. Surely students in most law schools would have found the course a hopeless hybrid that was neither law nor for that matter economics. But at the Uni-

---

1. On the changing attitudes on the role of the international monetary system vis-à-vis domestic economic policy, see Paul A. Volcker, "The Political Economy of the Dollar," *Federal Reserve Bank of New York Quarterly Review* 3 (Winter 1978–79): 1–12. See also Ralph C. Bryant, *Money and Monetary Policy in Interdependent Nations* (1980), 470–81.

versity of Chicago future lawyers somehow became almost overnight pas-
sionate and accomplished advocates for and against each successive wave of
international monetary proposals that absorbed the attention of contemporary
finance ministry, central bank, and International Monetary Fund officials.

Another debt is to a group of U.S. government officials with whom I
worked during the 1971–74 period, especially on the U.S. proposals to the
Committee of Twenty. It is an interesting comment on the intellectual vitality
of that group that they have continued to write and speak on international
monetary matters since leaving government. Of that number, who were led
by such major figures as George Shultz, Arthur Burns, and Paul Volcker
(the last of whom has of course returned to the forefront of international
monetary events as Chairman of the Federal Reserve Board), I recall particularly the analytical abilities and insights of Jack Bennett, Ralph Bryant,
Richard Erb, Arthur Laffer, J. Carter Murphy, Robert Solomon, and Marina
Whitman.

A particular word must be said about George Shultz, a former University
of Chicago colleague for whom I worked in the U.S. government and who
helped me immeasurably in understanding the international monetary events
of the early 1970s as we later reviewed, meeting by meeting and conference
by conference, the U.S. role in the swift succession of events from the
collapse of the Bretton Woods system to the demise of the Committee of
Twenty. The object of that review was the writing of the international
monetary chapter of our book *Economic Policy Beyond the Headlines*, but traces
of our joint work are also to be found in these pages. I should, of course,
warn the reader that my own experiences during the 1971–74 period account
not only for some of the necessarily undocumented statements I have made
about U.S. policy but also for certain biases in attitudes expressed toward
the issues of that period.

I have had the benefit of discussions with a number of Fund, U.S., and
British government officials. Since active officials have a right to anonymity
in return for discussing sensitive current issues, I shall mention only two—
Joseph Gold and Jacques Polak—who have recently retired from full-time
service with the Fund but whose unparalleled experience from the early
Bretton Woods period to the present made their assistance particularly valuable.

A note is warranted about the special contributions of Joseph Gold, the
Fund's former General Counsel, to the literature on the International Monetary Fund. His comprehensive writings on the meaning of the Articles of
Agreement, and on their interpretation by the various organs of the Fund,
not only have been invaluable to me but have relieved me of any need,
perhaps I should say any temptation, to provide a legal treatise on the law
of the Fund. More important, his writings provide for the outsider an in-

dispensable substitute for access to internal Fund documents. From my own experience when I did have access to Fund documents I realize that published documents often cannot be properly understood without access to prior drafts, to proposals and comments by national governments, and to memoranda by the Fund's legal and research departments. Gold's writings often extract the essence of these sources without betraying the spirit of confidentiality among participants that the Fund's niggardly publication policy seeks to protect.[2] At the same time his writings have over the years become so extensive and in some instances have come to cover the same ground from so many points of view that it may be useful to the reader to have at least a partial guide to the Gold writings. I have attempted to provide one, admittedly sketchy and imperfect, by setting forth a select list of those writings (see p. 362), and by referring to Gold's always authoritative and helpful published works when I have found them particularly striking in formulation or penetrating in insight.

Two British journalists with a scholarly interest in the history of money, Samuel Brittan and William Rees-Mogg, were generous with their time and knowledge. The value of conversations with Edward Bernstein, one of the architects of Bretton Woods and a highly informed commentator on the current scene, can only be fully appreciated by those who know this extraordinary economist and public servant. I have had the benefit of access to a comprehensive book-length, as yet unpublished, manuscript by Richard W. Edwards, Jr., dealing with the current law of the International Monetary Fund. Robert Aliber gave indispensable advice on historical sources and read a large portion of the manuscript. Samuel Brittan commented on several chapters.

Successive deans of the University of Chicago Law School, particularly the incumbent Gerhard Casper, made generous, even extravagant, concessions in adjusting my teaching duties to the demands of my research. The Law School library staff cheerfully met my unreasonable requests, especially for obscure and dated documents. The Law School's Law and Economics Program provided financial support. Without the research and editorial assistance of Barbara Donagan, a professional seventeenth-century British historian who admirably adapted her considerable talents to the twentieth century and to law and economics as well, I could not possibly have at-

---

2. In part, the gap created by the Fund's publication policy has also been filled by the official Fund history. See J. Keith Horsefield et al., *The International Monetary Fund, 1945–1965: Twenty Years of International Monetary Cooperation*, 3 vols. (1969), and Margaret Garritsen de Vries, *The International Monetary Fund, 1966–1971: The System under Stress*, 2 vols. (1976). But for outside scholars the Fund history is too little in the sense that most of the life has been drained from the disputes it chronicles, and too late in the sense that the most recent events described took place in December 1971, which in view of the tumultuous change of the 1970s must seem like the dawn of the modern era to most contemporary students of international monetary problems.

tempted, much less completed, this book. Glynis Gore researched various points, and Ralph Strohl typed all too many drafts of early chapters. Gayle McKeen ably turned her hand to research, typing, and preparation of the index.

University of Chicago
January 1981

ABBREVIATIONS

BIS   Bank for International Settlements
CRU   Collective Reserve Unit
C-20   Committee of Twenty
ECU   European Currency Unit
EEC   European Economic Community
EMCF   European Monetary Cooperation Fund
EMS   European Monetary System
EPU   European Payments Union
GAB   General Arrangements to Borrow
GATT   General Agreement on Tariffs and Trade
G-10   Group of Ten
IBRD   International Bank for Reconstruction and Development
IMF   International Monetary Fund
ITO   International Trade Organization
LDC   Less-developed country
LIBOR   London Inter-bank Offer Rate
MCI   Multi-currency intervention
OECD   Organization for Economic Cooperation and Development
OEEC   Organization for European Economic Cooperation
OPEC   Organization of Petroleum Exporting Countries
SDR   Special Drawing Right

ONE

The Role of Rules in the International Monetary System

The "rules of the game" was a phrase widely used in the 1920s to describe the workings of the pre-1914 international gold standard.[1] The notion was that the gold standard worked because there were certain rules and they were observed. Those who used the phrase, we now know, were mistaken about the nature of the rules that governed the gold standard.[2] But the concept of a set of rules, channeling the behavior of nations and their monetary authorities, is applicable not just to the pre–World War I gold standard but also to each of the distinct international monetary regimes that succeeded it. Beginning with the gold standard and ending with the present regime, which is sometimes deroga-

1. The phrase has been attributed to Keynes. Arthur I. Bloomfield, *Monetary Policy under the International Gold Standard, 1880–1914* (1959), p. 47. I find no evidence that Keynes originated the phrase.
2. See generally discussion pp. 14–19.

torily termed a "non-system,"[3] I shall attempt to answer a set of questions designed to expose to general view the dynamics of change in the international monetary system: What were the rules, what was their origin, and how well did they work?

Two more questions can be answered about earlier regimes but can only produce speculation, however informed, about the present regime: Why were the rules in the end changed, and how did the change occur? For the present system, the fundamental question is, in short, what kind of rule changes one can expect in the 1980s. It would be ridiculous to attempt to answer with any precision. But by analyzing the process of change in the past and the tensions in the present set of rules, one can at least postulate the options for change.

I. REFORM AND EVOLUTION

The distinction between reform and evolution provides an organizing principle in discussion of change. Reform, as used here, means intended, planned change. The Bretton Woods agreement of 1944 is one example. The creation of the Special Drawing Right (SDR) in the late 1960s is another.

Still other examples are of a somewhat different character. Efforts to nudge the existing system along a particular path by small planned changes in highly technical rules are an increasingly common type of reform. The present effort within the International Monetary Fund (IMF) to enhance the attributes of the SDR and thereby to make it the principal reserve asset is analytically a reform movement. But it is being promoted as a step in the evolution of the system because the notion of reform received bad marks in IMF circles as the result of the collapse of an effort in the first half of the 1970s at far-reaching, comprehensive reform under the auspices of the Committee of Twenty.[4] As in all other forms of politics, labels like reform and evolution have symbolic uses in international monetary affairs. But for analytical purposes it is preferable to reserve the term "evolution" to describe changes that occur as the result of external events or through the natural dynamics of the system. In any case, the contemporary tendency to describe all change as evolutionary corrupts the language because it leaves no scope for the contrasting notion of reform. Even with the relatively broad definition given here to reform, evolutionary change has been the more frequent, certainly up to the time of the Bretton Woods agreement and by any reasonable reckoning even thereafter.

That evolutionary change is unplanned does not mean that rules have no role in such change. Rules are needed to provide a foundation for any international monetary regime. Analogies to domestic law may help to clarify

3. John Williamson, *The Failure of World Monetary Reform, 1971–74* (1977), p. xiii.
4. See discussion pp. 216–21.

this point. The institution of private property was not planned by any governmental authority. Yet the efficiency and stability of this central institution depend upon complex, often arcane legal rules. Similarly, contracts were made and enforced before the full apparatus of contract law was brought to bear. But the rules of contract law developed hand in hand with the evolution of more complex forms of commercial contracts, supporting the development of new kinds of contracts and providing the certainty necessary to their increased use.

A similar process may be observed in the evolution from the gold standard to the gold exchange standard, as national statutes and regulations changed, not so much to create the new system as to cement it. After the Bretton Woods system collapsed in 1971, a number of changes in the rules adopted by the IMF were necessary simply to take account of the system of generalized floating that came into being in 1973. And in the 1980s one may safely assume that even if the system evolves into one based on multiple reserve currencies, many rule changes will be necessary to accommodate such a new system and to render it stable and workable. This use of rules to underpin change that is a response to external stimuli or that is the natural result of forces within the international monetary system will be an important theme in this book.

II. Types of Rules

The rules with which this book is concerned are of many kinds. Today nearly all of the key rules are international in character, though the rapid growth in international commercial banking, especially in offshore (Eurocurrency) markets, is bringing national rules back toward a central position as the responsibility for regulation of those markets devolves on national authorities. In earlier periods the international monetary system derived its structure from national rules, largely but not exclusively statutes. International rules today arise largely out of international organizations. The key organization is the International Monetary Fund. The Articles of Agreement, which are the Fund's charter, contain the more basic rules. The organs of the Fund, notably the Executive Board, take a variety of decisions that enunciate more specific rules.

Not all of the rules, even today, derive from the charter of an international organization. Consider, for example, the European Monetary System, one of the most important new elements in the international monetary system. Although formally it arose out of decisions of organs of the European Economic Community, it was from a political perspective a new international agreement reached at the highest level of its participant governments.

Even where new rules are attributable to international organizations, traditional legal categories provide a convenient framework for analysis. For example, the legal distinction between interpretation of general rules and creation of new rules by legislation has considerable utility in discussion of the way in which specific rules change. In chapter 5 this distinction, coupled with the legal concept of jurisdiction (dealing with who is entitled to interpret or legislate), is used to analyze the changes that occurred within the Bretton Woods system.

Substance and Procedure

Another distinction fundamental to the law is that between substantive and procedural rules. Substantive rules are those prohibiting or commanding particular behavior. The focus of economists studying the international monetary system has been almost exclusively on substantive rules and indeed on only a few key rules concerning the exchange rate regime (fixed versus floating exchange rates) and reserve assets (the relative role of gold and reserve currencies). These are, to be sure, among the most important substantive issues, but rules encompass a much wider set of issues. For example, the rules governing contributions to, and access to, IMF resources bear a direct analogy to a wide variety of rules in domestic corporate and commercial law.

Procedural rules play a particularly important and little appreciated role in the international monetary system. That is not merely because of the absence of a sovereign capable of coercing compliance with substantive rules. In domestic legal systems where coercion is available and regularly applied, legal procedures play a significant role (many lawyers would argue a dominant one) in preserving the system and in determining substantive outcomes. But procedures necessarily bulk large in the decentralized international arena where compliance must in the end rest on consent. In such circumstances the question *who* decides is often more important than *what* is decided. Moreover, the procedural technique of mandating consultation before unilateral action is taken, while leaving the nature of that action completely discretionary, looms much larger in international than in domestic legal systems. Consent to substantive international monetary rules is more likely to be forthcoming when consultation affords a fuller understanding of long-term costs and benefits and of mutual interdependencies among affected nations. Both substantive and procedural rules therefore warrant detailed study in an effort to understand the international monetary system.

Rules and Law

Lying just beneath the surface of this brief discussion of substantive and procedural rules is an issue that has bedeviled most discussions of law in international affairs. As often posed, that issue is whether international law is law. The literature on that issue is voluminous, and this is not the place to confront it.[5] However, for the present study, where the concern is for the interaction between the international monetary system in practice and the rules that embody and support it, the question whether those rules constitute "law" is barren and uninteresting. Suffice it to say that substantive and procedural international monetary rules have been observed a very large portion of the time (something that cannot be said for all rules of domestic law).

Instances in which the rules are not observed are, moreover, of particular interest in this study. Attention to systematic departures from formal rules provides a better understanding of the true nature of a particular international monetary regime (and thus, for example, helps to differentiate the gold standard as it actually worked from the idealized gold standard as handed down to us in economic textbooks).[6] Moreover, the transition from one international monetary regime to a new one occurs when the accumulation of such departures forces the international community to recognize that the system itself has changed.[7] And then a flurry of rule changes is likely to follow. That was what happened, as will be described at length in later chapters, when the Bretton Woods system collapsed in the early 1970s.

Some would argue that the system that followed Bretton Woods is a ruleless system. If one looks at the situation through the wrong end of the telescope, one can of course see the logic of that position. Certainly it is not possible to describe the current system by reference to a few simple propositions as one might have done, though at the risk of fatuous oversimplification, with the pre-1914 gold standard or the Bretton Woods system. The freedom of choice open to individual countries with respect to exchange rate practices and reserve holdings has been too great to allow such summary description. Yet it is striking how increasingly voluminous and complex the rules on the books have become.

Rules and Events

The multiple increase in rules at the end of World War II stemmed, of course, from the formation of an international organization, the International Monetary Fund. A cynic can say that the further increase in rules in the 1970s reflects the need for the employees of such an organization to justify their existence, especially as the organization loses relevance to the contemporary world. Yet, as will be seen when that period is discussed, the explanation is much more complex.

5. Readers not familiar with the literature may find illuminating the discussion, and the references, in Gidon Gottlieb, "The Nature of International Law: Toward a Second Concept of Law," in *The Future of the International Legal Order*, ed. Cyril E. Black and Richard A. Falk (1972), vol. 4, *The Structure of the International Environment*, pp. 331–83.
6. See discussion pp. 17–19.
7. The parallel to the process by which scientific paradigms change is striking. Thomas S. Kuhn, *The Structure of Scientific Revolutions* (1962), chap. 8, "The Response to Crisis," pp. 77–90.

Anyone concerned with the meaning and function of rules is necessarily led, in trying to explain their proliferation, to focus less on the conventional question of the influence of rules on events and more on that of how events determine the nature and scope of rules. The rules become, in such an inquiry, the dependent variable. Rules and events have been in an eternal struggle in the international monetary system, and events have been in the long run more powerful. It was the force of events that led to the abandonment of the gold standard at the beginning of World War I, to the dissolution of the gold exchange standard when Britain ceased gold payments in 1931, and to the collapse of the Bretton Woods system when the United States "closed the gold window" in 1971. The rules were changed, not because it was thought that the new rules were superior, but because the old rules no longer corresponded to monetary reality. As Giscard d'Estaing commented at the time of the breakdown of the par value system: "We are not living in a world of constitutions now, but in a world of events, so what will matter is what happens, not what is written."[8] One need not take as nihilistic a view of the role of rules as Giscard did at that crucial turning point in monetary history to appreciate the mutual dependence of rules and events.

III. INTERNATIONAL MONETARY SYSTEMS

The organization of this book is historical. In keeping with the conventions of the subject, four distinct periods are postulated. These four periods correspond roughly to four different international monetary systems. The first period, whose beginning can be disputed but which ended suddenly and unexpectedly with the beginning of the First World War, demarcates the life of the international gold standard. The second period covers the twenty-odd years between the two wars and can be thought of in connection with the gold exchange standard, though that system actually operated only from roughly 1925 to 1931. The third period, following World War II, spans the quarter century in which the Bretton Woods system was in effect. Thereafter, the years beginning not later than 1973 are usually characterized as a floating exchange rate period. And this book ends with the possibility that a transition may soon begin to a fifth period, centered either on the SDR or on multiple reserve currencies, depending upon the relative emphasis on reform and evolution that the 1980s bring. (A reader need not be particularly perceptive to detect the author's personal belief that evolutionary forces will drive the system further toward a multiple reserve currency system; predicting the future is not, however, one of the objectives of this study.)

As in all attempts to divide the seamless web of history into tractable bits, this division of international monetary history into periods may obscure as

8. Quoted in Joseph Gold, "Symmetry as a Legal Objective of the International Monetary System," *New York University Journal of International Law and Politics* 12(1980):475.

much as it reveals. To take but one instance, the Bretton Woods story that I shall tell is more concerned with the profound changes that occurred within that system in the 1946–71 period than with the continuities that allow it to be considered a distinct period.

Even more problematic is the notion that there were distinct systems corresponding to those periods. Take, for example, the gold exchange standard. Not only did monetary statesmen devote the first half of the decade of the 1920s to trying to create that system and most of the 1930s to picking up the pieces after its 1931 collapse, but the element in the gold exchange standard that distinguishes it from the gold standard—namely, the holding of foreign exchange in national reserves—was nearly as prominent a feature of the years leading down to the First World War as in the years immediately before Britain's 1931 cessation of gold payments. And the Bretton Woods system was based on what one can also call a gold exchange standard.

These objections to the narrative device of historical periods and to the organizational technique of classifying do not, however, outweigh their convenience. Again, since the emphasis here is on change within periods and from one period to another, rather than on continuity within periods, the reader would be well advised to regard the division into periods as merely an organizing device. So too the classification of different systems should be treated merely as points of reference. Indeed, much of the interest of a review of international monetary history is precisely in seeing how little the rules and events of the past correspond to the conventional stereotypes that underlie much contemporary analysis of current international monetary problems.

This study need not have been organized historically. It could have been organized around different kinds of rules. For example, different exchange rate regimes could have been analyzed in one chapter, different reserve asset arrangements in another and so forth. That approach would have had the advantage of providing the reader who is unfamiliar with the international monetary concepts a more structured presentation of the central issues. For such a reader a short explanation, largely confined to clarifying the mystifying terminology of the field, is provided in the remainder of this chapter. Other readers—for example those who already have a grasp of the current debate about fixed and floating exchange rates, reserve currencies and the like—will want to move directly to chapter 2.

IV. EXCHANGE RATE REGIMES

Perhaps the issue of greatest interest to academic economists has been whether a fixed or a floating exchange rate regime is superior. That issue is not addressed here. But it is worth noting that neither of the two regimes has been adhered to by all countries in any pure form. Even in the present floating world many currencies are pegged on other currencies. During the

Bretton Woods period, often thought of as a period of fixed rates, exchange rates were pegged only until such time as the peg was adjusted, and such adjustments became increasingly frequent in the final years. Perhaps the leading example of truly fixed rates is found in the gold standard period. But it appears to be one of the dark secrets concealed by history as taught in American schools that the United States was on floating exchange rates from 1862 to 1879.[9]

The term "fixed rates" is sometimes misunderstood by those unfamiliar with the foreign exchange market. All exchange rates are determined in the marketplace, between willing buyers and sellers (though sometimes national foreign exchange controls preclude some people from buying and force other people to sell). But under a fixed rate regime, national monetary authorities enter the market either on the buying or the selling side to assure that the market rate bears a close relationship to an officially specified rate. This latter rate is often referred to as the official rate, and the effect of such exchange market *intervention* is to peg the market rate to the official rate. If there is no obligation to intervene, exchange rates are said to float, and the system is said to be a floating (or fluctuating) rate system.

A key issue in the design of rules for a fixed rate system involves the degree of permissible fluctuation of market rates around the official rate. One issue is how far the market rate may diverge before intervention by the national monetary authorities becomes mandatory. If the *margins* around the official rate are very wide, then the distinction between fixed and floating rates tends to dissolve. Indeed, an issue analogous to the width of margins exists in a floating rate system. In the 1970s it was common for national monetary authorities to intervene to prevent the market rate from diverging too far from what those authorities had in mind as an appropriate rate. The extent of intervention in a floating system could be the subject of bilateral or multilateral agreement, or it could be left to unilateral decision. If such *managed floating* results in such extensive intervention that the market rate remains steady, then the distinction between fixed and floating rates again tends to dissolve.

Rules about intervention distinguish between mandatory and permissible intervention. The Bretton Woods rules were more concerned with specifying when national authorities must intervene in order to limit the divergence from the official rate. But more recently there has been some interest in limiting intervention that prevents the market rate from approaching an equilibrium rate. Because an exchange rate is the price at which one currency sells in terms of another and is therefore necessarily also the price at which the latter sells in terms of the former, it becomes important to specify which country has the obligation to intervene. In most periods the country with

9. See discussion pp. 22–23.

the weak currency (which normally is weak because the country is running a balance of payments deficit) had the obligation to intervene or otherwise to *adjust* (say by internal economic measures designed to stem the deficit) to prevent the market rate from diverging too far from the official rate. More recently, the thought has gained ground that this *asymmetry* between deficit and creditor countries should be rectified by imposing some of the *burden of adjustment* on the creditor country.

V. RESERVE ASSETS

If the weak currency country intervenes, it normally does so by purchasing its own currency in the foreign exchange markets. To do so, it must sell foreign exchange—that is, it must sell a foreign currency. To be able to intervene, monetary authorities therefore maintain *reserves*. Or they may borrow reserves, either from other countries, from commercial banks or, since World War II, from the International Monetary Fund.

Reserves may be held in several forms. The two most common forms are foreign exchange and gold. Though intervention could take the form of selling gold in return for domestic currency, it is more likely to be sold to obtain foreign exchange, which is in turn sold to buy the local currency. In recent decades countries that keep a substantial part of their reserves in gold have tended to keep the gold at the bottom of the "reserve barrel" and not use it at all except in dire emergency. Foreign exchange has one major advantage over gold. Since foreign exchange reserves can be and normally are held in the form of interest-bearing deposits or other short-term obligations, foreign exchange reserves, unlike gold, bear interest.

Foreign exchange reserves have normally been held in only a few currencies. A currency widely held by monetary authorities is called a *reserve currency*. Since reserve currencies are normally held for intervention purposes, the reserve currency is likely to be the one whose markets have the greatest liquidity. A reserve currency is therefore likely also to be an *intervention currency*. For several decades the U.S. dollar has been the principal reserve currency, but the German mark and Japanese yen are increasingly widely held and are often referred to as secondary reserve currencies. If this trend continues, as is widely predicted, the system will become a *multiple* reserve currency system.

The history of international monetary systems is therefore in part a matter of the shifting mix of *reserve assets*. Under the gold standard, gold was in principle the prime reserve asset, though even at the peak of the gold standard many governments held deposits in London, or in some cases in continental centers such as Paris and Berlin. These foreign exchange holdings became less the exception and more the rule under the gold exchange standard in the 1920s. After the Second World War, the dollar became the principal reserve asset, though sterling was also widely held for several decades, particularly by members of the British Commonwealth and by former British colonies. The dollar was also the principal intervention currency and, because most international transactions were denominated in dollars, the principal *transactions* currency as well. New types of reserve assets were created later in the Bretton Woods period, including certain kinds of claims on the International Monetary Fund and, in a remarkable development, the Special Drawing Right. As the 1970s proceeded, the dollar—though clearly remaining the principal reserve currency—became less dominant as the German mark and Japanese yen grew in importance.

In the 1960s, concern arose that countries might, in a period of payments imbalances, pursue unnecessarily deflationary policies or impose trade restrictions, because they did not have large enough reserves to surmount what might be purely transient balance-of-payments difficulties. To the extent that a shortage of reserves was a widespread condition, it became common to speak of a shortage of *liquidity*. The International Monetary Fund had been created to provide liquidity to particular countries (in the form of drawings on the Fund) to meet such short-term difficulties, and indeed certain claims on the Fund became unconditional sources of liquidity. But a major reform in the late 1960s was designed to generate liquidity for the international monetary system as a whole through the creation of a new reserve asset, the first truly manmade asset, the Special Drawing Right.

The fear of a shortage of liquidity, so large a part of the history of the 1960s, vanished in the 1970s as a vast growth in dollar holdings coupled with a massive expansion of international commercial bank lending generated a surfeit of liquidity and as inflation became the principal fear. Only following the 1973–74 and the 1979 rounds of international crude oil price increases did the fear of a shortage of liquidity revive, but the rhetoric took a new form, with most attention given to the size of the oil-exporting countries' payments surpluses and to the plight of oil-importing less-developed countries.

During the two periods when a gold exchange standard was fully in effect, that is in the 1925–31 period and again in the Bretton Woods period, a *confidence problem* arose from time to time. The principal weakness of a gold exchange standard was that countries holding reserves in foreign exchange might lose confidence in the future value of the principal reserve currency and decide to convert holdings of that currency into gold. This confidence problem would be exacerbated if the principal reserve currency country was seen as having inadequate gold to meet its external liabilities. Here a fundamental asymmetry in a gold exchange system may be perceived. Unlike other countries, the reserve currency country could finance, or as is sometimes said "settle," its balance-of-payments deficit by expanding its liabilities denominated in its own currency; other countries, in contrast, had to settle in assets—that is, in gold or reserve currencies.

During the 1925–31 period and again during the Bretton Woods period the principal reserve currency country (Britain and the United States, respectively) was able, for a time, to meet the confidence problem by prudent domestic economic policies and by standing ready to convert its currency into gold at a previously fixed price upon the request of foreign official institutions. But once a growth in size of external liabilities threw in doubt its ability to make such conversions, the confidence problem became acute, easily worsened by any payments deficit of the reserve center. When the reserve center decided that it was no longer able to continue conversions, the gold exchange standard came to an end. That occurred in 1931 when Britain "went off gold," and in 1971 when the United States "closed the gold window."

Any gold exchange system confronts an allied confidence problem when there is more than one reserve currency. The ability of countries to switch their reserve holdings from one currency to another is a source of instability for the system and places a special burden on the domestic economic policies of the reserve countries. Inflationary policies in one reserve country are likely to produce a loss of confidence leading to massive switches from one reserve currency to another.

In the late 1970s the attempt by foreign holders of the U.S. dollar to switch to the increasingly popular German mark and Japanese yen was often called *diversification*. Whatever the appellation, such switching is likely to become a major problem if the current international monetary system should evolve into a multiple reserve currency system. Indeed, the process of reserve switching from a smaller reserve currency, like the mark or the yen, into the dollar could produce even greater difficulties if only because a flow of a given amount bulks larger in a smaller economy. Coping with such flows and reflows may become a subject of new rules and perhaps new institutions in a multiple reserve currency system.[10]

A country running a substantial balance-of-payments deficit has, as suggested above, several adjustment options. One option involves permitting a *depreciation* in the value of its currency in the foreign exchange markets, which will tend to occur from the operation of market forces if the monetary authorities do not intervene in the exchange market. In a fixed rate system the country exercising such an option will normally announce a new *par value* for its currency. The par value is the value of a currency in terms of some *numeraire*, or common denominator, which would normally be a reserve asset—a reserve currency, gold, or the SDR. The result will be a new *parity*, which is simply the official rate equal to the ratio between the par value of

10. Still another kind of confidence problem involves commercial banks. The failure of a commercial bank can lead to a financial panic and thereby create an international monetary crisis. If the international monetary system relies heavily on commercial bank lending for new liquidity, then the system becomes correspondingly more vulnerable to commercial bank failures.

its own currency and that of another currency. The parity has usually been expressed as an exchange rate vis-à-vis the principal reserve currency.

A second adjustment option is to change domestic economic policy so that the balance-of-payments deficit is arrested. The components of such an approach would normally involve a stricter fiscal policy (reducing the budget deficit) and a tighter monetary policy. The ways in which fiscal and monetary policy affect the balance of payments, and its components such as the trade balance, constitute a subject of endless writing by, and no little controversy among, economists. In official circles emphasis is placed upon the interest rate and particularly upon the effects of higher interest rates in attracting short-term investments by foreigners and in discouraging short-term foreign investments by residents.

In passing, it should be noted that considerable emphasis is given at certain times to *cooperation* among countries, and particularly among central banks, as a solution to problems created by payments imbalances. What is normally meant is that through coordination of economic policies severe or prolonged payments imbalances among the principal trading nations can be avoided.[11] A further objective of cooperation, particularly in times when a fixed rate system was in effect, has been to permit maintenance of the existing set of exchange rate relationships among the world's principal currencies. Its prime relevance to this study is that cooperation is often thought of as an alternative to rules. Suffice it to say that it is difficult to know when cooperation in the sense of coordination of economic policies has been successful in averting payments crises, though one knows from the existence of such a crisis that cooperation either has failed or has not been attempted. But it is difficult to cite instances where major countries have pursued economic policies at variance with their national interest or even at variance with the dictates of domestic politics in order to help another country avert a payments crisis.

A third adjustment option is to act directly upon the components of the balance of payments by attempting to reduce the volume of transactions involving a payments outflow and to increase the volume of transactions involving a payments inflow. All adjustment options are likely to be controversial domestically, but measures under this third option are likely to be controversial with foreign countries as well. Whether they take the form of direct regulation or of financial techniques such as subsidies, such measures are likely to discriminate against foreigners in favor of residents, to distort trade and investment patterns, and generally to reduce the efficiency of the international economy. *Exchange restrictions* are one example of such measures. Extensive exchange restrictions may form a comprehensive *exchange control* system in which residents are required to have a license in order to make

11. At various times the term "cooperation" has also referred to schemes for bilateral lending, sometimes organized on a multilateral basis, as a way of providing reserve assets to a deficit country in order to allow it to weather a short-term problem without depreciation of its currency.

foreign payments and are required to surrender any foreign exchange that they acquire to a central authority. Exchange restrictions have been a particular concern of the International Monetary Fund, but the Fund's regulation extends only to exchange restrictions on *current* transactions (trade, services, interest and the like). Exchange restrictions on *capital* transactions, often called *capital controls*, have in general been permitted and at times even encouraged by international rules.

The terminology just reviewed has, in many instances, been developed since World War II and to a large extent in the secondary literature. Official documents often use more abstruse or more parochial terms, in part because of the influence of technical rules. Documents and secondary literature from earlier periods do not speak of reserve currencies, diversification and the like. Yet it is striking how similar the problems facing the international monetary mechanism have been from period to period, whatever the language used and whatever the formal nature of the system in effect at the time. A close look at actual national practice under the gold standard, for example, reveals remarkable parallels to more recent periods, even though the terminology and formal rules have almost nothing in common.

TWO

The
Golden Age

On one historical point most economists, bankers
and statesmen are in accord: the international monetary system worked exceptionally well before
World War I. And on two further points they are
nearly as agreed: that the system never worked as
well thereafter and can never be expected to again.
On the last point one may perhaps pick up a little
dissonance, especially among the laity. Perhaps,
one occasionally hears, if we could possibly, somehow, go back to a full-fledged gold standard, we
could recapture that golden age of international
economic relations that the world knew before the
Great War.

I. THREE PERSPECTIVES ON THE
GOLD STANDARD

What precisely was the gold standard? Before analyzing its legal foundation, it is useful to examine

the gold standard from three distances. Looking backward through the telescope of received mythology, the gold standard was an essentially automatic self-adjusting system that functioned without the aid of human hands, particularly those of central bankers and finance ministers. Taking a closer and more direct view, one can see the gold standard in idealized form as a sterling standard in which the Bank of England was central banker to the world, keeping all in equilibrium. On still closer inspection—which to be sure concentrates on the trees of individual country behavior, missing the beauty of the sylvan ensemble—one can see many features of the gold standard that we normally think of as recent developments: floating exchange rates, intervention in exchange markets, central bank foreign lending and borrowing, and the like. *Plus ça change!* Each of these three views: the myth, the idealization, and the reality warrant closer attention.

The Myth: A Self-Adjusting System

If the automatic self-adjusting concept of the gold standard is a myth, it is a myth that was widely believed at the time or at least was hastily created after the demise of the gold standard at the onset of World War I. The myth has its best statement in the 1918 report of the Cunliffe committee in England:

> When the balance of trade was unfavourable and the exchanges were adverse, it became profitable to export gold. The would-be exporter bought his gold from the Bank of England and paid for it by a cheque on his account. The Bank obtained the gold from the Issue Department in exchange for notes taken out of its banking reserve, with the result that its liabilities to depositors and its banking reserve were reduced by an equal amount, and the ratio of reserve to liabilities consequently fell. If the process was repeated sufficiently often to reduce the ratio in a degree considered dangerous, the Bank raised its rate of discount. The raising of the discount rate had the immediate effect of retaining money here which would otherwise have been remitted abroad and of attracting remittances from abroad to take advantage of the higher rate, thus checking the outflow of gold and even reversing the stream.[1]

[handwritten margin note: Money taken out of circulation - decrease in available supply of currency.]

In the Cunliffe committee's view, a balance-of-payments deficit led automatically to an outflow of gold, which the Bank of England stemmed through raising Bank Rate (that is, the rate at which the Bank would discount commercial paper in order to make funds available to financial institutions). The raising of the discount rate was less an act of public policy, as it might be today, than an internally motivated response to the decline of the reserve ratio of the Bank, which was a private institution. The raising of the discount rate forced up London interest rates, thus stemming the outflow of gold and even encouraging its inflow as the change in relative interest rates between

1. *First Interim Report of the Committee on Currency and Foreign Exchanges after the War* [Cd. 9182] (1918), p. 3.

London and abroad increased the supply of and dampened the demand for funds in London.

This was the first channel through which an initial outflow of gold under the gold standard tended virtually automatically to reestablish equilibrium in the balance of payments. But there was a second channel too, according to the Cunliffe committee. The rise in interest rates operated not merely on the supply and demand for short-term money but also on long-term investment and international trade:

> [T]he raising of the Bank's discount rate and the steps taken to make it effective in the market necessarily led to a general rise of interest rates and a restriction of credit. New enterprises were therefore postponed and the demand for constructional materials and other capital goods was lessened. The consequent slackening of employment also diminished the demand for consumable goods, while holders of stocks of commodities carried largely with borrowed money, being confronted with an increase of interest charges, if not with actual difficulty in renewing loans, and with the prospect of falling prices, tended to press their goods on a weak market. The result was a decline in general prices in the home market which, by checking imports and stimulating exports, corrected the adverse trade balance which was the primary cause of the difficulty.[2]

In short, the raising of Bank Rate tended to operate through employment and prices in such a way as to alter the trade and capital account balances.

Moreover, according to the Cunliffe committee, the gold standard equilibrated not merely the balance of payments but the domestic British economy. Overexpansion of credit would cause a gold outflow and hence lead to a contraction before inflation had taken hold:

> When apart from a foreign drain of gold, credit at home threatened to become unduly expanded, the old currency system tended to restrain the expansion and to prevent the consequent rise in domestic prices which ultimately causes such a drain. The expansion of credit, by forcing up prices, involves an increased demand for legal tender currency both from the banks in order to maintain their normal proportion of cash to liabilities and from the general public for the payment of wages and for retail transactions. In this case also the demand for such currency fell upon the reserve of the Bank of England, and the Bank was thereupon obliged to raise its rate of discount in order to prevent the fall in the proportion of that reserve to its liabilities. The same chain of consequences as we have just described followed and speculative trade activity was similarly restrained.[3]

2. Ibid. pp. 3–4.
3. Ibid. p. 4.

The great virtue of the gold standard in this view was that the effects were "automatic":

> There was therefore an automatic machinery by which the volume of purchasing power in this country was continuously adjusted to world prices of commodities in general. Domestic prices were automatically regulated so as to prevent excessive imports; and the creation of banking credit was so controlled that banking could be safely permitted a freedom from State interference which would not have been possible under a less rigid currency system.[4]

The Idealization: The Role of Discretion

Although the prewar existence of an automatic, self-adjusting gold standard was universal doctrine among central bankers in the 1920s—at least until they tried to reinstitute it[5]—and even found its way into elementary economics textbooks decades later[6] and hence into the public mind today, the crucial role played by increases and reductions of Bank Rate necessarily injected an element of discretion. As a private institution, the Bank of England had private incentives to maintain an appropriate ratio between its liabilities and its assets; yet private incentives were not necessarily enough, as the periodic difficulties of other financial institutions showed. In addition to acting as a central banker to other financial institutions, the Bank of England was also in the commercial banking business.[7]

A more serious problem, since the Bank apparently viewed its public role as primary,[8] was the inadequacy of Bank Rate by itself as an instrument for controlling interest rates in the money market. An increase in Bank Rate might not lead to a commensurate increase in money market interest rates, and in that event the Bank would have to use other methods to make Bank Rate effective. To the extent that the Bank's will and competence to control the money market was essential to its international payments role, the gold standard was far from automatic and self-adjusting.

---

4. Ibid.
5. See R. S. Sayers, *The Bank of England, 1891–1944* (1976), vol. 1, chaps. 6, 8.
6. See, e.g., Paul A. Samuelson, *Economics*, 8th ed. (1970), pp. 623–25; Theodore Morgan, *Introduction to Economics* (1950), pp. 745–48; Herbert Heaton, *Economic History of Europe*, rev. ed. (1948), pp. 596–97. For an account of "the classical analysis," see C. A. E. Goodhart, *The Business of Banking, 1891–1914* (1972), pp. 195–220.
7. See Sayers, *Bank of England 1891–1944*, 1:17–27. The Act of 1844 provided something of a public constraint. That act required the Bank of England to maintain gold coin and gold or silver bullion to "cover" all Bank note issues in excess of a statutorily specified "fiduciary" issue. 7 and 8 Vict., c. 32, § 1. This cover requirement provided a further constraint because the Bank had available for other purposes only so much of its gold as was not required to cover its note issue. When this requirement would have had its most drastic effect, it was suspended. See Albert Feavearyear, *The Pound Sterling*, 2d ed. (1963), pp. 272–305.
8. Sayers, *Bank of England 1891–1944*, 1:8.

A further discretionary aspect of the pre-1914 gold standard had to do with what in the 1920s came to be known as the "rules of the game." Under these "rules" the Bank of England (and other central banks as well) was not merely to respond to gold inflows and outflows pound-for-pound but was to do so more than once over. That is, if gold flowed out, then a central bank was supposed to act in such a way as to decrease its assets (say, by raising its discount rate, reducing the volume of discounted notes and thus tightening money market conditions) by more than the amount of the outflow, thereby hastening the process of equilibration. And if gold flowed in, a central bank was supposed to increase its assets disproportionately. But these rules of the gold standard game were strictly discretionary, and, as we shall see below, central banks not only did not always abide by them but sometimes acted perversely, reducing assets when the rules called for them to increase assets.

Even conceding the large discretionary element, we must acknowledge that the gold standard worked well for some decades. Consequently, a more modern interpretation than the Cunliffe myth has it that the Bank of England was the masterful director of what was actually a sterling, rather than a gold, standard. Keynes called it the Bank of England's "power to call the tune": "During the latter half of the nineteenth century the influence of London on credit conditions throughout the world was so predominant that the Bank of England could almost have claimed to be the conductor of the international orchestra."[9] Under this idealized portrait of the gold standard, the hegemony of London over the world's money markets permitted the Bank of England to act in effect as central banker to the world, a role which it supposedly discharged with competence and foresight.

For a variety of reasons, the tightening of money market conditions in London had immediate repercussions in other countries: London was the world's largest financial center, England was the world's principal capital exporter, commercial contracts even between third countries tended to be discharged by payments in sterling (so-called bills on London), the world's gold tended to flow to London, and the world's principal organized commodities markets were located there. London was the source of the world's liquidity, and a tightening of credit there meant that conditions would tighten quickly elsewhere. British funds that would otherwise have flowed abroad would tend to stay at home, attracted by higher local interest rates, and foreigners in turn could no longer afford to borrow in London. A loosening of credit in London would, in turn, increase the world's liquidity.[10]

9. John Maynard Keynes, *A Treatise on Money*, (1930), 2:306–7.
10. The text sets forth a highly compressed summary of the relation between London and foreign credit markets. For a fully developed account, see A. G. Ford, *The Gold Standard 1880–1914: Britain and Argentina* (1962), a discussion of the impact of British financial policy on the Argentine economy; Arthur I. Bloomfield, *Short-Term Capital Movements under the pre-1914 Gold Standard*, Princeton Studies in International Finance no. 11 (1963).

The Reality

The view of the gold standard as a worldwide sterling standard seems to be the dominant view today, perhaps because most of the writing on the subject has been by Anglo-Saxon authors. But the reality was much more complex.

In the first place, the gold standard as an international system did not last long. On the contrary, it did not come into existence in any meaningful sense until the 1870s and is best dated from 1879, when the United States went on the gold standard. And it was swept away in a few days by the financial tides accompanying the onset of World War I. In short, the gold standard was an incident in the history of international monetary organization, not all that much longer-lived than the Bretton Woods system, which lasted (at least nominally) from 1946 to 1971. This fact alone suggests that the gold standard was not self-adjusting. The common view that it dominated the nineteenth century is a product of British popular writing and of a confusion between the gold standard as an international monetary system and as a domestic monetary regime. Without at this point attempting to discuss its domestic aspects,[11] we can explain the common view by noting that the gold standard as a domestic regime dates back in England to 1819 and, if prepared to define the term loosely, we can think of it as dating back to at least 1717.[12]

Until 1879 the United States dollar was inconvertible. Indeed, using modern terminology, the dollar during the "greenback" period from 1862 to 1879 can only be described as floating against other currencies, notably the pound sterling.[13] During this period the dollar-pound exchange rate rose from the gold standard parity of $4.86 to more than $12 before eventually returning to parity when the United States resumed gold payments in 1879. And prior to the floating period, the dollar was on a bimetallic standard.

Before the 1870s most of Europe was also on a bimetallic standard. To the extent that a bimetallic country was de facto on silver rather than gold (and, for reasons set out below, a bimetallic country was essentially on either gold or silver at any particular time), such a country's currency was in effect floating against the currencies of gold standard countries.

II. BIMETALLISM AND GRESHAM'S LAW

The gold standard could not dominate the world economy until events eliminated its principal rival, the bimetallic standard. Under the bimetallic standard as practiced in the United States and in much of Europe, domestic legislation provided for coinage of both gold and silver coins of a specified weight and fineness. By comparing the metal contents of gold and silver coins

11. See pp. 24–28.
12. Feavearyear, p. 154.
13. Milton Friedman and Anna J. Schwartz, *A Monetary History of the United States 1867–1960* (1963), pp. 58–61, 85–86.

of a particular monetary unit (say, of the dollar), a ratio between gold and silver could readily be calculated. For example, at a ratio of 15½ to 1, which was the ratio maintained by France throughout the nineteenth century until the triumph of the gold standard, an ounce of gold was worth *at the mint* 15½ times as much as an ounce of silver. Since the ratio depended upon statute, it could be changed by legislation, as when the United States changed its ratio from 15–1 to 16–1 in 1834.[14] Because it was fixed by law, the ratio did not vary with the value of gold and silver in the bullion market. Therein lay the Achilles' heel of the bimetallic standard.

The difficulty lay in the often cited, but less often understood, economic principle known as Gresham's law. If gold is worth more in the bullion market than at the mint (that is, if the law undervalues gold), then a holder of gold can be expected to sell it in the market rather than to present it to the mint for coinage. Indeed, under such circumstances a holder of gold would sell it in the market even if he wanted newly minted coins, because with the proceeds of the sale he could purchase silver bullion that could be exchanged at the mint for coins of greater value than the mint value of the gold he originally held. Moreover, if gold was undervalued by the mint ratio in a given country at a given time, gold coins would tend to disappear; either they would be melted for their bullion content (so that the holder could profit by the exchange of the contained gold for already minted silver coins) or they would be exported to another country where gold was not undervalued at the mint. For Gresham's law to operate it is not necessary for each individual to make these calculations, much less to engage in these transactions. Specialists (bullion and coin dealers, for example) will seek to profit by the opportunities created by the disparity between the legislative ratio and the market ratio.

Since Gresham's law plays an important role in the history of the international monetary system, it is worth noting at this point that it has little to do with "bad" driving out "good," as popular versions of the law suggest. What is required is simply that relative prices between two objects be fixed by law and that relative market prices diverge from that fixed ratio.[15] Gresham's law is thus a statement about the effects of governmentally imposed price control where alternative markets at higher prices are available. In his proposal of a *sym*metallist system, Alfred Marshall pointed out that if a paper currency, convertible into gold and silver in fixed physical proportions, were issued instead of gold and silver coins existing side by side at a fixed coinage ratio, Gresham's law could not operate.[16] Alternatively, if there were some easily administrable way to permit the coinage ratio to

14. Coinage Act of 1834, 4 Stat. 699 (1834).
15. See Friedman and Schwartz, p. 27, n. 16.
16. Alfred Marshall, "Remedies for Fluctuations of General Prices (1887)," in *Memorials of Alfred Marshall*, ed. A. C. Pigou (1925), pp. 188, 204–6.

be determined from day to day in the marketplace, a two-metal system could function.

III. The Latin Monetary Union

The operation of Gresham's law upon the bimetallic standard was in fact the principal cause of the breakdown of one of the principal nineteenth century efforts at regional monetary organization, the Latin Monetary Union.[17] The 1865 treaty between France, Belgium, Switzerland, and Italy establishing the Union provided not only that the principal gold and silver coins of each country should be of the same weight, fineness, and diameter (thus differing among the member countries only by the devices affixed by the mints of each), but that the silver coins of each should be legal tender up to specified amounts in the other countries.[18] The Latin Union, which had been formed in part to solve certain Gresham's law problems stemming from the circulation in one another's countries of coins of differing weights and finenesses, failed not so much because of the common circulation and legal tender provisions as because the Union was based on a bimetallic standard.

The bimetallic standard of the Latin Union, based on the conventional fixed legislative ratio, succumbed to the fate of all earlier bimetallic standards; the coinage in any country at any particular time tended to be overwhelmingly in one metal or the other. When silver began to depreciate in the early 1870s and hence the statutory ratio undervalued gold relative to the market, gold stopped flowing in significant quantities to the mints in France and the other Latin Union countries. This was a complete reversal of the experience in the period prior to the formation of the Union when the French ratio had overvalued gold.[19]

The 1871 decision of Germany to adopt the gold standard created a large additional world demand for gold and exacerbated the Union's problems. To the disappearance from circulation of gold coins were added imports of silver of such rapidly escalating quantities that the mints of Union countries were increasingly becoming a principal support for the world silver market. France and Belgium reacted to the flood of silver by limiting its maximum daily coinage, itself a partial step toward a gold standard, and subsequent discussions among Latin Union members were dominated by the question whether or not to move entirely to a gold standard. By 1878, coinage of silver had

17. Similar nineteenth-century unions involving the German-speaking states were an important step in the unification of Germany. See Axel Nielsen, "Monetary Unions," *Encyclopaedia of the Social Sciences* (1933), 10:595–96; and Albert E. Janssen, *Les conventions monétaires* (1911), pp. 3–75.
18. For the text of the treaty, see *The Consolidated Treaty Series*, ed. Clive Parry, 132(1969):10–14. An English translation of the 1865 treaty, as well as of subsequent treaties, appears in Henry Parker Willis, *A History of the Latin Monetary Union* (1901), appendix 1, pp. 271–300.
19. See French coinage statistics in J. Laurence Laughlin, *The History of Bimetallism in the United States* (1886), appendix 7, p. 254.

been largely suspended in the Union countries (except for certain "token" coins containing a lesser proportion of silver and hence not bearing a 15½ to 1 ratio to gold). Because the issuing governments were at first unwilling or unable to agree to redeem their outstanding silver coins in gold, the Latin Union struggled on for some years, but its members were de facto on a gold standard (often called a "limping" gold standard). Events, largely the rapidly growing supply of silver stemming in large part from discoveries in the western United States and the increased demand for gold resulting from the movement of other countries to a gold standard, overwhelmed the plans of monetary statesmen.[20]

The decisive event in the formation of the gold standard was the resumption by the United States of gold payments in 1879. Prior to the Civil War the United States had been on a bimetallic standard that, because gold was overvalued at the mint, was de facto a gold standard.[21] Not long after the outbreak of the Civil War in 1861, commercial banks in the United States had been forced to suspend specie payments—that is, commercial banks would no longer pay their creditors (especially the holders of their bank notes) in gold coin. The U.S. Treasury thereupon also ceased specie payments on its obligations. The U.S. government followed in 1862 with the issuance, in an effort to finance the escalating costs of the war, of irredeemable U.S. notes—the controversial "greenbacks." The principal other form of currency was the national bank note; a dollar national bank note exchanged for a dollar greenback at par with rare exceptions.[22]

Until 1879, these and subsequent issues of greenbacks, together with national bank notes (which, unlike greenbacks, were not legal tender), displaced gold coin in general circulation, with gold coin being used only for special purposes.[23] At any given time there was a price for a greenback dollar in terms of gold. By late 1864 one could buy $100 in greenbacks for about $40 in gold coin,[24] although the price returned gradually to par with gold by

20. The text sets forth a highly condensed and necessarily oversimplified history of the Latin Union. For more detail and for the subsequent history of the Latin Union, see Willis. See also references to the Latin Union in Laughlin. The Latin Union went through several additional permutations and was not formally dissolved until 1926. Jacques E. Mertens, *La naissance et le développement de l'étalon-or* (1944), p. 276. A somewhat more successful experiment in international monetary integration was the Scandinavian Monetary Union, created by an 1872 treaty. For the text, see *Archives de Droit International* 1(1874):188–91; and for a brief description, see Nielsen, "Monetary Unions," p. 598. See also Janssen, pp. 105–47.

21. On the pre–Civil War standard, see Arthur Nussbaum, *A History of the Dollar* (1957), pp. 77–84; Laughlin, pp. 52–85.

22. Friedman and Schwartz, pp. 21–22, n. 8.

23. For a fuller description of the composition of the currency in the 1862–79 period, see Friedman and Schwartz, pp. 16–29. Only gold coin could be used, for example, to pay customs duties. Ibid. p. 27.

24. See gold price indices for greenbacks in Wesley C. Mitchell, *A History of the Greenbacks* (1903), appendix A, pp. 423–28.

the time specie payments were resumed in 1879.[25] The corresponding decline in the greenback price of gold reflected a severe decline in the U.S. price level over the same period.[26]

In present-day terminology the U.S. currency was floating from 1862 to 1879. Since the pound was tied to gold, the rate of exchange between green-backs (as well as national bank notes) and the pound sterling was determined by the greenback price in terms of a dollar in gold coin. Greenbacks and national bank notes were inconvertible because one could not receive a fixed amount of gold for them but could only obtain as much gold as they could command in the marketplace of the moment. But there were no domestic prohibitions on the purchase, sale, or export of gold by private individuals.

When the United States resumed specie payments, it redeemed paper currency (as before 1861) exclusively in gold. But the system was no longer a bimetallic system which de facto favored coinage of gold. The silver dollar had been omitted from the Coinage Act of 1873 (the "crime of '73").[27] When silver coinage was again authorized in the Bland-Allison Act of 1878, it was not free coinage but rather coinage of not less than $2 million nor more than $4 million per month.[28]

As the foregoing brief review of the development of the gold standard shows, the gold standard as an international system was not the result of any international agreement. To be sure, there were various international conferences, such as one resulting from the Bland-Allison Act of 1878, but these conferences tended to be oriented away from the gold standard and towards a bimetallic standard. The rise of the gold standard to international dominance thus owed little or nothing to diplomacy. On the contrary, it was the product of a series of national decisions, each taken primarily for reasons of national interest, without extensive regard to the needs of the international community.

In these national decisions, events played a large role. The demise of the de jure bimetallic standard in the United States was the outgrowth of the Civil War, which forced the country onto an inconvertible currency. The return to the gold standard, modified only slightly by the continued coinage of a limited amount of silver, reflected the outcome of a social and political struggle in the United States. Perhaps the most decisive event of all was the

25. Friedman and Schwartz, p. 74, chart 7, pp. 76–88.
26. Ibid. pp. 80–81; and see Wesley C. Mitchell, *Gold, Prices, and Wages under the Greenback Standard* (1908).
27. 17 Stat. 424 (1873).
28. 20 Stat. 25 (1878). This statute did call on the president to invite members of the Latin Union and other European nations to a conference with a view to adopting a bimetallic system based on a common gold-silver ratio. The conference did not lead to any international agreement. See A. Barton Hepburn, *A History of Currency in the United States*, rev. ed. (1924), pp. 283–85; and Willis, pp. 178–79.

political unification of Germany, which led to the decision to adopt the gold
mark in 1871. The enhanced demand for gold stemming from that decision,
as well as parallel decisions in other European countries and the greater
supply of silver attributable to new discoveries, together led to the breakdown
of an ambitious attempt to create a multilateral system based on agreed
rules—the Latin Monetary Union.[29]

IV. THE LEGAL FOUNDATIONS OF THE GOLD STANDARD

If the gold standard was not agreed upon as an international standard, can
it be regarded as an international rule at all? International lawyers might well
debate that issue, but it suffices here to underscore the extent to which the
international monetary system of the gold standard period rested fundamentally upon domestic law in each of the principal trading nations. These
domestic legal rules were similar, though not identical, in the various countries. The rules generally provided for free import and export of gold bullion
and coins by residents and nonresidents alike. In addition, national mints
stood ready to accept gold bullion and to turn it into gold coins as well as
to reverse the process upon demand. But there were many small differences
in national rules, and even the general principles were not unfailingly followed.

The British Gold Standard

A convenient place to start is Britain. From a legal point of view the cornerstone was the right of a private party to move freely from gold to currency
and back again and to import or export gold without limitation. Indeed, the
government, through the Bank of England, stood ready to facilitate such
transactions by redeeming at a fixed rate and without limit the official currency—Bank of England notes—in gold coin (the £1 gold sovereign).

As might be expected, the legal foundation for the Bank of England official
transactions was somewhat complicated. The three key statutes were Peel's
Act of 1819, an 1821 amendment to the 1819 statute, and the Bank Charter
Act of 1844.[30] Suppose, to start with, that an individual wanted gold for
export. He could, of course, acquire it in the private market, but under the

29. For some 30 years, from about 1855 to 1885, the production of gold fell somewhat while
the production of silver more than trebled. Roy W. Jastram, *The Golden Constant: The English
and American Experience 1560–1976* (1977), appendix C, p. 224.
30. 59 Geo. 3, c. 49 (1819); 1 & 2 Geo. 4, c. 26 (1821); 7 & 8 Vict., c. 32 (1844).

1819 act, as amended in 1821, he could present Bank of England notes[31] at the Bank of England and receive gold bullion (in bar form) or gold sovereigns at 77s. 10½d. per ounce.[32] In fact, the Bank was willing to provide either sovereigns or bullion, though it took the position that it need provide only sovereigns at the statutory 77s. 10½d. rate and therefore sometimes charged 77s. 11d. or even more for bullion. It would perhaps have charged still more than the all-time record of 78s. 1d.[33] if it were not for the fact that a higher price would simply have resulted in sovereigns being exported or melted into bars (with a consequent need to mint new sovereigns).[34] If the private party wanted to export gold to a particular country, he might ask for gold coin of that country, and the Bank, since it maintained an inventory of the principal foreign coins, would normally oblige him. But since the Bank had no statutory obligation to provide foreign gold coin, it would normally sell it only at a premium. The size of the premium was a matter of policy but was always limited by the possibility of the private party taking sovereigns or gold bars and having them minted into local coin in the country of destination.[35] Having acquired either gold bars or gold coin, the individual with whom we are concerned, whether a resident or nonresident, was guaranteed the right of export by the 1819 act.[36]

The statutory framework similarly facilitated the import of gold. The 1844 act assured the importer of the right to acquire notes from the Bank in exchange for gold bullion at a price of 77s. 9d.[37] If he imported foreign gold coin, the Bank would also normally buy it in exchange for Bank of England notes, but since it had no statutory obligation to do so, the price was a matter of Bank policy.

The statutory framework thus not only guaranteed but actually helped to facilitate the free import and export of gold. But this same legal framework, when viewed from a domestic rather than an international perspective, served two additional functions: (1) to "back" the official domestic paper currency, and (2) to permit circulation of an official gold coin. Anyone could present

31. British currency took three principal forms—Bank of England notes, coins (of which the principal coin was the £ gold sovereign) and private bank notes. The private bank notes gradually disappeared as a result of provisions of the Bank Charter Act that prevented new banks from issuing them and operated to reduce the number of existing banks that could continue to issue them. 7 & 8 Vict., c. 32, § 11, 12, 13 (1844).
32. 59 Geo. 3, c. 49, § 4, 6, 8 (1819); 1 & 2 Geo. 4, c. 27, § 1, 2, 3 (1821). The 1819 act had entitled the note holder to receive bullion, but the 1821 amendment permitted the Bank to substitute sovereigns.
33. R. S. Sayers, *Bank of England Operations 1890–1914* (1936), p. 82.
34. George Clare, *A Money-Market Primer*, 2d ed. (1903), p. 22; Sayers, *Bank of England Operations 1890–1914*, p. 82.
35. Sayers, *Bank of England 1891–1944*, 1:48–50.
36. 59 Geo. 3, c. 49, § 10, 11 (1819).
37. 7 & 8 Vict., c. 32, § 4 (1844).

Bank of England notes to the Bank and receive gold sovereigns at 77s. 10½d.[38]
Since Bank of England notes were not available in less than £5 denominations,
gold sovereigns played an important role in daily life, being widely used, for
example, in the payment of wages.

In view of the importance attached to Bank Rate in most interpretations
of the operation of the gold standard, an important question is how the legal
framework influenced Bank of England decisions as to the level of Bank Rate.
Since the Bank did not publicly explain its actions and did not even keep
records of its reasons for Bank Rate changes,[39] evidence must necessarily be
indirect. As previously mentioned, its banking operations were much like
those of any other bank, and therefore it would want to maintain a reserve,
but in fact it kept a much larger reserve than other British banks because of
its responsibilities under the Bank Charter Act of 1844.[40] The crux of the
1844 act was the requirement that the Bank maintain gold backing, pound
for pound, for all outstanding Bank of England notes beyond a defined
"fiduciary issue," which was backed only by securities. The fiduciary issue
was initially £14,000,000. Under the 1844 act it grew as country banks lost
their note issuing powers as a result of bank failures, merger with London
banks, and other contingencies specified by statute,[41] until by 1892 the fiduciary issue was £16,450,000.[42]

The Bank Charter Act divided the Bank of England into two departments,
the Issue Department, whose sole function was to issue notes, and the Banking Department, which carried on the private banking business of the Bank.
Although the Issue Department maintained gold coin and bullion against
note issues beyond the fiduciary issue, the Reserve—as it was known at the
time—was that portion of the assets of the Banking Department composed
of "cash"—that is, Bank of England notes and gold and silver coin. The
Reserve was thus cash maintained by the Banking Department as a reserve
against its deposit liabilities.

It was the practice of the Bank to attempt to maintain a "Proportion"
between the Reserve and deposits within a range decided upon from time
to time—a range that in the late nineteenth century was between 30 and 50
percent.[43] The Proportion was apparently one of the most important determinants of Bank Rate, and if the Proportion threatened to fall too low,

38. As previously noted, the Bank could still under the 1821 amendment have supplied gold
bars but it always chose to provide sovereigns to those who wanted them. It should also be
noted that private bank notes, as opposed to Bank of England notes, were backed only by the
credit of the issuing bank.
39. Sayers, *Bank of England 1891–1944*, 1:28–29.
40. 7 & 8 Vict., c. 32 (1844).
41. Ibid. § 11, 12, 16.
42. Clare, pp. 15, 58.
43. Ibid. p. 54. Clare calculated the average Proportion at 43 percent.

whether because of international gold flows or simply a domestic cash drain, then Bank Rate would normally be increased.[44]

The connection between the requirement of pound-for-pound backing of the note circulation (beyond the fiduciary issue) and the Proportion was indirect but inescapable. Parties seeking to export gold would normally obtain it from the Issue Department, which held the Bank's bullion and much of its gold coin. The provision of gold by the Issue Department left the Issue Department no worse off because both its gold and its note issue declined pound for pound. But to obtain gold from the Issue Department, the gold exporters would have to present Bank of England notes. However they obtained the Bank of England notes, this new note demand would tend to be met by the Banking Department (since other financial institutions kept Bank of England notes only in relatively small amounts). When the Banking Department paid out notes, the effect was to reduce the numerator (notes and coin) of the Proportion and hence to worsen it, even if the transaction took the form of a reduction of deposits liabilities, the denominator of the fraction. When the Proportion fell to a point where the Bank felt its Banking Department's ability to meet cash withdrawals by depositors was endangered, its response was conventionally to raise Bank Rate (thereby dampening the demand for gold for export).

The Issue Department could only come to the aid of the Banking Department by printing more Bank of England notes for transfer to the Banking Department so long as the limits imposed by the Bank Charter Act—the fiduciary issue plus notes issued pound-for-pound against gold—had not been reached. On three occasions, in each case more by reason of a domestic cash drain than any gold export crisis, the Banking Department's Reserve reached a dangerously low level, and the Bank was only able to restore order and confidence in the City by obtaining a letter from the Chancellor of the Exchequer pledging the government of the day to obtain legislation retroactively authorizing the Issue Department to increase the fiduciary issue beyond the Bank Charter Act limits in order to transfer new notes to the Banking Department.[45]

The famous "gold points" were a direct consequence of these statutory provisions and Bank of England policies. Though gold, whether in bullion or coin, could be freely imported and exported, the profitability of such transactions depended upon the cost of gold transport, insurance, and related transactions costs. These costs, together with the 1½d. difference between the statutory buying price and the nominal selling price for gold bullion, automatically set brackets above and below par, known as gold points, that

---

44. Ibid. p. 56; Sayers, *Bank of England 1891–1944*, 1:30.
45. These three "crises" occurred in 1847, 1857, and 1866. For a fuller description of the role of the Reserve in influencing Bank Rate policy, see Clare, pp. 45–71. See also Sayers, *Bank of England 1891–1944*, 1:28–33. Only in 1857 were the powers conferred actually used.

determined whether gold would be imported, exported, or—if the market price of gold in England was within the gold points—would neither be imported nor exported. With other major countries also linking their currency to gold, the analogy of gold points to margins under the Bretton Woods system was close.[46] The gold points set limits on the fluctuations in market rates of exchange between two gold standard currencies that could occur without gold movements being triggered. The gold movements under the gold standard were a response to the private incentives created by the Bank of England (and, at times, other central banks) standing ready to buy and sell gold at par. As we shall see later, the Bank began to use "gold devices" to affect these gold flows, and the effect of the gold devices was sometimes to widen slightly the gold points.

The United States

Although the United States can be said to have joined the international gold standard regime in 1879, the legal and institutional situation in the United States was different from that in England. In the first place, the United States had no central bank until the creation of the Federal Reserve in 1914. Second, the United States continued to coin silver even after 1879 under the terms of the previously discussed Bland-Allison Act of 1878[47] and to give a certain amount of lip service in legislation to bimetallism. Indeed, the Sherman Silver Purchase Act of 1890[48] increased the rate of silver purchases by the U.S. Treasury. It was not until the passage of the Gold Standard Act of 1900 that gold was declared to be the "standard unit of value" and hence the United States was unqualifiedly on the gold standard (though silver coinage in restricted amounts continued). It should be noted that the silver dollars coined after 1878, unlike gold coins, contained an amount of silver less than their face amount (though unlike copper and smaller silver coins their metal content was close to face value).[49]

Nonetheless, throughout the period beginning in 1879 the U.S. Treasury redeemed most kinds of Treasury-issued paper money in gold coin, and hence despite several kinds of currency and differences in statutory provisions, it was possible for private parties to obtain from the U.S. Treasury sufficient gold to permit the levels of gold outflow essential for the gold standard to work.[50] The United States version of the gold standard was so

46. For a discussion of margins under the Bretton Woods system, see pp. 93–94.
47. See discussion p. 23.
48. 26 Stat. 289 (1890). The Sherman Silver Purchase Act was repealed in 1893. 28 Stat. 4 (1893).
49. Laughlin, pp. 205ff.
50. See Nussbaum, pp. 143–48. Silver certificates were redeemable in silver coin under section 3 of the Bland-Allison Act, 20 Stat. 25 (1878). The Treasury had the option of redeeming U.S. notes (greenbacks) in silver, but insisted on redemption in gold even when the gold reserve ran low in the early 1890s. Paul Studenski and Herman E. Krooss, *Financial History of the United*

complex that in 1913 John Maynard Keynes, comparing the practices in other major countries to those in England, could only say that the U.S. "development and present position are anomalous, and have claimed no imitators."[51]

Other Countries

Some other countries attempted to model themselves on England, but either because they did not have as well developed a capital market as England or because they were debtor, rather than creditor, countries they could not rely on their central bank discount rate to attract gold or to stem its outflow to the extent that England could. Among the creditor countries France did not hesitate to restrict convertibility and to charge a premium on gold when the franc exchange rate was weak.[52] Debtor countries, such as Germany (which was a debtor vis-à-vis Britain if not against eastern European countries), Austria-Hungary, and Russia, were forced to resort to two additional steps. One was to hold much larger gold reserves than those with which Britain was able to survive economically. At the end of 1913, for example, Britain held $164.9 million of gold but Germany held $278.7 million, Austria-Hungary $251.6 million and Russia at least $786.2 million.[53] A second step for the debtor countries was the acquisition of large holdings of foreign exchange for use as reserves. The Bank of England, in contrast, saw no need to hold foreign currencies at all.[54]

V. THE GOLD STANDARD IN OPERATION

From what has already been set forth on the legal foundations of the gold standard, it can readily be seen that England played not only a key role but also a different role from that of other countries. Though the international monetary system can be said to have been centered in London, Britain did not play quite so central a role at the monetary periphery, particularly in central and eastern Europe. On the other hand, London played a profound role in shaping the international financial relations of Latin America.[55]

Britain was able to play this role for a number of reinforcing reasons. It was a large trading nation. As previously noted, the world's organized commodities markets were predominantly located there. London was the center

---

States (1952), p. 218. National bank notes were redeemable in U.S. notes and hence indirectly in gold.

51. John Maynard Keynes, *Indian Currency and Finance* (1913), p. 27, n. 1.
52. Ibid. pp. 20–21, n. 1; Harry D. White, *The French International Accounts* (1933), pp. 182–200.
53. Peter H. Lindert, *Key Currencies and Gold 1900–1913*, Princeton Studies in International Finance no. 24 (1969), pp. 10–11, table 1.
54. Foreign coins were, as previously indicated, sometimes acquired by the Bank of England. See discussion p. 25.
55. See Ford, *The Gold Standard 1880–1914*, on financial relations between Britain and Argentina.

of the world's gold market, with South Africa's output arriving each Monday.[56] On the investment side, Britain was the world's principal creditor nation. In the forty years before World War I about two-fifths of all British investment was made abroad. In some years, over 50 percent of its current savings went into foreign investment, a proportion that dwarfs anything in present-day British or U.S. experience.[57]

These factors led to the widespread use of sterling as the currency in which international obligations were discharged, often even between third countries. Both as a cause and an effect of sterling's role as a transactions currency, foreign enterprises engaged in international trade tended to keep their balances in London. And as debtor countries began to hold their reserves in foreign exchange, as well as gold, foreign government balances in the form of sterling securities and London bank balances grew. Today we would describe sterling of the gold standard period as the world's principal reserve currency. The combination of these factors permitted the Bank of England's Bank Rate to perform its role in equilibrating Britain's balance of payments. To describe the Bank of England as central banker to the world, then, is hardly to exaggerate. Certainly London as a financial center was the principal source of liquidity for the international monetary system of the time.

Yet the gold standard did not function in textbook fashion, even for the parts of the world within London's sphere of influence. How it did function, as a matter of economics, has been a matter of some controversy with some writers emphasizing gold flows, others interest rate changes, and still others prices and international trade. Most recently, writers in the tradition known as the monetary approach to the balance of payments have argued that the Bank of England played a small part and that the integration of world financial and trading markets made possible by fixed exchange rates and by the absence of exchange controls and trade quotas produced the gold standard's success.[58]

This is not the place to attempt to resolve these important economic issues. From the standpoint of a study of the rules governing the system, however, it is significant that the previously mentioned gold standard rules of the game, under which countries were to accentuate the effect of gold flows, were not regularly observed. Indeed, Bloomfield has shown that in the period 1880–1914 the contrary was the case. If the rules were being observed, then one would expect year-to-year changes in central bank domestic income-earning assets (discounts, advances, and securities)—which provide the monetary base for domestic bank credit—at the very least to be in the same direction as changes in holdings of international assets (gold, silver, and

56. Sayers, *Bank of England Operations 1890–1914*, p. 74.
57. A. K. Cairncross, *Factors in Economic Development* (1962), pp. 39–40.
58. See the references to the literature in Leland B. Yeager, *International Monetary Relations: Theory, History and Policy*, 2d ed. (1976), pp. 304–8; and Donald N. McCloskey and J. Richard Zecher, "How the Gold Standard Worked, 1880–1913," in *The Monetary Approach to the Balance of Payments*, ed. Jacob A. Frenkel and Harry G. Johnson (1976), pp. 357–85.

foreign exchange). Yet, as Bloomfield summarizes his evidence, "[i]n the case of *every* central bank the year-to-year changes in international and domestic assets were more often in the *opposite* than in the same direction, and in most cases *much* more often in the opposite direction."[59] In short, central banks tended to counteract the effects of gold inflows and outflows more often than they accentuated them.

Some differences in direction could be accounted for by the arbitrariness of using calendar years (which may combine periods of payments surplus and deficits) coupled with inevitable leads or lags in changing central bank discount rates. Nonetheless, the test Bloomfield uses is conservative because he looked only at the direction of changes and simply assumed that the banks would follow the supposed rule of accentuating inflows and outflows. Thus, a central bank that resisted an inflow to the extent of merely damping its effect on the growth of domestic assets would nonetheless be counted as having complied with the rule under the Bloomfield test because the direction of the two indicators would be the same. Especially noteworthy is the fact that even the Bank of England offset gold movements in more years than it permitted a movement of domestic assets in the same direction, though Bloomfield's results showed the Bank to come closer than any other central bank to complying with the gold standard rules.[60]

It is hard to escape the conclusion that the gold standard rules of the game were a post–World War I construct, not observed and probably not even widely recognized as relevant norms before the war. As we shall see, the rules that counted most were domestic rules and even the Bank of England looked first to its own accounts in making the Bank Rate decisions that conventional history puts at the center of the international operation of the gold standard.

Foreign Exchange under the Gold Standard

What is most remarkable in looking back at the gold standard against the experience of the 1930s and of the Bretton Woods era is the growth in the gold standard period of practices usually associated with later periods. The growth of foreign exchange holdings is often mistakenly thought to have been a product of the 1920s. Not only is that perception, which was widely held in the 1920s as well as today, inaccurate in the sense that exchange holdings were important under the gold standard, but it is wildly wrong. Foreign exchange holdings by monetary authorities were larger, as a percentage of international reserves, in 1913 than in 1925 if silver holdings are excluded

59. Arthur I. Bloomfield, *Monetary Policy under the International Gold Standard, 1880–1914* (1959), pp. 48–50. (Emphasis in original.)
60. Ibid. p. 50, n. 92.

from international reserves (that is, if international reserves are defined as gold plus foreign exchange).[61]

The development of foreign exchange holdings was not simply a twentieth-century development which could be thought to be uncharacteristic of the gold standard period as a whole. On the contrary, such holdings were already substantial at the beginning of the gold standard period in the early 1880s.[62] Foreign exchange was more important than gold as a reserve for all or nearly all of the gold standard period in Belgium, Sweden, Finland, and India.[63]

All of the major trading nations, with the exception of Britain, the United States, and France, held foreign exchange.[64] Moreover, contrary to the general impression handed down by several generations of British authors, sterling was not the sole reserve currency. French francs and German marks were widely held, particularly on the Continent. Although statistics are not available with respect to the currency in which a large proportion of total foreign exchange holdings was maintained, known holdings of francs and marks were roughly equal to those of British sterling and, on the Continent, franc and mark holdings far outstripped sterling holdings. At the end of 1913, Russia, one of the largest holders of foreign exchange, held $221.8 million in francs, $53.0 million in marks, and only $23.7 million in sterling. The statistical dominance of sterling in aggregate holdings stems largely from major sterling holdings maintained by India and Japan. One is forced to conclude that Britain, though doubtless the principal reserve currency country, not only was not the sole reserve center of what was already by the turn of the century a gold exchange standard, but that on the Continent, Britain did not even seem to be the center of the international monetary system.[65]

One explanation for the growth of foreign exchange holdings is that it was due to the very success of the gold standard. The certainty with respect to future exchange rates and the confidence in the stability of financial institutions engendered by the gold standard led not just firms and private individuals to make liquid investments in foreign countries but governments themselves to invest their reserves in foreign government securities and foreign bank deposits. (Foreign exchange, it will be noted, necessarily presupposed some form of investment because no government or central bank would

61. Lindert, *Key Currencies*, p. 14. The justification for excluding silver is that it was in the process of being effectively demonetized as an internationally usable reserve in 1913 and roughly half of the world's reserve holdings were in the U.S. Treasury, ibid. pp. 10–11, table 1, where their presence reflected the residue of nineteenth-century domestic politics rather than current international monetary policy. In any event, the inclusion or exclusion of silver does not change the general conclusion greatly. Ibid. p. 14.
62. Bloomfield, *Short-Term Capital Movements*, p. 9, chart 1.
63. Ibid. pp. 17–18, charts 2 and 3.
64. Lindert, *Key Currencies*, pp. 10–11, table 1. As Lindert's figures show, even France held some foreign exchange, but it constituted a small percentage of the very large French reserves in 1913. Britain held foreign coins. See discussion p. 25, above.
65. On foreign exchange holdings by currency, see Lindert, *Key Currencies*, pp. 18–19, table 2.

be likely to hold any significant amount of foreign paper currency in its vaults where it would earn no interest; and to the extent it held gold or silver coins, these would be counted as gold or silver and not as foreign exchange.) It is also true, however, that an important source of foreign exchange holdings in the gold standard period was the practice of a number of countries, when they first moved from an inconvertible currency to convertibility under the gold standard, of continuing to hold foreign exchange that had been acquired during their period of inconvertibility.[66]

An important consequence of the widespread holdings of foreign exchange was that Britain, just like the United States in the late 1960s and until 15 August 1971, was in the position of having total reserves (held in both instances almost entirely in gold) that were only a small fraction of its total liquid liabilities to foreign official institutions. And private institutions also had huge foreign liabilities which, even though matched by even greater claims on foreigners, were perhaps shorter-term than those foreign claims.[67] This "overhang" of foreign claims led to various near crises and to a certain amount of manipulation and borrowing from foreign institutions (to be discussed below); but the gold standard survived, as did Britain's relatively central position in it. Among the rival centers, Germany had large liquid liabilities, though France had a strong net reserve position.

The reasons for the growth of foreign currency holdings are uncertain and complex.[68] For example, lenders may have been as eager as borrowers to see this development; no doubt Britain, just like the United States in the 1960s, preferred growing liabilities to a gold outflow. And the desire to earn interest income on reserves was an influence even in the heyday of gold. But surely one important reason in some countries for a preference for holding part of the reserve in foreign exchange was a desire to be able to intervene in foreign exchange markets to maintain the exchange rate. Although direct information on the extent of exchange market intervention is scarce, Bloomfield's path-breaking studies led him to conclude that a number of Continental monetary authorities were "very active" in the foreign exchange market.[69] In the case of Finland, foreign exchange transactions were utilized to the virtual exclusion of gold flows to maintain the exchange rate.[70] And in Austria-Hungary, not only was exchange market intervention used to maintain the exchange rate once it joined the gold standard in the 1890s, but the central bank intervened

66. Ibid. p. 33.
67. Treasury Memorandum on the Gold Reserves, 22 May 1914, reprinted in Sayers, *Bank of England 1891–1944*, 3:3–30, appendix 2; Bloomfield, *Short-Term Capital Movements*, pp. 71–77; Lindert, *Key Currencies*, pp. 36–62.
68. For a discussion of various possible reasons, see Lindert, *Key Currencies*, pp. 27–35.
69. Bloomfield, *Short-Term Capital Movements*, p. 25. See also Bloomfield, *Monetary Policy*, p. 55.
70. Bloomfield, *Short-Term Capital Movements*, p. 23.

actively in *forward* markets in order, by altering the forward premium or discount, to influence gold movements.[71]

Gold Devices

Foreign exchange market intervention by peripheral countries can perhaps be defended as consistent with the gold standard model. Better known than exchange intervention, however, was a more technical manipulation of the implicit international rules of the gold standard which was developed into quite a fine art by the turn of the century at the supposed center of the gold standard world. The Bank of England learned that an outflow of gold might be arrested, or an inflow stimulated by acting directly on the gold market rather than trying to affect interest rates by increasing Bank Rate. Indeed, the indirect "second channel" effect of an increase in Bank Rate in slowing domestic economic activity came to be viewed as an inconvenience that could sometimes be avoided by the use of what came to be known as "gold devices." Gold devices had the effect of widening the gold points and thus permitting more flexibility in market exchange rates. Thus, when sterling was weak, an increase in market interest rates could be delayed by taking measures that lowered the gold outflow point. If it seemed desirable to rebuild the gold reserve when sterling was relatively strong, the Bank of England could in effect narrow the gold points in order to speed the process.

The most common gold device involved the manipulation of the Bank's buying and selling rates. It will be recalled that the Bank was required to buy gold bullion at par, which was 77s. 9d. per ounce. But nothing in British law precluded the Bank from paying more. And hence it frequently paid more.[72] The requirement that the Bank sell sovereigns at 77s. 10½d. did not prevent the Bank from charging more for gold bars, so long as it was willing to make sovereigns available at that price, when there was a shortage of bullion in the market (as when the flow of newly mined gold from South Africa was insufficient to meet demand). And so, in its efforts to discourage export of gold bullion, it often raised its selling price, twice reaching 78s. 1d.[73] Indeed, it could refuse to sell gold bars at all, forcing exporters to take sovereigns for which they had no use save through the expensive process of melting.[74] Similarly, the duty to sell sovereigns at not more than 77s. 10½d. did not preclude the Bank from raising the price at which it would sell foreign gold coins.[75] Since the exporter of foreign gold coins usually preferred the coins of the country to which he was exporting so that they could be used

71. Paul Einzig, *A Dynamic Theory of Forward Exchange*, 2d ed. (1967), pp. 405–19; Ludwig von Mises, "The Foreign Exchange Policy of the Austro-Hungarian Bank," *Economic Journal* 19(1909):201–11.
72. Sayers, *Bank of England Operations, 1890–1914*, p. 82.
73. Ibid.
74. Ibid. p. 79.
75. See discussion of Peel's Act of 1819, pp. 24–25.

there, a higher price for gold coins tended to deter gold export. At some price, of course, even those needing foreign gold coins would take sovereigns at 77s. 10½d. and have them melted and reminted into coins in the country of destination.[76] Since the Bank of England was the principal buyer and seller in England of gold bullion and coins, the manipulation of buying and selling rates tended to dominate the British gold market and to influence gold flows profoundly.

More esoteric gold devices were also used. A gold inflow could be accelerated by paying the gold importers' brokerage charges or buying the gold upon shipment, thus granting the importer what was in effect an interest-free loan.[77] If gold exports were to be discouraged, the Bank could offer foreign coins, or for that matter gold sovereigns, for sale that were as light as legally permissible, thus limiting their value in foreign markets.[78] This last technique, like the manipulation of the selling price for gold bars, was of course limited by the duty to sell sovereigns at 77s. 10½d.

England was not alone in using gold devices. The Bank of France often pursued a gold premium policy when gold exports would otherwise be profitable.[79] A number of central banks, including the Reichsbank, the Swiss National Bank, and the Austro-Hungarian Bank, used interest-free advances to gold exporters, as did the U.S. Treasury in 1906–7.[80] Some central banks used less formal and more coercive means of discouraging gold outflows when their country's exchange rate was weak.[81]

However significant the gold devices were within the context of the gold standard of the time, their effect can easily be exaggerated. What gold devices did was to increase slightly the flexibility of market exchange rates, but it was still a very modest flexibility compared to a floating system or even an "adjustable peg" system involving periodic devaluations.

A useful comparison can be made between gold points, even given the existence of gold devices, and margins under a fixed exchange rate system of the Bretton Woods variety.[82] Under the gold standard the spread between the gold import and gold export points depended upon the distance of the two financial centers in question, because the distance determined freight, insurance and interest costs. Thus, the author of one of the leading textbooks of the time provides calculations showing gold points some 1.2 percent apart for London–New York transactions but only about 0.9 percent apart for

---

76. For examples of manipulation of the price for gold coins, see Sayers, *Bank of England Operations, 1890–1914*, pp. 77ff.
77. Ibid. pp. 82–84.
78. Ibid. pp. 84–85.
79. White, *French International Accounts*, pp. 182–88.
80. Bloomfield, *Monetary Policy*, p. 53, including n. 97.
81. Ibid. pp. 54–55.
82. See discussion of Bretton Woods margins, chapter 4.

London-Paris transactions.[83] Taking these calculations as a base, one may add the following to the spread for various gold devices:

1. Raising the gold selling price from the usual price of
   77s. 10½d. to the maximum recorded of 78s. 1d.   +0.25 percent

2. Offering light foreign gold coins and/or raising their
   price[84]   +0.2 percent

It will be seen that, even with gold devices, the spread for London–New York would be no more than about 1.65 percent, which is less than the 2 percent maximum spread (1 percent margin on either side of par) under the Bretton Woods agreement.

Moreover, some gold devices, such as the subsidization of brokerage charges, were used to induce gold imports rather than to deter gold exports. The effect of those devices may be viewed as a slight devaluation, but if one puts that point aside and concentrates on the spread, then the effect was to narrow the spread. On the other hand, some spread-widening gold devices used in other countries, such as the French gold premium policy, were more substantial. The French premium reached 0.6 percent in 1880, 1887, 1888, 1891, 1893 and 1898, going over 0.7 percent only in 1887, but after the turn of the century the gold premium was seldom used and even then was rarely as high as 0.1 percent.[85] Thus, the French gold premium was a significant phenomenon, but it did not often do more than widen the franc-sterling spread (as we have seen, normally about 0.9 percent) to the width of the dollar-sterling spread (normally about 1.2 percent).[86]

83. Clare, pp. 110, 129–30. Clare, writing from a London standpoint, states that the import point from New York was $4.89 to $4.90 and the export point $4.84 to $4.83. For Paris he calculates the import point at 25.32½ francs and the export point at 25.10 to 25.15 francs. See also J. F. G. Bagshaw, *Practical Banking* (1920), p. 218.

84. This calculation is based on a statement in *The Statist*, quoted in Sayers, *Bank of England Operations 1890–1914*, p. 84, n. 5, that the selection of the minimum legal weight sovereigns for export made gold shipments unprofitable at 25.07½ francs. Since the duty to pay out sovereigns was an effective limit on the ability to raise the price of foreign gold coins and to select light foreign gold coins, one may compare the 25.07½ rate with 25.10 to 25.15 francs (taking an average of 25.125) as the normal gold export point. See note 83 above. The difference of 0.05 equals only 0.2 percent.

Another calculation would compare the American gold eagle's standard weight of 23.22 grains and its minimum weight of 22.97 grains, a difference of about 1.0 percent. However, for the $20 gold eagle, the standard weight was 464.4 grains and its minimum weight 463.9 grains, a difference of only about 0.1 percent. See Horace White, *Money and Banking*, 5th ed. (1914), p. 23. Since few American coins to be found in England were presumably still of standard "mint" weight, and since it would be difficult to select a sufficient volume of those eagles that were precisely at the minimum weight, these differences exaggerate the possible effect of such a policy.

85. White, *French International Accounts*, pp. 319–30, table 49.

86. Clare, p. 112. Clare states that between 1883 and 1888 the lowest recorded sterling-franc rate was 25.11½ and the highest 25.44½, a difference of about 1.3 percent. Ibid. p. 114.

Central Bank Cooperation

International lending for the purpose of keeping a country on the gold standard (or, as we would say today, to preserve the existing official rate of exchange) occurred during the gold standard period.[87] Such lending seems to have been much less common than during later periods of fixed exchange rates, such as the late 1920s and the Bretton Woods period. But it was on occasion necessary even to keep Britain convertible. How often foreign governments came to Britain's aid is a matter of some controversy. Certainly at the time of the Baring Bank crisis in 1890, the Bank of England borrowed several million pounds' worth of gold in Paris and sold £1½ million of securities to the Russian government.[88] The Bank of France came to the aid of the Bank of England in 1906–7, although the precise nature of its support remains more controversial than in the Baring Bank crisis.[89]

Floating Exchange Rates

Still another phenomenon of the gold standard period that was more common in later periods, floating exchange rates, is better understood not as part of the gold standard but as the result of reluctance of some countries to submit to it. The fact is that even after the United States went off floating in 1879, a number of countries had still not joined the gold standard. Seen from the parts of the world already on gold, the exchange rates of those countries still on silver were constantly fluctuating. The Indian rupee, for example, was on a silver standard until 1893, and the rate of exchange between India and gold standard countries depended upon the price of silver in terms of gold.[90] Throughout that period the rupee declined, from an average of 1s. 8d. in 1879–80 to 1s. 3d. in 1892–93.[91]

But there were other examples of floating that did not rest on the choice of silver as a standard. The Austro-Hungarian gulden floated until the passage of what purported to be gold standard legislation in 1891 and indeed even for a short time beyond, until the Austro-Hungarian Bank began intervening in defense of the exchange rate.[92] And Russia floated until it joined the gold standard in 1897.[93]

87. For instance, see Bloomfield, *Monetary Policy*, pp. 56–58.
88. John Clapham, *The Bank of England* (1945), 2:330; Sayers, *Bank of England Operations, 1890–1914*, pp. 102–3.
89. Compare White, *French International Accounts*, p. 195, with Sayers, *Bank of England Operations, 1890–1914*, pp. 102–15, and Sayers, *Bank of England 1891–1944*, 1:54–59.
90. *Royal Commission on Indian Currency and Finance*, Cmd. 2687 (1926), vol. 2, appendix 3, p. 9.
91. Ibid. appendix 3, p. 24.
92. Leland B. Yeager, "Fluctuating Exchange Rates in the Nineteenth Century: The Experiences of Austria and Russia," in *Monetary Problems of the International Economy*, ed. Robert A. Mundell and Alexander K. Swoboda (1969), pp. 61–62.
93. Ibid.; Bloomfield, *Monetary Policy*, p. 13.

VI. The Gold Standard in Retrospect

With all of its anomalies and exceptions, the gold standard "worked." While it worked and where it worked, it had certain clear-cut characteristics. The most important attribute of the gold standard was not gold flows, which are better understood as a means to an end, but rather fixed exchange rates. In the core period and area of the gold standard, rates were truly fixed and not just pegged, subject to change, as under the Bretton Woods system. They were so much fixed that the maintenance of gold parity between currencies came to be taken for granted. It is quite remarkable that from 1879 to 1914, a period considerably longer than from 1945 to the demise of Bretton Woods in 1971, there were no changes of parities between the United States, Britain, France, and Germany—not to speak of a number of smaller European countries.

That was also a period, of course, in which governments and central banks did not take it upon themselves to attempt to steer the economy, eliminate unemployment, or provide for the social needs and preferences of their peoples. For all the changes in Bank Rate and similar measures, the gold standard was *allowed* to work more than it was *made* to work. Yet one cannot merely say that the international monetary system worked because of the limited role of the state, for earlier eras had seen just as limited a state but disorder and even disaster in international monetary affairs.

More important than fixed exchange rates, which, like gold itself, are best seen as a means, not an end, the gold standard period witnessed a great expansion of trade and, it is worth emphasizing in view of the attitudes taken during the Bretton Woods period, a flow of private foreign investment on a scale the world had never seen and, indeed, relative to other economic aggregates, was never to see again.

All of this was particularly good for Englishmen. One of England's most illustrious economists described the results from just across the abyss of the Great War:

> What an extraordinary episode in the economic progress of man that age was which came to an end in August, 1914! The greater part of the population, it is true, worked hard and lived at a low standard of comfort, yet were, to all appearances, reasonably contented with this lot. But escape was possible, for any man of capacity or character at all exceeding the average, into the middle and upper classes, for whom life offered, at a low cost and with the least trouble, conveniences, comforts, and amenities beyond the compass of the richest and most powerful monarchs of other ages. The inhabitant of London could order by telephone, sipping his morning tea in bed, the various products of the whole earth, in such quantity as he might see fit, and reasonably expect their early delivery upon his doorstep; he could at the same moment and by the

same means adventure his wealth in the natural resources and new enterprises of any quarter of the world, and share, without exertion or even trouble, in their prospective fruits and advantages; or he could decide to couple the security of his fortunes with the good faith of the townspeople of any substantial municipality in any continent that fancy or information might recommend. He could secure forthwith, if he wished it, cheap and comfortable means of transit to any country or climate without passport or other formality, could despatch his servant to the neighboring office of a bank for such supply of the precious metals as might seem convenient, and could then proceed abroad to foreign quarters, without knowledge of their religion, language, or customs, bearing coined wealth upon his person, and would consider himself greatly aggrieved and much surprised at the least interference. But, most important of all, he regarded this state of affairs as normal, certain, and permanent, except in the direction of further improvement, and any deviation from it as aberrant, scandalous, and avoidable. The projects and politics of militarism and imperialism, of racial and cultural rivalries, of monopolies, restrictions, and exclusion, which were to play the serpent to this paradise, were little more than the amusements of his daily newspaper, and appeared to exercise almost no influence at all on the ordinary course of social and economic life, the internationalization of which was nearly complete in practice.[94]

Yet for all its bountifulness and conceptual beauty, the gold standard was swept away in a few days at the outset of the First World War. Galbraith has said that the first casualty of war may be not truth but money.[95] He was talking about the American Civil War, but the gold standard collapsed before the First World War was a month old. The refusal of London financial institutions to extend credit created a shortage of sterling for the payment by foreigners of short-term sterling debts. Sales of sterling securities in London bridged the gap for a few days until the London Stock Exchange closed. Shipment of gold from abroad stopped due to wartime risks. Even before war had been declared, in the last week of July, the pound sterling rose from near its mint par of $4.8665 to $6.35.[96] Although the dollar-sterling rate returned to par by December and was stabilized at approximately par for the course of the war, this result was accomplished only through extensive exchange control and pegging.[97] Meanwhile, the French franc, the Italian lira, and a variety of other currencies depreciated seriously.[98]

The international monetary history of the interwar period, to which we turn next, is very different from that of the gold standard period. In contrast

94. John Maynard Keynes, *The Economic Consequences of the Peace* (1920), pp. 10–12.
95. John Kenneth Galbraith, *Money, Whence It Came, Where It Went* (1975), p. 92.
96. William Adams Brown, *The International Gold Standard Reinterpreted 1914–1934* (1940), 1:7–23.
97. Ibid. pp. 59–65; Keynes, *Treatise on Money*, 1:19.
98. *Federal Reserve Bulletin*, 1918, pp. 837–39.

to the relative solidity and harmony of the gold standard epoch, the later period was marked by struggle and conflict in international monetary affairs. The first half of the 1920s is perhaps best seen as an extended effort, which ultimately proved a failure, to reconstruct what was so easily destroyed in a few days in August 1914.

THREE

The Interwar Years

The period between the two world wars can be viewed as a bridge between the era of the pre-1914 self-regulating gold standard and that of the post-1945 Bretton Woods system. Looking backward across the chasm of the Second War, statesmen often regarded the interwar period as a time of monetary anarchy that had been finally put behind them by the rules and institutions created at Bretton Woods. This optimistic picture of the progress achieved in international monetary affairs began to fade as some of the events of the interwar period reappeared in the 1970s—especially floating rates and trade-motivated devaluations. But it was a distorted view to begin with.

Properly situated between a less-idealized gold standard period (in which floating rates, exchange market intervention, and other "warts" mar the beauty of the model sketched in economic textbooks) and the early years of Bretton Woods (when exchange controls, bilateralism and the like were rampant), the interwar period represents far more continuity than discontinuity. A self-regulating gold standard was incompatible with the growing interventions of the state in domestic economies and international trade, and the international monetary system thus had to adapt to this changed environment. The outlines of one kind of adaptation are already visible in the mid-1930s. Nonetheless, the interpretation of the 1930s as a period of anarchy and chaos tended to dominate the thinking of the Bretton Woods architects. The fundamental principles of the Bretton Woods agreement—no floating rates, no competitive devaluations, exchange rate changes to be a matter of international rather than solely domestic concern, and exchange rate crises to be overcome when possible through the lending of international reserves rather than through contractionary domestic policies—were prescriptions for avoiding the perceived evils of the interwar period. Those principles were based in part on a distorted understanding of what had actually transpired in that period. An appreciation of the purposes and the weaknesses of Bretton Woods requires an understanding both of the events of the interwar period and of the contemporary understanding of those events.

I. Monetary Events between the Wars

The monetary history of the interwar period is complex. One simple measure of its complexity is that the most complete analytical treatment of the period, Brown's *The International Gold Standard Reinterpreted*, runs over 1,300 pages, yet carries the chronology only as far as 1934.[1] Although it would be convenient to be able to proceed directly to an analysis of the period as a whole, some sense of the historical flow of events is required. Hence, a capsule review of the events will be set forth here as a prelude. Such a review is facilitated by thinking of the interwar period as composed of four subperiods: the end of World War I to 1925, 1925–31, 1931–36, and 1936 to the beginning of World War II.[2]

World War I to 1925

The British fully expected the gold standard to be reestablished at the end of the Great War and London to remain its center. No reason thus appeared to change the legal form of the gold standard in Britain, and the necessary accommodations to the monetary realities imposed by the war were made

1. William Adams Brown, Jr., *The International Gold Standard Reinterpreted 1914–1934*, 2 vols. (1940).
2. Useful chronologies, shorter than Brown but longer than offered here, can be found in Leland B. Yeager, *International Monetary Relations: Theory, History, and Policy*, 2d ed. (1976), pp. 310–73; and R. G. Hawtrey, *The Gold Standard in Theory and Practice*, 5th ed. (1947), pp. 92–183. See also Gustav Cassel, *The Downfall of the Gold Standard* (1936), and Benjamin M. Anderson, *Economics and the Public Welfare* (1949).

without altering the formal interconvertibility of currency and gold on the same terms that governed before 1914. Even export of gold remained formally lawful until prohibited in 1919,[3] but informal means were successfully used to discourage such exportation.[4] Although the right to import gold was not legally impaired, the Bank of England arranged to purchase all Empire gold, and in 1916 the government requested all importers of other gold to sell it to the Bank of England. Thus, importation as well as exportation was effectively deterred.[5]

Yet there were legal changes that profoundly altered the conditions under which the return to gold in 1925 would occur. Inflationary finance in the form of currency notes (which were issued by the Treasury and which, unlike Bank of England notes, were beyond the fiduciary limits established by the Bank Charter Act of 1844)[6] had one major effect quite apart from the necessity of deflationary action to make possible the reestablishment of prewar parities on the return to the gold standard in 1925. The issuance of the currency notes in one pound and ten shilling denominations (unlike Bank of England notes which continued to be issued only in five pound and larger denominations) accustomed the populace to using paper currency rather than sovereigns for day-to-day transactions. The resulting new patterns of usage thus facilitated the "gold bullion" provision of the Gold Standard Act of 1925, which abolished the right to obtain gold from the Bank of England in the form of gold coins or in bars of less than approximately 400 ounces.[7]

Although the United States had sinned against the gold standard a bit during the war by placing an embargo on the exportation of gold coin and bullion, the lifting of the embargo in June 1919 placed it in the unusual position of being the only one of the belligerents firmly on the gold standard.[8] Of the major European belligerents, only Britain had a currency strong enough to make a return to the prewar parities thinkable. Although exchange rates between the dollar and the pound had been effectively pegged during the war through a combination of exchange and trade controls, purchase and sale of British treasury bills in New York and the extension of U.S. credits,[9] the pound floated from 1919 to 1925. By February 1920 sterling had depre-

3. Order in Council of 1 April 1919. See R. S. Sayers, *The Bank of England, 1891–1944* (1976), Appendixes, appendix 6, pp. 55–56.
4. Regulations issued in December 1916 under the Defence of the Realm Consolidation Act, 1914 (5 Geo. 5, c. 8), which prohibited the melting of gold coin, also served as a practical deterrent to export. Meanwhile exchange control was used to "limit the need for foreign remittances." Brown, 1:35, 180. A further important factor was the unavailability of insurance on ocean shipping of gold. D. E. Moggridge, *The Return to Gold, 1925* (1969), pp. 11–12.
5. Brown, 1:31.
6. The issue of currency notes was authorized by the Currency and Bank Notes Act, 1914, 4 & 5 Geo. 5, c. 14.
7. Gold Standard Act, 1925, 15 & 16 Geo. 5, c. 29, §1 (c) (2).
8. See the discussion of the embargo in *Federal Reserve Bulletin*, 1919, pp. 615–16.
9. Brown, 1:61–62, 71ff; S. E. Harris, *Monetary Problems of the British Empire* (1931), pp. 246–63.

ciated from the pegged wartime rate of about $4.76 to less than $3.40; thereafter it fluctuated within the $3.40 to $4.00 range until the end of 1921 (one incident of supposedly unstable floating rates) and then began a slow and persistent climb to the reestablished prewar parity of $4.86, with only one major setback in late 1923 and early 1924.[10]

The currencies of other major belligerents had depreciated beyond any possibility of stabilization at the prewar par. By November 1920 the French franc had depreciated to 31 percent, and the German mark to only 5 percent, of their prewar par value.[11] All major currencies were floating and stabilization of rates became a prime goal. Stabilization was first achieved in January 1923 in Austria.[12] Although usually thought of in terms of gold, stabilization was better conceived (to the extent that the gold standard was not returned to fully) as the adoption of fixed rates against the dollar and other stabilized currencies.

1925 to 1931

In 1925 Britain removed its embargo on the export of gold. Since the buying and selling price for gold was such, in comparison with the U.S. gold price, that the mint par between Britain and the United States was the same as before 1914, the effect was to place Britain back on gold at the prewar parity of $4.86. In retrospect this rate is almost unanimously considered to have overvalued sterling.[13] Indeed, the official experts' report recommending the step virtually conceded that such overvaluation would result but asserted confidently that "a courageous policy in currency matters surmounts apparently formidable obstacles with surprising ease."[14]

The consequences of Britain's return to the gold standard at an overvalued rate were compounded by the French franc's stabilization in the following year at an undervalued rate.[15] The franc, buffeted by highly inflationary fiscal and monetary policies since the war, had floated continuously, falling

10. See exchange rate tables, *Federal Reserve Bulletin*, 1928, p. 57 and graph, ibid. 1925, p. 371.
11. Brown, 1:216, table 16.
12. *Federal Reserve Bulletin*, 1928, p. 562.
13. *Report of the Committee on Finance & Industry*, Cmd. 3897, para. 113 (June 1931) (hereafter cited Macmillan report); Yeager, p. 322; Milton Friedman, "Money," in 12 *Encyclopaedia Britannica*, 15th ed. (1975), 12:351. The literature and the evidence, including arguments that sterling was not overvalued, are reviewed in D. E. Moggridge, *British Monetary Policy, 1924–1931* (1972), pp. 98–112. The most usual estimate of the degree of overvaluation is about 10 percent. See J. M. Keynes, "The Economic Consequences of Mr. Churchill" (1925), reprinted in *Essays in Persuasion* (1932), pp. 248, 250; and compare the view of Churchill's principal private secretary in P. J. Grigg, *Prejudice and Judgment* (1948), pp. 180–86, and R. S. Sayers, "The Return to Gold, 1925" in *Studies in the Industrial Revolution*, ed. L. S. Pressnell (1960), pp. 313–27.
14. *Report of the Committee on the Currency and Bank of England Note Issues*, Cmd. 2393 (1925), para. 32. Keynes characterized the report as "indolent and jejune." J. M. Keynes, "The Committee on the Currency," *Economic Journal* 35(1925):304.
15. Yeager, pp. 327–30.

to a low of under three U.S. cents in June 1926 (compared to a range of six to nine cents in 1920–22) and then rising after the formation of the Poincaré government in July 1926, until by the end of that year it reached a so-called de facto stabilization rate of roughly 3.95 cents.[16]

Between de facto stabilization in December 1926 and de jure stabilization in June 1928, the franc rate against sterling and the dollar was maintained by means of foreign exchange transactions by the Bank of France. The recovery of confidence in France under the Poincaré government led to a reversal of the previous capital flight, with the consequence that France accumulated large holdings of foreign exchange during the de facto stabilization period. By 1928 its foreign exchange reserves had increased from $14 million to nearly $1.3 billion (while gold reserves were increasing from $0.7 billion to nearly $1.25 billion). The statute that converted de facto into de jure stabilization and placed France back on the gold standard, made gold the sole permissible backing for note issues.[17] Although the statute did not prohibit the Bank of France from continuing to hold foreign exchange, the French authorities nevertheless set about reducing foreign exchange holdings and acquiring gold. By 1930, French foreign exchange holdings fell to $1.0 billion while gold holdings increased to more than $2.0 billion. Thereafter, the conversion to gold accelerated and by 1932 foreign exchange constituted only 5 percent of the total French reserves of nearly $3.5 billion.[18]

Between the return of Britain to the gold standard in 1925 and the French de jure stabilization in 1928, most of the other principal countries of the world had returned to the gold standard.[19] The U.S. Federal Reserve was able to announce in August 1928 "the practical completion of the world's monetary reconstruction."[20] But the reconstruction was short-lived. It had been fueled with large-scale U.S. capital exports, which helped to provide the stabilizing countries with the requisite liquidity, but the capital export flow virtually stopped in 1928 as funds were diverted into short-term financing of the New York Stock Exchange boom.[21]

16. *Federal Reserve Bulletin*, 1928, pp. 57–58. The lowest quotation was 2.03 cents. Yeager, p. 327. On the inflationary internal French policies, see Eleanor Lansing Dulles, *The French Franc, 1914–1928* (1929), and Martin Wolfe, *The French Franc between the Wars, 1919–1939* (1951), pp. 26–72.
17. Monetary Law of 25 June 1928, Art. 4 (English translation), *Federal Reserve Bulletin*, 1928, p. 570.
18. For French reserve figures, see League of Nations, *International Currency Experience* (1944), p. 234, appendix 2. Some, but surely not all, of these foreign exchange sales may have been required to acquire gold sufficient to meet the statutory requirement of 35 percent gold backing of the currency. Monetary Law of 25 June 1928, Art. 4, in *Federal Reserve Bulletin*, 1928, p. 570.
19. Despite some restrictions, four countries (Austria, Colombia, Sweden, and Germany) can be said to have returned to gold before Britain. For a summary by country of the return to gold, see *Federal Reserve Bulletin*, 1928, p. 562.
20. Ibid. p. 541.
21. Macmillan report, paras. 158–61; Yeager, pp. 336–37.

The drop in U.S. capital exports, coupled with the growth of French reserves and their conversion into gold, put strong pressure on the pound. British gold reserves were probably even less ample than before World War I and now Britain suffered from an overvalued currency to boot. When the 1931 Macmillan report showed, in an attempt to reassure the foreign exchange markets, that Britain's net short-term liabilities were only £254 million,[22] the market found the news anything but reassuring in view of the fact that the Bank of England's total holdings of gold were only about £150 million and most of that was required as domestic backing for the pound.[23] In July alone the Bank of England lost nearly £32 million of gold.[24] Despite foreign credits, withdrawal of foreign balances beginning in mid-July reached £200 million by mid-September.[25] On September 21 the British government suspended payments of gold against legal tender currency, and Britain thereby left the gold standard.[26]

1931 to 1936

The effect of the suspension of gold payments was a sharp depreciation of sterling against all gold standard currencies. A number of countries, chiefly those in the British Commonwealth and including some other countries that held reserves primarily in sterling, elected to allow their currencies to depreciate with the pound. Thus was born the sterling area.[27]

The September 1931 decision was in essence a devaluation of sterling, but the means was to let sterling float. Given the prevailing uncertainty, about both currency markets and the possibilities of recovery from the still worsening world depression, sterling did not promptly come to rest, fluctuating in 1932 between $3.27 and $3.74.[28] The British authorities decided in 1932 to create an Exchange Equalisation Account,[29] which would permit intervention in the foreign exchange markets while insulating the domestic money

---

22. Macmillan report, paras. 259–60.
23. Ibid. para. 324, giving the April 1931 figure as £145 million, and appendix 2, p. 303, giving the average May 1931 figure as £149.4 million. At the end of May, gold holdings were £151 million and reached £165 million in early July, after which they declined rapidly. Sayers, *Bank of England 1891–1944*, Appendixes, appendix 37, p. 355. See discussion pp. 66–68 below.
24. Paul Einzig, *The World Economic Crisis, 1929–1931*, 2d ed. (1932), p. 133.
25. Text of press notice issued 20 September 1931, in Sayers, *Bank of England 1891–1944*, Appendixes, appendix 23, pp. 264–65.
26. The Gold Standard (Amendment) Act, 1931, 21 & 22 Geo. 5, c. 46, suspended the operation of the gold payment provisions of the Gold Standard Act, 1925.
27. BIS, *The Sterling Area* (1953), pp. 13–15.
28. Board of Governors of the Federal Reserve System, *Banking and Monetary Statistics* (1943), p. 681.
29. Finance Act, 1932, 22 & 23 Geo. 5, c. 25, Part IV. See Susan Howson, *Sterling's Managed Float: The Operations of the Exchange Equalisation Account, 1932–39*, Princeton Studies in International Finance no. 46 (1980), pp. 4–14.

supply from the otherwise direct influence of those transactions.[30] Another precedent was set, this time for the principle of managed floating and for the purposeful insulation of the domestic economy from the international monetary system.

Unlike the British, who adhered to the gold standard as long as their dwindling gold reserves permitted, the incoming Roosevelt administration, though enjoying undiminished gold reserves,[31] elected to engineer a depreciation of the dollar in the foreign exchange markets. The goal was to force up depreciating domestic prices, especially for internationally traded agricultural commodities. The means was a gold-buying program.[32]

Even earlier the administration had signaled its intention to manage the foreign exchange value of the dollar by imposing exchange controls and a gold export embargo,[33] thereby taking the dollar off the gold standard, and by ordering delivery of private holdings of gold coin, bullion, and certificates to the Federal Reserve.[34] In order to pursue his administration's forced depreciation policy, Roosevelt, in the summer of 1933, purposely torpedoed the London World Economic Conference, which had been the arena for negotiation of a stabilization arrangement among the United States, Britain, and the gold standard countries.

The gold value of the dollar declined from the pre-1933 parity of $20.67 per ounce to more than $34 in mid-January 1934. Viewed from the foreign exchange point of view, the dollar depreciated commensurately against gold standard currencies and even against the floating pound sterling. Indeed, the pound-dollar rate rose from $3.43 in March 1933 to $5.14 in November of that year and averaged just over $5.00 in 1934.[35] The gold-buying program having achieved its exchange market goals, the president acted in late January 1934 to peg the gold price at $35 per ounce.[36] To maintain the dollar at the

30. Sayers, *Bank of England 1891–1944*, 2:426–30. On the Account's operations see N. F. Hall, *The Exchange Equalisation Account* (1935); Leonard Waight, *The History and Mechanism of the Exchange Equalisation Account* (1939); and Howson, *Sterling's Managed Float*, pp. 15–44.
31. During the latter half of the 1920s the U.S. monetary gold stock had fluctuated around $4.5 billion. After rising to $5 billion in 1931, it fell by more than $1 billion in the first half of 1932, but had risen to nearly $4.3 billion when Roosevelt assumed office. See *Federal Reserve Bulletin*, 1933, p. 212.
32. On the gold-buying program, see Milton Friedman and Anna J. Schwartz, *A Monetary History of the United States* (1963), pp. 462–83.
33. Presidential Proclamations no. 2039 (6 March 1933), and no. 2040 (9 March 1933); Executive Orders no. 6111 (20 April 1933) and no. 6260 (28 August 1933). See *The Public Papers and Addresses of Franklin D. Roosevelt* (1938), 2:45–46, 141–43, 345–52 (hereafter cited *FDR Papers*), and 48 Stat. 1691 (1933).
34. Exec. Order no. 6102 (5 April 1933), *FDR Papers*, 2:111–14.
35. *Banking and Monetary Statistics* (1943), p. 681.
36. Proclamation no. 2072 (31 January 1934), *FDR Papers*, 3:67–70. The president acted under the authority of Section 12 of the Gold Reserve Act of 1934, 48 Stat. 337, 342 (1934), which

new price, the United States stood ready not merely to buy gold freely and to sell it freely to foreign central banks at $35 per ounce,[37] but also to enter into foreign exchange transactions. To facilitate the latter transactions, an Exchange Stabilization Fund was created out of a portion of the profits of the devaluation of the dollar in terms of gold.[38] The Fund bore an obvious resemblance to the British Exchange Equalisation Account. However, in view of the $35 gold commitment, the role of the U.S. Fund was less crucial to the stabilization of the dollar.[39]

Despite the return of the United States to the gold standard, the world was effectively divided into monetary blocs. European countries adhering to the gold standard had formed a "gold bloc" upon the collapse of the 1933 World Economic Conference. Although the governments of France, Belgium, Italy, the Netherlands, Poland, and Switzerland agreed that their central banks should cooperate to maintain the existing gold parities,[40] the gold bloc was little more than a name for those European countries remaining on gold. A second regional group was the sterling area, whose members tended to float with sterling.[41] Meanwhile, though the dollar was once again on gold, the gold bloc currencies were substantially overvalued relative not just to sterling area currencies but to the dollar as well. The 28 percent devaluation by Belgium in March 1935 sealed the fate of the gold bloc,[42] but it was not until the end of September 1936 that the French franc left the gold standard. The other gold bloc countries had no alternative but to follow the French example.[43]

together with Section 43 of the 1933 Agricultural Adjustment Act, which it amended, empowered the president to fix the gold weight of the dollar between 50 and 60 percent of its prior weight. The new $35 official price of gold involved fixing the gold weight of the dollar at 59.06 percent of its former weight.

37. Statements of the secretary of the treasury, *Federal Reserve Bulletin*, 1934, p. 69.

38. Gold Reserve Act of 1934, ch. 6, §10, 48 Stat. 341–42 (1934).

39. On the Fund's rationale and transactions, see Arthur I. Bloomfield, "Operations of the American Exchange Stabilization Fund," *Review of Economics and Statistics* 26(1944):69–87. The practice of offsetting or "sterilizing" gold imports did not begin until December 1936. Ibid. pp. 71–72. Moreover, the sterilization technique was used for all gold imports whether or not passing through the Fund. Nonetheless, the creation of the Fund, following on the establishment of the British Exchange Equalisation Account, was an important precedent leading other countries to create stabilization funds for more explicit stabilization purposes.

40. See declaration of 3 July 1933, and communiqué of 8 July 1933, in *Documents on International Affairs, 1933*, ed. John W. Wheeler-Bennett (1934), p. 45.

41. *Bank for International Settlements 5th Report* 1935, pp. 7–8 (hereafter cited BIS).

42. See "Belgian Legislation on Currency and Foreign Exchange," *Federal Reserve Bulletin*, 1935, p. 290. See also Paul Einzig, *World Finance, 1935–1937* (1937), p. 10: "the devaluation of the belga . . . constitutes one of the most important landmarks in the history of financial developments since 1914. . . . It was the starting-point of the death-struggle of the Gold Bloc."

43. See *Federal Reserve Bulletin*,1936, pp. 759–61, 852, 878–81, 979; and *BIS 7th Report* 1937, pp. 18–24, for details.

1936 to World War II

The way in which France left the gold standard was important. Because of the political sensitivity of devaluation in France, the French government sought some kind of international arrangement to accompany the devaluation. Meanwhile, both the American and British governments were interested in limiting the amount of the French devaluation. Out of those mutual interests came the Tripartite Agreement among the three governments.[44]

The agreement itself did not result in any single document. Each of the three governments issued a separate declaration.[45] Although the Tripartite Declarations have been characterized as "nothing but words,"[46] the chief underlying multilateral agreement, though achieved in two sets of bilateral agreements, represented a move toward multilateralism and toward a recognition that exchange rates were matters for international and not merely domestic concern. Moreover, the Tripartite Agreement was implemented by a "twenty-four hour" understanding that led to ongoing working relationships among the international monetary authorities of the three countries. Under the umbrella of the Tripartite Agreement each government committed itself to convert any balances of its own currencies acquired by the other governments at an announced price, which was subject to change at any time, so long as the conversion was made within twenty-four hours; the conversion would be at the price in effect at the time of acquisition of the currency, not at the time of conversion.[47] This technical arrangement eliminated any exchange-rate risk in dealing in other adherents' currencies.

Although the arrangement facilitated cooperation among exchange stabilization funds, including the newly created funds of France, the Netherlands, and Switzerland, whose governments also adhered to the principles of the agreement, nothing fundamental was altered.[48] The French franc, now off the gold standard, resumed its depreciation in 1937.[49] But the sterling-dollar rate remained relatively stable (near $5.00) until mid-1938. It then was pegged at $4.68, through Exchange Equalisation Account foreign exchange inter-

44. On the complex of interests and the negotiating history, see Stephen V. O. Clarke, *Exchange-Rate Stabilization in the Mid-1930's: Negotiating the Tripartite Agreement* (1977), and Howson, *Sterling's Managed Float*, pp. 27–29.
45. For the U.S. Declaration, see *Federal Reserve Bulletin*, 1936, pp. 759–60.
46. James Daniel Paris, *Monetary Policies of the United States, 1932–1938* (1938), p. 35.
47. Clarke, *Exchange-Rate Stabilization*, pp. 53–54.
48. See generally Ian M. Drummond, *London, Washington, and the Management of the Franc, 1936–39*, Princeton Studies in International Finance, no. 45 (1979). On the various funds, see Bloomfield, "American Exchange Stabilization Fund," pp. 75–80; Robert Marjolin, "The French Exchange Fund," and Paul Bareau, "The Belgian, Dutch and Swiss Exchange Funds," *The Banker* 48(1938):25–40. On the adherence of the French, Dutch, and Swiss governments, see *Federal Reserve Bulletin*, 1936, p. 940.
49. *BIS 8th Report* 1938, p. 22.

vention, from January 1939 until late August, just before the outbreak of the war.[50]

II. INTERNATIONAL INSTITUTIONS

In the foregoing brief history, one can perceive a number of trends that led to the international regime of Bretton Woods. One was the largely unsuccessful groping toward some form of international organizational regulation of monetary affairs. An international conference of experts at Brussels in 1920 recommended the establishment of what became the Economic and Financial Commission of the League of Nations.[51] Although this was the only one of the recommendations of the Brussels Conference that was implemented, it led to the 1922 Genoa Conference, which was a meeting of governments rather than experts. The great importance of the Genoa Conference was that it popularized the notion of "gold economy," an idea that, as discussed below, played an important role in the evolution of the interwar gold standard.[52]

As the 1920s went on, most of the international organization activity took place within the Economic and Financial Commission of the League of Nations. In part because the United States was not a member of the League, it took no formal part in either the Brussels or Genoa Conferences, which were sponsored by the League,[53] or in the reconstruction work of the Economic and Financial Commission.[54] The most successful Commission ventures were the stabilization loans to Austria and Hungary in the early 1920s,[55] but the U.S. preference for working outside the League was one factor favoring central bank cooperation as the vehicle for later stabilization loans during the rest of the decade.[56]

The 1930s saw a resurgence of interest in an international organization approach to monetary problems. This movement culminated in the 1933 London World Economic Conference, which the United States attended despite the conference's League of Nations sponsorship. The conference might well have resulted in a dollar-pound-franc stabilization agreement had

50. *Banking and Monetary Statistics* (1943), p. 681; *BIS 10th Report* 1940, pp. 18–19; Howson, *Sterling's Managed Float*, pp. 30–32.
51. See resolutions of the Brussels Conference reprinted in *Federal Reserve Bulletin*, 1920, p. 1286 (Commission on International Credits Res. VIII), p. 1287 (Annex), and p. 1291 (New Credits Organization); see Brown, 1:341–42.
52. See Report of the Financial Commission of the Genoa Conference, reprinted in *Federal Reserve Bulletin*, 1922, p. 678 (Currency) (hereafter cited Genoa Conference report).
53. See Lester V. Chandler, *Benjamin Strong, Central Banker* (1958), pp. 250–51.
54. Ibid. p. 263.
55. Martin Hill, *The Economic and Financial Organization of the League of Nations* (1946), pp. 26–29.
56. League of Nations, *International Currency Experience*, p. 32. See discussion in Richard Hemmig Meyer, *Bankers' Diplomacy* (1970), pp. 3–4 and n. 4, and p. 12; and Stephen V. O. Clarke, *Central Bank Cooperation, 1924–31* (1967), pp. 27–44, 112–19, 123–24, 150–51.

the incoming Roosevelt administration not decided in the middle of the conference that it preferred forced depreciation of the dollar and autonomy for its future course. Thereafter, international meetings were abandoned in favor of more traditional methods of financial diplomacy.

The collapse of international initiatives coincided with a growth in monetary and trade blocs. Even before the London World Economic Conference the sterling area had been formed and reinforced by the Ottawa trade agreements providing for a system of imperial preference under which Commonwealth countries would accord tariff preferences to one another.[57] The gold bloc was a direct response to the failure of the London conference.[58] And in the 1930s a more ominous bloc involving exchange controls and bilateral trade and clearing arrangements was organized by Nazi Germany.[59]

At the beginning of the 1930s, however, the long struggle over German reparations for World War I led to the creation of a new kind of international organization, which played a major role in later international monetary developments. In order to administer the Young loan to Germany, the Bank for International Settlements located in Basle, Switzerland, was granted broad powers. The shareholders were central banks. Even though the U.S. Federal Reserve did not become a shareholder, the Bank became an important forum for central bank cooperation. The periodic meetings of central bank representatives in Basle became, especially in the Bretton Woods period, vehicles for multilateral consultation and negotiation out of the glare of publicity and freed from the bureaucracy of international conferences. The term "central bankers' club" conveys the atmosphere created.[60]

Domestic politics prevented U.S. participation in an international organization approach to monetary problems in the interwar period. By the time the change of heart of the U.S. public in World War II made it possible for an international organization—the International Monetary Fund—to be created, the regional approach represented by the 1930s blocs had taken a firm hold and was to constitute a major problem for the Fund. Moreover, a rival organization, the Bank for International Settlements, was already in place.

III. CENTRAL BANK COOPERATION

The notion that central banks should maintain close relations with one another was foreign to the pre-1914 gold standard. Since that system was

57. Ottawa Agreements Act, 1932, 22 & 23 Geo. 5, c. 53.
58. See discussion pp. 47–48.
59. League of Nations, *International Currency Experience*, pp. 167–83; Yeager, pp. 366–71.
60. On the early BIS, see Henry H. Schloss, *The Bank for International Settlements* (1958); Roger Auboin, *The Bank for International Settlements, 1930–1955*, Princeton Essays in International Finance no. 22 (1955); Eleanor Lansing Dulles, *The Bank for International Settlements at Work* (1932).

supposed to be self-regulating, and such management as might be required was supposed to be the task of the Bank of England, cooperation among central banks had little ostensible role to play.[61]

After the war there was no international gold standard in place, and the goal was to reestablish the conditions for the return to gold. The British, and particularly the governor of the Bank of England, Montagu Norman, believed that central banks had a key role to play in achieving that goal. Moreover, Norman wanted to deal with central banks, not with treasuries, in the reconstruction task. It became a central tenet of Bank of England and British Treasury policy that every country should have a central bank independent of the government.[62]

The principle of central bank independence found expression in the resolutions of the Brussels Conference and again, in more elaborated form, in the Genoa resolutions.[63] The principle of central bank independence involved two separate desiderata: the creation of a central bank in countries not yet having such an institution, and rehabilitation on an independent basis in many other countries.[64] Consequently, the establishment and rehabilitation of central banks became an important issue in the reconstruction loans of the 1920s, whether carried out under the League of Nations or by cooperation among the central banks of the principal creditors.

Cooperation among central banks proved to be more practical and personal than legal or formal. It was concerned both with reconstruction and with policy coordination among the principal monetary powers of the day. Its foundations were the zeal of Montagu Norman and his close friendship with Benjamin Strong, the head of the New York Federal Reserve Bank, which at that time was more important than the Federal Reserve Board in Washington, particularly in international affairs.[65] The style of central bank cooperation was bilateral, with the U.S.-British and British-French relationships being the most important.[66] Indeed, only one multilateral central bank meeting of any consequence was held in the 1920s; in that instance—a meeting in a private home on Long Island in July 1927 (which included central bank representatives from the United States, Britain, Germany, and France)—the

61. Clarke, *Central Bank Cooperation*, pp. 27–29.
62. Sayers, *Bank of England 1891–1944*, 1:156–60.
63. Brussels Conference, Commission on Currency and Exchange (Resolutions III, XIV), and Report: Recommendations: Central Banks of Issue, reprinted in *Federal Reserve Bulletin*, 1920, pp. 1285, 1291; Genoa Conference report, Currency (Resolutions 2, 3, 9), in ibid. 1922, p. 678.
64. The U.S. Federal Reserve had been established only in 1914, and the British Dominions did not establish central banks until the 1920s. Sayers, *Bank of England 1891–1944*, 1:201–10.
65. On the Norman-Strong friendship, see Sir Henry Clay, *Lord Norman* (1957); and Chandler, *Strong*.
66. On the latter, see the diary of Émile Moreau, *Souvenirs d'un gouverneur de la Banque de France* (1954).

participants met collectively only for meals and social occasions, and business meetings were strictly bilateral.[67]

When Strong died in 1928, the peak of central bank cooperation in the interwar years had probably already been reached. The monetary debacles of the early 1930s strengthened the hands of treasuries. It is symptomatic that by 1936 the negotiation of the Tripartite Agreement was completely in the hands of governments.[68]

The subjection of central banks to political authority was publicly acknowledged in the immediate aftermath of the Tripartite Agreement by Montagu Norman, who had been the leading exponent of central bank independence in the 1920s, when he declared: "I assure Ministers that if they will make known to us through the appropriate channels what it is they wish us to do in the furtherance of their policies, they will at all times find us as willing with good will and loyalty to do what they direct as though we were under legal compulsion."[69] Political control of monetary affairs was not necessarily a step forward in professionalism, as evidenced by the transcript of the following telephone conversation between the U.S. secretary of the treasury, Henry Morgenthau, Jr., and Merle Cochran, financial secretary of the U.S. Embassy in Paris on 1 May 1936:

> C: And so the pressure is rather strong today.
> HMjr: There's what?
> C: The pressure—
> HMjr: Yes.
> C: The pressure on the franc is bad.
> HMjr: I don't get that.
> C: I say, the franc is weak.
> HMjr: The franc is weak?
> C: Yes, the pressure on the franc is—is heavy.
> HMjr: I'm sorry, I don't get it.
> C: Well, the franc is weak, that I said [sic].
> HMjr: The what?
> C: There are many people who want to sell their francs.
> HMjr: Yes.
> C: So it is weak as a result.
> HMjr: I don't get that.
> C: Well, you do have it that they want to sell their francs?

67. Sayers, *Bank of England 1891–1944*, 1:336–42. To be sure, multilateral action was often the outcome of initially bilateral negotiations, as in reconstruction loans. See e.g. Meyer, p. 3; [League of Nations] Economic, Financial and Transit Department, *The League of Nations Reconstruction Schemes in the Inter-war Period* (1945).

68. On the displacement of power to treasuries, see Paul Einzig, *Bankers, Statesmen and Economists* (1935), pp. 47–59.

69. *The Economist*, 10 October 1936, p 69.

```
HMjr:   Yes.
   C:   Well, that's the point.
HMjr:   I see, all right.
   C:   They are afraid.
HMjr:   I see. Now,—anything new on the political situation?[70]
```

Whatever the consequences, the decline of central banks' importance was an inevitable concomitant of the growth of governments' increased intervention in domestic economies. Domestic management by political representatives engendered management of external economic relations.

One important manifestation of treasury dominance was the proliferation of exchange stabilization funds. They were normally run by treasuries with treasury money, even where central banks carried out the exchange market transactions. In the case of the first such fund, the Exchange Equalisation Account, the motives for this transfer of responsibility were complex. In England the desire for secrecy of accounts conflicted with the difficulties that would be faced by a private institution (which the Bank of England nominally remained until after World War II) if it was expected to incur exchange market losses in pursuit of a purely public objective.[71]

The decline of central banks in favor of treasuries in international monetary affairs had a direct impact on the negotiation of the Bretton Woods agreement. It was assumed from the very beginning that the structure of the postwar international monetary system was an issue for governments, and specifically for treasuries, and that central banks would play a strictly subordinate role.

IV. THE TRANSMUTATION OF THE GOLD STANDARD

During the interwar years the gold standard, to the extent it was in effect, remained a collection of internal national rules without any explicit international rules. But the nature of the national rules had changed. Before World War I they involved a domestic monetary standard that had certain external implications. These implications were so uniform from country to country

70. Reported in Clarke, *Exchange-Rate Stabilization*, pp. 13–14; cf. Drummond, pp. 43–52. One might also compare the following exchange: "H: . . . Did you get the report that the British floated the pound? P: No. I don't think so. H: They did. P: That's devaluation? H: Yeah. Flanigan's got a report on it here. P: I don't care about it. Nothing we can do about it. H: You want a run-down? P: No, I don't. H: He argues it shows the wisdom of our refusal to consider convertibility until we get a new monetary system. P: Good. I think he's right. It's too complicated for me to get into. (*Unintelligible*) I understand. H: Burns expects a 5 percent devaluation against the dollar. P: Yeah. O.K. Fine. H: Burns is concerned about speculation about the lira. P: Well, I don't give a (*expletive deleted*) about the lira. (*Unintelligible*)." Excerpt from transcript of meeting between President Nixon and H. R. Haldeman on 23 June 1972, released pursuant to order of U.S. Supreme Court in *United States v. Nixon*, 418 U.S. 683 (1974). Quoted in Andreas F. Lowenfeld, *The International Monetary System* (1977), p. 1.
71. Sayers, *Bank of England 1891–1944*, 2:426–27.

that one can speak of an international gold standard system. By the time of the ultimate collapse, with the devaluation of the gold standard currencies in 1936, the nature of the national rules had evolved to the point where they were primarily external in character with only vestigial internal rules remaining. By 1936 it was thought sufficient, in order that a country might be said to be on the gold standard, that foreign central banks could redeem that country's currency in gold bullion. It no longer mattered that nationals had no similar right of redemption or that gold coins did not circulate or even that it was illegal to hold gold for other than industrial purposes. Indeed, a country could still be said to be on the gold standard even though the amount of gold had no direct influence on the money supply.[72] The cat had slowly faded away; only the gold standard grin remained.[73]

The evolution to the mid-1930s gold standard was partly intended by governments and central banks and partly the consequence of events. The intentional part can be found spelled out in the resolutions of the Genoa Conference and is best conveyed by the now archaic term "gold economy."

A widespread view immediately after World War I was that the principal difficulty in returning to the gold standard would be a shortage of gold. This view was especially popular in Britain, which had had to function before the war with comparatively small gold reserves, and had seen the amount of British currency in circulation roughly doubled during the war.[74]

The Cunliffe committee, reporting in 1918, made a number of recommendations designed to increase the holdings of gold by the Bank of England and to decrease the public's demand for gold. The most important was that gold coin should not circulate as money and that paper currency should replace it. This was already the de facto situation, inherited from the wartime period when Treasury-issued currency notes had displaced the sovereign.[75] Such a monetary system, under which only gold bullion could be withdrawn from the Bank of England in redemption of notes and in which gold coin would not circulate, was generally known as a "gold bullion" standard. With a gold bullion standard and with adoption of a further Cunliffe committee recommendation that banks should transfer their gold holdings to the Bank of England, all gold in England would be effectively concentrated in the

72. In the United States it was illegal with certain limited exceptions, after 1933, for a resident to hold gold coins or gold bullion. Exec. Order no. 6260 (28 August 1933) *FDR Papers*, 3:345–52. Moreover, though there was a nominal gold cover requirement for the currency, the amount of gold held was so far in excess of the currency outstanding that the requirement was superfluous. And the money supply, when defined to include bank deposits, was not effectively constrained by the level of gold holdings. See Friedman and Schwartz, pp. 473–74; Milton Friedman, "Real and Pseudo Gold Standards," *Journal of Law and Economics* 4(1961):66–79.
73. The discrepancy between retention of the "façade" of the gold standard and the economic reality is developed at length in Brown, 2:779–91, 1221, 1313–15.
74. *First Interim Report of the Committee on Currency and Foreign Exchanges after the War* [Cd. 9182] (1918), para. 13 (hereafter cited Cunliffe report).
75. Ibid. para. 23. See discussion of currency notes, p. 43.

Bank of England and therefore available in support of sterling in foreign
exchange markets.[76] Under this system, the essence of the gold standard
would be preserved, in the committee's view, because gold would still be
withdrawable in large-quantity transactions from the Bank of England for
export.[77]

The Cunliffe committee's recommendations became British government
policy, and the gold bullion standard was formally adopted on the occasion
of the return to gold in 1925. The Gold Standard Act of 1925 provided that
notes would be redeemable only in transactions larger than 400 ounces of
fine gold.[78] Meanwhile, the virtual discontinuance of the minting of gold
sovereigns in 1917 precluded a resurgence of gold coin circulation after the
war.[79] Some other countries followed, and by 1925 the world circulation of
gold coin was $2.7 billion less than in 1913.[80] But the United States carried
the gold bullion standard to its furthest extent in the 1930s, forbidding not
merely the circulating of gold coin but also the private holding of gold
bullion.[81]

The Cunliffe committee's recommendations became British government
policy; but the Genoa resolutions, heavily shaped by British thinking,[82] carried the concept of gold economy well beyond recommending the gold bullion
standard. Resolutions 9 and 11 called for an international convention establishing a gold exchange standard.[83] Although an international convention did
not prove feasible, a gold exchange standard could be adopted de facto by
individual country action. The principal historical role of the Genoa conference was to place a formal stamp of respectability on the gold exchange
standard.

Holding reserves in the form of foreign exchange was already common
before World War I, as previously discussed.[84] But now it was emphasized
that gold economy could be achieved if there were a limited number of gold
centers. The gold center countries would be on the gold standard in the
sense that their currencies would be redeemable in gold, and these countries

76. Ibid. para. 25. This transfer had begun in 1915. See Brown, 1:42, 109; E. Victor Morgan,
Studies in British Financial Policy, 1914–25 (1952), p. 226.
77. Gold would only be exportable if withdrawn from the Bank of England for that purpose.
Hence, the incentive for private gold holdings would be minimized. Cunliffe report, para. 24.
The Gold and Silver (Export Control, &c.) Act, 1920, 10 & 11 Geo. 5, c. 70, confirming the
1919 Order in Council, prohibited export of gold coin and bullion (with certain exceptions) until
the end of 1925.
78. Gold Standard Act, 1925, 15 & 16 Geo. 5, §1(2).
79. John Craig, *The Mint* (1953), pp. 351–52.
80. League of Nations, *International Currency Experience*, p. 7.
81. See discussion p. 47.
82. The Genoa conference recommendations were essentially those of the British government
draft. Stephen V. O. Clarke, *The Reconstruction of the International Monetary System: The Attempts
of 1922 and 1933* (1973), p. 13.
83. Genoa Conference report, Currency (Resolutions 9, 11), *Federal Reserve Bulletin*, 1922, p. 678.
84. See discussion pp. 31–34.

would maintain free gold markets. Other countries would hold their reserves in the form of short-term liquid assets in the gold centers. These other countries would maintain their currencies at par with a gold center by foreign exchange transactions in the currency of the gold center country.[85] Gold economy would result because a given quantity of gold in the vaults of a central bank in a gold center would serve as reserves, not simply for the gold center country but also at one remove for those countries that held its currency as foreign exchange reserves.[86]

Although the convention envisaged at Genoa did not come into being, European central banks' foreign exchange holdings grew rapidly for a few years in the 1920s, both absolutely and as a proportion of total reserves. Ragnar Nurkse, in his influential 1944 report, estimated that in 1913 the principal European central banks had held 12 percent of their reserves in foreign exchange; by 1925 the figure had risen to 27 percent and by 1928 to 42 percent.[87] Moreover, some countries that previously had held reserves almost exclusively in gold, most notably France, began holding large quantities of foreign exchange.[88] Thus, France, itself a gold center, also became a potential claimant on other gold centers' gold reserves.

A more accurate description of the system would perhaps be a "gold *or* exchange" standard rather than a "gold exchange" standard. If major countries began to lower the percentage of reserves held in the form of foreign exchange, as France did at the same time that its total reserves were growing at the end of the 1920s, the effects on the gold centers were potentially great. Here lay, as discussed below, one of the major lessons of the interwar years that was not taken into account in the drafting of the Bretton Woods agreement.

A further aspect of gold economy involved national "gold cover" requirements specifying the amount of gold required to "back" paper currency and bank deposits. There were extensive debates on the virtues of various stat-

---

85. Genoa Conference report, Currency (Resolution 11), *Federal Reserve Bulletin*, 1922, pp. 678–79.
86. See the explanation of one of the Genoa draftsmen, R. G. Hawtrey, in "The Genoa Resolutions on Currency," *Economic Journal* 32(1922):293–94. On Hawtrey's role see C. W. Guillebaud, "Hawtrey, R. G.," *International Encyclopedia of the Social Sciences* (1968), 6:328–29.
87. League of Nations, *International Currency Experience*, p. 29; IMF, *International Reserves and Liquidity* (1958), p. 16, table 1, and p. 31, table 4. 1913 figures are for fifteen European central banks; 1925 and 1928 figures are for twenty-four European central banks. World foreign exchange reserves, as a percentage of total reserves, did not change as dramatically as European, rising from 19 percent of total reserves in 1913 to 24.5 percent at their highest point in 1928. See discussion p. 32, above. The increase in foreign exchange holdings of major European central banks represented a change in proportional world distribution. In 1913 the major holders of foreign exchange had been Russia, Japan, and India. Peter H. Lindert, *Key Currencies and Gold, 1900–1913*, Princeton Studies in International Finance, no. 24 (1969), pp. 13–15.
88. Nurkse estimated that foreign exchange represented 2 percent of France's total reserves in 1924, 51 percent in 1928, and 5 percent in 1932. See League of Nations, *International Currency Experience*, pp. 234–35, appendix 2, for statistics of foreign exchange as a percentage of reserves for twenty-four European central banks, 1924–32. By 1928, France accounted for 40 percent of total world foreign exchange reserves. Lindert, *Key Currencies*, p. 15.

utory schemes, of which the two chief kinds were a ratio requirement (specifying a minimum percentage relationship of gold to currency and/or deposits)
and a fiduciary limit (such as the £14,000,000 fiduciary limit under the 1844
Bank Charter Act).[89] During the late 1920s and early 1930s efforts were
made, notably through the League of Nations Gold Delegation, to reduce
cover requirements in order to avoid an increased demand competing for an
anticipated reduced supply of gold.[90]

As with so many other anticipated shortages of commodities, the prospective shortage of gold was taken care of by a price increase. The effect
of the 1931–36 round of depreciation of the world's currencies was to increase
the price of gold measured in currencies and hence, particularly when measured against falling prices for other commodities during much of the 1930s,
to raise relative prices for gold even more. Gold production responded; by
1938 it was twice as great as a decade earlier.[91]

The "gold economy" movement inevitably changed the essential nature
of the gold standard. Without gold coins in circulation and with severe
limitations on the permissible amounts and circumstances of paper currency
redemption in gold, the gold standard had a limited internal effect. This was
particularly the case when it became apparent to the public that gold cover
requirements could simply be reduced whenever they might prove incon-
venient.

A more subtle, less intentional change in official attitudes also affected the
economic substance of the gold standard. Although the gold standard had
been much admired during the immediate postwar period, when it was not
in effect for its self-regulating character, government officials—who were
increasingly being held responsible for the economy—found that a standard
regulating their decisions was not at all comfortable. Even so fervent a disciple
as Montagu Norman became disillusioned within a few years of the 1925
return to the gold standard, and began at least as early as 1929 to offset
British gold losses by open market operations in bills in order to maintain
existing domestic credit conditions.[92]

Offsetting was, of course, not new. Violations of the traditional "rules of
the game" had, as we have seen, been common even before 1914.[93] But the
United States, experiencing an unprecedented level of gold reserves, sought
to make a public virtue out of not complying with the traditional "rules of
the game." In order to prevent gold imports from having inflationary effects,
the Federal Reserve began to make open market sales of government securities

89. Ibid. pp. 10–11, 94–98. The British pre-1914 fiduciary limit is described p. 26, above.
90. Lindert, *Key Currencies*, pp. 96–98; League of Nations, *Second Interim Report of the Gold
Delegation of the Financial Committee* (1931), p. 17; Macmillan report, paras. 144–50, 322–29.
91. League of Nations, *International Currency Experience*, p. 233, appendix 1. Higher prices also
discouraged industrial consumption. In 1938 it was only one-fourth the level of 1928. Ibid.
92. Sayers, *Bank of England 1891–1944*, 1:312–13, 334–35; Clay, pp. 254–55.
93. See discussion pp. 30–31.

gold inflow ↑   *domestic money supply ↑*
prices ↑
inflation

transactions

Offsetting payments imbalances

in order to offset the increase in member bank reserves accruing from the gold imports. In justifying this policy, the Board openly argued that in view of the influx of gold, reserve ratios had "lost much of their value as administrative guides" and that it was therefore "necessary . . . to devise other working bases."[94]

Once countries left the gold standard in the 1930s and began to manage floating currencies by intervention in foreign exchange markets, they felt free to be even more explicit about offsetting the effect on the domestic money supply of changes in international reserves resulting from that intervention. As has been discussed, the desire to engage in such offsetting transactions was one of the purposes behind the creation of the British Exchange Equalisation Account after Britain left the gold standard in 1931. Not all exchange stabilization funds offset their transactions, however, nor did any of them do so at all times.[95]

A stabilization fund was not actually needed for such offsetting, and when the United States decided to offset part of the gold influx that followed the collapse of the gold bloc, the U.S. Treasury announced a "sterilization" policy involving the use of the proceeds of the sale of government securities to the public to acquire the newly imported gold.[96] Although the United States purported to be on the gold standard, the sterilization policy, coupled with its explicitness and the publicity given to it, shows how far the idea of a gold standard had departed from the pre-1914 concept, which assumed that international exchange rate stability would be achieved by automatic internal adjustments. The sterilization policy, coupled with the extreme form of the gold bullion standard embodied in the prohibition against private holding of gold and thereby of private transactions in gold, constituted a complete repudiation of the basic tenets of the pre-1914 form of gold standard. Such a systematic offsetting policy broke the link of international transactions to the domestic economy.

An even more serious departure from the concept of the pre-1914 gold standard was the attempt to break the related link between domestic economic conditions and the international economy through exchange control.[97] By the use of direct controls on private transactions, many governments attempted in the 1930s to prevent changes in internal price levels from generating

94. Federal Reserve Board, *Annual Report for 1923* (1924), p. 30, quoted in League of Nations, *International Currency Experience*, p. 74. For the background, see ibid. pp. 73–75, and Chandler, *Strong*, pp. 188–246.
95. See discussion, pp. 46–48, 54. For treatments of the complicated subject of the effect of exchange stabilization funds on domestic credit conditions, see League of Nations, *International Currency Experience*, pp. 150–54; Yeager, pp. 282–85; and R. S. Sayers, *Modern Banking*, corrected ed. (1939), pp. 200–10.
96. *Federal Reserve Bulletin*, 1937, p. 1. According to this announcement, the loss of gold would likewise be sterilized through Treasury purchase of government securities from the public.
97. On exchange controls in the 1930s, see generally League of Nations, *International Currency Experience*, pp. 162–89; League of Nations, *Report on Exchange Control* (1938).

payments imbalances. The essence of exchange control was to require exporters and other recipients of foreign exchange to surrender it to the central
bank where it would be made available at an official rate of exchange to
private parties whose proposed use ranked highest in the government's priorities.[98] It was, in essence, a rationing scheme involving a commodity—foreign
exchange—whose price no longer equilibrated supply and demand.

The motivation was to permit governments to pursue inflationary policies
while avoiding the losses in gold that would otherwise occur. The rationale
was often that exchange controls would permit countries to stay on the gold
standard by arresting capital outflows.[99] Hence exchange control tended to
discriminate against capital transactions in favor of trade transactions. It
became an accepted notion that the gold standard, or in its absence any
existing set of exchange rates, was threatened by rapid movements of disequilibrating flows of short-term "hot money."[100] Thus, by the time of Bretton
Woods, the use by governments of controls on capital transaction was viewed
by many influential people as not only compatible with a stable international
monetary system but actually a prerequisite to it and hence something to be
institutionalized in the Bretton Woods system. This attitude is a measure of
how far the world had come from the pre-1914 system in which capital flows
in and out of Britain were viewed as a principal method of adjustment
facilitating the operation of the gold standard.

V. THE LESSONS OF THE INTERWAR EXPERIENCE

The growing limitations on the economic significance of the gold standard
took their toll on its symbolic prestige. In the 1920s it had meant "order,
international law, security, international confidence, and discipline."[101] Yet
by the end of the 1930s the gold standard had become a symbol of undesirable
constraints on enlightened government management of domestic economies.
But if the gold standard had lost its attraction, the periods when the gold
standard was not generally in effect were regarded as highly unstable—
especially the early 1920s and the five years between Britain's 1931 departure
from the gold standard and the 1936 Tripartite Agreement. Those who
sought, during World War II, to design a new international monetary system,
sought to gain the fixed rate benefits of the gold standard without subjecting

98. William Adams Brown, Jr., "Gold: Master or Servant?" *Foreign Affairs* 19(1941):837.
99. Whatever the rationale, exchange controls became more pervasive, often being used to
regulate trade in goods and commodities. Indeed, they sometimes corresponded to and reinforced
an increase in tariffs and the use of quantitative trade restrictions. The results were protectionist,
and the underlying purpose for governments was to permit greater management of the domestic
economy.
100. See, for an example of this view, League of Nations, *International Currency Experience*, p. 16.
See, for a criticism, pp. 61–62, below.
101. Robert Mundell, "The Monetary Consequences of Jacques Rueff," *Journal of Business*
46(1973):387.

national economies to its constraints. In their work they reflected the conclusions that officials and bankers had drawn from the interwar experience.
Some of those conclusions were not fully supported by the evidence. Nor
did the Bretton Woods draftsmen take account of all of the lessons that the
interwar experience afforded.

Floating Rates

A lesson drawn by some observers that proved to be highly influential in the
construction of the Bretton Woods system can be simply stated: What was
good about the gold standard was that exchange rates were pegged. What
was bad about the breakdown of the gold standard was not that gold standard
discipline on domestic economic policy was lost but rather that countries
allowed their exchange rates to float. If this formulation is oversimplified as
a matter of economics, it nonetheless captures the psychological essence of
the Bretton Woods preference for fixed rates and abhorrence of floating.
Floating rates were viewed as inherently destabilizing. The lesson of history
was, to those holding this view, that they engendered destabilizing speculation and disequilibrating short-term capital flows.

Perhaps no publication was more influential in popularizing this view than
Ragnar Nurkse's 1944 report for the League of Nations, *International Currency
Experience.*[102] He stated his conclusions in the folowing uncompromising
terms: "If there is anything that interwar experience has clearly demonstrated, it is that paper currency exchanges cannot be left free to fluctuate
from day to day under the influence of market supply and demand."[103] This
conclusion has been widely criticized in recent years as not consistent with
the historical evidence.[104] Certainly the evidence in Nurkse's report is extremely slim. The only incident discussed in any detail is the depreciating
French franc of 1922–26.[105] That three-paragraph discussion is remarkable
in its total failure to consider the domestic political and economic factors
within France that led to the depreciation.[106] To make a convincing case he
would have had to explain why the exchange market speculation, to which
his strongest objections were voiced, would not have been present if a policy

102. See especially pp. 117–22. This book is generally credited to Nurkse, though, as the
preface, p. 5, states, he did not write all of it. On the influence of the Nurkse report, see Milton
Friedman, "The Case for Flexible Exchange Rates," in *Essays in Positive Economics* (1953), p. 176
n. 9.
103. League of Nations, *International Currency Experience*, p. 137.
104. Yeager, pp. 252–62, 328; S. C. Tsiang, "Fluctuating Exchange Rates in Countries with
Relatively Stable Economies," *IMF Staff Papers* 7(1959):244–73; J. K. Whitaker and Maxwell
W. Hudgins, "The Floating Pound Sterling of the Nineteen Thirties: An Econometric Study,"
Southern Economic Journal 43(1977):1478–85. See also Robert Z. Aliber, "Speculation in the
Foreign Exchanges: The European Experience, 1919–1926," *Yale Economic Essays* 2(1962):171–75,
188, 240–45.
105. League of Nations, *International Currency Experience*, pp. 117–19.
106. See e.g. D. T. Jack, *The Restoration of European Currencies* (1927), pp. 120–29; Wolfe,
pp. 33–43; Tsiang, pp. 271–73.

of discrete exchange rate changes rather than a policy of allowing the franc
to float had been adopted by the French government. Even if Nurkse was
right in characterizing French franc speculation as destabilizing, the balance
of the accumulated evidence points the other way for other important currencies that had been thought at the time to be the victims of destabilizing
speculation.[107] Perhaps the reason that little evidence was offered by Nurkse
is that his verdict on floating was not thought to require evidence because,
by the time he wrote, the abhorrence of floating was almost universal in
official and banking circles.[108]

This is not the place to review the evidence on floating exchange rates in
the interwar period. But several points are worth bearing in mind. The first
is that governments did not adopt floating rates as an explicit long-term
policy. In each case the announced policy was either that there would be a
return to pegged rates (usually by means of a return to the gold standard)
or that the exchange rate would thenceforth be managed by official intervention in foreign exchange markets. This point is important because if
stabilization is expected, speculation is engendered by the prospect of an
approaching pegged rate different from the market rate. If the authorities
are in the market, then private exchange transactions are influenced by the
anticipated direction and amount of official exchange transactions. There is
no a priori reason to believe that private speculation based on an anticipated
change in official intervention policy is any more "destabilizing," whatever
content that term might have in such a context, than private speculation in
a truly free floating situation.

This point is illustrated by three of Nurkse's principal examples. The
British post-1931 float was accompanied by a declaration of intention to
return to the gold standard and later by a declared intention to manage
sterling rates through the Exchange Equalisation Account.[109] The U.S. 1933
case is different in the sense that it is not clear whether Roosevelt at first
intended to repeg the dollar rate, but it is a leading illustration of speculation
engendered by an erratic government intervention policy—in this instance
in the world gold market rather than in foreign exchange markets.[110] The

107. For differing interpretations of the 1922–26 French float, see Robert Z. Aliber, "Speculation
in the Flexible Exchange Revisited," *Kyklos* 23(1970):303–12, and the opinion of Milton Friedman
in Milton Friedman and Robert V. Roosa, *The Balance of Payments: Free versus Fixed Exchange
Rates* (1967), pp. 106–7. On other currencies, see notes 104 above and 108 below.
108. Nurkse later granted that the movement of private speculative funds had been equilibrating
in the early years after World War I. League of Nations, *The Course and Control of Inflation*
(1946), pp. 44–46.
109. The Chancellor of the Exchequer, introducing the Gold Standard (Amendment) Bill,
emphasized that its provisions were temporary. See his speech as reprinted in Philip Snowden,
An Autobiography (1934), 2:1054–55. For the Exchange Equalisation Account, see Clay,
pp. 402–3, and for an account of its operations, see *The Economist*, 19 December 1936,
pp. 588–89.
110. Lester V. Chandler, *American Monetary Policy, 1928–1941* (1971), pp. 272–77.

French 1937 float again involved a governmentally managed exchange rate, in which speculation centered around the level to which the French government would allow or force the franc to depreciate.[111]

The second point to be made about floating rates in the interwar period is a corollary of the first. Floating rates were the product of a breakdown of a pegged rate system in which exchange rates had been far out of equilibrium. Adjustment to a new set of equilibrium rates not only took time but was hampered in most cases by severe internal economic and sometimes political instability.

To take Nurkse's principal instances: the French float of 1922–26 followed on the drastic depreciation of the French franc and the internal devastation of World War I and was accompanied by highly inflationary domestic economic policies that would have surely engendered intense speculation against any pegged rate.[112] The British float after 1931 resulted from Britain's departure from the gold standard and the consequent drastic depreciation of the pound. The dollar float in 1933 presents a different case, but the villain here was a deliberate government policy of exchange depreciation. The French float in 1937 was another example of depreciation, reflecting the fact that the devaluation accompanying the 1936 Tripartite Agreement was insufficient.[113]

Competitive Depreciation

A related lesson from the interwar period drawn by the Bretton Woods draftsmen was that competitive depreciation is a prime evil to be avoided. This policy prescription had an antecedent in the Tripartite Declaration's expressed "trust" that "no country will attempt to obtain an unreasonable competitive exchange advantage and thereby hamper the effort to restore more stable economic relations."[114] It was believed that in the 1930s some countries forced a depreciation of their currencies below an equilibrium level in order to promote exports.[115]

The United States and Britain are the offenders most open to this charge. In the U.S. case there is little doubt that the United States intentionally

111. Paul Einzig, *World Finance, 1937–1938* (1938), pp. 93–105. Government exchange market activity appears to have played a less important role in the French 1922–26 float than in Nurkse's other examples. Brown, 1:434–44.
112. Dulles, pp. 151–202. Wholesale prices more than doubled from 1922 to 1926. Ibid. p. 510.
113. Einzig, *World Finance 1937–1938*, pp. 86–87.
114. Printed in *Federal Reserve Bulletin*, 1936, pp. 759–60. Haberler includes in his definition of competitive depreciation not merely government acts "pushing down" the value of the currency but also deliberate government acts "keeping it down if it has temporarily been pushed down by capital flight or speculation" in order to reflect the French stabilization actions in the 1926–28 period. Gottfried Haberler, *The World Economy, Money, and the Great Depression, 1919–1939* (1976), p. 34.
115. Harry G. Johnson, "The International Monetary Crisis of 1971," *Journal of Business* 46(1973):16; Stephen V. O. Clarke, *Exchange-Rate Stabilization in the Mid-1930s: Negotiating the Tripartite Agreement*, Princeton Studies in International Finance no. 41 (1979), p. 2.

attempted to force a depreciation below the level that a free exchange market
would produce. Although the prime motive was to achieve a higher level of
domestic prices rather than an increase in exports,[116] the trade effect was
what mattered to other countries—particularly the gold bloc countries still
adhering to the gold standard and therefore to correspondingly overvalued
exchange rates. In the case of Britain, the creation of the Exchange Equalisation Account fueled suspicions that its purpose and effect were not simply
to iron out minor fluctuations in the sterling exchange rate but to affect its
general level. And there is evidence that at times the Account was used to
prevent sterling from rising in the exchange markets.[117]

The Vulnerability of the Gold Exchange Standard:
An Unlearned Lesson

Not all of the lessons that might have been drawn from the interwar experience were learned by the Bretton Woods planners. Problems leading to its
eventual demise were overlooked in the construction of the Bretton Woods
system. These problems involved the fundamental vulnerability of any gold
exchange standard.

The essence of the gold exchange standard as actually practiced was that
central banks might hold their international reserves in two forms—gold and
foreign exchange—in whatever proportion they chose. Indeed, central banks
might change that proportion as they saw fit. Moreover, they were not
required to maintain the foreign exchange component in any one currency
but might switch from one "reserve currency" to another. The vulnerability
of the gold exchange standard may thus be discussed under two headings.
The first, involving the weakness arising out of the ability of a central bank
to vary the proportion of foreign exchange and gold, materialized as soon as
France began to convert some of its claims on London into gold in 1927.[118]
The second, involving the ability of a central bank to shift its foreign exchange
assets held in the form of claims on one reserve center to claims on another
foreign exchange center, became a steadily increasing factor as New York
became a rival of London as a financial center.

Although it is justifiable to think of a gold exchange standard as inherently
vulnerable for these two reasons, it is not true that a gold exchange standard
need be unstable at any particular time. A great deal depends upon the
economic policies of the reserve currency country. So long as assets denominated in its currency are sufficiently attractive to foreign central banks, a
gold exchange standard need not be at all unstable, at least so long as there
is only one reserve currency. Such assets have one great advantage over gold

116. See discussion, p. 47, and *FDR Papers*, 2:266, 426–29.
117. Brown, 2:1116–30; John H. Williams, *Postwar Monetary Plans*, 3d ed. (1947), p. 210.
118. Clarke, *Central Bank Cooperation*, p. 117; Roger Dehem, *De l'étalon-sterling à l'étalon-dollar*
(1972), p. 87.

to start with and that is that they are obligations that earn interest, a factor that will be of some concern to almost all central banks and perhaps of great concern to some. Moreover, since foreign exchange assets can be held in obligations of impeccable credit rating (government bills, if desired), they need involve no significant risk of nonpayment. The dominant risk a central bank in the interwar period took in holding foreign exchange rather than gold was an exchange risk: the reserve center's currency might depreciate in terms of gold. This depreciation might occur either by a devaluation in terms of gold or by the reserve currency country electing to leave the gold standard, permitting its currency to float downward.

The probability at any given time of depreciation of the reserve currency (which would determine the willingness of foreign central banks to hold obligations denominated in that currency in preference to gold) turned on three principal factors. The first involved the domestic economic policies of the reserve currency countries; the more inflationary those policies, the more likely it was that depreciation would occur. The second involved the present level of the exchange rate, which under a gold standard was by definition a fixed rate against other currencies on that standard. If the reserve currency was significantly overvalued, then depreciation was a possibility; and the greater the degree of overvaluation the higher the probability that future events, particularly inflationary domestic policies, might trigger depreciation.

The third principal factor affecting a foreign central bank's willingness to hold obligations of the reserve center is somewhat different in kind from the first two. It stems from the fact that the reserve center has certain characteristics of a bank. The reserve center's holdings of gold are its reserve assets, and the foreign central bank's holdings of its obligations are its reserve liabilities. Sometimes these are actual liabilities, as when obligations of the government are held by the foreign central banks, but even if private bank deposits or commercial paper is held, those private obligations are readily convertible into gold and therefore must be considered as reserve liabilities of the reserve center. For this reason it is convenient in some contexts to speak of a reserve center, rather than a reserve currency country, in order to make clear that private obligations to foreign central banks are included.[119] When the liabilities of a reserve center grow too large relative to its reserve assets, the desire of foreign central banks to hold obligations may decrease or even vanish.

In the light of these three factors, a review of Britain's position as a reserve currency country between 1925 and 1931 helps to reveal the dimensions of

119. The concept of a reserve center would also imply that, with respect to assets, gold held by residents of the reserve country might be counted. However, such private holdings are not readily available to the reserve currency country's central bank. This circumstance explains Britain's desire to concentrate the gold holdings of the country in the Bank of England by discouraging commercial banks from maintaining substantial gold reserves and its measures to prevent the reemergence of gold coins after World War I. See Cunliffe report, paras. 23–25.

the vulnerability of a gold exchange standard. The policies of Britain were not notably inflationary. On the contrary, in this period before Keynes had popularized deficit spending, British domestic policy did little to attempt to reduce the unprecedentedly high unemployment rate. In fact, Britain reduced its national debt by about £83 million between 1925 and 1931.[120] Nevertheless, in 1931 Britain was running a budget deficit, and the exaggeration of the amount and implications of this deficit in the July 1931 report of the May committee was a factor in the collapse of the gold standard in Britain.[121] The Bank of England kept its discount rate above the U.S. discount rate throughout most of these years and above the French rate during the crucial 1928–29 period.[122] Here too, however, a reduction of Bank Rate to historically low levels in 1930 and 1931 played a role in the 1931 debacle.[123]

As for the second factor, the nearly unanimous view of observers at the time, and of scholars looking back to the years 1925–31, has been that sterling was overvalued against other major currencies. The usual estimate of the degree of overvaluation is about 10 percent.[124] Moreover, it is interesting that from 1925 to 1931, the average annual sterling exchange rate reached par only once, in 1928, indicating a persistent weakness of sterling in exchange markets.[125]

Britain's unexpansionary fiscal and monetary policies were successful in countering the overvaluation of sterling to the extent that Britain maintained its gold holdings more or less intact until 1931. Britain's gold reserves in June 1931 were in fact greater than at the end of 1925[126] and fell below that level only occasionally and then only rarely by more than 10 percent.

Britain's gold holdings should be viewed, however, in the context of its net liabilities to foreigners. Although these liabilities apparently did not grow

---

120. Moggridge, *Monetary Policy*, p. 143.
121. *Committee on National Expenditure Report*, Cmd. 3920 (July 1931). On the May report, see Sayers, *Bank of England 1891–1944*, 2:394–95; Clay, pp. 389–90; Charles P. Kindleberger, *The World in Depression, 1929–1939* (1973), pp. 158–59. Keynes is reported to have called the May report "the most foolish document I have ever had the misfortune to read." R. F. Harrod, *The Life of John Maynard Keynes* (1951), p. 438. In fact, the 1931–32 accounts ended with a small surplus through the use of devices such as withdrawal of £12,750,000 from a special fund, the Dollar Exchange Reserve, and accelerated collection of income tax, and also through the draconian economy measures of the September 1931 emergency budget. For budget figures and for debate over the true significance of the 1931 deficit estimates, see Snowden, pp. 938–42, 967–69; *Lloyds Bank Limited Monthly Review*, n.s. 3(1932):139; R. Bassett, *Nineteen Thirty-One: Political Crisis* (1955), pp. 222–23; Colin Cross, *Philip Snowden* (1966), pp. 270–71, 278–89; H. F. Fraser, *Great Britain and the Gold Standard* (1933), pp. 99–101.
122. Moggridge, *Monetary Policy*, p. 150, fig. 3; Sayers, *Bank of England 1891–1944*, 1:218–19, 224–25, and Appendixes, appendix 36, p. 347; Macmillan report, paras. 165, 169–71.
123. Sayers, *Bank of England 1891–1944*, 1:228–34.
124. See discussion p. 44; and see Sir Frederick Leith-Ross, *Money Talks: Fifty Years of International Finance* (1968), pp. 91–93; Donald Winch, *Economics and Policy: A Historical Study* (1969), pp. 81–89.
125. Brown, 1:603.
126. *Banking and Monetary Statistics* (1943), p. 551.

during this period,[127] they were considerably larger than the gold reserves. For example, as previously noted, at the end of May 1931 the gold holdings of the Bank of England were £151 million,[128] and net foreign short-term liabilities of London (defined as deposits and sterling bills held in London on foreign account minus sterling bills accepted on foreigners) were £254 million, according to the Macmillan report. The gross liabilities were, of course, even larger—£407 million.[129] Moreover, because of cover requirements, the Bank of England's gold holdings were not regarded as fully available for the defense of sterling. The Macmillan report pointed out that at certain times of the year "£120 millions of the gold held by the Bank . . . is immobilized and . . . only £25 millions is actually available."[130] Disclosure in the Macmillan report that, in this sense, only £25 million of gold might be available against liabilities about ten times that great apparently came as a shock to the world's financial community. This was one factor leading to the loss of confidence in sterling and the spiral of withdrawals from London that reached such a point in September that Britain was forced to leave the gold standard.[131]

In short, though Britain maintained a generally conservative domestic economic policy and though it succeeded in preventing the ratio of net liabilities to gold from rising until 1931, the fact that net liabilities exceeded substantially its gold reserves (particularly those gold reserves that could be exported without exhausting the Bank of England's domestic reserves against outstanding notes) caused the gold exchange standard in the end to collapse. At a difficult moment there occurred what may be regarded as a run on the British gold bank. Claims exceeded reserves, and when confidence in sterling waned (in part because the Bank of England's borrowings in New York and

127. Macmillan report, paras. 259–60.
128. *Banking and Monetary Statistics* (1943), p. 638. The Bank of England also held dollars in the amount of about £26 million. Sayers, *Bank of England 1891–1944*, Appendixes, appendix 37, pp. 354–55. See p. 46 and n. 23, above.
129. Macmillan report, para. 260. Subsequent investigation showed that the Macmillan committee underestimated Britain's foreign short-term liabilities. See J. M. Keynes, "Reflections on the Sterling Exchange," *Lloyds Bank Limited Monthly Review*, n.s. 3(1932):148–49. See also *Reserves and Liabilities 1931 to 1945*, Cmd. 8354, p. 5, table III (1951); and David Williams, "London and the 1931 Financial Crisis," *Economic History Review*, 2d ser. 15(1963):525, 527–28.
130. Macmillan report, para. 324. These figures are based on the Bank's gold holdings of £145 million in April 1931. Between January 1929 and June 1931, the Bank's holdings ranged from £131 to £162 million. *Banking and Monetary Statistics* (1943), p. 638.
131. Macmillan report, paras. 259–60, 324, 347–52. The report also made the point that the £254 million in net liabilities should be reduced by the amount of foreign balances held by British financial institutions. The committee had no estimates of this amount. Ibid. para. 262. For an argument that the foreign reaction to the Macmillan report was unjustified, see Clay, pp. 395–97. However, it was also argued that the concern aroused by the Macmillan report's revelation of the extent of short-term foreign indebtedness was intensified by the German banking crisis, as London banks were deeply involved in Germany. Leith-Ross, pp. 136–38.

Paris came to be interpreted as weakness), the run was on.[132] Without a reestablishment of confidence in sterling, the run was not to be stemmed, and the end came only three months after the June 1931 publication in the Macmillan report of the state of Britain's foreign accounts.

The difficulties faced by London as a reserve center were exacerbated by the growth of New York as a second reserve center. Not only did foreign private institutions hold balances in New York but some central banks too came to hold part of their foreign exchange reserves in New York. To the extent that such foreign balances in New York grew, the indirect effect might often be to reduce balances in London. Although the reduction in foreign balances in London would lower the net liquid liabilities of Britain and hence future claims on British gold, they would also tend to reduce the Bank of England's gold holdings.[133]

The very existence of two reserve centers thus created doubts about the viability of the center less adequately endowed with gold—namely London. Moreover, the existence of two centers provided the motivation for diversification of reserve holdings by central banks. The Bank of France, for example, held its foreign exchange in sterling, dollar and even German reichsmark assets.[134] When central banks switched foreign exchange reserves from sterling to dollars, they undermined the strength of sterling. The extent to which central banks entered into such transactions, and the resulting influence on the strength of sterling, is impossible to determine because of the secrecy with which banks treated not merely individual transactions but even the currencies in which they held foreign exchange reserves.[135]

The additional complexities introduced by the existence of two reserve centers were perhaps swamped by the more obvious vulnerability stemming from the ability of foreign central banks to convert sterling balances into gold in England. Certainly the decline of the gold exchange standard at the end of the 1920s and beginning of the 1930s can be measured by the decreasing percentages of reserves held in foreign exchange, whether in London or New

132. On these and earlier loans, see Sayers, *Bank of England 1891–1944*, 2:390–99, 405–6; and Clarke, *Central Bank Cooperation*, p. 206; Clay, pp. 384–87; Moggridge, *Monetary Policy*, pp. 135, 139; Snowden, 2:1050–51; *Federal Reserve Bulletin*, 1931, p. 435.
133. Brown, 1:588–91, 637, 2:784–91; *Federal Reserve Bulletin*, 1930, pp. 1–3; Sayers, *Bank of England 1891–1944*, 1:220–28; *The Gold Exchange Standard* (BIS, Monetary and Economic Department, C.B. 60) (1932), pp. 18–21.
134. On Bank of France balances in Berlin, see Clarke, *Central Bank Cooperation*, pp. 164–65.
135. See, for example, the reporting on foreign exchange in Bank of France Annual Report for 1931, reprinted in English translation in *Federal Reserve Bulletin*, 1932, pp. 161–66. See also central bank statistics, ibid. pp. 172–74; *Gold Exchange Standard*, pp. 8–10. Most informed comment on reserve diversification in the interwar period has been quite general. See e.g. League of Nations, *International Currency Experience*, p. 46. It is noteworthy that one function the BIS hoped to perform was to "offer to the depositary Central Banks certain advantages in the administration of [foreign exchange] reserves, in the revenue therefrom, and in the rapid convertibility from one currency to another." *BIS 1st Report* 1931, p. 4.

York.[136] The important point is that there was nothing in the mechanism of the gold exchange standard to provide defenses against these twin weaknesses. Other than domestic economic measures to assure confidence in the reserve currency, central bank cooperation provided the only buttress for the system. And such cooperation in the end proved unequal to the task.[137]

Liquidity

As Robert Mundell has observed, in the 1920s "[n]either academic economists nor monetary officials had stumbled onto the world liquidity problem in any explicit form."[138] The concern about a gold shortage can, of course, be interpreted as a concern about liquidity, but it would be stretching a point to find in that concern a precedent for events in the Bretton Woods period. Several developments in the interwar period may nevertheless be considered to have been forerunners of post–World War II practices.

Intergovernmental lending was an important part of the stabilization programs of a number of countries rejoining the gold standard in the 1920s.[139] Even Britain obtained assistance from the U.S. Federal Reserve in connection with the return to gold in 1925.[140] An important precedent was the ultimately unsuccessful attempt to bolster the pound in 1931 through loans by the United States and France to England.[141] One lesson to be derived from the experience was that intergovernmental lending was pointless and even counterproductive, especially where the rate was pegged, if the loans were viewed by the market as inadequate to permit the borrowing country to survive a foreign exchange crisis.[142] Another lesson was that central banks alone did not have the resources to preserve pegged-rate relationships without the intervention of treasuries and hence government-to-government lending, arguably on some previously institutionalized basis.[143]

In 1933, shortly before the World Economic Conference, attention was briefly given to a plan to establish a joint U.S.-British-French exchange

136. League of Nations, *International Currency Experience*, pp. 39–41; *Gold Exchange Standard*, p. 18.
137. See generally Clarke, *Central Bank Cooperation; Gold Exchange Standard*, pp. 28–29.
138. Mundell, p. 386.
139. See discussion p. 45. Clarke, *Central Bank Cooperation*, chap. 4; Moggridge, *Monetary Policy*, pp. 191–92.
140. Sayers, *Bank of England 1891–1944*, 1:141–47; *Federal Reserve Bulletin*, 1925, pp. 372–73; Clarke, *Central Bank Cooperation*, pp. 81–85; Moggridge, *Monetary Policy*, pp. 81–83. For Britain's worsening liquidity position 1929–31, see Williams, pp. 525–26.
141. See pp. 67–68.
142. Clay, pp. 397–98. Cf. *The Economist*'s comment (8 August 1931, p. 256) when the loans were first made: "The size of the credits need not arouse any surprise or misgivings. If such credits are to be opened at all, it is best for them to be so big as to make it clear beyond question that they are able to give the protection they promise."
143. See Clay, pp. 390–95; Bassett, pp. 131–36. For some contemporary responses to this problem, see e.g. *Gold Exchange Standard*, pp. 18–19; *BIS 2d Report* 1932, pp. 7–10, 21; "The Sterling Pool," *Lloyds Bank Limited Monthly Review*, n.s. 3(1932):66–67.

account as part of a de facto stabilization of the three currencies. Such a pooling of reserves would have been a major new institutional departure.[144] But the concept of a pooling of reserves apparently played no role in the Tripartite Agreement discussions in 1936, and the stabilization task was left to the national governments.

In the late 1930s the Bank for International Settlements developed facilities for reciprocal credits among central banks, but the purpose was more to make credit available to exporters than to permit governments to avoid exchange rate changes.[145] Moreover, the United States began to make bilateral stabilization loans to certain Latin American countries.[146] Although one can find precedents in the BIS arrangement and the U.S. bilateral loans for the much larger scale of public international lending in the post–World War II period, neither appeared to be motivated by any concern about liquidity.

144. On the 1933 joint exchange discussion, see Sayers, *Bank of England 1891–1944*, 2:456–57, and Appendixes, pp. 276–79; *Documents diplomatiques français 1932–1939* (1967), vol. 3, no. 258, pp. 456–57.
145. *BIS 8th Report* 1938, p. 109; Auboin, p. 12; J. Keith Horsefield, *The International Monetary Fund 1945–1965* (1969), 1:7.
146. Ibid. 1:6–7.

FOUR

The Bretton Woods Agreement

The legal and institutional framework for the international monetary system throughout several decades after World War II was provided by the Bretton Woods agreement. Unlike earlier changes in the international monetary system, which had been dictated by events, this change was dictated by men—the wartime planners of the postwar world. The war was, at most, an impetus for the key international monetary policy decision of the century—namely, the decision of nearly all of the countries outside the emerging communist bloc to regulate the international monetary system through a comprehensive treaty with a potentially powerful central organ, the International Monetary Fund.

This decision would surely not have been taken apart from the general postwar planning in Britain and especially in the United States. The Fund was only one of the international organizations that grew out of that planning. On the economic side, an International Bank for Reconstruction and Development and an International Trade Organization were also agreed upon.[1] And all of this economic planning was part of the work that led to the United Nations and its many specialized agencies. A strong motive for the creation of the Fund was an idealism, favoring international organization, that has characterized U.S. executive branch policies for much of the twentieth century.[2] The perceived lessons of the thirties thus shaped the Bretton Woods system but were not a sufficient condition for its creation.

I. Britain and the United States

The dominant role of the United States and Britain in postwar economic planning affected the Bretton Woods system in important ways. The anticipated economic position of the two countries at the end of the war put bounds on the proposals that received serious consideration. And since the U.S. influence was stronger than the British, the style of the drafting of the Articles of Agreement of the Fund, together with positions adopted on the role of the Fund staff, reflected U.S. executive branch views of that time.

U.S. economic strength had been growing relative to the strength of other major countries, including Britain, since the nineteenth century. The physical devastation of continental countries and the economic stress placed on Britain by extensive borrowing and wartime dislocations accelerated the culmination of these trends in postwar U.S. economic hegemony. The United States realized that it would be the most powerful country after the war, and other countries realized it as well. Consequently, the United States self-confidently set out to impress on the postwar international monetary system its particular view of the desirable which, as one would expect, corresponded to U.S. perceived self-interest.

The U.S. government anticipated that it would be a creditor nation for the indefinite future.[3] It was already the largest holder of gold, and U.S. gold holdings could be expected to grow after the war.[4]

1. On postwar economic planning, see generally Richard N. Gardner, *Sterling-Dollar Diplomacy*, new ed. (1969). On the International Trade Organization, its failure to come into being, and its transmutation into the General Agreement on Tariffs and Trade, see Kenneth W. Dam, *The GATT: Law and International Economic Organization* (1970), pp. 10–16.
2. Richard N. Gardner, "The Political Setting," in *Bretton Woods Revisited*, ed. A. L. K. Acheson, J. F. Chant, and M. F. J. Prachowny (1972), p. 21.
3. See Gardner, "The Political Setting," in *Bretton Woods Revisited*, p. 24. See also *Bretton Woods Agreements Act*, Hearings on H.R. 2211 Before the House Committee on Banking and Currency, 79th Cong., 1st Sess., 1945, 2:558–60 (evidence of H. D. White, 19 April 1945) (hereafter cited House Bretton Woods Hearings); H. D. White, "The Monetary Fund: Some Criticisms Examined," *Foreign Affairs* 23(1945):203–5; and Roy Harrod, *Reforming the World's Money* (1965), pp. 141–42: "It was thought at that time that the U.S. would be the one creditor country in the world, and that all other nations would be indebted to it. . . . I argued *at the time* that to regard . . . credits as hand-outs was quite the wrong way of looking at the matter. The system would be fully mutual. A nation that was in credit for a number of years might be in debit for

Within the U.S. government, the dominance of the Treasury over bureaucratic rivals reinforced the importance of the U.S. creditorship position
in shaping U.S. proposals. The more forthcoming, expansive positions that
might have come out of State Department dominance had little influence
once President Roosevelt gave Secretary Morgenthau the lead on international
monetary negotiations in 1943.[5] The Federal Reserve, and specifically the
Federal Reserve Bank of New York, which then was much more important
than the Federal Reserve Board in Washington, might have been an important
policy rival for the Treasury had it not been that Roosevelt considered the
New York "Fed" part and parcel of the New York financial community and
therefore as much an enemy of the Roosevelt administration as part of it.[6]
At Bretton Woods, treasury secretary Morgenthau expressed the administration's attitude when he declared that he was unable to feel "any sense of
dismay" at the prospect of driving "the usurious money lenders from the
temple of international finance."[7] Consequently, a Federal Reserve plan named
after Harvard professor and New York Federal Reserve Bank vice-president
John Williams, never had a significant chance to form the basis for the U.S.
negotiating position. The Williams "key currency" plan would have built the
postwar system around a U.S.-U.K. agreement on the pound-dollar exchange
rate and would have emphasized central bank cooperation.[8]

The Treasury view prevailed, and within the Treasury the leading views
were those of Harry Dexter White, a civil servant whose doctoral dissertation
had been written on French international accounts in the gold standard
period[9] and who had achieved intellectual dominance within the department

---

a following number of years—so I argued. Americans at that time were entirely sceptical about
the second eventuality; they were apt to smile."
4. U.S holdings of gold more than doubled between February 1934 and October 1941 (from
$7.4 billion to $22.8 billion), when they constituted nearly 70 percent of total gold reserves of
all countries. Much of the increase reflected capital flight from Europe. Board of Governors of
the Federal Reserve System, *Banking and Monetary Statistics* (1943), pp. 537–38; *BIS 13th Report*
1943, p. 124; Frank D. Graham and Charles R. Whittlesey, *Golden Avalanche* (1939), pp. 41–66.
During World War II, U.S. gold reserves declined slowly to $20.2 billion (55 percent of total
gold reserves) in June 1945, as the United States drew on its gold stock to support reserve
operations and to finance a shift from commercial exports to lend-lease shipments. *BIS 15th
Report* 1945, pp. 126–27. Thus, the U.S. decline could not be expected to continue in the
immediate postwar period.
5. On the president's decision, see *Postwar Foreign Policy Preparation 1939–1945*, Department of
State Publication 3580 (1949), p. 191. On Treasury dominance over the State Department, see
Gardner, *Sterling-Dollar Diplomacy*, pp. 71–72; Gardner, "The Political Setting," in *Bretton Woods
Revisited*, p. 23; and John Morton Blum, *From the Morgenthau Diaries: Years of War 1941–1945*
(1967), 3:241–42.
6. H. F. W. Plumptre, "Canadian Views," in *Bretton Woods Revisited*, pp. 42–43.
7. *Proceedings and Documents of the United Nations Monetary and Financial Conference, Bretton Woods,
New Hampshire, July 1–22, 1944* (1948), 1:1119 (hereafter cited *Bretton Woods Proceedings*).
8. See a similar view favoring an "Anglo-Saxon financial understanding and not . . . some
universal approach" by the president of the First National Bank of New York, Leon Fraser,
"Reconstructing World Money," *Proceedings of the Academy of Political Science* 20(1944):372.
9. White, *The French International Accounts 1880–1913*, Harvard Economic Studies 40 (1933).

and tended to be more influential on technical matters than the more politically inclined secretary.[10]

Moreover, the negotiating position of the United States would be affected,
both favorably and adversely, by its peculiar constitutional separation of
powers. Any postwar system would have to be approved by two-thirds of
the U.S. Senate under the treaty clause of the Constitution and by simple
majorities in both houses of Congress as well, to the extent supporting legislation was necessary. The executive branch would thus be limited by what
it could expect to sell to the Congress but would also be given a bargaining
tool to strengthen its refusal to accept proposals from other countries, for in
close cases it could say (with little possibility of disproof) that there was little
point in the U.S. negotiators approving a proposal that could not achieve
congressional support.[11]

The British government's position was determined by both economic and
political factors. Unlike the dollar, the pound sterling was expected to be
weak in the postwar period. The principal reason for this anticipated weakness was that the British investment account had been turned on its head by
the war.[12] Britain had traditionally enjoyed an inflow of investment income
that tended to offset trade deficits and long-term capital outflows. The shift
to war production coupled with wartime shipping difficulties reduced exports. The need to import war material and to continue food imports in the
face of reduced exports, in what Keynes termed Britain's "reckless single-
mindedness to wage and win the war,"[13] forced the British to sell foreign
assets to obtain hard currency, thereby reducing the international asset base
available to generate investment income after the war.

The British bought goods throughout the war from countries within the
sterling bloc, and, since sterling was a reserve currency, they were able to
pay in sterling. The consequence was the creation of large "sterling balances"
on which interest would have to be paid after the war. Moreover, the sterling
balances would constitute large short-term indebtedness that would represent
a potential call on British gold holdings.[14] The importance of this weakening
in the British international asset-liability balance in conditioning official Brit-

10. On White's role in the Treasury, see Blum, pp. 229–30; and Gardner, *Sterling-Dollar Diplomacy*, p. 73. See generally David Rees, *Harry Dexter White* (1973).
11. As the chief lawyer to the Bretton Woods delegation, Ansel Luxford, put it, "Let me admit
that Bretton Woods' sails had to be trimmed to the point where public and Congressional
acceptance might be possible—but only then after a life and death fight." Quoted in Gardner,
"The Political Setting," in *Bretton Woods Revisited*, p. 32. Some flavor of the congressional role
in Bretton Woods issues can be derived from Blum, pp. 228–71, 427–36; Gardner, *Sterling-Dollar
Diplomacy*, pp. 129–43. For the statutory terms of U.S. participation in the Bretton Woods
system, see Bretton Woods Agreements Act, ch. 339, 59 Stat. 512–17 (1945).
12. For wartime assessments, see T. Balogh, "Britain's External Problem," *The Banker* 72(1944):7;
and ibid. 73(1945):6–7.
13. Quoted in Balogh, 72:8.
14. See R. S. Sayers, *Financial Policy, 1939–1945* (1956), pp. 438–40.

ish perceptions of the probable postwar strength of sterling is perhaps best understood in the light of the events of 1931, when the size of British liabilities played a role in Britain's departure from the gold standard.[15]

Also affecting British views were the links with the Commonwealth that had been established in the 1930s and had come to be viewed, especially as the result of Commonwealth solidarity in the war, as a necessary and permanent feature of British postwar economic policy. The Imperial Preference system established in Ottawa in 1931 was particularly important in the International Trade Organization negotiations but also affected British monetary thinking. The political importance of that system reinforced the view that the sterling area monetary arrangements, under which Commonwealth members held their foreign-exchange reserves in London in sterling-denominated assets, were for Britain an alternative to a more universal monetary system.[16] The British came to view the sterling area as an institution that required discrimination not merely in tariffs but more particularly in exchange controls. Exchange controls on an area-wide basis would be needed, it was believed, to permit control-free transactions to occur within the sterling area and to induce sterling area members not to diversify out of sterling assets.[17] Such diversification might weaken the sterling exchange rate and lead to a loss of gold.

A final factor conditioning British views was a general disposition toward the use of government controls to regulate private economic activity. Economic planning could not be made effective if international transactions were free of controls.[18]

A remarkable feature of British preparations for the postwar monetary system was the intellectual dominance of John Maynard Keynes. When Harry Dexter White visited London in 1942, he stated, "I don't want to talk with anyone except Keynes."[19] Not only did the British proposal, which contemplated an International Clearing Union, bear the unmistakable mark of his economic brilliance and literary lucidity but Keynes became, for most of the period leading to and including the Bretton Woods conference, the

15. See chapter 3 above.
16. League of Nations, *International Currency Experience* (1944), pp. 47–65.
17. The foregoing paragraph states the author's interpretation of somewhat less forcefully stated views expressed by various British officials and bankers at various times. See e.g. Armand Van Dormael, *Bretton Woods: Birth of a Monetary System* (1978), pp. 21–28; D. E. Moggridge, "New Light on Post-War Plans," *The Banker* 122(1972):340–42; Gardner, *Sterling-Dollar Diplomacy*, pp. 122–24, 154–58; Paul Bareau, "The Sterling Area—Its Use and Abuse," *The Banker* 73(1945):131–36; "The Regional Solution," *The Economist*, 5 February 1944, pp. 169–70. On sterling area controls during World War II, see Raymond F. Mikesell, *Foreign Exchange in the Post-War World* (1954), pp. 14–18.
18. Moggridge, "New Light," pp. 340–42. One member of Parliament summed up a common British view of American policy as based on "rampant individualism" in a 1944 debate on postwar monetary plans. 399 House of Commons Debates, col. 1996 (10 May 1944).
19. E. F. Penrose, *Economic Planning for the Peace* (1953), p. 48; Van Dormael, p. 62.

leading British negotiator.[20] To be sure, Keynes's views reflected widely held British views on the postwar position of sterling and British attitudes toward planning and controls, but Keynes was one of the leading spokesmen and proselytizers for those views.

Keynes's thinking on demand management, reflected in his General Theory,[21] led him to view international monetary arrangements not as ends in themselves but rather as potential constraints on expansionary economic policies. Therefore, a prime criterion was that the postwar system should not restrain British domestic policy and, in particular, that any system resembling the gold standard should be avoided at all costs.[22] Moreover, Keynes thought that exchange controls, far from being merely a necessary evil, were desirable and, at least for capital transactions, should become a permanent feature of the postwar system.[23] Despite the fact that the Roosevelt administration was more interventionist than any previous U.S. administration, these views were not at all shared by the U.S. Treasury and certainly not by a majority in the U.S. Congress. A conflict in ideologies concerning the functions of economic policy and the role of the government in economic life complicated agreement on the details of postwar international monetary organization.

Other governments had views on these matters and had their own concerns about the postwar positions of their currencies, but they played little role in the shaping of Bretton Woods. Only two other national plans were offered. The Canadian plan was close enough to the White plan to be dubbed "off-White,"[24] and the French plan was so sketchy that it played no direct role in the negotiations, perhaps because it placed primary emphasis on an agreement among "the principal nations," analogous to the Tripartite Agreement, and treated an international institution as "optional"—a view of world postwar organization that was at odds with both the Keynes and White visions.[25]

20. See Van Dormael passim. See also the comments of Lord Robbins, then head of the Economic Section of the Cabinet Office, in *Autobiography of an Economist* (1971), pp. 192–96.

21. J. M. Keynes, *The General Theory of Employment, Interest and Money* (1936).

22. See e.g. Keynes's defense, in his 1944 House of Lords speech, of the joint U.S.-British plan against the charge that it was a return to the gold standard. 131 House of Lords Debates, cols. 844–46 (23 May 1944).

23. Van Dormael, pp. 8–9. For similar views on quantitative restrictions on trade, see Lord Kahn, "Historical Origins of the International Monetary System," in *Keynes and International Monetary Relations*, ed. A. P. Thirlwall (1976), pp. 3, 7.

24. For a retrospective view of the distinctive characteristics of the Canadian plan by Canada's delegate to Bretton Woods, see Louis Rasminsky, "Canadian Views," in *Bretton Woods Revisited*, p. 36.

25. J. Keith Horsefield, *The International Monetary Fund, 1945–1965* (1969), 1:37 and 3:97–102. The text of the French plan appeared in two slightly different versions. That reprinted in Horsefield provided for a Monetary Stabilization Office as the organ of central monetary authorities, and cited the Franco-British monetary agreement of December 1939, as a precedent for methods of cooperation. Ibid. 3:98, 100. The version printed in the *New York Times*, 9 May 1943, section 5, pp. 7, 9, referred to an International Clearing Office, and cited the Tripartite Agreement of 1936 as precedent.

II. THE TWO PLANS

The International Clearing Union

Keynes's proposal for an International Currency Union, as it was called in his early drafts, is especially interesting in a historical perspective because it saw the key problem as a lack of liquidity and its solution as the provision of more liquidity. In his proposal, questions involving exchange rates took a back seat.

By the time of the official publication in April 1943 of the British government's proposal,[26] the Keynes plan had already begun to be shaded to be more acceptable to the United States. It is useful therefore to review briefly earlier drafts to capture the essence of his views.[27]

Although the word "liquidity" had not yet been adopted as a convenient shorthand expression,[28] the central notion of the Union was that a new kind of "international bank-money" called "bancor"[29] would permit "the substitution of an expansionist, in place of a contractionist, pressure on world trade."[30] The role of bancor in the Keynes plan is difficult to understand in the present-day context of free exchange markets. It assumed comprehensive exchange controls in which "the provision of foreign exchange for remittance either to member or nonmember states will be concentrated in the hands of [the state's] central bank which would deal with the public through the usual banks."[31] Central banks would thus have a monopoly of foreign exchange within their own country. They would "buy and sell their own currencies among themselves only against debits and credits to their accounts" at the Union.[32] These accounts would be denominated in "the bank money of the Clearing Bank," later christened "bancor"; at the outset the balance would be zero and thereafter deficit countries would acquire debit balances with

26. Proposals for an International Clearing Union, Cmd. 6437 (April 1943); reprinted in Horsefield, *IMF 1945–1965*, 3:19–36.
27. The fourth draft was subsequently published by the International Monetary Fund in Horsefield, *IMF 1945–1965*, 3:3–18. More recently, earlier versions have been published in *The Collected Writings of John Maynard Keynes*, vol. 25, *Activities 1940–1944: Shaping the Post-War World, The Clearing Union*, ed. Donald Moggridge (1980), pp. 21–100. For the "electrifying effect" of Keynes's original document in British official circles, see Robbins, p. 196.
28. Ragnar Nurkse used the term "liquidity" in referring to the "main function" of the IMF in his 1945 essay, "Conditions of International Monetary Equilibrium," Princeton Essays in International Finance, no. 4 (1945), reprinted in *Readings in the Theory of International Trade*, ed. H. S. Ellis and L. A. Metzler (1950), p. 19. On the faulty understanding of the liquidity problem by the Bretton Woods architects, see Harry G. Johnson, "The International Monetary System and the Rule of Law," *Journal of Law and Economics* 15(1972):286–87, 291.
29. Horsefield, *IMF 1945–1965*, 3:3, para. 1.
30. Ibid. p. 4, para. 4.
31. "Proposals for an International Currency Union," appendix A.3 (18 November 1941), in Keynes, *Collected Writings*, 25:61. This was the second draft of the Keynes plan.
32. "Proposals for an International Currency Union," A.2 (8 September 1941), in ibid. p. 34. This was the first draft of the Keynes plan.

the Union and surplus countries credit balances. The Union would not acquire any foreign currencies but would deal solely in bancor.[33]

The process by which a central bank in deficit would acquire foreign currencies without any review at the time of the transaction was analogous to the British overdraft system of private borrowing from commercial banks.[34] In his thinking, Keynes linked the overdraft technique to what he called the "essential principle of banking, as it is exhibited within any closed system." This banking principle was "the necessary equality of credits and debits, of assets and liabilities. If no credits can be removed outside the clearing system but only transferred within it, the Union *itself* can never be in difficulties."[35] Keynes, who had grown up with the overdraft system, believed that the deficit country should have an automatic, or nearly automatic, right to draw bancor up to a previously specified limit.[36] The unfamiliarity of Americans with what Keynes called the "banking principle"[37] was a major barrier to acceptance of the Keynes plan, but the overdraft could have been restructured as simple lending as part of a line of credit, if Keynes had been more interested in American understanding than in abstract elegance.[38] As the British Treasury later conceded: "These two arrangements [the Keynes and White plans] represent alternative technical setups, capable of performing precisely the same functions. . . . It has, however, proved easier to obtain agreement on the mechanism of the [White plan], which has the appearance of being closer to what is already familiar."[39]

In his plan, Keynes characterized the underlying question concerning what became known as the "automaticity issue" as one of rules versus discretion: "Perhaps the most difficult question to determine is how much to decide by rule and how much to leave to discretion."[40] Since a central international

---

33. Ibid. A.2 and A.4.
34. On the relation of the Keynes plan to the British banking overdraft principle, see Penrose, p. 42; John Parke Young, "Developing Plans for an International Monetary Fund and a World Bank," *Department of State Bulletin* 23(1950):780–81.
35. Horsefield, *IMF 1945–1965*, 3:3, para. 2. See the link made between the overdraft technique and the banking principle in a speech by Keynes on 26 February 1943. Keynes, *Collected Writings*, 25:210–12.
36. Horsefield, *IMF 1945–1965*, 3:4, para. 5.
37. Keynes, *Collected Writings*, 25:160.
38. D. H. Robertson, "The Post-War Monetary Plans," *Economic Journal* 53(1943):358.
39. Joint Statement by Experts on the Establishment of an International Monetary Fund (Explanatory Notes by United Kingdom Experts) in Horsefield, *IMF 1945–1965*, 3:129. According to Robbins, White was not unsympathetic to the overdraft plan, but thought it was not politically feasible. In a memorandum of 23 June 1943, on "the heart of the problem—the question of subscriptions *versus* overdrafts," Robbins recorded that White "assured us that there was no hope of compromise on the subscription principle. The American public would never accept even the appearance of unlimited liability which the overdraft principle involved. . . . 'Don't think I say this because I am out of sympathy with your point of view,' he said. 'Personally I am very attracted by it and if I had my own way, I would go a long way to meet you. But I know that we can never get it across.' " Robbins, p. 199.
40. Horsefield, *IMF 1945–1965*, 3:6, para. 15.

organization was contemplated, however, discretion had two dimensions. The first was the discretion to be accorded national governments, and the second was the discretion to be accorded what Keynes termed the "central management," by which he seemed to mean the staff of the new international organization:

> If rule prevails, the liabilities attaching to membership of the system are definite, whilst the responsibilities of central management are reduced to a minimum. On the other hand, liabilities which would require the surrender by legislation of too much of the discretion, normally inherent in a Government, will not be readily undertaken by ourselves or by the United States. If discretion prevails, how far can the ultimate decision be left to the individual members and how far to the central management? If the individual members are too free, indiscipline may result and unwarrantable liberties be taken. But if it is to the central management that the discretions are given, too heavy a weight of responsibility may rest on it, and it may be assuming the exercise of powers which it has not the strength to implement. If rule prevails, the scheme can be made more watertight theoretically. But if discretion prevails, it may work better in practice.[41]

Keynes thus linked the question of automaticity of drawing rights to the question of the discretionary powers of the central organization. Although Keynes did not spell out the organizational implications explicitly, the nature of the organization's staff and executive board was to become an important issue dividing the British and the Americans.[42]

Keynes viewed the exchange rate regime as raising fundamental issues about the responsibility for adjustment. Under the gold standard, even during the interwar period, it was simply assumed that deficit countries had, and should have, the burden of adjusting their domestic economies so as to make adherence to existing exchange rates feasible. This view was widely accepted, even though the classical view of the pre-1914 gold standard was that it operated not simply by causing recessions in deficit countries but also in part through the expansionary effect of gold inflows in surplus countries. Keynes argued for placing "part of the responsibility for adjustment on the creditor country as well as on the debtor."[43] The mechanism for doing so would be a charge on credit balances, and not just deficit balances, of bancor.[44] The duty to pay a charge on credit balances would induce surplus countries to eliminate payments surpluses in order to avoid higher charges on increasing holdings of bancor. Such a provision, Keynes explained, would "recover the advantages which were enjoyed in the nineteenth century when a favourable

41. Ibid.
42. See discussion pp. 110–13.
43. Horsefield, *IMF 1945–1965*, 3:6, para. 16, and see Kahn, p. 16.
44. Horsefield, *IMF 1945–1965*, 3:6–8, para. 17.

balance in favour of London and Paris, which were the main creditor centres, immediately produced an expansionist pressure in those markets, but which have been lost since New York succeeded to the position of main creditor, the effect of this change being aggravated by the breakdown of international borrowing credit and by the flight of loose funds from one depository to another."[45] Moreover, adjustment might take the form of exchange rate changes, including appreciations of surplus currencies.[46] Thus, an exchange rate change—say, the devaluation of sterling after the war—would be a virtue, in contrast to the 1931 sterling devaluation, which was seen as evidence that the international monetary system was collapsing.

No doubt Keynes's position was affected by the anticipated postwar weakness of sterling.[47] However, Keynes's views also significantly influenced thinking about the international monetary system by introducing into general discussion the very concept of the responsibility for adjustment, as well as the policy issue of the relative burdens of adjustment to be placed on surplus and on deficit countries. Though not resolved at Bretton Woods, that issue continued to grow in importance in postwar discussions until it became a central issue in the negotiations of the 1970s following the collapse of the Bretton Woods system.

Keynes favored comprehensive controls on capital transactions by all countries even though he recognized that the United States would not accept any requirement that capital controls be imposed:

> It is widely held that control of capital movements, both inward and outward, should be a permanent feature of the post-war system—at least so far as we [i.e., the British] are concerned. If control is to be effective, it probably involves the *machinery* of exchange control for *all* transactions, even though a general open license is given to all remittances in respect of current trade. But such control will be more difficult to work . . . by unilateral action than if movements of capital can be controlled *at both ends*. It would therefore be of great advantage if the United States and all other members of the Currency Union would adopt machinery similar to that which we have now gone a long way towards perfecting in this country; though this cannot be regarded as *essential* to the proposed Union.[48]

45. Ibid. p. 6, para. 16.
46. Ibid. p. 8, para. 17(5). Other possible steps that a creditor country with balances exceeding half its quota would be required to discuss with the Union's governing board included such then-radical measures as "expansion of domestic credit and domestic demand; . . . reduction of excessive tariffs . . . ;" and "international loans for . . . backward countries." Ibid.
47. In a memorandum accompanying his first draft of 8 September 1941, Keynes quoted a gloomy assessment by H. D. Henderson of Britain's probable postwar balance-of-payments position. Keynes, *Collected Writings*, 25:25.
48. Horsefield, *IMF 1945–1965*, 3:13, para. 45. Keynes stated that his plan "presumes that member countries will operate an official monopoly of exchange transactions." "A Comparative

He was particularly concerned about "speculative movements or flights out of deficiency countries or from one surplus country to another" (phenomena that later came to be referred to as "destabilizing capital flows") and argued that one of the virtues of his Clearing Union would be that it would facilitate capital controls.[49]

The Stabilization Fund

White's April 1942 proposal for a Stabilization Fund, which became the basis for the official U.S. proposal published on 10 July 1943, reflects a considerably different view of the purpose of the postwar monetary organization.[50] Although the very concept of a Fund implies agreement with Keynes's view that liquidity was a key problem, the purpose of the Fund was not to substitute "expansionist, in place of contractionist, pressure" as Keynes sought.[51] Rather, the first objective listed was the stabilization of exchange rates.[52]

This emphasis on the exchange rate regime was not logically inconsistent with the purposes of the Clearing Union, whose resources would also be used to support existing exchange rates, but Keynes's provision for adjustment by exchange rate changes was notably missing from the White proposal. The United States expected to have the strongest currency in the postwar period and therefore to be providing, one way or the other, the bulk of international credit. As Senator Robert Taft later complained, the United States was "putting in the fund all the valuable money," yet it was likely to be "pouring money down a rat hole."[53] From this expectation of permanent creditor status flowed a concern with exchange rate stability. The White plan saw exchange depreciation as a threat to private foreign investment as well as to trade.[54]

White did not accept Keynes's banking principle under which deficit countries could run overdrafts. Perhaps he feared that the Congress would never be able to understand the British overdraft system, for to an American of that era, an "overdraft" suggested an inability to keep one's spending under control as well as a propensity of debtors to take advantage of creditors. This can be only a partial explanation of the White plan, which in some versions did in fact countenance an international unit, the "unitas."[55] Both Keynes and White saw some differences in form between unitas and bancor, and

---

Analysis of the British Project for a Clearing Union (C.U.) and the American Project for a Stabilisation Fund (S.F.)" (1 March 1943), in Keynes, *Collected Writings*, 25:221, para. 12.
49. Horsefield, *IMF 1945–1965*, 3:13, para. 46(b).
50. Ibid. pp. 85–96; see ibid. pp. 37–82 for White's "Preliminary Draft Proposal" of April 1942.
51. See discussion p. 77.
52. Horsefield, *IMF 1945–1965*, 3:41, 46.
53. *Congressional Record* 91(16 July 1945):7573. See Gardner, *Sterling-Dollar Diplomacy*, pp. 129–31.
54. Horsefield, *IMF 1945–1965*, 3:46.
55. Ibid. 1:41. See part III:1 of the 10 July 1943 Draft Outline, ibid. 3:87.

these differences in form took on at least great symbolic value. The unitas was to be a *unit of account* for recording obligations incurred in transactions in national currencies. The bancor, on the other hand, was to be a *medium of exchange;* that is, bancor itself was to be advanced to debtors by the Union even though bancor was only a bookkeeping entry that would have to be used to acquire national currencies. The April 1944 Joint Statement by the U.S. and British experts explained the differences in form between Keynes's Union and White's Fund in terms of who would be on the opposite sides of any lending transactions:

> Under the *Clearing Union* the member countries might have been said to bank with the Union with which they were to keep balances or to run overdrafts. Under the *International Monetary Fund*, on the other hand, the Fund may be said to bank with the member countries, which undertake to grant to the *Fund* facilities to hold and to draw on their local funds. Thus if under the *Clearing Union* a member country drew resources from the *Union* this meant that its own balance with the *Union* would be diminished and the balance of some other member would be increased; whereas, if a member country draws resources from the *Fund*, this means that the *Fund's* balances with that member are increased and its balances with some other member are decreased.[56]

The differences between bancor and unitas are easily exaggerated, and it is worth underscoring not simply that unitas were not a factor of the original White plan but also that neither bancor nor unitas played any role in the final Articles of Agreement. One can therefore conclude that bancor and unitas were more symbols of different attitudes toward the role of the new institution than controlling technical mechanisms. Bancor, being created by agreement, could be liberally dispensed. In contrast, unitas, being a bookkeeping unit of account for transactions in gold and currencies, implied a more conservative policy. Keynes recognized that the prime objection to his plan, even among his British colleagues, was the difficulty of combining constraints on the amount borrowed with the automatic overdraft technique.[57]

The presumption that the United States would be in a permanent creditor position, as well as the necessity for congressional approval, led White to envision a Fund with much less lending capacity than Keynes's Union would have had. White was primarily interested in the total U.S. contribution, most or all of which could be expected to be advanced by the Fund to deficit countries and which therefore was a measure of what the United States would be lending indirectly to those countries. The White plan involved

56. Ibid. 3:128.
57. See e.g. correspondence with R. F. Harrod and D. H. Robertson, in Keynes, *Collected Writings,* 25:226–32.

aggregate subscriptions of "at least $5 billion" (implying a U.S. share of $3.2 billion),[58] whereas the Keynes plan envisioned a Union with aggregate quotas of over $30 billion. Since the quota played somewhat different roles in the Stabilization Fund and in the Clearing Union, Keynes himself used the rule of thumb that "the quota under S.F. corresponds for most purposes to *half* the quota under C.U."[59] Moreover, the ratio of $5 billion to $30 billion understates the relative potential U.S. obligation because under the White plan, the potential call on U.S. goods and services would be limited to its quota, $3.2 billion, and hence to about 64 percent of the $5.0 billion total Fund. Under the Keynes plan, however, it was theoretically possible that, although the U.S. quota might amount to no more than $3 billion, the corresponding call on U.S. resources could be well over half of the possible quota total of $30 billion or more. This differential potential obligation would arise if the United States became the only creditor, and the remaining members, all being under this assumption debtor countries, were to incur debt balances equal to three quarters of their entire quotas.[60]

Perhaps because the United States expected to be in persistent surplus the White plan, as originally drafted, unlike the Keynes plan, did not contain provisions designed to put part of the burden of adjustment on surplus countries. Moreover, the creditor's view of the international economy is also evident in the White plan's position that existing capital controls were to be "reduced" and new capital controls "prevented" in order to "encourage the flow of production capital,"[61] a position that contrasts with Keynes's enthusiasm for capital controls.

58. Preliminary Draft Outline, part IV, in Horsefield, *IMF 1945–1965*, 3:73–74, and 1:22; see 1:43, 58 for later suggested figures.
59. Keynes, "A Comparative Analysis of the British Project for a Clearing Union (C.U.) and the American Project for a Stabilisation Fund (S.F.)," (1 March 1943), in Keynes, *Collected Writings*, 25:216, para. 3 (emphasis in original).
60. See calculations in Joan Robinson, "The International Currency Proposals," *Economic Journal* 53(1943):163, 165. On the basis of average world trade figures for the last three prewar years of $48 billion, Robinson calculated that if the whole world joined the Clearing Union the sum of quotas (three-quarters of the trade figures) would be $36 billion. If all countries except the United States drew on their quotas to the maximum extent permissible without stringent penalties (i.e., three-quarters of the total quota), "the upper limit which the debit account of the world might reach is three-quarters of $33,000 million," ($36 billion less the U.S. quota of $3 billion) or about $24 billion. For other estimates, see e.g. Jacob Viner, "Two Plans for International Monetary Stabilization," *Yale Review* 33(1943–44):87–88, who estimated $31 billion in total borrowing quotas if the "sole contributing country" were the United States; R. F. Harrod, *The Life of John Maynard Keynes* (1951), pp. 548–49, who estimated credits available as approximately $25 billion. Unlike Robinson and Harrod, Viner did not allow for reduction in total credits available to three-quarters of total quotas. See Horsefield, *IMF 1945–1965*, 3:7, para. 17(2)(c). See Penrose, p. 42 for the rising scale of penalties, culminating in declaration of default if the overdraft exceeded three-quarters of the quota for more than two years. On proposed quota totals, see also p. 103 below.
61. Horsefield, *IMF 1945–1965*, 3:47.

III. The Process of Agreement

The differences in the two plans were the subject of intensive negotiations, mostly at the expert level, between the two governments.[62] For an understanding of the text of the Articles of Agreement, it is useful to think of the process of negotiations leading to the final text at Bretton Woods in terms of key interim documents. These documents comprise the *travaux préparatoires*, or legislative history, for the Articles of Agreement.

The final version of the Keynes plan was published by the British government in April 1943.[63] The final White plan appeared in July 1943 in the form of a "Preliminary Draft Outline of a Proposal for an International Stabilization Fund."[64] Although both of these documents had already been honed by the British and American treasuries in the light of discussion between them,[65] negotiations began in earnest only after publication. Following prolonged negotiations in Washington in September and October of 1943, a draft statement of principles was prepared, which was then released in a number of capitals in April 1944.[66] In fact, it remained largely a U.S.-British joint product.[67] This document, styled "Joint Statement by Experts on the Establishment of an International Monetary Fund," was published by the British government with the caveat that "it in no way commits the Governments concerned," but rather summed up principles agreed to at the technical level.[68] Nonetheless, the preceding negotiations had been at a sufficiently high level, with Keynes and White both involved, for each government to be effectively precluded from independently recurring to positions abandoned in the process of drafting the Joint Statement.[69] From this point on, the negotiating process was largely one of drafting more specific language to flesh out agreed principles and of obtaining agreement by other countries.

Once the Joint Statement was published in April 1944, the two governments turned their attentions to an international conference to be held at Atlantic City, New Jersey, in June 1944 in preparation for the July 1944 Bretton Woods Conference. In preparation for the Atlantic City conference, the U.S. Treasury released a key document entitled "Questions and Answers

---

62. On the negotiations, see Van Dormael, chaps. 4–13; Young, pp. 778–86; Gardner, *Sterling-Dollar Diplomacy*, parts 1 and 2; *Postwar Foreign Policy Preparation*, pp. 191–92, 240–42; Penrose, chaps. 1–3; and Horsefield, *IMF 1945–1965*, 3:3–118.

63. Proposals for an International Clearing Union, Cmd. 6437, reprinted in Horsefield, *IMF 1945–1965*, 3:19–36.

64. Published by the U.S. Treasury as revised 10 July 1943, reprinted in Horsefield, *IMF 1945–1965*, 3:83–96.

65. Van Dormael, pp. 59–70; Penrose, pp. 14–20, 39–52.

66. See Young, pp. 782–84. The Joint Statement by Experts was printed as a British command paper, Cmd. 6519 and reprinted in Horsefield, *IMF 1945–1965*, 3:128–35.

67. See Van Dormael, pp. 115–26, on the participation of third countries.

68. Horsefield, *IMF 1945–1965*, 3:128.

69. Gardner, *Sterling-Dollar Diplomacy*, p. 110.

on the International Monetary Fund," which set forth at considerable length an explanation and defense of the principal features of the emergent Fund.[70]

The proceedings of the Atlantic City conference were not published.[71] The negotiations there revolved about the Joint Statement, though the previously mentioned Canadian and French plans and various amendments to the Joint Statement offered by other countries were also before the delegates. No final document was published at the end of the Atlantic City conference on 30 June, but delegates, who went directly from Atlantic City to Bretton Woods, New Hampshire, found a "Preliminary Draft of Suggested Articles of Agreement for the Establishment of an International Monetary Fund," prepared by the Bretton Woods Conference secretariat and dated 1 July, awaiting them on their arrival.[72] The Preliminary Draft, setting forth a variety of alternative language formulations, reflects not merely the results of the Atlantic City meeting but also apparently behind-the-scenes work by the U.S. delegation.[73]

The proceedings of the Bretton Woods Conference, though running to two volumes, throw remarkably little light on the meaning of particular provisions,[74] in part because several of the more important clauses were drafted by the U.S. delegation alone and at the last meeting of the conference. Indeed, even Keynes, the head of the British delegation, did not read one key provision until after he had signed the Final Act, an oversight that nearly led the British government to refuse to ratify.[75] Nonetheless, the Bretton Woods proceedings do contain a variety of documents that illuminate some provisions. These documents include the Preliminary Draft with which the conference opened, amendments formally considered in the course of the conference, and various reports of Commission I (which had responsibility for the Fund)[76] and of its committees. What is missing from the written record, on the whole, is any reasoned argument for choosing one form of language over another.

The fact that the International Monetary Fund was to be a universal organization, established at an international conference as part of the United Nations system, led to a form of drafting that makes a number of provisions exceptionally opaque to the uninitiated reader. Despite provisions for weighted voting, all nations and all currencies are placed on an equal footing by the Articles of Agreement. One finds, with exceptions to be noted in a

70. Reprinted in Horsefield, *IMF 1945–1965*, 3:136–82.
71. Joseph Gold, *Interpretation by the Fund*, IMF Pamphlet Series no. 11 (1968), p. 19.
72. *Bretton Woods Proceedings*, 1:21.
73. See Horsefield, *IMF 1945–1965*, 1:88.
74. See the guarded comments on the usefulness of the *Bretton Woods Proceedings* by Joseph Gold, the Fund's general counsel, in his *Interpretation by the Fund*, p. 18.
75. Van Dormael, pp. 202–3, 224–39.
76. Commission II was concerned with the Bank for Reconstruction and Development, and Commission III with "Other Means of International Financial Cooperation." *Bretton Woods Proceedings*, 1:13.

moment, no mention of dollars, of sterling, of reserve currencies, of developing (or, in the terms of the time, "backward") countries, or of the other categories so essential to communicative speech and so common in the policy-oriented and scholarly writing of the period and of today. The terms "member" and "currency" are used without further precision.

This drafting convention, which has sometimes been referred to under the somewhat broader heading of the "principle of uniformity,"[77] has two exceptions and one near-exception that illustrate the difficulties inherent in such a mode of drafting, however essential it may be for achieving international agreement. The exceptions involve two references in the Bretton Woods agreement to the U.S. dollar. The first is the Article III, Section 3(b) requirement that each member pay in the form of gold the smaller of either 25 percent of its quota or 10 percent of its "net official holdings of gold and United States dollars." This provision, as originally drafted, referred to "gold and gold-convertible exchange" rather than gold and U.S. dollars.[78]

The second reference to the U.S. dollar, found in Article IV, Section 1, permitted a member to express the par value of its currency either in terms of gold or "the United States dollar of the weight and fineness in effect on July 1, 1944."[79] One version of this provision read gold or "a gold-convertible currency unit of the weight and fineness in effect on July 1, 1944."[80] White later remarked, "We ended up by getting gold as the unit and calling it dollars."[81] It was understood that "gold-convertible exchange" referred to the U.S. dollar (though only monetary authorities were entitled to demand conversion of U.S. currency into gold). The draft agreement bore a footnote indicating that the term "gold and gold-convertible exchange" was "subject to definition,"[82] despite Keynes's protest that "all our researches into the technical legal position and the opinions of the experts we have consulted support the view that no such currency at present exists."[83] When Dennis Robertson, one of the members of the British delegation, suggested that "gold-convertible exchange" be changed to "dollars," contrary to the instruction of Keynes (who preferred the bland "reserves"),[84] White jumped at the opportunity.

77. Joseph Gold, *Legal and Institutional Aspects of the International Monetary System: Selected Essays* (1979), pp. 469–519 (hereafter cited Gold, *Selected Essays*).
78. Articles of Agreement of the International Monetary Fund, Article III, Section 3(b), *original;* Joint Statement, II, Section 3. See Horsefield, *IMF 1945–1965*, 3:132, 188. This requirement was deleted in the Second Amendment to the Articles of Agreement, which went into effect in 1978.
79. Article IV, Section 1, *original.*
80. *Bretton Woods Proceedings*, 1:185.
81. House Bretton Woods Hearings, 1:152 (15 March 1945).
82. *Bretton Woods Proceedings*, 1:26, n. 1.
83. Van Dormael, pp. 159–60.
84. Ibid. pp. 165, 202.

Keynes did not become aware of the change until after the Final Act had been signed.[85]

The near-exception to the uniformity principle involves the provision in Article IV, Section 5(e), permitting a member to change the par value of its currency without Fund concurrence "if the change does not affect the international transactions of members of the Fund." This provision was drafted to apply specifically to the Soviet Union, even though there were strong arguments that the par value of the Soviet ruble would affect, at least indirectly, international transactions of other countries.[86] Since the Soviet Union did not join in the Fund, the provision had little impact, although it did play a role in the Fund's subsequent declaration of Czechoslovak ineligibility to use the resources of the Fund.[87] This near-exception to the principle of uniformity is merely a vivid example of a general tendency in international monetary legal drafting to attempt to dress up in generalized language a provision intended to apply to a particular country, a tendency caricatured by spelling "scarce currency" in what became Article VII as "$carce ¢urrency."[88]

As Harry G. Johnson observed, this drafting technique has significant political and intellectual consequences:

> The result [of Bretton Woods] was an international monetary constitution that treated all national currencies as equals—though the American negotiators were careful to ensure that in the International Monetary Fund as in the United Nations voting power was distributed according to the principle of the pigs of Orwell's *Animal Farm*, that "All animals are equal, but some are more equal than others." This fictitious legal principle of equality among nations has continued to dominate discussion and analysis of international monetary problems, where both academic and official experts like to start debate from the postulate of an anonymous surplus or deficit country, despite the arrant absurdity of refusing to name the delinquent in a club so small that everyone including the delinquent knows who he is. Of course, the fiction of anonymity is useful, and indeed socially necessary, if any member of the club may find himself a delinquent at any time. But it is apt to mislead the unwary into dilating at length on the content and implications of democratic rules that everyone knows will not be enforceable in a pseudo-democratic situation.[89]

85. On the "gold-convertible exchange" versus "United States dollar" issue, which had considerable symbolic importance to some countries, see ibid. pp. 112–13, 132, 135–37, 149–50, 159–60, 201–3.
86. Article IV, Section 5(e), *original;* Gold, *Selected Essays*, pp. 534–35.
87. Joseph Gold, *Membership and Nonmembership in the International Monetary Fund* (1974), pp. 345–72.
88. Horsefield, *IMF 1945–1965*, 1:46.
89. Johnson, pp. 284–85.

IV. The Exchange Rate Regime

As we saw in the last chapter, a principal lesson drawn from the interwar experience by the Bretton Woods planners, particularly those in the U.S Treasury, was that the postwar international monetary system should eliminate floating rates and competitive devaluations. They believed, moreover, that exchange rate changes should be a matter for international regulation.[90] As the rapporteur for Commission I at Bretton Woods put it, one principle on which general agreement was reached "at a relatively early stage in the preliminary discussions" was that "an exchange rate in its very nature is a two-ended thing, and that changes in exchange rates are therefore properly matters of international concern."[91] For White in particular, exchange stability was the "cardinal point" of the Bretton Woods agreement.[92]

Keynes did not wholly share White's views on the primacy of exchange stability, even though he was not an advocate of floating exchange rates. Certainly the expectation that the pound would be weak and British reserves exhausted after the war led Keynes to stress the need to permit devaluation whenever justified. One early version of the Keynes plan would have permitted a deficit country to depreciate its currency by 5 percent a year indefinitely.[93] Even if Keynes had not favored permitting British devaluation, his government could hardly support an international commitment that tied its hands on the sterling exchange rate in view of the anticipated postwar position of sterling. In any case, Keynes felt that a commitment that would have had the effect that the gold standard was thought to have had in 1931—of delaying a needed devaluation—would have been unacceptable to British public opinion.[94] Moreover, Keynes's prescriptions for dealing with a depressed domestic economy required that any given exchange rate be abandoned if necessary. Indeed, he argued in the House of Lords that an exchange rate should reflect the domestic price level rather than vice versa; he believed that it would be a mistake, when a currency was overvalued, to require the country to reduce the domestic price level by deflationary policies and that it would be preferable to permit devaluation instead.[95] Given his advocacy of strong governmental management of the domestic economy, exchange stability was necessarily a secondary objective. The U.S. Treasury was consequently aware that some provision would have to be made for changes in exchange rates.

The two principal questions that had to be resolved in marrying the British and U.S. conceptions on change of exchange rates were the substantive issue

90. See discussion, p. 54.
91. *Bretton Woods Proceedings*, 1:867.
92. Van Dormael, p. 163. See Horsefield, *IMF 1945–1965*, 1:16.
93. Louis Rasminsky, "Canadian Views," in *Bretton Woods Revisited*, p. 35.
94. Van Dormael, pp. 163–64.
95. 131 House of Lords Debates, col. 846 (23 May 1944). See further discussion, p. 96, below.

of the conditions under which a change might be made and the procedural issue of the role of the Fund in passing on any proposed change. Under the initial U.S. position, which was that a member's par value was to be fixed by agreement between that member and the Fund, the Fund would effectively have a veto and hence the substantive and procedural issues merged.[96] The ultimately adopted substantive criterion, namely, that no change be made except to correct a "fundamental disequilibrium," was added to the White plan in November 1942.[97] (The "fundamental disequilibrium" standard will be discussed below.) But that version also required an 80 percent qualified majority vote of approval of any exchange rate change,[98] a position from which the United States gradually retreated in order to gain British agreement to the U.S. plan as a whole. This retreat on the procedural role of the Fund was one of the few crucial U.S. concessions that induced Keynes and the British government to abandon the Clearing Union plan.[99]

Although the British and Americans had agreed on the Joint Statement, that document nevertheless did not meet British requirements for unilateral control over the sterling exchange rate. The Joint Statement retained the U.S. principle that "changes shall be made only with the approval of the Fund" but made that principle subject to the requirement that the "Fund shall approve a requested change . . . if it is essential to correct a fundamental disequilibrium." The Joint Statement also permitted one 10 percent change without approval and made clear that a country's "domestic social or political policies" were not to serve as a basis for refusing approval.[100] But despite these limitations of the principle of Fund approval, Keynes found the principle difficult to accept.

At Atlantic City the British offered an amendment to the Joint Statement's formulation to the effect that nothing therein "shall affect the right of members to modify their exchange rates as they may consider necessary or advisable."[101] In Keynes's view the core of the issue was not so much whether a country formally had such a unilateral right since the essence of the right could always be asserted by withdrawal from the Fund. Rather, he emphasized the sanction that would be applied if a country devalued in the face of Fund opposition. Therefore, he proposed that a country be unable to use the facilities of the Fund—that is, that the country would become ineligible

96. Horsefield, *IMF 1945–1965*, 1:46.
97. Ibid.
98. Ibid.
99. Herbert Feis, "Keynes in Retrospect," *Foreign Affairs* 29(1951):571.
100. Joint Statement, IV, Sections 3 and 4. See also IV, Section 2. The Joint Statement also provided that the "extreme uncertainties" prevailing at the time of the establishment of initial par values were to be taken into account. Ibid. IV, Section 3. Horsefield, *IMF 1945–1965*, 3:133.
101. Ibid. 1:83.

to borrow from the Fund—so long as its exchange rate was not approved by the Fund.[102]

Although Keynes and White could not agree at Atlantic City,[103] and although White, after Atlantic City, advised Treasury Secretary Morgenthau that "we should not budge one bit" in the face of British demands "to increase the flexibility and ease of alterations of exchange rates,"[104] the British and Americans were able in the course of the Bretton Woods Conference to table agreed language amending the Joint Statement formulation.[105] Under the new formulation a member altering its par value "despite the objection of the Fund, in cases where the Fund is entitled to object," would become "ineligible to use the resources of the Fund unless the Fund otherwise determines." If, after a "reasonable period" of time, the difference between the member and the Fund continued, then some as yet unagreed provisions in the withdrawal article were to come into effect. Further negotiation was required to arrive at a final compromise. As a Canadian delegate observed, the final formulation, "allow[ing] a member country to change its rate without the approval of the Fund, and yet remain a member in good standing," reflected "a compromise between international agreement and control on the one hand and national autonomy on the other."[106]

The tortuousness of this compromise is both a tribute to the skill of the draftsmen and evidence that major countries are loath to concede substantial power to a universal organization when they consider important national interests likely to be at stake. Under the compromise, "fundamental disequilibrium" remained nominally the substantive standard insofar as a "member shall not propose a change in the par value of its currency except to correct a fundamental disequilibrium," and the Fund was required to concur if it was satisfied that the change was in fact necessary for that purpose.[107] The member was required to consult with the Fund before making any change, and assuming that the increase or decrease exceeded 10 percent, the Fund was required to concur or object to the change.[108]

If the Fund objected, then the member might nonetheless change its par value, but the consequence was that the member became ineligible to use the resources of the Fund unless—and here was another concession to the British—the Fund should "otherwise determine."[109] If the "difference be-

---

102. Van Dormael, pp. 162–65. See also Joseph Gold, "Unauthorized Changes of Par Value and Fluctuating Exchange Rates in the Bretton Woods System," *American Journal of International Law* 65(1971):116.
103. Van Dormael, pp. 164–65.
104. Horsefield, *IMF 1945–1965*, 1:84.
105. *Bretton Woods Proceedings*, 1:270–71, 2:1798 (p. 1798 establishes the new language as a joint U.S.-British submission). See also, for a later joint U.S.-British amendment, ibid. 1:463, 2:1798.
106. Article IV, Section 6, *original; Bretton Woods Proceedings*, 1:557.
107. Article IV, Section 5(a) and (f), *original*.
108. Article IV, Section 5(b) and (c), *original*.
109. Article IV, Section 6, *original*.

tween the member and the Fund" continued, then "after the expiration of a reasonable period," the provisions of Article XV, Section 2(b) became applicable.[110] This last reference, which deserves recognition in the annals of creative obscurity, was intended to permit the Fund, by majority vote, to force the offending member to withdraw from the Fund while at the same time preserving the formal legal position that the change in par value, though unauthorized, was nonetheless not a violation of a member's obligations.[111] In short, an unauthorized par value change was not a violation of the Articles of Agreement, although the Fund could, if it chose, withhold access to its resources and, in the end, force the member to withdraw. The illusion of Fund preeminence and of an international legal rule remained, but the substance was that the artful concessions to the British had vitiated the principle of central Fund control of exchange rates espoused by the Americans.[112]

Since the question of violation did not arise, and since access to the Fund resources by the member in question (and in the end its continued membership) was discretionary with the Fund, the substantive requirement of a "fundamental disequilibrium" was relegated to a shadow existence, playing a role perhaps in debate and negotiation, but ultimately no decisive substantive legal role. That being so, it is hardly surprising that the pragmatic draftsmen abandoned attempts to define what, in the event that Fund approval had become a precondition to a par value change, would have been a central legal concept.[113] Nor would it have been easy to construct a definition for a term that attempted in two words to capture a vague, and perhaps ill-considered, economic notion. As White later wrote:

> In the drafting of the Articles of Agreement no attempt was made to define fundamental disequilibrium. This, as we know, was not an oversight. It was generally agreed that a satisfactory definition would be difficult to formulate. A too rigid or narrow interpretation would be dangerous; one too loose or general would be useless in providing a criterion for changes in currency parities. It was felt too that the subject matter was so important, and the necessity for a crystallization of a harmonious view so essential that it were best left for discussion and formulation by the Fund.[114]

But though the Executive Directors were asked on one occasion for an interpretation (under the Article XVIII interpretation power) that raised issues

110. Ibid.
111. The derivation of this legal result depends upon the fact that the reference in Article IV is to Section 2(b), rather than to Section 2(a)—the latter alone applying to a failure to perform obligations. Article XV, Section 2(a) and (b), *original*. See generally Gold, "Unauthorized Changes," pp. 118–19.
112. For a detailed exegesis of the resulting treaty language, see Gold, *Selected Essays*, pp. 520–73.
113. White later devoted many pages of an unpublished manuscript to attempting to interpret the fundamental disequilibrium condition. Horsefield, *IMF 1945–1965*, 1:139.
114. Quoted in Gold, *Selected Essays*, p. 526. And cf. *BIS 15th Report* 1945, p. 109, n. 1.

under the "fundamental disequilibrium" language,[115] and in another instance published a decision bearing on the definition, the resulting interpretations are singularly unenlightening. Perhaps the most illuminating definition, albeit circular, was offered by the Bank for International Settlements in its 1945 annual report: "The practical test will probably be that a disequilibrium which cannot be eliminated by any other method than an alteration of exchange rates must be regarded as fundamental."[116]

Further light on the compromise is thrown by the subsequent experience. On only one occasion did the Fund ever elect to treat an exchange rate change as unauthorized.[117] Indeed, the Fund on some occasions did not even require a member to assert that it was in "fundamental disequilibrium" when passing upon a proposed change in par values.[118] As time went on and it became apparent that a key problem under Bretton Woods was not the instability that White had feared but rather an unwillingness of members to make par value changes promptly enough, considerable effort was expended on making it clear that the "fundamental disequilibrium" requirement was not really a limitation on prompt and small exchange rate changes.[119]

Finally, upon the thorough redrafting of the Articles involved in the 1976 Jamaica Second Amendment, when a par value system was relegated to the status of a possible future system,[120] the concept of a fundamental disequilibrium (still undefined) was retained but the concept of an unauthorized change disappeared. According to the Second Amendment, any future par value regime will involve reversal of the presumption that a member devaluing without Fund concurrence would automatically become ineligible to have access to Fund resources in the absence of an affirmative Fund decision to the contrary. Any offending member will continue to be eligible until the Fund decides otherwise.[121] As Joseph Gold has observed, the very concept of an unauthorized change with any automatic sanctions "vanished in the [Jamaica] negotiations with no clamor to retain it and indeed with hardly any notice of its passing."[122] Thus has the legal pragmatism of the Bretton Woods negotiators in drafting the U.S.-U.K. compromise been justified by subse-

115. Decision no. 71-2 (26 September 1946), and Decision no. 278-3 (1 March 1948), *Selected Decisions of the International Monetary Fund*, 8th Issue (1976), pp. 30–32. For the background of the former, see Gold, *Interpretation by the Fund*, p. 4, and of the latter, see Joseph Gold, "Constitutional Development and Change," in Horsefield, *IMF 1945–1965*, 2:549 (hereafter cited Gold, "Constitutional Development"). See also IMF, *The Role of Exchange Rates in the Adjustment of International Payments* (1970), pp. 47–51.
116. *BIS 15th Report* 1945, p. 109, n. 1.
117. The Fund refused to concur in the French change of 26 January 1948, which was accompanied by discriminatory multiple currency practices. Gold, "Unauthorized Changes," p. 120.
118. Gold, *Selected Essays*, p. 56.
119. IMF, *Role of Exchange Rates*, pp. 47–51, 71–74.
120. Article IV, Section 4, *second*.
121. Schedule C(7), and Article XXVI, Section 2, *second*. See Gold, *Selected Essays*, p. 13.
122. Ibid.

quent history and taken still another step in the par value provisions of the Second Amendment.

Because of their importance in the subsequent history of the Fund and particularly in the breakdown of the Bretton Woods system, it is useful to review briefly three further aspects of the Bretton Woods provisions on the exchange rate regime. The first involves the provisions for margins around par, the second the special exchange rate provisions for the U.S. dollar, and the third the role of gold.

Margins

Par values are not the same as market exchange rates. Exchange rates are determined in the marketplace. A par value is an abstract concept. A key issue therefore was how far the market exchange rate between two currencies might deviate from parity, which is the ratio of their two par values expressed in some common numeraire.

As a solution to the problem, the analogy between gold points under the gold standard and a maximum margin on either side of par commended itself to the U.S. Treasury.[123] The June 1944 "Questions and Answers on the International Monetary Fund" contained an extensive discussion of that analogy.[124] The Treasury concluded that under contemporary conditions the spread between gold points for New York–London transactions would be 1.6 percent. This calculation was based on the fact that the United States imposed a ¼ percent charge on both buying and selling gold (which gave a ½ percent spread in New York) and on the assumption that the United Kingdom might impose similar charges; these ½ percent spreads would sum to 1 percent, to which should be added another ⅗ percent for transportation, insurance, and the like. The U.S. Treasury argued that the spread under the new system should be wider in order to induce "a country to utilize its own gold and exchange resources rather than to draw upon the resources of the Fund to meet normal and moderate needs for foreign exchange."[125] Ergo, a 2 percent spread would be desirable, which would equate to a one percent margin on either side of par.

From a legal point of view, the margins might, in principle, be enforced in several ways. One would be that each member might be given a monopoly over transactions within its territory, and it would then transact only within the margins.[126] Keynes envisaged that Britain would retain such a monopoly

123. See discussion of gold points under the gold standard, chap. 2, above.
124. Answer to Question 19, Horsefield, *IMF 1945–1965*, 3:158–60.
125. Ibid. 3:159.
126. The phrase "within the margins" is widely used, though strictly speaking the Bretton Woods one percent margins were maximums, so that transactions at the margins would be lawful.

(or at least, comprehensive exchange control),[127] but the United States looked forward to free exchange markets.[128] A second possibility would be that transactions outside the margins would be illegal. This would be an application to currency markets of the principle of price controls and could be expected to lead to evasion and to enforcement difficulties. The third possibility, and the one finally adopted, was to permit private parties to transact at the market price (subject to the right of any particular country to establish a monopoly or price control for transactions within its territory), but to impose upon member governments the obligation to intervene—that is, to buy and sell foreign exchange—in order to prevent the market rate from rising above the upper margin or falling below the lower margin.[129] The intervention requirement was not, however, made explicit in the Articles. Rather, each member was required to "undertake" to "permit" transactions within its territory only within the prescribed margins.

The Dollar Exchange Rate Regime

Article IV, Section 4(b) provides that a "member whose monetary authorities, for the settlement of international transactions, in fact freely buy and sell gold within the limits prescribed by the Fund . . . shall be decreed to be fulfilling" the foregoing undertaking.[130] The price for such gold transactions was to be par plus or minus a special gold margin. The United States was the only country to elect this particular manner of complying with the undertaking, and others elected to use exchange market intervention.[131] In line with the expectation that the dollar would be the strongest currency, it was assumed that a weak currency country would intervene to sell dollars (or gold) in exchange for its own currency, thereby keeping its own currency within the prescribed margins. The fundamental purpose of the Fund qua fund would be to provide weak currency countries with the financing to permit such transactions (unless, in the event of a fundamental disequilibrium, devaluation was appropriate).

Under such a system, though the United States could in theory sell dollars to support weak currencies, such "ceiling intervention" would not be required. "Floor intervention" by weak currencies would suffice, and the United States could remain passive, not participating in any way in exchange markets. In Joseph Gold's phrase, the "system of par values *in practice* was

127. Van Dormael, p. 229. The September 1941 draft does not fully support Van Dormael's blanket statement that there would be "no free currency markets." Ibid. That draft recognized the possibility of an "open general licence" to "authorised dealers." Keynes, *Collected Writings,* 25:34, footnote.
128. Answer to Question 19, Horsefield, *IMF 1945–1965,* 3:158–60.
129. Article IV, Section 4(b), *original.*
130. Ibid.
131. Article IV, Section 2, *original.* It was anticipated that the gold margins would be the same as for spot currency transactions. Article IV, Section 3, *original.* Gold, *Selected Essays,* p. 80. See also testimony of Harry D. White, House Bretton Woods Hearings, 2:592–93 (19 April 1945).

a solar system in which the U.S. dollar was the sun."[132] In keeping with the principle of uniformity, this special position of the U.S. dollar was not mentioned in the text of the Articles of Agreement. Rather, an option was established—the buying and selling of gold—which only the United States would elect.[133]

The Role of Gold

The role that gold would play in the Bretton Woods system was both a political and a technical question. The British view was nicely enunciated in an *Economist* article entitled "Ten Years Off Gold," published in September 1941 on the tenth anniversary of Britain's departure from the gold standard: "It would be easier to-day to persuade the electorate and the Commons to accept the Corn Laws than the gold standard."[134] Yet *The Economist* recognized that gold had somehow to be a part of the system:

> [As] the international precious substance, there may still be a use for gold. The decision rests with the United States Government; for in any forseeable time, dollars will be sought after by the rest of the world, and so long as gold remains a sure means of acquiring dollars, gold will be desired by the whole world. No currency, not even the dollar, is now on the gold standard; but gold is on the dollar standard, and it is in the general interest, and specifically the British interest, that it should remain there. The Emperor has abdicated, but he still rules his St. Helena at Fort Knox, Kentucky, the pensioner of a stronger power. Ten years after Waterloo, there is no desire to see a return.[135]

When the April 1943 Joint Statement was found to contain numerous references to gold, Keynes felt compelled to defend the Joint Statement and himself in the House of Lords. Beaverbrook had already submitted the following memorandum to the War Cabinet:

> This is the Gold Standard all over again. And at a moment when the United States has all the gold and Great Britain has none of it.[136]

Keynes's defense was twofold. First, referring to his own role in persuading his countrymen to turn their backs on traditional economic ideas that had underlain the gold standard, he asked rhetorically:

> Was it not I, when many of today's iconoclasts were still worshippers of the Calf, who wrote that "Gold is a barbarous relic?" Am I so faithless,

132. Gold, *Selected Essays*, p. 80 (emphasis in original).
133. House Bretton Woods Hearings, 2:565–66 (19 April 1945).
134. *The Economist*, 20 September 1941, p. 346.
135. Ibid. p. 347.
136. Quoted in Van Dormael, p. 131. The Beaverbrook memorandum was dated 9 February 1944, before the Joint Statement was published but after the outlines of the joint plan had been settled.

so forgetful, so senile that, at the very moment of the triumph of these ideas when, with gathering momentum, Governments, Parliaments, banks, the Press, the public, and even economists, have at last accepted the new doctrines, I go off to help forge new chains to hold us fast in the old dungeon?[137]

Second, he argued that the Joint Statement plan was "the exact opposite" of the gold standard because gold's role was merely that of a standard of value:

The gold standard, as I understand it, means a system under which the external value of a national currency is rigidly tied to a fixed quantity of gold which can only honourably be broken under *force majeure;* and it involves a financial policy which compels the internal value of the domestic currency to conform to this external value as fixed in terms of gold. On the other hand, the use of gold merely as a convenient common denominator by means of which the relative values of national currencies—these being free to change—are expressed from time to time, is obviously quite another matter.[138]

Yet he recognized that gold could not be demonetized completely. To do so "would obviously be highly objectionable to the British Commonwealth and to Russia as the main producers, and to the United States and the Western Allies as the main holders of it."[139]

Gold would be held as monetary reserves, and since "there must be *some* price for gold . . . , it is most advisable that the current rates of exchange and the relative values of gold in different currencies should correspond."[140] Since Keynes intended that a country should be free to devalue, he emphasized that in lieu of the gold standard principle that "the internal value of a currency should conform to a prescribed *de jure* external value," the new system would permit the external value to "be altered if necessary so as to conform to whatever *de facto* internal value results from domestic policies, which themselves shall be immune from criticism by the Fund." Keynes's view was that the Fund would therefore be a triumph for his ideas about domestic economic policy. If, he asked, the Joint Statement proposals "lay down by international agreement the essence of the new doctrine, far removed from the old orthodoxy . . . in terms as inoffensive as possible to the former faith, need we complain?"[141]

Though Keynes's House of Lords speech was a model of elegant advocacy, it did not persuade everyone. Monetary commentator Paul Einzig declared in the *Daily Express* shortly after Bretton Woods that "once the plan is trans-

137. 131 House of Lords Debates, col. 844 (23 May 1944).
138. Ibid. col. 845.
139. Ibid. col. 846.
140. Ibid. cols. 845–46 (emphasis in original).
141. Ibid. col. 846.

lated into intelligible English and is denuded of all camouflage, every layman of normal intelligence is bound to realize that it is the gold standard, the full gold standard and nothing but the gold standard."[142] One of the reasons that this charge could not be lightly dismissed was that U.S. officials implied to the Congress and the public that many of the advantages of the gold standard had been preserved. Dean Acheson, then Assistant Secretary of State, summed up the situation candidly: "The British like to say that this is a departure from the gold standard. We like to say that this resembles the gold standard. Neither one of us has any differences as to what the plan provides. We differ in the words we like to use about it."[143]

The truth was that gold was much more than a standard of value. Before analyzing gold's additional functions, however, it is useful to explore its standard-of-value role. The U.S. dollar had an official definition in terms of gold, and hence, even if a second currency's par value was expressed (under Article IV, Section 1) in terms of the U.S. dollar rather than gold, it would nonetheless have an implicit value in terms of gold. Moreover, gold's standard of value was intentionally anchored at the existing level. Unless the dollar was to be devalued, a step no one apparently envisaged, gold had a guaranteed price. That price was guaranteed by the U.S. undertaking to buy and sell gold at $35 an ounce. Though it is true that the price of gold could be changed through the device of a uniform change in par values, such a change required not merely a majority of the total voting power of the Fund but also the affirmative vote of every member with at least 10 percent of the total of quotas, a requirement that permitted the United States, which had more than 30 percent of the vote, a veto over any change in the price of gold by international action.[144]

In addition to its standard-of-value role, gold was to be a reserve asset. Indeed, at the outset it was the principal reserve asset. In 1948, for example, total world holdings of gold (outside the Soviet bloc) totaled $32.8 billion, and foreign exchange reserves came to only $13.4 billion.[145]

In addition, gold was to be, as a result of the subscription provisions, an important asset of the Fund itself. Each member was to pay to the Fund in gold the lesser of (1) 25 percent of its quota or (2) 10 percent of its net official

142. Quoted in Van Dormael, p. 227.
143. *Bretton Woods Agreements Act*, Hearings on H.R. 3314 before the Senate Committee on Banking and Currency, 79th Cong., 1st Sess. (1943), p. 23 (hereafter cited Senate Bretton Woods Hearings).
144. Article V, Section 7, *original*. White later testified that the 10 percent clause was designed to give the United States a veto. House Bretton Woods Hearings, 2:581 (19 April 1945). On the U.S. voting percentage, see discussion p. 110 below.
145. *International Reserves and Liquidity: A Study by the Staff of the International Monetary Fund* (1958), p. 16, table 1. The Fund and its members accounted for almost the whole of these totals. The only significant nonmember gold reserve was Switzerland's ($1.4 billion). *BIS 19th Report* 1949, p. 150.

holdings of gold and United States dollars.[146] As of June 1947, subscription payments in gold totaled $1.3 billion compared to $2.1 billion in dollars and $3.1 billion in other currencies (many of which were inconvertible).[147] And most of the charges on drawings were, in the early years, paid in gold.[148]

Over the years, first as the dollar's dominance became clearer and then as the dollar became overvalued, the issue would be debated whether the value of the dollar rested on the tie to gold or vice versa. But at the outset of the Fund's operations an objective observer might be forgiven for noting that gold seemed more central to the international monetary system than at any time since 1931.

V. Exchange Controls

The Articles of Agreement make a fundamental distinction between current transactions (in popular usage called "current account" transactions) and capital transactions. In general, exchange controls are not permitted for current transactions but are permitted, and may even be encouraged in certain circumstances, for capital transactions. The distinction throws a good deal of light on the purposes of the Bretton Woods agreement.

As previously mentioned, Keynes considered exchange control a desirable feature of an international monetary system and, in particular, favored controls over capital movements because of his concern with speculative capital flows out of deficit currencies.[149] Here one sees again Keynes's worries about the anticipated weakness of sterling after the war. But one can also perceive the belief that later became fashionable that destabilizing capital flows, or "fugitive funds" in Keynes's phrase,[150] would be a threat to the entire par value system. It was a "vital object" to "have a means . . . of controlling short-term speculative movements or flights of currency whether out of debtor countries or from one creditor country to another." Though he viewed long-term capital flows from creditor countries for investment as desirable, he wanted to restrict even such flows "out of debtor countries which lack the means to finance."[151] And Keynes apparently also believed that exchange control would be a desirable instrument of national policy. In 1944 he argued in the House of Lords that pervasive capital controls might be necessary to permit control of domestic capital markets.[152] Nevertheless, he recognized that it was neither feasible nor essential to the operation of his Union to

146. Article III, Section 3, *original*.
147. *IMF Annual Report 1947*, appendix VIII(ii), pp. 66–67.
148. Horsefield, *IMF 1945–1965*, 2:364, table 11.
149. See discussion pp. 80–81.
150. Horsefield, *IMF 1945–1965*, 3:31.
151. Ibid. 3:32.
152. 131 House of Lords Debates, col. 845 (23 May 1944).

mandate capital controls in member countries and the "degree of such control should therefore be left to the decision of each member State."[153]

White, in contrast, favored examination of a requirement that countries be required to agree "to abandon, not later than one year after joining the Fund, all restrictions and controls over foreign exchange transactions with member countries, except with the approval of the Fund."[154] Yet he considered "unrealistic and unsound" the "tendency to regard foreign exchange controls, or any interference with the free movement of funds and of goods as, ipso facto, bad."[155]

Whatever White's views, attitudes at higher U.S. government levels were hostile to exchange controls. The U.S. concern with exchange controls, which to Europeans with a more *dirigiste* point of view may have seemed an obsession, is partly to be explained by the belief that Nazi Germany's aggression in Europe had been furthered by currency controls. Secretary of the Treasury Morgenthau wrote in 1945:

> The decade of the 1930's was almost unique in the multiplicity of ingenious schemes that were devised by some countries, notably Germany, to exploit their creditors, their customers, and their competitors in their international trade and financial relations. It is necessary only to recall the use of exchange controls, competitive currency depreciation, multiple currency practices, blocked balances, bilateral clearing arrangements and the host of other restrictive and discriminatory devices to find the causes for the inadequate recovery in international trade in the decade before the war. These monetary devices were measures of international economic aggression, and they were the logical concomitant of a policy directed toward war and conquest.[156]

[handwritten margin note: Nazi Germany]

Severe limitations on exchange controls were therefore seen as part of planning for the peace within the United Nations system as well as more technical planning for the monetary system.

White's plan exempted capital transfers from the requirement imposed on members to abandon existing exchange restrictions when feasible or to obtain Fund approval of new restrictions.[157] The U.S. Treasury had come around to the view that the experience of the interwar period showed that the "gold and foreign exchange resources of a country should be reserved primarily for the settlement of international balances on *current* account."[158]

153. Horsefield, *IMF 1945–1965*, 3:31.
154. This language is taken from the April 1942 draft of his stabilization fund proposal. Horsefield 3:63.
155. Ibid.
156. Henry Morgenthau, Jr., "Bretton Woods and International Coöperation," *Foreign Affairs* 23(1945):185.
157. Horsefield, *IMF 1945–1965*, 3:95.
158. Questions and Answers, answer to Question 33, ibid. 3:176 (emphasis supplied).

The Joint Statement would have permitted the Fund to "*require* a member country to exercise control to prevent" the "use [of] the Fund's resources to meet a large or sustained outflow of capital."[159] This particular formulation was modified at Bretton Woods to permit the Fund to "*request* a member to exercise controls" to prevent the use of the Fund's resources for such a purpose.[160] The change had the effect of considerably limiting the power of the Fund vis-à-vis member countries, though perhaps more in concept than in practice, since a country might still be inclined to comply with such a request to obtain Fund financing.

Although any formal power to mandate capital restrictions was thus eliminated, the freedom of members to impose such restrictions was made explicit in Article VI, Section 3. The only restriction on "such controls as are necessary to regulate international capital movements" was that such controls should not be exercised "in a manner which will restrict payments for current transactions or which will unduly delay transfers of funds in settlement of commitments."[161]

Once the distinction is made between current and capital transactions, the question of definition becomes important. A definition of "payments for current transactions" as "payments which are not for the purpose of transferring capital" was included in Article XIX(i), but the difficulty of making a distinction was emphasized by using the device of listing examples of current transactions to give content to the definition while at the same time stating that the examples had been included "without limitation."[162]

More significant to the influence of the Fund, however, was a transitional provision to deal with the practical difficulty that most members were already using comprehensive controls on current as well as capital transactions. Under Article XIV, Section 2, members might during "the post-war transitional period . . . maintain and adapt to changing circumstances . . . restrictions on payments and transfers for current international transactions." This language subjected any new restrictions to the prohibition of Article VIII against restrictions, imposed "without the approval of the Fund," on the making of payments and transfers for current international transfers. For a country already imposing comprehensive restrictions, however, the power under Article XIV to "adapt" existing restrictions provided a means to continue to apply an evolving exchange control system to current transactions. No country had to submit to the rigors of Article VIII once it notified the Fund of its intention to avail itself of the transitional arrangements of Article XIV, until such time as it notified the Fund that it was "prepared to accept" the

159. Ibid. 3:133–34 (emphasis supplied).
160. Article VI, Section 1(a), *original* (emphasis supplied).
161. Article VI, Section 3, *original*.
162. Article XIX(i), *original*.

obligations of Article VIII.[163] Only a minority of members have accepted Article VIII status, and new members have a choice between the Article VIII and the transitional Article XIV regimes.[164]

VI. THE IMF AS A FUND

From a lawyer's point of view, one of the most distinctive aspects of the Bretton Woods agreement was that it created a Fund. The Fund was, of course, an organization, but it was also a fund of money and other assets. These assets were to be "lent" to member countries of the organization, which were in turn to "repay" the "loan." (The quotation marks here indicate the begging of interesting issues concerning how properly to characterize Fund transactions.) The terms and conditions under which the IMF was to obtain the assets that would make up this fund, under which it might make those assets available to members, and under which the members would thereafter be required to return them to the fund are directly comparable to the kinds of issues with which lawyers grapple daily in domestic legal systems.

Two immediate domestic law analogies spring to mind. The subscriptions by members and the methods of voting on use of the resulting assets bear a close resemblance to issues in corporation law. The "loans" to members and their "repayment" are analogous to banking law or at least to banking practice, where terms of loans and their repayment are spelled out in contracts and often limited by statutes and regulations. Consequently, though the policies of the Fund with regard to quotas and the use of the Fund's resources can be and usually are discussed from an economic viewpoint, the establishment of the Fund and the mechanics of its activities required a level of specificity of rules spelling out the rights and obligations of both members and of the organization that is characteristic of a legal system.

Quotas

In considering the legal bases of the Fund, it is useful to treat issues concerning the Fund's sources of assets separately from issues concerning members' drawing rights to those assets. However, it is well to recognize at the outset that the Articles of Agreement were so drafted that a single concept unites both aspects: the quota. Indeed, the quota is also central to the governance of the Fund, a subject discussed separately below. As one IMF staff publication states, quotas are "multipurpose":

163. Article VIII, Section 2; Article XIV, Sections 2 and 3, *original*. See discussion in Dam, *GATT*, pp. 152–54.
164. Gold, "Constitutional Development," pp. 555–57. As of 30 April 1980, 50 of 140 members had accepted Article VIII status. *IMF Annual Report* 1980, pp. 83, 122, table I.14.

> A quota determines the subscription or contribution of each member
> to the capital of the Fund; and the total of the quotas of all members
> determines the size of the Fund's financial resources. . . . Quotas de-
> termine, or at least greatly affect, the amount and the rate of member
> drawings (borrowing) from the Fund. . . . The quotas that determine
> the members' drawing rights and subscriptions also determine their
> relative voting strength, which is intended to reflect approximately their
> relative economic significance in the Fund.[165]

Determination of quotas by negotiation, rather than by application of some
predetermined rule, was perhaps inevitable. The fact that the quotas would
have such central functions made their negotiation perhaps the most significant and time-consuming aspect of the Bretton Woods conference. Since
the factors that influenced the size of the respective quotas and particularly
the efforts to resolve issues by economic formulas have been discussed at
length by others, it is not necessary to recover that ground here.[166] It is worth
stressing that negotiations must be undertaken each time that quotas are
increased.[167] Quotas were made renewable each five years under Article III,
Section 2, and consequently seven renegotiations of varying complexity have
occurred since Bretton Woods.[168]

Resources

Subscriptions called for by quotas were the principal source of assets for the
Fund. Each member was required to pay the amount of its quota partly in
gold and partly in its own currency.[169] As a consequence of the subscription
formula, the Fund received gold plus what Keynes pejoratively called a
"mixed bag of national currencies."[170] At a time when the U.S. dollar was
the only major currency that was convertible and therefore members seeking
payments assistance would want to draw dollars, only the United States
would be providing dollars. Most of the rest of the currency subscriptions
would be of little or no value since the drawing of inconvertible currencies
would be pointless. One of the principal advantages of Keynes's Union would
have been that the aggregate amount of drawing rights to bancor would all
be available for balance-of-payments financing, unlike the aggregate amount
of currency subscriptions under the Bretton Woods agreement. The subscription of inconvertible currencies was not a burden on the subscribing

165. Oscar L. Altman, "Quotas in the International Monetary Fund," *IMF Staff Papers*
5(1956):129–30, 132, 134.
166. Ibid. pp. 136–42; Van Dormael, pp. 179–83; Horsefield, *IMF 1945–1965*, 1:94–100.
167. A related process determines quotas for new members. Altman, "Quotas," pp. 142–43.
168. *IMF Annual Report 1980*, pp. 68, 70, 83. See Horsefield, *IMF 1945–1965*, 2:354–63; Margaret Garritsen de Vries, *The International Monetary Fund 1966–1971* (1976), 1:287–305.
169. Article III, Section 3(b), *original*. See discussion of the gold subscription provision,
pp. 97–98, above.
170. Van Dormael, p. 112.

countries, it should be noted, since the Fund was empowered to accept non-negotiable, non–interest-bearing demand notes for currencies not needed for Fund operations.[171] And of course members could in effect simply print the additional currency to be subscribed, knowing that it would not enter into circulation so long as the Fund had no use for it.

The gold plus mixed-bag-of-currencies solution involved a rejection not merely of Keynes's bancor proposal but also of an earlier White proposal that subscriptions include interest-bearing government securities.[172] White's intention had been that the Fund should have the "means of conducting open-market operations in any given country when desired."[173] White's Fund would thus be able to influence local interest rates by means of open-market purchase and sale of securities. Such a role for the Fund, which would have made it a far more important institution than the one that emerged from Bretton Woods, was totally at odds with Keynes's view that the institution should be "passive."[174] The limitation of the subscription provisions to exclude such transferable securities thus reflected both an important U.S. concession and a sharply reduced role for the Fund.

The total amount of resources at the disposal of the Fund was much smaller than Keynes had proposed. Although Keynes did not specify the size of his Union but rather proposed that quotas be "fixed by reference to the sum of each country's exports and imports on the average of (say) the three pre-war years, and might be (say) 75 percent of this amount," Joan Robinson calculated in a widely cited article that this formula would result in quotas totaling $36 billion with an "upper limit which the debit account of the world might reach" of $24 billion.[175] White, in contrast, envisaged a Fund of "at least $5 billion."[176] At Bretton Woods it was agreed that quotas would total $8.8 billion.[177] Because of the mixed bag of currencies, only a small part of this $8.8 billion would, as a practical matter, be available for drawings by members. Subscriptions of gold and U.S. dollars were, at the time of Bretton Woods, expected to be only about $3 billion.[178]

Subscriptions were not, however, the only source of Fund assets. The Fund would derive income from charges on member drawings. These charges

171. Article III, Section 5, *original*. Of the 34 original members who declared par values by 30 June 1947, 18 elected to substitute notes for part of their national currency subscription. *IMF Annual Report* 1947, p. 30.
172. Blum, p. 231.
173. White plan (April 1942 version), Horsefield, *IMF 1945–1965*, 3:73.
174. Blum, p. 244. See also Van Dormael, pp. 102–3.
175. Keynes plan (April 1943 version), Horsefield, *IMF 1945–1965*, 3:22; Robinson, p. 165. For these and other estimates, see note 60 above.
176. White plan (April 1942 version), Horsefield, *IMF 1945–1965*, 3:73.
177. Articles of Agreement, Schedule A, *original*.
178. Estimate by Jacob Viner, cited in Altman, "Quotas," p. 144, n. 28. The amount could not be known with precision in advance because of the provisions on gold subscriptions, which made a country's gold subscriptions turn on its holdings of gold and U.S. dollars in its reserves. See discussion, pp. 97–98, above.

(analogous to, but not the same as, interest payments) were to be imposed on drawings and hence only on deficit countries. Keynes's notion that pressures would be placed on creditor countries through charges on credit balances of bancor[179] had no counterpart in the White plan and did not survive to Bretton Woods. In addition to a one-time service charge of ¾ percent on each transaction, the Articles of Agreement provided for a sliding scale of periodic charges based on the relation of the amount of drawings to the drawing country's quota and on the elapsed time from the date of the drawing.[180] The amounts of the charges were specified in the Bretton Woods agreement itself, rather than being left to the Fund's "management" or even to a majority vote; the charge schedule might, however, be changed by a three-quarters majority.[181] Charges were payable in gold, though members with monetary reserves less than one-half of quota (whose currencies were thus unlikely to be useful to the Fund) were permitted to pay a portion of the charge in local currency.[182] Charges were thus intended to be a source of income in gold, except on transactions with the weaker currency countries. White believed that the charge provisions would permit the Fund to be "quite a money-maker."[183]

The Articles of Agreement envisaged two other kinds of transactions designed to increase the Fund's assets (or at least to improve their composition): borrowing and replenishment by sale of gold. Investment of Fund assets was a possible third source not specifically provided for in the Articles of Agreement. A fourth source of assets was implicit in the maintenance-of-value provisions. That the Fund was conceived as an institution of specifically delegated and limited powers meant that the ability to rely on each of these four sources depended on the wording of the Articles of Agreement.[184]

The Fund was given power to borrow currencies of particular members, either directly from the member or elsewhere with that member's consent.[185] Since this provision appears in Article VII, an article entitled "Scarce Currencies," an inference is that such borrowing could only occur if the member's currency was scarce (a concept to be discussed below). That inference is strengthened by the requirement that the Fund must deem "such action appropriate to replenish its holdings" of the currency to be borrowed.[186]

179. Keynes plan (February 1942 version), para. 17(3) in Horsefield, *IMF 1945–1965*, 3:7.
180. Article V, Section 8(a) and (c), *original*.
181. Article V, Section 8(e), *original*.
182. Article V, Section 8(f), *original*.
183. House Bretton Woods Hearings, p. 94 (9 March 1945). Another source of assets would be the currencies that a drawing country would be required to pay upon purchase of the currencies it drew. See discussion, p. 107, below.
184. The U.S. lawyer, Ansel W. Luxford, explained in congressional hearings: "The fund is an instrumentality of delegated powers. It has only those powers that are given to it, the same as our own Constitution." House Bretton Woods Hearings, p. 153 (15 March 1945).
185. Article VII, Section 2, *original*.
186. Ibid.

Within the same article and subject to the requirement of a replenishment purpose is a provision that the Fund require a member to sell its currency to the Fund for gold.[187] Such a transaction would not, of course, increase Fund assets but rather would simply change the composition of assets to enhance the usefulness of those assets to the Fund.

Although the Fund would have large holdings of gold and of member currencies, it was not specifically empowered to increase those holdings by investment. On the other hand, no provision prohibited such investment. And so the question of investment, which could generate a substantial flow of resources for the Fund, became a legal issue that would be of some consequence during periods when income from charges was low.[188]

The Fund was conceived of as a revolving fund of constant gold value.[189] Consequently, the Articles of Agreement provided for the maintenance of the gold value of currencies held by the Fund.[190] White conceived of this provision as a "gold value guaranty."[191] A member that reduced the value of its currency was required to pay an amount in its own currency "equal to the reduction in the gold value of its currency held by the Fund."[192] Although the Articles of Agreement provided for a par value system with maximum margins around par, the Articles also envisaged that members, rather than formally devaluing, might simply permit their currencies to depreciate below the lower margin. In that event, the Fund might, if in its opinion a member's currency had "depreciated to a significant extent within that member's territories," require a similar maintenance-of-value contribution.[193] The Articles of Agreement also provided for a return of currency by the Fund to a revaluing member, though (by implication) not to a member that, rather than revaluing, merely allowed its currency to appreciate.[194]

Drawing Rights

The purpose of creating a Fund was, of course, to make the resources of the Fund available to members in balance-of-payments difficulties, though the Fund would also be a source of finance for the staff itself in carrying out its various functions. A fundamental choice was made to specify in considerable detail the terms, conditions, and amounts of drawings. Even if the Bretton

187. Ibid.
188. The income derived from this source was severely limited. See Horsefield, *IMF 1945–1965*, 2:365–73.
189. Testimony by Harry D. White, House Bretton Woods Hearings, 1:83 (12 March 1945).
190. Article IV, Section 8, *original*. See generally Joseph Gold, *Maintenance of the Gold Value of the Fund's Assets*, IMF Pamphlet Series no. 6 (1965).
191. Senate Bretton Woods Hearings, p. 59 (14 June 1945). The term "gold clause" appears in the Second Report of Committee 2 to Commission I at Bretton Woods. *Bretton Woods Proceedings*, 1:313.
192. Article IV, Section 8(b), *original*.
193. Ibid.
194. Article IV, Section 8(c), *original*.

Woods provisions left considerable scope for interpretation and discretion, the approach followed excluded to that extent two other logically possible, but competing, principles.

The first competing principle was the "owned reserves" principle, under which the drawing country might determine how much it would draw, treating its own subscription as equivalent to reserves that it owned. Keynes would have preferred this to be the dominant principle. In the September–October 1943 bilateral discussions with the United States, he took the position that a member "should have access to the reserves of the Fund without limitation until it had withdrawn resources equivalent to its quota."[195] Aside from being a device to assure that Britain would be able to borrow without Fund interference with its domestic economic policy, Keynes also believed that "it would be very unwise to try to make an untried institution too grandmotherly."[196] The second competing principle was that the Fund staff, or alternatively the members acting collectively, might set the terms, conditions, and amounts at their discretion. White favored a solution giving great discretion to the Executive Directors over members' access to Fund resources.[197]

In the end a compromise was reached between the Keynes and White principles. But since the terms, conditions, and amounts of drawing were not fully specified, a crucial question would become, in the postwar interpretation of the Articles and in the evolving practice of the Fund, to what extent the owned reserves and Fund discretion approaches would play a role in fact. This question will be deferred to the next chapter. Here the inquiry will be the extent to which the Bretton Woods negotiators purported to specify the terms, conditions, and amounts of future drawings.

One of the basic concepts of the Fund is that balance-of-payments assistance takes the legal form of a purchase of a strong currency for the members' own currency rather than the borrowing of the strong currency. Similarly, when the time to reverse the transaction occurs, the member repurchases its own currency. Thus, the language of credit (repayment, interest and the like) is missing from the Articles of Agreement. It is unclear why the language of purchase rather than that of credit was used. White tended to use the purchase concept from an early date, and the explanation may simply be that he was thinking of the foreign exchange market, where foreign currencies are acquired by buying them with one's own currency.[198] Keynes, in contrast, had used the language of credit, albeit of the British overdraft variety, where

195. Young, p. 783. Keynes recognized the member should not be able to draw down the entire amount of the quota at one time. Keynes plan (April 1943 version), in Horsefield, *IMF 1945–1965*, 3:23, and see ibid. 1:67.
196. Keynes, letter to Jacob Viner, quoted in ibid. 1:72.
197. Young, p. 783.
198. See e.g. the discussion in the April 1942 draft, Horsefield, *IMF 1945–1965*, 3:48–49. See also White's testimony in 1945, House Bretton Woods Hearings, p. 95 (12 March 1945).

a line of credit is established and then drawn down simply by transactions with third parties rather than with the bank itself. In one sense, the White purchase concept was not congenial to his preference for giving the Executive Directors discretion over member drawings. Language of credit would be more calculated to reinforce that view of the Executive Directors' powers since a financial institution should normally have discretion over the decisions whether to make a loan and over its terms and conditions. The International Bank for Reconstruction and Development, for example, was to make loans, and no member was to have a "right" to borrow from that institution.[199]

Whatever the motivations, the decision to use the language of purchase had certain consequences. Since repurchase was not the repayment of a loan, the timing of repurchase was left flexible, with no fixed term. Moreover, sale by the Fund of any of the currency with which a member had purchased currency of other members reduced the obligation to repurchase by a corresponding degree, a provision which further distinguished Fund transactions from loans. Similarly, since a loan and interest payments were not involved, it was easier to justify the system of charges escalating with the amount of the purchase and period outstanding before repurchase.[200] A more mechanical incident of the purchase form of the transaction was that the Fund received, as the consideration for the purchase, that member's currency rather than merely a note or an account receivable. In theory, this currency was available for sale to other members, though the currency of a country in balance-of-payments difficulties was unlikely to be in demand.

Perhaps the most important consequence of using terms such as "purchase," "repurchase," and "charges" is that the text of the Articles is not easily understood, even by financial experts or lawyers. Technical discussions of the Fund's operations strike anyone who has not mastered the special vocabulary as arcane. Conversely, the normal language of credit used by the uninitiated appears amateurish to the international monetary lawyer. The result is a separation between international monetary policy and international monetary law that has not been to anyone's advantage.

The purchase provisions, as previously mentioned, do not follow either the Keynes or the White principle. Indeed, part of the difficulty that arose

199. See e.g. Article III, Section 4 of the Bank's Articles of Agreement, *Bretton Woods Proceedings*, 1:1054–55. For discussion of choice of language of purchase rather than of loan, see Harrod, *Reforming the World's Money*, pp. 123–24; Fritz Machlup, *International Payments, Debts, and Gold* (1964), pp. 288–92; Fritz Machlup, "The Cloakroom Rule of International Reserves: Reserve Creation and Resources Transfer," *Quarterly Journal of Economics* 79(1965):340.

200. Gold, "Constitutional Development," p. 525; Gold, *Selected Essays*, pp. 417–18. White emphasized that the factors allowing escalation of charges were important incidents of purchase rather than borrowings. House Bretton Woods Hearings, p. 95 (12 March 1945). From 1952, it became declared Fund policy that drawings should be repurchased in three to five years. J. Keith Horsefield, "Charges, Repurchases, Selection of Currencies," in Horsefield, *IMF 1945–1965*, 2:446.

later in their interpretation[201] derives from the fact that, as is so often the case in diplomatic negotiations where fundamental differences of view are "papered over," the Articles include language supporting both principles. The Keynes principle is espoused in the flat declaration that "a member shall be *entitled* to buy the currency of another member from the Fund in exchange for its own currency" but that language is immediately followed by the condition that requires the purchasing member to "represent" that the other member's currency "is presently needed for making in that currency payments which are consistent with the provisions of this Agreement."[202]

Not only is the latter clause ambiguous as to whether the correctness of the representation is subject to challenge by the Fund, but it also raises issues as to which provisions of the Articles are drawn into consideration by the "consistent with" requirement. As Joseph Gold has pointed out, one interpretation favored by "some negotiators of the original Articles" was that a request for purchase could only be turned down if the member had been formally declared ineligible to use the resources of the Fund and that such a declaration could be made only on the basis of past improper use and not on the basis that the prospective use would be improper.[203] This view was not to prevail, but it illustrates the failure to resolve the fundamental cleavage between the Keynes and White views.

The Articles of Agreement contain a variety of other provisions specifying the amounts and purposes of purchases. In the absence of a waiver, the provisions limit the rate of purchase to roughly 25 percent of quota per year up to a maximum of 200 percent of quota.[204] Currencies may not be purchased "to hold against forward exchange transactions" without Fund permission, nor can members "make net use of the Fund's resources to meet a large or sustained outflow of capital" without risking ineligibility.[205] The repurchase requirements, which have the effect of determining the period of the drawing, are so complex that they became the subject of an annex to the agreement, Schedule B, but at the same time they are indefinite since no repurchase is required at all in certain circumstances.[206]

Scarce Currencies

In view of the expected dominance of the dollar in the postwar period, the anticipated weakness of almost all other currencies, the relatively small size

201. See discussion p. 119.
202. Article V, Section 3, *original* (emphasis supplied).
203. Gold, *Selected Essays*, p. 46. As Gold points out, there are some specific conditions, not relevant here, that might bar a purchase in the absence of waiver. See, for example, Article V, Section 3(iii), *original*.
204. Ibid.
205. Article V, Section 3(b), and Article VI, Section 1, *original*.
206. See the admirably concise summary of the repurchase provisions of Article V, Section 7, in Horsefield, *IMF 1945–1965*, 2:383. Schedule B deals with the assets (gold and particular currencies) to be used to make the repurchase.

of the Fund compared to the Clearing Union proposal, and the mixed-bag-of-currencies feature of the Fund, there was widespread concern that the Fund might run out of usable resources (gold and dollars) and be left only with large amounts of currencies of no use for balance-of-payments financing. To be sure, as U.S. Treasury officials publicly emphasized, this result was unlikely unless there was a general dollar shortage in the world extending beyond the immediate postwar period,[207] but that was precisely what many observers feared.[208]

The U.S. response to the problem of a shortage of dollars was to include in the White plan the provision that became the scarce currency clause of Article VII, Section 3. That clause permitted other members "to impose limitations on the freedom of exchange operations in the scarce currency."[209] That it was drawn with the United States almost exclusively in mind is underscored, as previously mentioned in connection with the uniformity principle, by the jocular spelling "$carce ¢urrency."[210] Although in one sense it may be true that the clause was "included in the original Articles largely as a result of the insistence of the United Kingdom,"[211] it also appears to have been inserted in the White plan unilaterally by the United States. In March 1943 Keynes wrote to R. F. Harrod that until Harrod had pointed out the scarce currency provision to him he had paid little attention to it:

> I interpreted it as a half-baked suggestion, not fully thought through, which was certain to be dropped as soon as its full consequences were appreciated. I cannot imagine that the State Department really would put forward as their own solution the rationing of purchases from a scarce currency country. . . . I should expect that the moment emphatic attention was drawn to this alternative, it would be withdrawn.[212]

Although the scarce currency provision was never implemented, in large part because of the liquidity furnished first to European countries by the Marshall Plan and then to the Fund by the General Arrangements to Borrow,[213] the provision contained a germ of several ideas that were to reemerge in the 1970s. The first was Keynes's idea that pressures should be placed on surplus

207. Senate Bretton Woods Hearings, pp. 159–66, especially pp. 163–64 (18 June 1945); House Bretton Woods Hearings, pp. 91–92, 555–66 (12 March and 19 April 1945); White, "Monetary Fund" (1945), pp. 201–5; E. M. Bernstein, "Scarce Currencies and the International Monetary Fund," *Journal of Political Economy* 53(1945):3–4, 12–14; letter of H. D. White to Representative A. H. Andresen, 10 April 1945, *Congressional Record* 91(1945):A2669.
208. At least in 1946, Keynes did not expect a long-term dollar shortage. See Keynes, "The Balance of Payments of the United States," *Economic Journal* 56(1946):172–87.
209. Article VII, Section 3(b), *original;* Horsefield, *IMF 1945–1965,* 3:195.
210. Horsefield, *IMF 1945–1965,* 1:46.
211. Gold, *Selected Essays,* p. 208.
212. Letter dated 4 March 1943, in Keynes, *Collected Writings,* 25:230.
213. Johnson, p. 289. For legal reasons why the scarce currency clause may not have been invoked, see Gold, *Selected Essays,* pp. 209–10; Roy Harrod, "Problems Perceived in the International Financial System," in *Bretton Woods Revisited,* pp. 17–18.

as well as debtor countries, an idea that found no other significant resonance in the Bretton Woods agreement.[214] The second was that such pressures might take the form of discrimination against a persistent surplus country. Not only was the Fund to ration its supplies of a currency declared by the Fund to be scarce,[215] but such a declaration constituted authority for other members to impose exchange controls on current transactions that discriminated against the scarce currency. The clause thus authorized an action that, in the absence of the Fund authorization via the scarce currency declaration, would be in violation of the nondiscrimination rules of Article VIII, Section 3.[216] Thus, the notion of discriminatory retaliation as a pressure, if not indeed as a sanction, found a place in the Articles of Agreement.

VII. GOVERNANCE

The IMF was to be an international organization. Unlike many other such organizations, decisions were to be made by weighted voting rather than by one-country, one-vote procedures. Both the United States and Britain agreed on this point because weighted voting would assure them jointly a dominating voice in decisions. Voting strength was to be determined by the size of the quota, though not precisely proportional thereto since each member received 250 votes (in a concession to the principle of equality of states) plus one additional vote for each $100,000 (U.S.) of quota.[217] This arrangement gave the United States 31.46 percent and Britain 15.02 percent of the vote.[218] As a supplement to the power gained under weighted voting, Britain and the United States acquired a veto over certain decisions under special voting requirements.[219] For example, uniform changes in par values required, in addition to a majority of all votes, the affirmative vote of all members with at least 10 percent of the total of the quotas.[220]

The British and the Americans had rather different views of the appropriate management of the Fund. Their differences of view came to revolve more

214. Kahn, pp. 16–18.
215. Article VII, Section 3(a), *original.*
216. See Questions and Answers, reply to Question 32, in Horsefield, *IMF 1945–1965*, 3:175.
217. Article XII, Section 5, *original.* See also the provisions of Article XII, Section 5(b), for adjustment of voting power for countries that, as a result of Fund transactions, are not users of Fund resources or other members whose currencies have been sold by the Fund and not yet restored to it. See, for a detailed explanation, Joseph Gold, *Voting and Decisions in the International Monetary Fund* (1972), pp. 30–43.
218. The percentage figures are as of 30 June 1947, *IMF Annual Report* 1947, appendix I, p. 45. Gold notes that U.S. voting power on 27 December 1945 (the date on which the articles took effect) was 37.9 percent of the total, but by 30 April 1946 had declined to 33.1 percent. Gold, *Voting and Decisions,* p. 26.
219. Article XII, Section 5(a), *original.* See also the special rules for certain votes in Article XII, Section 5(b). Gold, *Voting and Decisions,* pp. 36–38; Senate Bretton Woods Hearings, pp. 43, 125–27 (12 and 16 June 1945).
220. Article IV, Section 7, *original.*

about the choice of the types of appointments to be made to the executive director positions than over such other potential issues as the composition of the staff or the details of weighted voting. Under the Fund structure as adopted at Bretton Woods, the Board of Governors, composed in practice of the finance ministers of member countries, would normally meet only annually and would delegate all but the most important decisions to the Executive Directors.[221] The Managing Director, to be selected by but not from the Executive Directors and, a fortiori, not from the staff, would not have legal powers of decision.[222] The Executive Directors would be appointed by member countries, though only the five countries with the largest voting power would have their own Executive Director and other members would be grouped in constituencies (which would each elect an Executive Director) so that their meetings could be limited to a manageable size.[223]

The decisions on the Executive Director positions were only partially resolved at Bretton Woods and arose again at the inaugural meeting of the Board of Governors at Savannah, Georgia, in March 1946. The crucial decisions concerned how often the Executive Directors were to meet, where they were to reside, and how high their salaries were to be. These issues addressed the functions of the officials who were to fill the Executive Director positions, but they were so hotly contested because they were actually proxies for the role of the Fund itself.

The British had, early in negotiations, hoped for a governing board independent of member countries, which would provide expert management and be free of political control. This appeared in their submission at Atlantic City: "So far as practicable . . . we want to aim at a governing structure doing a technical job and developing a sense of corporate responsibility to all members, and not the need to guard the interests of particular countries."[224] In the face of U.S. opposition these views were modified, and at the Savannah meetings Keynes argued for part-time directors with financial expertise and a high standing in national treasuries, who would bring to the Fund's policy decisions both expert knowledge of national needs and conditions and a commitment to the international aims of the Fund.[225] Thus the Managing Director, who should be "a thoroughly able and discreet man," should run

---

221. Article XII, Sections 1 and 2, *original*.
222. Article XII, Section 4, *original*. Although the Articles of Agreement referred to the organ of the Fund responsible for conduct of its general operations as "the Executive Directors," it became more common in the Fund to refer to this body as "the Executive Board," the members of which were the Executive Directors or their Alternates. De Vries, *IMF 1966–1971*, 1:622, n. 8.
223. Article XII, Section 3, *original*.
224. Horsefield, *IMF 1945–1965*, 1:86; J. Keith Horsefield, "Proposals for Using Objective Indicators as a Guide to Exchange Rate Changes: A Historical Comment," *IMF Staff Papers* 20(1973):837.
225. Harrod, *Keynes*, pp. 633–34.

the Fund "day in and day out" with the aid of an efficient technical staff, while the directors performed a different function.[226] They should

> remain in the background, meeting only occasionally to determine broad policies of the Fund and to protect their respective national interests. The men best fitted to perform these functions of executive directors when called for it would be top flight men active in the affairs of their own central banks or governments. Such men could be made available on a part-time basis. But they could not be spared for the daily work of the Fund and, even if they could, they would not find enough to do unless they proceeded to interfere with the management of the Fund itself and make it a football of international politics.[227]

The American view that Fund resources had to be husbanded and that the Fund should play a major role in exchange rate changes was reflected in the U.S. preference for full-time directors meeting in what they termed "continuous session." This American view was reinforced by the U.S. preference for Washington over New York for the headquarters of the Fund. The antipathy that Morgenthau and White, and Roosevelt as well, felt for the "money changers" of Wall Street was well known.[228] Permanent Executive Directors, especially if located in Washington, would be more likely to be bureaucrats than bankers.

The difference between the British and American positions was papered over at Bretton Woods with a compromise providing, in accordance with the U.S. view, for the Executive Directors to "function in continuous session at the principal office of the Fund" (whose location was left undetermined), but, in a bow to the British view, specifying that they should "meet as often as the business of the Fund may require."[229] The question of continuous presence at headquarters was still open at the time of the inaugural meeting in Savannah, Georgia, in 1946. Keynes then interpreted the "continuous session" provision to require only that the Executive Directors be available for meetings at the Fund headquarters, not that they necessarily reside in Washington.[230] The American preference for continuous presence (subject to provision for an alternate for each Executive Director) was imposed, ap-

226. Van Dormael, p. 296; Harrod, *Keynes*, p. 633.
227. Van Dormael, p. 296. Cf. the views of a Dutch delegate at Bretton Woods, who had argued that the Fund "would need an organ composed of the highest monetary officials, who would reside and continue to function in their own countries. If they were required to remain at the headquarters of the new organization, they would be compelled to sit and study economics or statistics, or in order to escape boredom they would be tempted to intervene in affairs into which they should not intrude." Gold, *Selected Essays*, p. 249.
228. Ibid. pp. 249–50; A. F. W. Plumptre, "Canadian Views," in *Bretton Woods Revisited*, p. 42; *Bretton Woods Proceedings*, 1:1118–19; Gardner, *Sterling-Dollar Diplomacy*, pp. 258, 265.
229. Article XII, Section 3(g), *original*.
230. Horsefield, *IMF 1945–1965*, 1:131–32.

parently rather brutally, on the British.[231] A bylaw was adopted providing that Executive Directors should "devote all the time and attention to the business of the Fund that its interests require, and [shall] be continuously available at the principal office of the Fund."[232] The collateral American preference for relatively high salaries, permitting full-time presence of Executive Directors with high-salary alternates (who presumably would not be merely technicians), was also imposed on the British. Keynes abstained on the final salary vote in the subcommittee charged with the issue.[233]

Finally, the decision to establish the Fund in the country with the largest quota having been taken at Bretton Woods, the United States insisted on a sovereign right to locate it in Washington. Keynes complained, "In the light of the unyielding attitude taken up by the American representative, we are prepared to accept the proposal of the United States, but I am afraid that the arguments employed have not persuaded us that a mistake is not being made."[234] He later said privately, referring to the uncompromising positions taken by Secretary of the Treasury (later Chief Justice) Fred Vinson, "I went to Savannah to meet the world, and all I met was a tyrant."[235]

Keynes feared that the consequences of these decisions would be to make the Fund a "political" rather than a technical financial institution. Though the decisions of the Fund were inevitably political in the sense that they would have a profound impact on issues vitally important to the internal economies of member states, the appellation "political" had to Keynes a darker side. He sought to warn the Savannah delegates in an oft-quoted speech. Warming to the theme of good fairies who would bring gifts to the new twins, Master Fund and Miss Bank, he brought his eloquent analogy to a head with the warning:

231. See chapter 21 in Van Dormael, pp. 286–303, entitled "Savannah: Pax Americana." Joseph Gold regards the provision for continuous availability of either the Executive Director or his Alternate as a compromise, but notes that the British merely regarded it as "an aggravation of . . . error." *Selected Essays*, pp. 254–55.

232. By-Law 14(g), in Horsefield, *IMF 1945–1965*, 3:282.

233. Ibid. 1:134–35; Gardner, *Sterling-Dollar Diplomacy*, p. 260. In a Treasury Memorandum of 27 March 1946, Keynes observed that "an obstacle to successful opposition lay in the fact that the majority of the individuals taking part in the salary discussion were expecting to receive their jobs. Moreover, political and financial patronage was being created of the first order of attraction for South American (and other) countries—life in Washington with no defined or onerous duties and a grand tax-free salary." Quoted in Kahn, p. 25.

234. Horsefield, *IMF 1945–1965*, 1:130. Keynes, in his Treasury Memorandum, wrote: "We had not conceived it possible that either institution [Fund or Bank] would be placed away from New York. . . . No rumour reached us until a day or two before we left Washington for Savannah, when Mr. Vinson . . . told me that the American Delegates had decided that both institutions should be placed in Washington and that this was a final decision the merits of which they were not prepared to discuss." Quoted in Kahn, p. 23.

235. Quoted in lecture by Paul Bareau, in turn quoted by Van Dormael, p. 302.

I hope that Mr. Kelchner[236] has not made any mistake and that there is no malicious fairy, no Carabosse, whom he has overlooked and forgotten to ask to the party. For if so, the curses which that bad fairy will pronounce will, I feel sure, run as follows:—"You two brats shall grow up politicians; your every thought and act shall have an arrière-pensée; everything you determine shall not be for its own sake or on its own merits but because of something else.

If this should happen, then the best that could befall—and that is how it might turn out—would be for the children to fall into an eternal slumber, never to waken or be heard again in the courts and markets of mankind.[237]

Keynes's eloquence was lost on Vinson. He was overheard to mutter: "I don't mind being called malicious, but I *do* mind being called a fairy!"[238]

This short survey of the principal issues concerning the management of the Fund[239] highlights the way in which attitudes toward the role of the Fund in the international monetary system tended to dominate attitudes toward Fund governance. These issues were to emerge again in the 1970s when the reform of that system once more came to the center of the world economic stage. But in the meantime the evolution of the Fund and of the principal rules of the Bretton Woods agreement was to dominate during the 1950s and 1960s. The next chapter is devoted to that evolutionary process.

236. Warren Kelchner, chief of the Division of International Conferences, U.S. Department of State (see *Bretton Woods Proceedings*, 1:3).
237. Quoted in Harrod, *Keynes*, p. 632.
238. Gardner, *Sterling-Dollar Diplomacy*, p. 266, n. 4.
239. For further analysis, see Gold, *Selected Essays*, pp. 249–57.

FIVE

The International Monetary Fund as a Legal Institution

Once the Bretton Woods machinery was in place, it began to evolve, shaping economic events as well as being shaped by them. By the time the United States closed its "gold window" in 1971, the Bretton Woods system had collapsed. (Some would identify the decisive event as the adoption of a two-tier gold system in 1968 and others as the movement to generalized floating in 1973.) Discussion of the evolution and eventual collapse of the Bretton Woods system will be deferred until the next chapter.

In this chapter the focus will be narrower. Here the inquiry will be into the efforts of the International Monetary Fund, as an institution providing balance-of-payments assistance and as administrator of a system of rules, to shape economic events. A legal perspective is well suited to this study. As seen in the last chapter, the Articles were formulated as a set of rules analogous to rules in a domestic legal system. By focusing attention on the experience with the rules themselves during the period when the Bretton Woods system remained more or less intact, we can gain a better appreciation of the role of rules in an international monetary system.

In this legally oriented discussion of the Bretton Woods system, it will be useful to use three relatively simple legal concepts that are likely to be reasonably familiar to the reader whose interests in the international monetary system lie in the economic or political sphere. The first concept is *interpretation*. The rules had to be interpreted by the organs of the Fund, and the interpretation of the Fund's powers, as it evolved over time, largely defined what the Fund would do in practice. To be sure, the causation ran both ways: what member countries wanted the Fund to do tended to determine the Fund's policies and thereby the way in which the Fund's powers would be interpreted. But legal interpretation and policies interact. In section I of this chapter, which considers interpretation, emphasis will be placed on access to the Fund's resources, on the Fund's code of conduct, and on the role of gold.

The second legal concept is *legislation*. When the member countries wanted the Fund to do something beyond any reasonable interpretation of the Fund's powers, they were forced to legislate. Since there was, however, no legislature in the Fund system, an amendment of the Articles of Agreement was required. In the discussion of legislation in section II of this chapter, the creation of the Special Drawing Right will be the centerpiece of analysis. But the need to amend the Articles of Agreement led the drafters of the First Amendment (agreed in 1968, entered into force in 1969) to make other minor changes to the basic operating rules of the Fund.

The third legal concept is that of *jurisdiction*. The Fund and the international monetary system were not coterminous. The Fund did not have, or at least did not exercise, jurisdiction over everything that happened in that system. And the Fund had competitors. Consequently, the discussion of jurisdiction in section III will be organized around the three major competing institutions: the European Payments Union, the Group of Ten, and the Bank for International Settlements.

The illustrations of these three legal concepts will be limited here almost exclusively to the period from the formation of the Fund to 1971. Other illustrations from the years after 1971 will be deferred to later chapters in order to provide the reader with the underlying factual context necessary to understand the later use of the techniques of interpretation and legislation and the later issues with respect to the fund's jurisdiction.

I. Interpretation

The history of interpretation of the Fund's Articles of Agreement is nothing more, and nothing less, than the record of the evolution of the rules of the Fund.[1] Perhaps the most interesting evolution has occurred with respect to those rules dealing with access to Fund resources and, in particular, what has come to be known in Fund parlance as "conditionality." That term refers to the conditions that the Fund may impose on access to its resources and on their subsequent use by member countries.

Conditionality

As seen in chapter 4, the British and the Americans had reached a compromise at Bretton Woods between their contrasting views as to the conditions under which a country might have access to the Fund's resources. The British preference for unfettered access, at least to the extent of a country's quota, found expression in the declaration that "a member shall be entitled to buy the currency of another member from the Fund in exchange for its own currency." Although the Americans would have preferred considerable Executive Board discretion, they fought for and obtained their fallback position, which was that a member country drawing from the Fund would have to "represent" that the currency obtained "is presently needed for making in that currency payments which are consistent with the provisions" of the Articles.[2] The question whether the Executive Board could go behind the representation to evaluate the degree of need, and perhaps thereby to impose conditions on use, was left entirely open.[3] If the Executive Board could do so, then there was the possibility that it might be able to exercise some discretion under cover of an assessment of need (and thereby move toward the U.S. preferred position).

Over the course of the first decade after Bretton Woods, the Fund sought to resolve the ambiguity of the Articles by adopting the unconditional alternative for that portion of the quota that was contributed in gold (the gold tranche) and by moving in the direction of imposing conditions on drawings beyond the equivalent of the gold contribution (the credit tranches). Although

1. The discussion of interpretation will use that concept quite broadly. I shall largely ignore the more limited notion, important though it is to Fund lawyers, of interpretation under Article XVIII. On this narrower subject, see Joseph Gold, *Interpretation by the Fund*, IMF Pamphlet Series no. 11 (1968). And I am using "rules" in a broad sense to refer to all legal norms and not simply the specialized and particular provisions known as the "Rules and Regulations of the International Monetary Fund" which were adopted explicitly to "supplement the Fund Agreement and the By-Laws adopted by the Board of Governors." See J. Keith Horsefield, *The International Monetary Fund 1945–1965* (1969), 3:287 (hereafter cited Horsefield, *IMF 1945–1965*).
2. Article V, Section 3(a), *original*.
3. See discussion pp. 105–8.

this approach might seem politically to be the wisdom of Solomon, it was legally problematical. A gold tranche "unconditionality" policy would have to face up to the problem that if the word "represent" were construed to permit representations contrary to fact as to need, then the Articles would be open to contempt and abuse. And a credit tranche "conditionality" policy, as detailed below, not only lacked explicit authority in the Articles, but under normal standards of interpretation did not seem to be justified by their text. The techniques by which the Fund overcame both legal hurdles illustrates the way in which it grew to become an institution of economic and political significance transcending the legalistic limitations of the Articles of Agreement.

The Gold Tranche Policy

This policy, under which a member is accorded an unconditional right to draw up to the amount of its gold tranche, was motivated by a desire on the part of the Fund to encourage members to use its resources for balance-of-payments financing.[4] Drawings in 1950 had been nil, and in 1951 only Brazil and Iran had drawn.[5] Consequently, on 13 February 1952 the Executive Directors, seeking to alleviate any anxiety that the Fund would seek to go behind a representation by a member that the currency it sought to draw was needed for payments, but being legally unable to commit themselves absolutely never to question a representation,[6] adopted the following formulation of policy: "Each member can count on receiving the overwhelming benefit of any doubt respecting drawings which would raise the Fund's holdings of its currency to not more than its quota."[7] Put in policy rather than legal terms, the Executive Directors did not intend to challenge any drawing within the gold tranche.

The language used to define how large any drawing might be and still be entitled to the "overwhelming benefit of any doubt" reveals a difficulty in defining the size of the gold tranche. The theory behind the decision was that a member should be entitled to draw unconditionally amounts up to the net economic contribution it had made to the Fund.[8] A member's own currency, unlike the amount contributed in gold (normally 25 percent of quota), might have little value to the international community. Indeed, in 1952 very

4. Joseph Gold, "Constitutional Development and Change," in Horsefield, *IMF 1945–1965*, 2:524.
5. Ibid. 2:460–63, table 22.
6. Indeed, the Executive Board had decided in 1948 that the Fund could challenge a representation. See discussion of Decision of 10 March 1948, p. 120, below.
7. Decision of 13 February 1952, para. 3, *IMF Annual Report* 1952, p. 89. The objection that the gold subscription reduced members' reserves ceased to be valid once the gold tranche could be counted and used as reserves. Edward M. Bernstein, "The History of the International Monetary Fund 1966–71," *Finance and Development* 14(December 1977):17.
8. Joseph Gold, *The Stand-By Arrangements of the International Monetary Fund* (1970), p. 13.

few currencies were freely convertible into other currencies. But if another member were to draw the first member's currency, that fact not only demonstrated the economic value of that currency but also constituted the creation of a claim on goods and services of the first member (since that currency could be used by the drawing member to pay for imports from that country). Hence, a member's net economic contribution would include not merely the gold contribution but also any net drawings of that member's currency (gross drawings minus repayments). At a later time an informal distinction was sometimes made between the gold tranche and the *super* gold tranche, the latter term being used to refer to a member's unconditional right to draw equal to any net drawings of its currency.[9]

To understand the language of the 1952 decision one must bear in mind that a drawing of a currency is a purchase of that currency paid for with the drawing member's currency. Therefore, in a simple case where the only relevant transaction was a drawing equal to the 25 percent gold contribution, the Fund would, upon completion of the drawing, hold an amount of the drawing member's currency equal to 100 percent of quota—the 75 percent of quota originally contributed in currency plus another 25 percent used to purchase the other member's currency. In short, the transaction would, in the words of the 1952 decision, "raise the Fund's holdings of its currency to not more than its quota."[10] And in the complicated case where the drawing country's currency had previously been drawn by a third country in an amount equal to, say, 10 percent of the first member's quota, the Fund would at the outset hold the first member's currency in an amount equal to only 65 percent of that member's quota. Hence that member could, under the gold tranche policy, purchase unconditionally an amount equal to 35 percent of its quota. It should be noted that the use of the language of purchase rather than that of credit thus led to a definition of the gold tranche that, however technically precise, tended to obscure the nature and location of the dividing line between unconditional entitlement and conditional credit. Although the 1952 decision made gold tranche drawings de facto unconditional, de jure status had to await the First Amendment of the Articles. This was one of several amendments that accomplished easily by legislation what had to be done cumbersomely by the process of interpretation.[11]

9. See e.g. Margaret Garritsen de Vries, *The International Monetary Fund 1966–1971* (1976), 1:312 (hereafter cited de Vries, *IMF 1966–1971*).
10. Decision of 13 February 1952, para. 3, *IMF Annual Report* 1952, p. 89.
11. The Amendment to Article V, Section 3, needed to make gold tranche purchases unconditional, was however less than transparent. For an explanation, see "Establishment of a Facility Based on Special Drawing Rights in the International Monetary Fund and Modifications in the Rules and Practices of the Fund (April 1968). A Report of the Executive Directors . . . ," para. 32 (hereafter cited Executive Directors' First Amendment Report), reprinted in de Vries, *IMF 1966–1971*, 2:68. See also Joseph Gold, *The Reform of the Fund*, IMF Pamphlet Series no. 12 (1969), pp. 19–20.

Credit Tranche Policies

The Fund also faced legal hurdles in imposing conditions on drawings beyond the gold tranche—that is, in the credit tranches. (The use of the plural "tranches" reflected a conceptualization of the quota as normally divided into four 25 percent slices, first the gold tranche and then three successive credit tranches.) The clause in Article IV, Section 3, declaring that a member was "entitled to buy the currency of another member," was subject to four specific conditions. This clause did not purport to give the Fund any discretion to impose additional conditions and certainly not any conditions having to do with a member's future economic policies. Nevertheless, the Fund found a way, through interpretation, to impose those kinds of conditions.

The first step involved the representation required of a drawing country that the purchased currency was "presently needed for making in that currency payments which are consistent with the provisions of this Agreement."[12] In a decision taken on 10 March 1948, the Executive Board confirmed the Fund's power to challenge the correctness of a representation "on the grounds that the currency is not 'presently needed,' or because the currency is not needed for payment 'in that currency,' or because the payments will not be 'consistent with the provisions of this Agreement.' "[13] A related decision, taken seven days later, interpreted the "provisions of this Agreement" to refer not merely to explicit substantive provisions but also to the "purposes" of the Fund set out in Article I.[14] This reference to "purposes" was a veiled way of referring to the provision of Article I that defines one purpose of the Fund as being to "give confidence to members by making the Fund's resources available to them under adequate safeguards." The reference to "purposes" also evoked a 1946 decision in which the Executive Board had interpreted that language to mean that the Fund was "to give temporary assistance in financing balance of payments deficits on current account for monetary stabilization operations."[15]

From these decisions, it was thus possible to reason that the Fund could look behind a representation to verify whether, in view of the member's policies, the assistance provided could be expected to be temporary. Exactly this approach was used in a 1952 decision that declared that the following statement by the Managing Director was to "be the framework for his discussions with members on use of the Fund's resources":

Access to the Fund should not be denied because a member is in difficulty. On the contrary, the task of the Fund is to help members that need temporary help, and requests should be expected from members

12. Article V, Section 3, *original*.
13. Decision of 10 March 1948, *IMF Annual Report* 1948, p. 98.
14. Decision of 17 March 1948, in ibid. p. 99.
15. Decision of 26 September 1946, *IMF Annual Report* 1946, p. 106.

that are in trouble in greater or lesser degree. The Fund's attitude toward the position of each member should turn on whether the problem to be met is of a temporary nature and *whether the policies the member will pursue will be adequate to overcome the problem within such a period. The policies, above all, should determine the Fund's attitude.*[16]

On the basis of the 1952 decision, the Fund announced in various annual reports its policies for the credit tranches. By 1962 the following formulation had evolved:

> The Fund's attitude to requests for transactions within the "first credit tranche"—that is, transactions which bring the Fund's holdings of a member's currency above 100 percent but not above 125 percent of its quota—is a liberal one, provided that the member itself is making reasonable efforts to solve its problems. Requests for transactions beyond these limits require a substantial justification. They are likely to be favorably received when the drawings or stand-by arrangements are intended to support a sound program aimed at establishing or maintaining the enduring stability of the member's currency at a realistic rate of exchange.[17]

The legal upshot of this pastiche of decisions and pronouncements was that the Fund would, in its discussions with members, discuss their proposed economic policies in order to make certain that the use of the drawn currency would turn out to be temporary. But that position, though a considerable legal leap from the text of the Articles in justifying conditions on a member's right to draw, did not provide the only fulcrum for applying Fund leverage. Another was Article V, Section 3 (iii), which limited drawings to 25 percent of quota in any twelve-month period. Any country seeking to draw more than that amount would have to obtain a waiver under Section 4 of Article V. This waiver provision explicitly permitted the Fund to impose "terms which safeguard its interests." When waivers were required, the Fund thus had clear authority to impose conditions as to domestic policy that assured that repurchase would be possible.[18]

As with the change from de facto to de jure unconditionality of gold tranche drawings, the Fund's conditionality practices were endorsed textually in the First Amendment. The most important of several changes in support of this drafting goal was the provision of Article V, Section 3(c), calling on the Fund to "adopt policies on the use of its resources that will assist members to solve their balance of payments problems in a manner consistent with the

---

16. Decision of 13 February 1952, para. 1, *IMF Annual Report* 1952, p. 87 (emphasis supplied).
17. *IMF Annual Report* 1962, p. 31.
18. The 25 percent provision of Article V, Section 3(iii) was only one provision affording a basis for waivers. Another was the provision in the same subsection limiting total drawings to 200 percent of quota.

purposes of the Fund and that will establish adequate safeguards for the temporary use of its resources."[19]

Stand-By Arrangements

The chief legal vehicle for conditionality was not, however, either of the two techniques just reviewed, but rather the stand-by arrangement. In fact, because the stand-by arrangement was more conducive to conditionality, the Fund made little or no use of its waiver authority to impose conditions concerning domestic economic policies.[20] The stand-by arrangement was, however, an even more remarkable example of the role of interpretation in the growth of the Fund's powers and the development of its policies.

The stand-by arrangement had its genesis in the same 13 February 1952 decision that announced the intention to consider domestic policies in the discussions leading to a conventional drawing. In that decision the Executive Board incorporated a statement by the Managing Director (partially quoted above) that outlined future policies regarding access to resources.

In aid of expanding access, the Managing Director suggested that "discussions between the member and the Fund may cover its general position, not with a view to any immediate drawing, but in order to ensure that it would be able to draw if, within a period of say 6 or 12 months, the need presented itself."[21]

A stand-by arrangement might be quite unexceptional if the Fund were an international banking organization; but under the Articles, and particularly under the decision confirming the Fund's power to challenge a drawing member's representations, it was legally somewhat anomalous. The reason was that the legal essence of a stand-by arrangement lies in the Fund's agreement *not* to challenge a representation and indeed to close its eyes to the need for the drawing at the time the drawing occurs. Indeed, a stand-by arrangement presents the contradiction that the drawing country does not have to establish need at the time the arrangement is entered into and the Fund in effect waives any power to judge need at the time the drawing is made. During the early years of stand-by arrangements, the Fund's decisions insisted that the "Fund will agree to a stand-by arrangement only for a member that is in a position to make purchases of the same amount of exchange from the Fund."[22] Although this formal position thus avoided the legal anomaly described above, the actual practice of the Fund began to downplay any requirement of a need shown at the time that the stand-by

---

19. For a discussion of this and related changes, see Gold, *Reform*, pp. 27–30.
20. Gold, "Constitutional Development," pp. 530–33.
21. Decision of 13 February 1952, para. 1, *IMF Annual Report* 1952, p. 88.
22. Decision of 23 December 1953, para. 2, *IMF Annual Report* 1954, p. 132.

arrangement was entered into. As Joseph Gold, the Fund's general counsel, observed:

> One of the purposes of stand-by arrangements is to make resources available should the need for them arise in the future, and practice shows that it is not essential that a need for them should exist at the time when the stand-by arrangement is requested or approved. Although there may be no need for resources at the date of the request for or approval of a stand-by arrangement, normally the objective of a stand-by arrangement is to assist a member to deal with particular problems that could arise during the period of the stand-by arrangement. The member's policies must be designed to overcome these problems within a reasonable period if they should arise. In this way, the member can demonstrate that the Fund will have adequate safeguards when making its resources available to the member.[23]

What is revealed in this language is that the Fund, after resolving the legal issue by formally deciding that need had to be shown at the time the arrangement was entered into, then departed from that requirement in its actual practice. The Fund did so because it found that there were sufficient safeguards for the Fund through its conditionality policies to justify an arrangement when a need might reasonably be expected to arise in the future, when the member was willing to make certain commitments with regard to its economic policies at the time the arrangement was entered into, and when it was willing to declare a need at the time the drawing occurred even if that declaration was not subject to challenge by the Fund.[24] In short, interpretation by practice tended to be more flexible and expansive than interpretation by Executive Board decision.

More interesting than these legal issues about the Fund's powers is the way the Fund's conditionality policies were applied in practice in stand-by arrangements. The underlying notion was simple. Whatever a member's legal entitlement to draw, there was no legal entitlement to a stand-by arrangement. Since the Fund was not required to enter into such an arrangement (which would be a future claim on its resources), it could reasonably require a member seeking such an arrangement to undertake certain commitments as part of the bargain. The most important of these commitments took the form of "performance criteria."

For stand-by arrangements going beyond the first credit tranche, performance clauses until recently have normally been included in the letter of intent that, under standard Fund practice, is annexed to each stand-by agree-

---

23. Gold, *Stand-By Arrangements*, p. 27.
24. On the last point concerning a declaration of need at the time of drawing, see "Form of Request for Purchase Under a Stand-By Arrangement," in Gold, *Stand-By Arrangements*, appendix H, p. 271.

ment.[25] In that letter of intent the member declares its intention with regard to particular economic policies. These performance criteria cover, at a minimum, a ceiling on credit expansion and, usually, commitments with respect to avoidance of restrictions in current payments and in imports.[26] Frequently declarations with respect to future performance are quantitative and precise.[27] For example, in 1969 the United Kingdom made quantitative commitments on public expenditure, the central government borrowing requirement, and domestic credit expansion. The commitment with respect to domestic credit expansion (defined as "broadly speaking, the net addition to the borrowing of the public and private sectors taken together"),[28] which at the time was politically unpopular in Britain, illustrates the flavor of commitments given in letters of intent:

> 8. As was . . . stated in the Budget speech, the Government attaches the greatest importance to monetary policy, which provides an essential support to fiscal policy. The rise in money supply in 1968 of £986 million was broadly in line with the growth of G.N.P.; but the increase in credit in the economy was too high, and the Government intends not to permit credit to be supplied to the economy on anything like this scale in 1969–70.
>
> 9. The Government will therefore watch closely the development of domestic credit expansion during the year. The Government's objectives and policies imply a domestic credit expansion for the private and public sectors in the year ending 31st March, 1970 of not more than £400 million, compared with some £1,225 million in 1968–69. It is the Government's policy to ensure that the course quarter by quarter of domestic credit expansion as a whole, and of the Central Government borrowing requirement within it, is consistent with the intended result for the year as a whole, and to take action as appropriate to this end.[29]

Apparently additional less formal commitments are sometimes made; in the British case, the Chancellor of the Exchequer declared in Parliament that, with respect to the quarterly domestic credit commitments referred to in the last sentence of paragraph 9:

---

25. Decision of 20 September 1968, conclusions 3 and 4, *IMF Annual Report* 1969, p. 183; Joseph Gold, *Financial Assistance by the International Monetary Fund, Law and Practice*, IMF Pamphlet Series no. 27 (1979), p. 16. See Decision of 20 May 1980, *IMF Annual Report* 1980, pp. 148–50, for revised form of stand-by arrangements, and Joseph Gold, *The Legal Character of the Fund's Stand-By Arrangements and Why It Matters*, IMF Pamphlet Series no. 35 (1980), pp. 26–27.
26. Gold, *Financial Assistance*, pp. 14–15.
27. For a model letter of intent from a fictional country, Patria, see Gold, *Stand-By Arrangements*, pp. 60–64.
28. Statement of Chancellor of the Exchequer Jenkins, 785 House of Commons Debate, col. 1002 (23 June 1969).
29. Ibid. col. 1010. For an analysis of this commitment, see "Dear Mr. Schweitzer . . . ," *The Economist*, 28 June 1969, pp. 13–14.

In addition to the annual figure, I have made estimates, of which I have informed the I.M.F., of an appropriate quarterly path for domestic credit expansion and for the Government borrowing requirement within it. I do not propose to publish these quarterly figures. Were I to do so, I would be encouraging speculation in a way that would make more difficult the management of the gilt-edged market.[30]

The sensitivity of commitments in letters of intent, reflected in the Chancellor's statement just quoted, is usually met by not publishing any of the letter of intent. Any publication of the letter of intent that occurs is at the option of the member.[31]

Performance clauses have involved the Fund in controversy. The Fund has been in the position of requiring more restrictive commitments from members than has been politically popular in many countries. The foregoing U.K. domestic credit commitment, for example, was rigorously criticized in Britain. To be sure, finance ministers have frequently welcomed privately being forced publicly into pursuing a more restrictive fiscal policy than the spending ministers in their own governments would have wished. But at the same time the commitments have had important social as well as economic effects in countries forced by balance-of-payments crises under the Bretton Woods system to turn to the Fund for assistance. Particularly in less developed countries, therefore, the Fund's insistence on the curbing of spending and on a restrictive monetary policy has sometimes seemed to be interference in domestic politics and to be biased toward conservative policies.[32]

Because letters of intent have dealt with policies that go to the heart of domestic politics and because governments struggling for political survival are not always able to meet budgetary and monetary targets even with great effort, commitments are not always met. This fact of political life raises the legal issue of the status of the letter of intent commitments. The Fund has been quite unambiguous in stating that the stand-by arrangement is not an agreement in the contract sense. Hence, a failure to carry out commitments in the appended letter of intent is a fortiori not a breach of any agreement and certainly not a violation of international law.[33] And, to eliminate doubts on this score, the Executive Board concluded in 1968 that "in view of the

30. 785 Commons Debates, col. 1002.
31. Gold, *Stand-By Arrangements*, pp. 53–54. See ibid. appendix G, pp. 269–70, for citations to the relatively few letters of intent that had been published through 1969.
32. See e.g. Columbia University School of Law, *Public International Development Financing in Chile*, Public International Development Financing: A Research Project, Report no. 8 (1964), pp. 45, 115–16. See also "The Politics of IMF Aid," *Financial Times*, 15 August 1979; Peter Field, "The IMF Now: De Larosière's Troubled Institution," *Euromoney* 10(October 1978):14–29; Bernard D. Nossiter, "New Pragmatism at the I.M.F.," *New York Times*, 5 February 1980. See also Gold, *Legal Character of Stand-Bys*, pp. 36–37.
33. See Joseph Gold, *Legal and Institutional Aspects of the International Monetary System: Selected Essays* (1979), pp. 464–66 (hereafter cited Gold, *Selected Essays*); Gold, *Financial Assistance*, pp. 17–18; Gold, *Conditionality*, IMF Pamphlet Series no. 31 (1979), pp. 19–21.

character of stand-by arrangements, language having a contractual flavor will
be avoided in the stand-by documents."[34] The Fund took this position because
of a fear that members would otherwise be deterred from seeking Fund
assistance in view of the difficulty any government (at least in a democratic
society) would face in meeting performance commitments with respect to
fiscal and monetary policies. No government wants to be in a position of
defaulting on a contractual commitment.[35]

The fact that failure to carry out performance clauses is not considered a
breach of an agreement in any formal sense does not mean that performance
criteria have no purpose. They still are the heart of the consensual arrangement between the member and the Fund. Consequently, an intentional failure
to live up to a performance commitment could be expected to affect the
disposition of the Fund staff toward future drawings in the credit tranches.
Moreover, performance arrangements normally provide for phasing of drawings under the arrangement, and until 1980 the letter of intent might itself
provide that in the event that certain performance commitments were not
met, then the member would not request any further drawing under the
stand-by arrangement without reaching a new understanding with the
Fund.[36] The effect of such provisions is presumably to give the member a
powerful incentive to meet its performance commitments in order to remain
eligible to draw under the stand-by arrangement.

As time went by, the stand-by arrangement became the normal form of
relationship between a member seeking assistance and the Fund, at least for
drawings in the credit tranches.[37] It provides the framework for strong Fund
influence on members' economic policies, particularly with respect to smaller
and less-developed countries. One of the institutional reasons for this influence was that a Fund stand-by arrangement came to be viewed by private
sector banks as a seal of approval justifying private loans to the drawing

34. Decision of 20 September 1968, conclusion 7, *IMF Annual Report* 1969, p. 184, and see
Gold, *Legal Character of Stand-Bys*, pp. 17–19.
35. See Gold, *Selected Essays*, pp. 465–66. For an account of the Fund's "retreat from an open
display of toughness" see Susan Strange, *International Monetary Relations*, vol. 2 of *International
Economic Relations of the Western World, 1959–1971*, ed. Andrew Shonfield (1976), pp. 92–97, and
Guidelines on Conditionality, Decision of 2 March 1979, *IMF Annual Report* 1979, pp. 136–38.
36. Following the decision of 20 May 1980, the stand-by arrangement itself, rather than the
letter of intent, was commonly relied on to declare performance criteria. *IMF Annual Report*
1980, pp. 148–50; Gold, *Legal Character of Stand-Bys*, p. 26. For earlier practice, see model stand-
by arrangement, paragraph 4(ii), and model letter of intent, paragraph 9, in Gold, *Stand-By
Arrangements*, pp. 58–63. See also ibid. pp. 144–46, and Gold, *Conditionality*, pp. 38–48 (on
stand-by arrangements reflecting the Second Amendment). See Gold, *Legal Character of Stand-
Bys*, p. 34, on the "sanction of discredit" for "poor performance," and Manuel Guitián, "Fund
Conditionality and the International Adjustment Process: The Early Period 1950–70," *Finance
and Development* 17(December 1980):26–27 on Fund targets and assessment of implementation.
37. Gold, *Selected Essays*, p. 463.

countries.[38] Thus, Fund assistance had a multiplier effect in increasing balance-of-payments financing to deficit countries. All in all, the stand-by arrangement represents an excellent example of the use of interpretation in expanding the effective powers and role of an international organization.

New Facilities

Despite the flexibility that the Fund gained through interpretation of its powers, it nevertheless felt constrained in responding to growing pressures to do something extra for less-developed countries. The Fund resisted efforts to provide development capital through balance-of-payments financing since the World Bank and its growing family of special development institutions were available for development financing. Nevertheless, some response seemed called for in view of the persistent and severe balance-of-payments problems faced by some developing countries. The pressure to act was great in view of the volatility of prices in commodities markets and the then popular theory that producers of primary commodities faced a permanent and growing deterioration in their terms of trade (that is, in the ratio of the prices of their exports to the prices of their imports, particularly imports of manufactured products). However, the principle of uniformity, under which no members were to be singled out for special treatment, seemed to preclude any special policy for particular members.[39]

One response was to create a compensatory financing facility with special rules for countries suffering from a shortfall in export proceeds from primary commodities. This approach was deemed to satisfy the uniformity principle because the facility was available to all members suffering from this particular balance-of-payments problem.[40] Under a 1963 decision, members, "particularly primary exporters," that satisfied the Fund that they were suffering an export "shortfall . . . of a short-term character . . . largely attributable to circumstances beyond the control of the member" and that they would "cooperate with the Fund in an effort to find, where required, appropriate solutions for [their] balance of payments difficulties" would benefit from easier access.[41] Specifically, they would be able to draw up to 25 percent of

38. Gold, *Stand-By Arrangements*, pp. 37–39; Christopher Prout, "Finance for Developing Countries: An Essay," in Strange, *International Monetary Relations*, pp. 390–94; Raymond F. Mikesell, *The Economics of Foreign Aid* (1968), pp. 164–66.

39. On the principle of uniformity, see discussion pp. 85–87.

40. Gold, *Selected Essays*, pp. 489–91; Louis M. Goreux, *Compensatory Financing Facility*, IMF Pamphlet Series no. 34 (1980), p. 10.

41. Decision of 27 February 1963 II B(5), *IMF Annual Report* 1963, p. 198. See "Compensatory Financing of Export Fluctuations (February 1963): A Report by the International Monetary Fund on Compensatory Financing of the Fluctuations in Exports of Primary Exporting Countries," in Horsefield, *IMF 1945–1965*, 3:442–57; Goreux, pp. 7–10.

their quota (increased in 1966 to 50 percent),[42] and, if necessary, the Fund would waive the normal limit of Fund holdings of a member's currency to 200 percent of quota. The effect of the decision was thus to permit the drawing country to avoid the performance commitments involved in a stand-by arrangement and to permit members to draw even though they had already exhausted their credit tranches by conventional drawings.[43] Moreover, as a result of a floating feature introduced in the 1966 liberalization, a drawing under the compensatory financing facility did not affect a member's tranche position. Thus, a member not having drawn previously could draw under the facility while leaving its gold tranche intact and fully available for future drawings.[44]

Exchange Rate Changes

The Bretton Woods agreement established a par value system under which changes in par value were to be made only in the event of "fundamental disequilibrium."[45] Nothing could be more at odds with such a system than floating exchange rates. Yet some members insisted on floating, either temporarily en route to a new parity or as a permanent exchange rate regime. The ways in which the Fund dealt with floating rates throw light on the difficulties of regulating such an important aspect of sovereignty as a country's exchange rate through an international agreement and by an international organization.

The legal difficulty faced by the Fund in dealing with what in Fund parlance were then called "fluctuating rates" stemmed from a felt need to maintain a general posture hostile to floating rates while at the same time permitting, or even encouraging, smaller countries to abandon exchange market intervention in several circumstances. One such circumstance was presented when a "free rate" was a step toward the abolition of multiple exchange rates.[46] The Fund also recognized that a period of floating might be useful in determining the appropriate level of a new par value. On the other hand, any use of floating rates by a major developed country could

42. Decision of 20 September 1966, *IMF Annual Report 1967*, pp. 159–61. The 1966 decision provided that the 50 percent compensatory financing drawings were to be made at a rate not exceeding 25 percent in any twelve-month period. See generally "Compensatory Financing of Export Fluctuations—Developments in the Fund's Facility (September 1966). A Second Report by the International Monetary Fund . . . ," in Horsefield, *IMF 1945–1965*, 3:469–96; and Goreux, p. 37.
43. Horsefield, *IMF 1945–1965*, 2:422; Goreux, pp. 41–47.
44. Gold, *Selected Essays*, pp. 423–24; and Gold, *Conditionality*, pp. 6–7. The floating feature of the compensatory financing facility was explicitly endorsed in the subsequent First Amendment, Article XIX(j), *first*. See discussion pp. 168–69, below. A related but much less utilized facility was the buffer stock facility created in 1969. See de Vries, *IMF 1966–1971*, 1:261–86, for a description and references to the relevant documents.
45. See discussion pp. 89–91.
46. Multiple exchange rates are discussed at greater length pp. 131–33.

undermine the credibility of the Bretton Woods system and lead to wide-spread disregard for its rules.

The Articles of Agreement, at least as interpreted by the Fund, created the anomaly that the Fund could approve a floating rate in certain situations but not in others. Although a floating rate would be a violation of the member's duty (under Article IV, Section 4) to maintain its rate within the margins around par, and the Fund had no power to waive this duty, none-theless the Fund could approve a multiple exchange rate system and therefore it could approve a free rate as part of such a system. The Fund also approved, as part of stand-by arrangements, temporary cessation of intervention for a short period of depreciation en route to a new par value.[47] The approval in such cases was tacit, though unmistakable, because the decision to enter into the stand-by arrangement was taken in full knowledge of the member's in-tentions. The justification offered by the Fund's general counsel was that "the member was making progress towards the establishment of an effective par value and the observance of the purposes of the Fund."[48]

After a good deal of backing and filling by the Fund during 1949 and 1950 with respect to the temporary resort to floating rates by Mexico, Belgium, and Peru,[49] the entire Bretton Woods system was challenged in a more fun-damental way by Canada's decision in 1950 to unpeg its exchange rate. Since Canada was a major trading country, and did not assert that its departure from parity would be temporary (and, in the event, Canada continued to float until 1962), the Fund could not take refuge in the multiple exchange rate or stand-by arrangement rationale.

The Canadian case was complicated by the fact that it was the first instance of what would come to be an important problem for the system. Canada, far from having a weak currency, was faced with continual capital inflows that threatened to force a revaluation of its currency. Unlike most later cases, however, the persistent capital inflows involved primarily long-term invest-ment capital rather than short-term speculative flows (though speculative flows joined the investment inflows to force the abandonment of the existing parity). Moreover, Canada faced a recurring trade deficit.[50] Despite a dis-position by the Fund staff to disapprove the Canadian adoption of floating rates, that view was not sufficiently widely held among the Executive Di-rectors to permit any definitive decision on the Canadian case. The Executive Board's formal decision was simply that "the Fund recognizes the exigencies of the situation which have led Canada [to float] and takes note of the intention

47. *IMF Annual Report* 1962, p. 63.
48. Gold, "Constitutional Development," p. 550.
49. Margaret G. de Vries, "Fluctuating Exchange Rates," in Horsefield, *IMF 1945–1965*, 2:153–59.
50. A. F. W. Plumptre, *Three Decades of Decision: Canada and the World Monetary System, 1944–75* (1977), pp. 142–51, 156–73. See the discussion of the Canadian case in Leland B. Yeager, *International Monetary Relations: Theory, History and Policy*, 2d ed. (1976), pp. 543–65.

of the Canadian Government to remain in consultation with the Fund and to re-establish an effective par value as soon as circumstances warrant."[51] In short, the Fund recognized that Canada was in violation of the Articles of Agreement but at the same time decided to accept that violation in lieu of the even less attractive alternatives of either forcing a showdown with Canada or purporting to approve what it had no legal power to approve. In an ensuing annual report, the Executive Directors articulated the Fund's policy toward such violations of the par value and margin rules:

> The circumstances that have led the member to conclude that it is unable both to maintain the par value and immediately select a new one can be examined; and if the Fund finds that the arguments of the member are persuasive it may say so although it cannot give its approval to the action. The Fund would have to emphasize that the withdrawal of support from the par value, or the delay in the proposal of a new par value that could be supported, would have to be temporary, and that it would be essential for the member to remain in close consultation with the Fund respecting exchange arrangements during the interim period and looking toward the early establishment of a par value agreed with the Fund. No other steps would be required so long as the Fund considered the member's case to be persuasive, but at any time that the Fund concluded that the justification for the action of the member was no longer sustainable, it would be the duty of the Fund so to state and to decide whether any action under the Fund Agreement would be necessary or desirable.[52]

This pragmatic toleration of floating rates by a major country amounted to a de facto waiver.[53] But it had legal implications because of the need to have some method of valuing a floating currency when no par value existed or when the market rate departed seriously from parity. A 1954 decision specified how to calculate the market rate without referring to the legal issue of whether that rate was a lawful one.[54] Although Britain came close to floating the pound in 1952,[55] no major currency followed Canada, and therefore the Canadian case could be viewed as an aberration rather than a precedent. But the increasingly tolerant Fund attitude toward the adoption of floating rates by less developed countries experiencing high rates of inflation reached the point that by 1962–63 it began to advise such members to float rather than to use exchange restrictions to maintain a par value.[56]

51. Horsefield, *IMF 1945–1965*, 1:274.
52. *IMF Annual Report 1951*, p. 40.
53. Gold, *Selected Essays*, pp. 366–69.
54. Decision of 15 June 1954, *IMF Annual Report 1955*, pp. 125–27.
55. See Earl of Birkenhead, *The Prof in Two Worlds* (1961), pp. 284–92, and Milton Gilbert, *Quest for World Monetary Order* (1980), pp. 59–60.
56. Gold, *Selected Essays*, p. 369.

Multiple Exchange Rates

If floating rates were a fundamental challenge to the fixed parity principle of the Bretton Woods system, the maintenance of more than one rate might appear to be an even greater derogation of that principle. To be sure, multiple rates might each be stable (though frequently at least one of the multiple rates floated freely in the market). But the existence of more than one rate cannot easily be reconciled with the notion of all exchange transactions occurring within a narrow margin around par.[57]

In contrast to floating rates, however, multiple rates were specifically mentioned in the Bretton Woods agreement. Article VIII, Section 3 provided that no member should "engage in . . . any . . . multiple currency practices except as . . . approved by the Fund." Thus, the Fund could approve multiple currency practices but not floating rates, although the power to approve multiple rates was construed to include the power to approve a floating rate if it was only one rate within a multiple rate system.[58]

Unlike floating rates, which provided only an occasional challenge to the Bretton Woods system, multiple currency practices were rampant after the war and even acquired a certain vogue in Latin America and to a lesser extent in Europe. Even as late as 1956, twelve of the sixty members maintained significant multiple rate practices and only twenty-four conducted all of their current transactions at exchange rates within 1 percent of parity.[59] This pattern improved only partly in the 1960s,[60] and as late as 1971 a major member, France, introduced a new multiple rate system.[61] Meanwhile, another major member, the United Kingdom, maintained a separate investment currency rate until 1979.[62]

In the early days of the Fund, when drawings were small and occasional, review of the multiple exchange rate systems constituted a major portion of the work of the staff and of the Executive Board.[63] Yet the Fund rarely failed to give its approval and normally was placed in the position of passing on a multiple currency practice after it had already been instituted. Indeed, the only case in which the Executive Board explicitly disapproved a multiple rate practice, a 1948 incident involving France, ended rather ignominiously for the Fund.

As part of a January 1948 devaluation of the franc, the French government elected to adopt a new par value with respect to inconvertible currencies (a

57. Ibid. p. 550.
58. See discussion p. 129.
59. Margaret G. de Vries, "The Par Value System: An Overview," in Horsefield, *IMF 1945–1965*, 2:47–48.
60. Ibid. p. 49.
61. IMF, *23d Annual Report on Exchange Restrictions* (1972), pp. 2, 5; *International Financial News Survey* 23(1971):271–72.
62. *Bank of England Quarterly Bulletin* 19(1979):370–71.
63. Margaret G. de Vries, "Multiple Exchange Rates," in Horsefield, *IMF 1945–1965*, 2:137.

category that at that time involved almost all currencies) but to allow the rate for the convertible U.S. dollar and Portuguese escudo (and later the Swiss franc) to be determined in a free market. Under this unusual kind of multiple rate practice the result would be broken cross-rates—that is, actual rates between any convertible and any inconvertible currency would be inconsistent with those implied by those two currencies' exchange rates with the French franc. The result was not only a considerable incentive for triangular trade transactions in order to take advantage of the fact that purchases through a third country might result in a lower price to the buyer than direct purchases but also a considerable distortion of trade patterns to the detriment of international efficiency.[64] It was this trade-distorting aspect of the French multiple rate that caused the Executive Board to declare France ineligible to use Fund resources. This was one of the few occasions, if not the only one, in which the Fund invoked this Article IV, Section 6, sanction,[65] but the sanction failed to induce the French to adopt a unitary rate. In October 1948 the French government did, however, eliminate the broken cross-rate aspect for trade transactions and in 1949, following a further devaluation, the French restored a stable rate, though not a new par value. The Fund therefore continued France's ineligibility status until 1954. Thus, the invocation of the severe and unusual ineligibility sanction, though perhaps influential in modifying French practices, was perceived as a failure, and the sanction was never invoked again.[66]

One of the principal difficulties in applying the rules of the Articles to multiple rate practices was that those practices took such varied forms and had such diverse purposes that no simple rule could distinguish those that the Executive Board would oppose from those the Board might allow or even favor. For example, the French practice had been highly unusual because it involved different rates for different members rather than, as in the usual case, different rates for different kinds of transactions.

Even in the latter situation, however, diversity abounded. Though many multiple currency practices involved unfavorable rates for particular imports and thus were analogous to exchange restrictions on current payments under Articles VIII and XIV, others involved favorable rates for particular exports

64. For examples, see "Multiple Exchange Practices," *The Economist*, 6 November 1948, pp. 758–60.
65. Article IV, Section 6 could be applied because the adoption of the multiple currency practice encompassed a change in par value which, because it was tied to the multiple currency practice, was instituted over Fund objection and hence was "unauthorized" under that provision. Where a par value change was not involved, only the compulsory withdrawal sanction under Article XV, Section 2 would appear to apply.
66. On the French multiple rate case, see Gold, *Selected Essays*, pp. 397–402; Horsefield, *IMF 1945–1965*, 1:200–205; de Vries, "Multiple Exchange Rates," in ibid. 2:130. One of the reasons for the weakness of the ineligibility sanction was that France had access to bilateral Marshall Plan funds. R. A. Mundell, "The International Monetary Fund," *Journal of World Trade Law* 3(1969):477.

and hence were more analogous to export subsidies. Still others involved unfavorable rates for particular exports and hence were more analogous to domestic tax devices; such schemes were used by some primary exporting countries as a way of taxing their principal exporting industries. And many multiple rate schemes, by differentiating between current and capital transactions (the latter, for example, being left to find their own rate in a free market), would not be considered restrictions on current payments under Articles VIII and XIV. In fact, such "dual rate" systems might be protected by the capital transfer provisions of Article VI, Section 3, and even considered desirable by those in the Fund who feared "disequilibrating" or "disruptive" capital flows and hence believed that regulation of capital flows contributed to the preservation of the par value system.[67]

In view of these many types of multiple rate practices (and this is not an exhaustive list),[68] it is not surprising that the Fund developed internally what Joseph Gold has called "an immense jurisprudence."[69] But, at least to the extent that it has been published, it is not an illuminating jurisprudence.[70] The Fund's most conspicuous efforts, a 1947 memorandum[71] and a 1957 decision,[72] provide neither intellectual nor practical legal guidance. Indeed, the Executive Board recognized in the 1957 decision that rather than trying to adjudicate each individual proposal to come before it, the Fund's efforts would be better devoted to pressing for simplification of existing multiple rate systems.[73] Simplification efforts were somewhat successful, though much of the progress was an indirect effect of the general movement toward convertibility in the period beginning in 1958.[74]

Gold

The Bretton Woods agreement was based on a much diluted form of a gold exchange standard. Gold was the ultimate numeraire (that is, unit of account) of the system because all currencies were required to declare a par value expressed in terms of either gold or "the United States dollar of the weight and fineness in effect on July 1, 1944."[75] Thus, the only dollar in terms of which a par might be declared was a dollar worth one-thirty-fifth of an ounce of gold. This point, of little operative significance at the time of Bretton Woods when a dollar devaluation in terms of gold was hardly conceivable,

67. J. Marcus Fleming, "Dual Exchange Markets and Other Remedies for Disruptive Capital Flows," *IMF Staff Papers* 21(1974):1–27.
68. For one taxonomy, see Horsefield, *IMF 1945–1965*, 1:177.
69. *Selected Essays*, p. 550.
70. See, for example, the complex analysis of the rules in Hans Aufricht, "Exchange Restrictions under the Fund Agreement," *Journal of World Trade Law* 2(1968):310–15.
71. *IMF Annual Report* 1948, pp. 65–72.
72. Decision of 26 June 1957, *IMF Annual Report* 1957, pp. 161–62.
73. Ibid.
74. De Vries, "Multiple Exchange Rates," in Horsefield, *IMF 1945–1965*, 2:141–46.
75. Article IV, Section 1(a), *original*.

nonetheless underscores the crucial unit-of-account role of gold in the Bretton Woods system.

More important, gold was to be one of the principal reserve assets. Although this did not appear unambiguously in the Articles of Agreement, the Articles as a whole seemed to presume that gold would be the ultimate reserve asset to a greater degree than turned out to be the case. The role reserve currencies were to play in the postwar period cannot be detected from the text of the Bretton Woods agreement.

Moreover, gold was to be a major asset of the Fund. Subscriptions were to be made in part (normally 25 percent) in gold, and to the extent that subscriptions were in a member's currency the gold value of that currency was to be maintained.[76]

Finally, a link between gold and currencies was implicit in the provision that members could discharge their obligation with respect to exchange stability by freely buying and selling gold within a margin around par.[77] The gold sale provision was drafted in the anticipation that the United States would avail itself of that option in lieu of exchange market intervention.[78] The United States did so, alone among members, and the U.S. commitment to buy and sell gold at the official $35 per ounce price became the cornerstone of the Bretton Woods system in practice—a cornerstone whose removal signaled the collapse of the system.[79]

The Bretton Woods gold exchange standard was, to be sure, a pale imitation of a full-scale gold exchange standard, not to speak of a gold standard of the pre-1914 variety. Gold coins did not circulate, gold could not universally be freely imported and exported, national currencies could not be converted into gold at central banks or mints, and, in the United States, citizens could not even own gold for most purposes.[80]

The Fund nonetheless regarded gold as central to the Bretton Woods system. The Fund was therefore concerned about any institutional changes that might cause the free market price of gold to depart from the official price. The Articles themselves tended to discourage members from entering into transactions that might move free market gold prices away from the $35 per ounce level. Article IV, Section 2, which required the Fund to establish a margin "above and below par value for transactions in gold by members," provided that "no member shall buy gold at a price above par value plus the prescribed margin, or sell gold at a price below par value minus the prescribed margin." Thus, in essence, members could not buy

76. See discussion pp. 97–98 and 105.
77. Article IV, Section 4(b), *original*.
78. See discussion p. 97.
79. See discussion pp. 187–89.
80. See discussion of the transmutation of the gold exchange standard in the 1930s, pp. 54–60.

gold above par nor sell it below par.[81] Though this rule allowed what might be thought stabilizing transactions (that is, transactions tending to drive the market price toward par by buying gold below par and selling it above par), a central bank could not enter into any gold transaction with another central bank other than at par without one or the other violating the Articles.

The Fund, concerned even about stabilizing transactions because they would be seen as endorsing a market price other than the official price, had a good deal of difficulty with the question of premium sales of gold. The Articles did not regulate private transactions in gold, whereas private transactions in currencies were indirectly regulated by the requirement of Article IV, Section 4(b) that a member permit exchange transactions within its territory only within the exchange rate margins. The Fund's only leverage in the private gold market was consequently restricted to whatever influence it could bring to bear on transactions to which a member was a party. The Fund feared that premium sales by monetary authorities, even if stabilizing in the short run, might divert substantial quantities of gold from international reserves to private hoards and thereby undermine the role of gold in the international monetary system. Acting on this fear, the Managing Director stated in 1947 that the "Fund strongly deprecates international transactions in gold at premium prices and recommends that all of its members take effective action to prevent such transactions in gold with other countries or with the nationals of other countries."[82]

This recommendation, which might be thought to go beyond the Fund's powers under the Articles (though the Fund later attempted to justify it under the "exchange stability" and "orderly exchange arrangement" language elsewhere in the Articles),[83] provides an instructive contrast with the Fund's position on subsidies to domestic gold producers. Though they were analogous to premium purchases and therefore no less and no more at odds with the Articles, such subsidies were widespread among members. Subsidies tended, moreover, to increase the quantity of gold potentially available for international reserves—a factor that would be increasingly important as inflation tended to lower the real value of the $35 official price. The Fund took the position that so long as the subsidy did not cause the price formally paid by the member for gold to rise above par, the subsidies did not violate the

---

81. The gold margin was set by the Fund at 0.25 percent plus certain handling charges. In 1954 members were given the option of a one percent margin. Mary H. Gumbart, "Gold Transactions at Premium Prices," in Horsefield, *IMF 1945–1965*, 2:202.
82. Horsefield, *IMF 1945–1965*, 3:310.
83. Gumbart, "Gold Transactions," in Horsefield, *IMF 1945–1965*, 2:179. The Preamble made it a "purpose" of the Fund to "promote exchange stability" and to "maintain orderly exchange arrangements among members," and members were required by Article IV to "collaborate with the Fund" with respect to those purposes. See Article I(iii) and Article IV, Section 4(a), *original*.

Articles. In short, form was preferred to substance in order to permit increases in gold production.[84]

The Fund position on premium sales was challenged by South Africa, the leading source of newly mined gold, which wanted to be able to sell at the highest available price in private markets but which as a member would not be able to do so under the 1947 statement. The South African case took on special force because the Fund's legal position was weak[85] and because the effect of the Fund's position was to place price controls on South Africa's leading export at a time when it was in balance-of-payments difficulties.

South Africa continued to make premium sales to private parties on the theory that the sales were for industrial rather than monetary use. The suspicion was, however, that much of the premium gold, though usually in semiprocessed form and hence not directly usable for monetary purposes, was finding its way into private hoards. The differences of view between the Fund and most members, on the one hand, and South Africa, on the other, came to a head during the Korean war.[86] Although a Fund staff working party recommended more stringent measures to limit premium sales, the Executive Board rejected its recommendations, in part on the ground that premium prices were a symptom and not a cause of underlying financial difficulties.[87] The consequence was a new gold policy statement that kept the 1947 principle of opposition to premium gold sales formally in place but left the implementation of those principles to the individual members.[88] The new statement represented a major shift of priorities from the 1947 position of seeking to prevent premium sales in private markets to a new position emphasizing the desirability of maximizing the flow of gold to monetary reserves. Perhaps because 1949 devaluations in South Africa and other gold-producing countries increased the return to gold mining and because the end of the Korean war as well as European economic recovery engendered a calmer international economic climate and hence reduced gold hoarding, gold

84. J. Keith Horsefield, "Subsidies to Gold Producers," in Horsefield, *IMF 1945–1965*, 2:203–14.
85. In addition to the fact that Article IV, Section 2 failed to restrict premium sales, Article V, Section 6(b) specifically protected the right of a member to sell newly mined gold in any market and did not limit that privilege by any condition as to price. This latter provision was intended to permit postwar restoration of the London private market, one of the traditional outlets for South African gold. See Joseph Gold, "A Comparison of Special Drawing Rights and Gold as Reserve Assets," *Law and Policy in International Business* 2(1970):336.
86. The fact that the South African dispute was with other members (and not merely with the Fund staff) was highlighted by a statement by Executive Director Melville, an Australian who represented a constituency composed of both South Africa and Australia: "As a South African I am, of course, in favour of premium sales of gold. As an Australian I must add that my instructions are to oppose them." Quoted by Gumbart, "Gold Transactions," in Horsefield, *IMF 1945–1965*, 2:196–97.
87. Ibid. 2:198.
88. Decision of 28 September 1951, *IMF Annual Report* 1952, p. 95. On the 1947 and 1951 statements, see generally Gumbart, "Gold Transactions," in Horsefield, *IMF 1945–1965*, 2:174–202, and Gold, *Selected Essays*, pp. 402–6.

prices in private markets fell and the premium gold issue disappeared from the international monetary agenda until the 1960s.[89]

When substantial premiums reappeared in the early 1960s as a result of worries about the U.S. balance of payments, the institutional response occurred not within Fund structure but rather through cooperation outside the Fund structure between the United States and the principal European governments. Moreover, the emphasis was not on either limiting premium transactions or on increasing the quantity of gold in monetary reserves. Rather it was on supplying the private gold market with larger quantities of gold, from national monetary reserves if necessary, in order to satisfy private demands, whether for industrial purposes or for hoarding.

The impetus for this extra-Fund initiative was the fear that, with the U.S. dollar having slipped from hegemony to weakness, private market prices well above $35 per ounce might cause an increased demand for U.S. reserve gold at $35 per ounce. By 1962, U.S. gold reserves had already fallen from a level of $24 billion in 1948 to $16 billion.[90] U.S. official liabilities to foreign official institutions had reached more than $12 billion by 1962.[91] Since some foreign central banks might be tempted to arbitrage between the U.S. $35 official price to foreign official institutions and the substantially higher prices available in the private market, the United States had a powerful incentive to try to force down the private market price in order to preserve the U.S. commitment to sell gold to foreign official institutions at the official price. The United States elected to do so by "supplying the market instead of starving it as the Fund had recommended" in the 1947–51 period.[92]

In 1961 the United States enlisted the principal European countries in the establishment of a London gold pool in order to spread the burden of supplying the private market. The Gold Pool was not a new organization; it was officially described as a "kind of gentlemen's agreement."[93] The underlying documents have not been published. Indeed, initially at least, there were no documents. An official of the New York Federal Reserve Bank has written that an agreement was reached at a Bank for International Settlements meeting in Basle in November 1961 to activate the Gold Pool immediately without any documentation: "In the traditional spirit of the BIS meetings, not a scrap of paper had been initialed or even exchanged; the personal word of each governor was as binding as any written contract."[94]

89. Strange, *International Monetary Relations*, pp. 70–71.
90. IMF, *International Financial Statistics*, 1972 Supplement, pp. vi–vii, and see Gilbert, pp. 120–21.
91. U.S. Treasury Department, *Statistical Appendix to Annual Report . . . for the Fiscal Year Ended June 30, 1975*, pp. 326–27, table 95. See table 2, p. 145 below.
92. Gold, "Constitutional Development," p. 564.
93. "The London Gold Market," *Bank of England Quarterly Bulletin* 4(1964):18.
94. Charles A. Coombs, *The Arena of International Finance* (1976), p. 63.

The essence of the Gold Pool was an agreement among the central banks of Belgium, France, Italy, the Netherlands, Switzerland, West Germany, and the United Kingdom to contribute, in accordance with agreed quotas, 50 percent of the gold to be supplied to the private market in London with the United States supplying the other 50 percent.[95] When the price began to fall and fears of a gold surplus arose, the same group of countries agreed to join to buy gold in London whenever the market price fell below the official price. Thus, the Gold Pool became, in effect, a stabilization pool, operated through the Bank of England as agent, to keep the market price at roughly the official price.[96] The Gold Pool's members were, however, often referred to as the BIS or Basle group in recognition of the origins of the Gold Pool and the increasing importance of the BIS as a rival to the Fund as an organizer and regulator of the international monetary system.[97]

The Gold Pool operated successfully until 1967, even acquiring net some gold from the private market.[98] But in late 1967 and early 1968 concern about the stability of the U.S. dollar led to large private purchases, and therefore, equally large sales from reserves through the Gold Pool. Total sales to the pool between the November 1967 devaluation of sterling and mid-March 1968 came to $3 billion. During this period the United States and Britain lost 18 percent, and the Gold Pool countries as a whole lost one-eighth of their gold holdings.[99]

Consequently, in March 1968, after gold sales of well over one-half billion dollars in four days,[100] the members of the Gold Pool (minus France, which had become inactive in 1967)[101] agreed to disband the pool and to substitute a commitment among themselves as to their future transactions in gold.

Under this arrangement, which became known as the two-tier system, an effort was made to separate the official gold market from the private gold market. The essence of the idea was to permit the private gold price to rise substantially and perhaps permanently above the official gold price and yet to prevent any leakage of official gold into the private gold market in response to the financial opportunity for profit by arbitrage between the two markets. The arrangement had in the planning stage been known as the "green stripe plan"; the idea was that "figuratively, a green stripe would be painted on each bar of monetary gold; monetary authorities would then buy and sell—at the official price of $35 per ounce—only gold with a green stripe on it," and those authorities "would stay out of the free market as either buyers or sellers."[102]

95. "London Gold Market," pp. 19–20.
96. See e.g. ibid. pp. 20–21; Coombs, pp. 62–68.
97. Gold, *Selected Essays*, p. 219. See further discussion pp. 170–72, below.
98. De Vries, *IMF 1966–1971*, 1:402.
99. Robert Solomon, *The International Monetary System, 1945–1976* (1977), p. 119.
100. Coombs, p. 166–67.
101. Gold, *Selected Essays*, p. 219.
102. Solomon, p. 116.

The two-tier gold agreement was embodied in a communiqué dated 17 March 1968, issued by the seven central banks involved. This agreement, though in form one among central banks, was perceived as an international agreement among the seven countries involved.[103] The communiqué stated that the central bank governors had "decided no longer to supply gold to the London gold market or any other gold market," and that they had "agreed" not to "sell gold to [other] monetary authorities to replace gold sold in private markets."[104] On the buying side, the commitment was not phrased in terms of decision or agreement but rather in terms of a feeling: "as the existing stock of monetary gold is sufficient in view of the prospective establishment of the facility for Special Drawing Rights, they no longer feel it necessary to buy gold from the market."[105] As one of the American draftsmen of the communiqué later commented, this more tentative language reflected an inability of the United States to negotiate "a stronger commitment from the European governors to refrain from market purchases" in view of "deep-seated views on gold . . . held by some Europeans."[106] These buying and selling commitments were endorsed in one form or another by fifty-nine countries.[107]

The conflict between the United States and some European governments on gold had a third dimension in the desire of South Africa, which then accounted for about 70 percent of the noncommunist world's gold production,[108] to be able to sell some of its newly produced gold at the official $35 price if the private market price should fall below that level. The South Africans found support for their position in the reciprocal desire of some European governments to be able to buy South African gold if necessary to maintain the official gold price, especially since a collapse of the private gold market price might be interpreted as a step toward demonetization of gold and would no doubt be politically unpopular in European countries where private ownership of gold was widespread. South Africa, not a supporter of the two-tier arrangement, also wanted to be able to sell gold at above $35 an ounce to willing European monetary authorities in order to avoid being forced to sell all its gold on the private market, thereby depressing the private market price.

The South African government argued that it had a legally protected right to sell gold to the Fund at the official price under Article V, Section 6(a),

---

103. See discussion of this issue of "legal classification" in Gold, *Selected Essays*, pp. 221–23.
104. *Federal Reserve Bulletin*, 1968, p. 254.
105. Ibid. On special drawing rights, see discussion p. 151 ff.
106. Solomon, p. 122.
107. *The International Monetary Fund's Special Drawing Rights Proposal and the Current International Financial Situation*, Hearing before the Subcommittee on International Finance of the House Committee on Banking and Currency, 90th Cong., 2d Sess., 12 April 1968 (1968), pp. 6–8.
108. David Williams, "The Gold Markets 1968–72," *Finance and Development* 9(December 1972):13.

which stated that "any member desiring to obtain, directly or indirectly, the currency of another member for gold shall, provided it can do so with equal advantage, acquire it by the sale of gold to the Fund." Although the Managing Director of the Fund supported South Africa's legal position,[109] the United States apparently took the position that the operative principle should be derived from the two-tier agreement which created two entirely different circuits for gold, and that any arrangement that permitted new gold to enter the international reserve circuit at $35 per ounce would, in effect, support the private market price.[110] The U.S. legal position rested on the proviso in Section 6(a) that the member must be able to acquire the "currency of another member . . . with equal advantage"; if the private market price was above $35, then the advantage to South Africa from gold sales to the Fund at $35 was not equal to the advantage of private sales above $35.[111]

The legal issue came to a head when the private market price, after having ranged upwards of $40 per ounce, fell to $35 at the end of 1969.[112] By that time the United States had come to see the wisdom of preventing private gold prices from falling below the official price, and the issue of South African sales to European monetary authorities at premium prices had disappeared from the immediate agenda. The U.S. and South African authorities consequently were able to negotiate a bilateral settlement,[113] and their agreement was promptly endorsed in a decision of the Executive Board.

The Executive Board decision is legally interesting both because it appended South African and U.S. letters that had been negotiated bilaterally (albeit addressed to the Fund) and because the Executive Directors expressly reached their decision as "a matter of policy" and "without prejudice to the determination of the legal position under the Articles of Agreement."[114] The decision distinguished, without any apparent justification in the Articles of Agreement, between periods when the private market price was $35 or less and those when it was above $35 as well as between newly mined gold and previously mined gold held in inventory. In a period when the price was at

109. De Vries, *IMF 1966–1971*, 1:410.
110. This is an interpretation of the U.S. legal position derived from secondary sources. See e.g. Solomon, pp. 124–25; C. Gordon Tether, "Sth. African Gold—Fund's Embarrassing Position," *Financial Times*, 18 June 1968. The U.S. legal position on sales to governments above $35 an ounce was stronger since any such sales would involve a contravention by the buying countries of the two-tier agreement and, as a purchase above par, might also violate Article IV, Section 2.
111. Strange, *International Monetary Relations*, p. 307.
112. *IMF Annual Report* 1970, pp. 128–29. The private market price fell below $35 in January 1970. Ibid. p. 129.
113. The only Fund involvement was the presence of the U.S. Executive Director, who was appointed by the United States alone and therefore as a practical matter was operating under U.S. instructions. Also present at the U.S.-South African negotiations was a representative of the Bank for International Settlements. Solomon, p. 126.
114. Decision of 30 December 1969, *IMF Annual Report* 1970, pp. 184–89. This decision was terminated at the request of South Africa on 7 December 1973. *IMF Annual Report* 1974, p. 63.

or below $35, South Africa was permitted to sell to the Fund enough gold to meet its "current foreign exchange needs for that period."[115] However, regardless of the private market price, South Africa could sell gold to the Fund "up to the extent that [it] has a need for foreign exchange over a semiannual period beyond the need that can be satisfied by the sale of all of its current production of newly-mined gold on the market or by sales to the Fund."[116] In addition, South Africa was permitted to sell out of inventory up to $35 million per calendar quarter.[117] With respect to private market sales, South Africa was not directly restricted by the decision but the decision was qualified by "the understanding that members generally do not intend to initiate gold purchases directly from South Africa."[118] Thus, South Africa could not sell freely in private gold markets, but whether Fund members could, as a matter of Fund law, purchase in those markets in transactions other than with South Africa was left open. (Such a purchase, regardless of whether or not it was a premium transaction, would presumably violate the buying country's two-tier commitment, assuming that country had made such a commitment.)

The South African case illustrates the interplay between the Fund and other legal arenas within the international monetary system. At stake in the South African case was the preservation of the two-tier arrangement which, as a legal matter, was entirely outside the Fund's sphere. South Africa opposed the two-tier arrangement because it was contrary to its national interest as an exporter of gold (especially since South Africa hoped that higher private market prices would lead to an increase in the official price). It used as a legal weapon in support of its policy position its right under the Articles of Agreement to sell gold to the Fund. But whatever the abstract legal right that South Africa might have, it could not enforce that right unless it could obtain sufficient support among the Executive Directors, who represented other nations and constituencies.

Although the principal protagonists, the United States and South Africa, negotiated a compromise entirely outside the Fund, the issue of Fund law had to be passed upon formally through the Fund machinery. Moreover, the Fund itself had a considerable stake in the two-tier agreement, which was regarded as essential to the continued U.S. ability to sell gold at $35 an ounce to official purchasers. In the face of the murky legal situation, the U.S. letter to the Managing Director that was appended (together with the South African letter) to the Executive Board decision attempted to convey the reality of the Fund interest and to construct a link between the Fund and the two-tier arrangement by reminding the Managing Director that he had attended the

---

115. Decision of 30 December 1969, *IMF Annual Report* 1970, p. 184, para. 2(a)(i).
116. Ibid. para. 2(a)(ii).
117. Ibid. p. 185, para. 2(c).
118. Ibid. para. 3.

central bankers' meeting at which the two-tier arrangements had been agreed upon.[119] In this situation one can observe the Fund Managing Director and staff giving their support to an extra-Fund arrangement that they found to be in the interest both of the Fund and of the Bretton Woods system as it had by then evolved.

II. LEGISLATION

Amendment

Liquidity

The impetus for amending the Articles of Agreement in 1968 was the desire to make a major effort through the Fund to do something about what was regarded as the "international liquidity problem." Any analysis of the content of the First Amendment warrants a brief discussion of the liquidity issue and of the reasons why so far-reaching a solution as the creation of the special drawing right was decided upon.

The Liquidity Question

During the mid-1960s a widespread worry in international monetary circles was that the monetary system might soon face a liquidity crisis. Although with hindsight such a fear may seem shockingly misplaced in view of the great inflation of the 1970s, the belief that liquidity would be inadequate was honestly and firmly, though by no means universally, held. This belief was most strongly held in the United States; it was challenged in some European countries, particularly France.

One of the characteristics of the resulting liquidity debate was that the concept of liquidity was not widely understood. For purposes of discussing the First Amendment to the Articles, liquidity can be thought of as the total of international reserves held by all countries (or at least Fund members) plus credit available from the Fund. This is a convenient but inexact definition.

The term "international reserves" should be distinguished from "national reserves," the latter referring to those assets that under domestic law may be said to back the currency. "International reserves" refers simply to those assets owned by a country (including its monetary authorities such as the central bank) that can be used to support the exchange rate of its currency. Thus, the principal forms of international reserves are gold, foreign exchange (at least in the form of holdings of reserve currencies, e.g., the dollar), and unconditional claims such as gold tranche positions in the Fund.[120] "Liquidity" would then include not merely such reserves, which are unconditionally available, but also resources that can readily be borrowed. Hence, credit conditionally available from the Fund should be included. And although credit available to members from private banks was not usually mentioned

119. Ibid. pp. 188–89.
120. Also included would be creditor positions under the General Arrangements to Borrow, which are discussed pp. 149–50.

in the 1960s discussion, this source of liquidity became extremely important in the 1970s.

In the 1960s the main source of growth in liquidity was the deficit in the U.S. balance of payments. Under the par value system, countries with corresponding balance-of-payments surpluses frequently intervened in exchange markets to prevent their currencies from appreciating. Since the principal intervention currency was the dollar, the result of such intervention (which took the form of sale of national currency in exchange for dollars) was that the surplus countries added to their holdings of dollars. Increases in dollar holdings provided more than half of the 22 percent increase (from $60.3 billion to $73.6 billion) in international reserves between 1960 and 1967 (see table 1). Moreover, dollar holdings grew by more than half during that period, from $11.1 billion to $18.3 billion. Gold production was a comparatively minor source of new international reserves, since most production went into industrial uses and private hoarding, and after 1965 total gold held in international reserves declined slightly (see table 1). Still other sources were the expansion from time to time of Fund quotas, which increased the unconditional reserves in the form of gold tranche reserve positions as well as conditional reserves in the form of increased credit tranches.[121]

The persistent U.S. deficit was severely criticized by European countries on a number of grounds. First, it tended to force European countries to

Table 1
International Reserves, 1960–67
(billions of U.S. dollars)

	Foreign exchange		Gold	Reserve positions in Fund	Total international reserves
	Dollar liabilities	Total foreign exchange			
1960	11.1	18.7	38.0	3.6	60.3
1961	11.8	19.3	38.7	4.2	62.4
1962	13.0	20.0	39.3	3.8	63.0
1963	14.6	22.2	40.2	3.9	66.4
1964	15.7	23.7	40.8	4.2	68.7
1965	15.8	23.3	41.9	5.4	70.5
1966	15.0	24.7	40.9	6.3	72.0
1967	18.3	28.3	39.5	5.7	73.6

Source: IMF, *International Financial Statistics* (January 1970), pp. 13–15. Later IMF estimates made minor adjustments to these figures (see tables 3 and 4). All figures are year-end. They have been rounded to the nearest decimal point; hence totals show minor discrepancies. Reserve positions in Fund "are the amounts that a member, when experiencing a balance of payments deficit, may draw essentially automatically under the Fund's Gold Tranche policy." Ibid. p. 12.

121. Conditional reserves in the form of credit tranches are not shown in table 1 because the totals have little meaning in view of the fact that not all countries could be in the position to draw at the same time.

revalue their currencies, which was politically unpopular because of effects on export industries. Second, in order to prevent appreciation of the currency, countries found it necessary to intervene in exchange markets, which added to the local money supply and was therefore inflationary (a process referred to as the "importing of inflation" from the United States). Third, the U.S. deficit could be continued only because, as a reserve currency country, the United States simply increased its liabilities rather than having to face the exhaustion of its international reserves as would other countries.

The last of these three points was a source of political irritation because some countries, notably France, regarded the reserve currency mechanism as permitting the United States to act imperialistically both in economic matters (e.g., purchase of key French companies) and in the military sphere (e.g., the Vietnam war). But the reserve currency mechanism also led to increases in perceived liquidity when the United States ran a deficit. Since international reserves tended to be counted "gross" rather than "net," the dollar holdings by foreigners constituted international reserves but the increased U.S. liabilities were not usually subtracted from U.S. gold holdings in calculating U.S. reserves. This led the United States to view its deficits as a desirable source of additional liquidity and to argue that a problem would arise for the system if the United States ended its deficit. The argument was that U.S. payments balance would eliminate a principal source of additional liquidity or, worse, that if the United States ran a surplus, liquidity would contract.

The United States became the principal advocate of finding a new, supplementary source of liquidity. In contrast, Europeans, especially the French, argued that the United States deficit would have to end before any new form of liquidity could be created. Much of the liquidity debate thus centered on the need for new liquidity, without, however, much public enlightenment on the purposes and uses of liquidity. Much of the discussion tended to confuse international liquidity with the availability of financing for international trade; thus, it was argued that international liquidity had to grow at the same pace as international trade. But the main importance of international liquidity was to permit countries to intervene in the exchange markets in support of their currency's exchange rate. Thus, most of the public discussion failed to recognize explicitly that a shortage of liquidity was important only if it led to the imposition of exchange or trade controls as a substitute for exchange market intervention or if countries were forced to pursue unduly restrictive economic policies (with resulting unnecessary unemployment) merely in order to avoid the exchange rate consequences of, say, short-term reversible export shortfalls.

A related problem concerned the composition of reserves. Not all countries were content with their accumulations of dollars and preferred to hold some of their increased reserves in the form of gold. The principal source of additional gold for surplus countries' reserves was the United States under its policy of selling gold to foreign monetary authorities at $35 per ounce. The additional liquidity generated by U.S. deficits provided the basis for a sharp disagreement on the composition of reserves for particular countries. The tension rose as U.S. liabilities came to exceed the U.S. gold supply at the start of the 1960s and became twice as large in 1965 (see table 2). A situation analogous to domestic banking in the United States in the 1930s was thus created on an international scale since a run on the U.S. "gold bank" could be started at any time if a particular creditor country were to demand gold. This dependence on the solvency of the reserve countries is, as observed in chapter 3, an Achilles' heel of a gold exchange system that was not widely perceived when the Bretton Woods planners drew their lessons from the interwar experience.[122]

This dependence put considerable pressure on many countries to refrain from converting their dollar holdings into gold. The French under de Gaulle, however, adopted the policy of systematically converting dollars to gold when

Table 2
U.S. International Reserves and Liabilities, 1950–71
(billions of U.S. dollars)

	Total reserves	Gold	Total external liabilities	External liabilities to monetary authorities and governments
1950	24.3	22.8	8.9	4.9
1955	22.8	21.8	13.5	8.3
1958	22.5	20.6	16.8	9.6
1959	21.6	19.6	19.4	10.1
1960	19.4	17.8	21.0	11.1
1961	18.7	16.9	22.9	11.8
1962	17.2	16.1	24.3	12.7
1963	16.8	15.6	26.4	14.4
1964	16.7	15.5	29.3	15.8
1965	15.4	14.1	29.6	15.8
1966	14.9	13.2	31.0	14.9
1967	14.8	12.1	35.7	18.2
1968	15.7	10.9	38.5	17.3
1969	17.0	11.9	45.9	16.0
1970	14.5	11.1	47.0	23.3
1971	13.2	11.1	67.8	50.6

Source: IMF, *International Financial Statistics*, pp. 2–3 (1972 Supplement). All figures are year-end. Total reserves include gold, foreign exchange, reserve position in the Fund and, beginning in 1970, SDRs. Gold is valued at $35 per ounce.

122. See discussion pp. 64–69.

they enjoyed payment surpluses.[123] France's foreign exchange holdings fell
from $1.4 billion at the end of 1964 to $0.5 billion at the end of 1966, at the
same time that its gold holdings were rising from $3.7 billion to $5.2 billion.[124]
This situation led to the argument that a new form of liquidity should be
found that would not have the disadvantage of generating disputes over the
composition of reserves and that would not threaten the very underpinnings
of the Bretton Woods system.

Additional liquidity could be provided in a number of ways other than
the creation of a new asset. In fact, three different means had already been
utilized before discussion of a new asset had begun: quota increases, the
General Arrangements to Borrow, and bilateral swap agreements.

Quotas had been enlarged on several occasions. During each five-year
period quotas were reviewed; and, in 1959, quotas were increased 50 percent
to make a 1960 total of $14.7 billion, almost twice the December 1945 total
of $7.6 billion.[125] Another 25 percent increase followed in 1966.[126] Quota
totals also increased from time to time as new members joined and as adjustments were made in individual country quotas.[127] By the end of April
1966, aggregate quotas reached $19.4 billion.

Quota enlargements increased both conditional and unconditional liquidity
(that is, both gold and credit tranches). For most countries the quota increases
by themselves were painless. Although some countries had difficulty making
the required gold contribution, the gold contribution was matched by an
increase in the unconditionally available gold tranche, and the currency contribution could in effect be printed for the occasion. On the other hand, by
enlarging quotas a creditor country laid itself open to drawings of its currency,
and thus quotas constituted contingent claims on goods and services of such
a country. This consequence might either be welcome as a stimulus to exports
or unwelcome to the extent that the resulting increase in the money supply
or the increased demand for goods and services had inflationary effects.

A more subtle liquidity aspect of quota increases was that Fund drawings
themselves enlarged international liquidity. Thus, if a member drew currency, the drawing did not diminish the reserves of the drawing country,
since it now had foreign exchange that it did not previously have to offset

123. From 1957 to 1963, French gold reserves rose from $581 million to $3,175 million (although
this represented a decline from 90 percent to 71 percent of total reserve holdings of gold and
foreign exchange). Poul Høst-Madsen, "Gold Outflows from the United States, 1958–63," *IMF
Staff Papers* 11(1964):254, table 4. By the end of 1967, French gold reserves were $5,234 million:
IMF, *International Financial Statistics*, 1973 Supplement, p. 138. See also Fred Hirsch, *Money
International*, rev. ed. (1969), p. 276, chart, on the complementary curves of U.S. and French
gold reserve holdings up to 1967, and see ibid. p. 381, table 24, on French gold acquisitions.
124. IMF, *International Financial Statistics*, 1973 Supplement, pp. 137–38.
125. J. Keith Horsefield, "Derivation and Significance of the Fund's Resources," in Horsefield,
IMF 1945–1965, 2:358–60, 378–80, table 14.
126. Ibid. 2:362–63.
127. Ibid. 2:354–63.

its use of its Fund drawing power. Indeed, if the drawing was not in the credit tranches, the effect of the drawing would be to increase the calculated reserves of the drawing country.[128] (Since the gold tranche was normally counted as part of reserves, the effect was merely the loss of the gold tranche position balanced by the equivalent increase in foreign exchange holdings.) Meanwhile, the country whose currency was drawn, which as a strong currency country would almost certainly have part or all of its gold tranche still available, would enjoy an increase in unconditional liquidity in the form of an increase in its gold tranche position (the super gold tranche). Thus, drawings increased liquidity and insofar as larger quotas encouraged further drawings, the effect of quota enlargement was to increase liquidity by at least as much as the total increase in quotas. By how much liquidity would be increased could not be determined in advance.

One of the weaknesses of quota enlargements as a source of liquidity stemmed from the "mixed bag of currencies" approach adopted at Bretton Woods.[129] Most of the currencies that would be contributed to the Fund would be those of deficit countries and would therefore be useless, except perhaps in the case of the United States (and possibly Britain) whose reserve currency might still be useful for exchange market intervention transactions. Thus, the quota totals grossly exaggerated the resources available to the Fund. Moreover, at the beginning of the 1960s it seemed likely that the 1950s pattern of drawings mostly by less developed countries would be superseded by large-scale drawings by the United States, the United Kingdom, and other major developed countries with large quotas. For these purposes the usable resources of the Fund might be quite modest.

Until 1958, when the major European currencies became externally convertible for current transactions, the Fund had only two kinds of assets—gold and dollars—that could readily be used for lending.[130] Prior to 1958 less than 10 percent of total drawings from the Fund had been in other than U.S. dollars.[131] As the U.S. balance-of-payments problem became more serious and therefore large U.S. drawings became a possibility, and particularly after the United Kingdom in August 1961 drew various currencies equal to $1.5 billion and entered into a stand-by agreement for another $500 million, several

---

128. John Williamson, *The Failure of World Monetary Reform, 1971–74* (1977), pp. 16–17. For a more elaborate analysis, see Hannan Ezekiel, "The Present System of Reserve Creation in the Fund," *IMF Staff Papers* 13(1966):398–418.

129. See discussion p. 102.

130. Gold would not be used directly but rather would be sold by the Fund to obtain the currencies to be drawn.

131. National Advisory Council on International Monetary and Financial Problems, *Special Report to the President and to the Congress on Special Borrowing Arrangements of the International Monetary Fund* (January 1962), p. 8, table 4 (hereafter cited National Advisory Council, *Special Report*).

weaknesses of the "mixed bag of currencies" structure of Fund assets became evident.[132]

The first weakness was that neither of the two currencies representing the largest quotas, the United States ($4.125 billion) and the United Kingdom ($1.950 billion), would be of general use if the United States were to draw. U.S. dollars could not be used by the United States as U.S. reserves, and British pounds sterling were of dubious value to the United States so long as sterling was weak. Indeed, if the United States were to draw sterling and then sell it to buy dollars in support of the dollar rate, the effect would be to weaken sterling further.

The second weakness was that the eight other principal industrialized countries, whose currencies would be the major source of Fund assets for any U.S. drawing, had quotas totalling only $3.795 billion. (The great bulk of Fund quotas, on the order of $5.0 billion, were accounted for by less developed countries' currencies that, simply because they were inconvertible, were of little use for lending.)[133] At any given time, some of those eight countries would be in deficit and might have Fund drawings outstanding. As in the case of the pound sterling, the drawing and sale in the exchange market of a weak currency could weaken that currency further. The Fund's holdings of those eight currencies had, moreover, been reduced to $1.7 billion as a consequence of the British drawing.[134] This amount was insufficient for a major U.S. drawing in view of the size of the U.S. quota and the U.S. deficit.[135]

This particular liquidity problem could not be solved by an increase in quotas, at least without a major shift in quota proportions and hence in voting power among countries, which the European members themselves did not favor.[136] Given existing quota proportions, more than one-third of any quota enlargement would be accounted for by the United States and the United Kingdom, thereby increasing their drawing rights, and another third would be accounted for by less developed countries with inconvertible currencies. Thus, quota enlargements increased the drawing rights of the two reserve currency countries, both of which were now experiencing balance-of-payments deficits, more rapidly than it would generate currencies of value for U.S. and U.K. drawings.

132. Ibid. p. 9.
133. *IMF Annual Report* 1962, appendix I, pp. 179–82. Inconvertible currencies had occasionally been drawn prior to 1958, but the amounts were small and the currencies were those of major industrialized countries. Horsefield, *IMF 1945–1965*, 1:452, table 5.
134. National Advisory Council, *Special Report*, p. 9, table 5.
135. The U.S. overall balance-of-payments deficit had exceeded three billion dollars in 1958–60. Ibid. p. 6, table 2. See also Solomon, p. 43.
136. S. E. Brittan, "International Financial Diplomacy in 1961," in *Royal Institute of International Affairs, Survey of International Affairs, 1961*, ed. D. C. Watt (1965), p. 318.

The General Arrangements to Borrow (GAB)

The solution to the Fund liquidity problem arrived at in the General Arrangements to Borrow was for the Fund to be put in a position to borrow from the industrialized convertible-currency countries other than the United States and the United Kingdom. Though Article VII, Section 2 empowered the Fund to borrow from a member, it also provided that no member should be obliged to lend to the Fund, and therefore some new arrangement had to be made. Though the idea behind the GAB came from the Fund staff,[137] the negotiations occurred largely outside the Fund among the ten major industrialized countries, which became known thereafter as the Group of Ten (United States, Britain, Germany, France, Italy, Netherlands, Belgium, Sweden, Japan, and Canada).

The form of the GAB was significant. Although it was negotiated by representatives of the signatory countries and the Managing Director and his staff outside normal Fund channels,[138] the form of the agreement was such that it could be subsequently incorporated in a decision of the Executive Board approving the GAB under the provisions of Article VII, Section 2 involving replenishment of scarce currencies.[139] This decision was somewhat deceptive, however, because as Joseph Gold has observed, the Executive Board may normally amend its own decisions, but the GAB could not be amended during its term without the concurrence of the members who negotiated it as well as the Fund.[140] This was one factor that led Gold to analyze whether the GAB could be classified legally as an international agreement among the participants and the Fund.[141]

As a practical matter, the importance of the GAB was that its negotiation created the Group of Ten, an international body that assumed a life of its own, and that it created a special Fund facility available only to certain members and, above all, controlled by those particular members. This last aspect is illustrated by the fact that, in addition to the Executive Board decision, the GAB was enshrined in a series of identical letters from the French finance minister to the finance ministers of each of the participating countries. These letters spelled out procedures, especially those by which the participants decided whether and how much the participants were willing

---

137. Ibid. p. 315.
138. Horsefield, *IMF 1945–1965*, 1:511–12; Gold, *Selected Essays*, p. 224. The representatives were finance ministers except in the case of Germany and Sweden, where for constitutional reasons the commitments were made by central banks. Strange, *International Monetary Relations*, p. 113.
139. Decision of 5 January 1962, *IMF Annual Report* 1962, pp. 234–45.
140. Gold, *Selected Essays*, pp. 451, 457–58.
141. Ibid. pp. 448–62. Gold discusses in this respect the legal aspects of the later association of Switzerland, which was not a Fund member, with the GAB. Ibid. pp. 460–62. For the text, which took the form of an exchange of letters between the Swiss ambassador to the United States and the Managing Director, see Horsefield, *IMF 1945–1965*, 3:254–55.

to lend to the Fund in response to any proposal from the Managing Director for borrowing to finance a drawing by a participant.[142]

The immediate financial effect of the GAB was to increase the potential usable financial resources of the Fund by the equivalent of $6.0 billion, of which $2.0 billion was committed by the United States and $1.0 billion each by the United Kingdom and the German Bundesbank. The GAB facility was not in fact used until 1965, when the United Kingdom drew under a $1.0 billion stand-by arrangement.[143]

Swap Arrangements

An alternative to the GAB was being developed at the same time that the GAB was being negotiated. That alternative, the reciprocal credit arrangement or "swap," was a creation of central banks, operating through the Bank for International Settlements. Thus, swap arrangements were developed completely outside the framework of the Fund.

The fundamental idea was very simple, however esoteric the swap device might have seemed to the uninitiated. Two central banks would simply open stand-by credits in each other's name for a fixed period, say one year, subject to renewal. The credits could be drawn with short notice, say two days. Swaps thus increased the liquidity available to both parties. Since any central bank would be borrowing the currency of its opposite number and would normally have to pay back in that currency, the borrower would be giving the lender an implicit exchange guarantee so that the borrower would be taking the risk of any exchange rate change in the interim. However, the parties sometimes agreed to share the exchange risk. The swap arrangements normally called for the reversal of any borrowing thereunder at the end of three months, subject to any agreed renewal. To the extent that foreign currency was borrowed but not used in exchange transactions, the borrowed funds would be invested for the account of the lender and the lender could call for its return on short notice. Thus, a swap borrowing would bear interest only to the extent not used in exchange transactions.[144]

The first swap arrangement was entered into between the Federal Reserve Bank of New York and the Bank of France in early 1962.[145] A network of swap arrangements was built up among the central banks of developed coun-

142. See sample letter in Horsefield, *IMF 1945–1965*, 3:252–54.
143. Ibid. 1:512, 568–69.
144. For a description of swaps, see "Treasury and Federal Reserve Foreign Exchange Operations" (March 1961–August 1962), *Federal Reserve Bulletin*, 1962, pp. 1147–48. I have also relied upon the text of a December 1978 swap agreement between the Federal Reserve Bank of New York and the German Bundesbank, provided to me by the general counsel of the Board of Governors of the Federal Reserve System.
145. Coombs, p. 75.

tries.[146] U.S. swap arrangements totaled $900 million by the end of 1962[147] and were at the $22 billion level in 1978.[148]

The Special Drawing Right

The quest for new forms of liquidity continued throughout the mid-1960s. In part, this search was based on the notion that the GAB and swaps were too ad hoc and only useful for developed countries' liquidity needs. A more bureaucratic motivation was that they were either partially (the GAB) or wholly (swaps) extra-Fund institutions. Moreover, swap arrangements appeared useful only for short-term imbalances.[149] So the Fund staff and many academic economists studied various schemes for the creation of liquidity through the Fund. Many of the ideas built on one aspect of the GAB that was not central to the initial GAB idea, namely, that lending to the Fund by GAB participants created a liquid claim on the Fund—a claim that was equivalent to a gold tranche position—and therefore could be counted as an unconditional claim on the Fund and hence part of the international reserves of the lending countries. From this idea developed a variety of schemes involving borrowing by the Fund or other means for expanding automatically available claims on the Fund (say by expanding the unconditional portion of the quota—until then the gold tranche only—into the credit tranches).[150] Because these schemes are primarily of historical interest, attention here is better devoted to the outcome of the extensive proposals and analyses, the Special Drawing Right (SDR). Indeed, since the history of the negotiation of the SDR has been admirably recounted elsewhere, it too can be passed over here.[151]

The SDR differed from nearly all prior proposals in one crucial respect. Previously it had been thought essential that any new international reserves created through the Fund, and particularly any new reserve asset, be "backed" by some other asset (such as a liquid claim by the Fund on national

---

146. Ibid. pp. 69–91.
147. Solomon, p. 41.
148. "Treasury and Federal Reserve Foreign Exchange Operations" (February–July 1978), *Federal Reserve Bank of New York Quarterly Review* 3(Autumn 1978):47–48, table 1.
149. Group of Ten, *Report to Ministers and Governors by the Group of Deputies* (7 July 1966), para. 26–27, p. 6.
150. The basic Fund documents, reprinted in de Vries, *IMF 1965–1971*, 2:3–29, are "Creation of Additional Reserves through the International Monetary Fund (March 3, 1966)"; "Creation of Additional Reserves through the International Monetary Fund—Supplementary Notes (March 28, 1966)"; "Outline of an Illustrative Reserve Unit Scheme (February 23, 1967)"; and "Outline of an Illustrative Scheme for a Special Reserve Facility Based on Drawing Rights in the Fund (February 28, 1967)." See also the analysis in ibid. 1:43–53. Academic plans are reviewed in John Williamson, "Surveys in Applied Economics: International Liquidity," *Economic Journal* 83(1973):713–17. See also Herbert T. Grubel, ed., *World Monetary Reform: Plans and Issues* (1963).
151. See de Vries, *IMF 1966–1971*, 1:11–205; Stephen D. Cohen, *International Monetary Reform, 1964–69* (1970). See also the discussion of the Group of Ten, pp. 172–74, below.

governments). The SDR, in contrast, was created out of (so to speak) whole cloth. It was simply allocated to participants in proportion to quotas, leading some to refer to the SDR as "manna from heaven."[152] Thereafter it existed and was transferred without any backing at all (aside from technical arrangements for the possible future winding up of the entire SDR scheme, at which time presumably "the new units would have to be turned in for something").[153] A ready analogy is to "fiat" money created by national governments but not convertible into underlying assets such as gold. In one sense the dropping of the backing concept was an intellectual breakthrough in planning for the reform of the international monetary system. It certainly was a moral victory for enlightened economists who viewed the supposed need for backing as a myth. As Fritz Machlup put it at the time of the SDR agreement:

> Now the forward-looking experts of the Fund and the negotiating governments have proved that their reputation for backwardness in economic thinking had been undeserved. (I propose that they be granted honorary doctor's degrees by the great universities.)
>
> All that matters for the acceptability of anything as a medium of exchange is the expectation that others will accept it. If over a hundred central banks or national monetary authorities including those of the major trading nations of the world agree to accept SDR's from one another in exchange for convertible currencies, this is all that is needed to establish the moneyness of the SDR's in inter-central-bank transactions. Money needs takers, not backers; the takers accept it, not because of any backing, but only because they count on others accepting it from them.[154]

Despite Machlup's enthusiasm, the elimination of any backing for the SDR gave many central and private bankers the feeling that SDRs were "funny money" not fully competitive with gold and reserve currencies as international reserves. The failure to provide backing, however cosmetic it might be, may therefore paradoxically have created some of the difficulties surrounding the full acceptance of the SDR mechanism in the 1970s. In sum, the absence of backing may thus have been a victory of economic reasoning over statecraft. Charles Coombs of the Federal Reserve Bank of New York, a leading member of the central banking community, put the point as follows in his memoirs:

152. As Polak observes, this phrase was usually used in a "slightly deprecatory vein," implying that "those who regarded the allocations in this way were as ill-informed as the children of Israel 'who said to one another, It is manna: for they wist not what it was' (Exodus, 16:15)." J. J. Polak, *Some Reflections on the Nature of Special Drawing Rights*, IMF Pamphlet Series no. 16 (1971), p. 9.
153. De Vries, *IMF 1966–1971*, 1:118–19.
154. Fritz Machlup, *Remaking The International Monetary System: The Rio Agreement and Beyond* (1968), pp. 65–66.

For my own part, I could not help feeling that the SDR edifice, however carefully constructed, would nevertheless be balanced on a razor's edge. If, on the one hand, the fiat money attribute of the SDR were to be emphasized, I found it hard to believe that money issued by the International Monetary Fund or any supranational agency would prove to be a generally acceptable alternative to the dollar, much less gold. And if, as was eventually agreed, the SDR was endowed with a categorical gold guarantee to enhance its acceptability, the SDR would inevitably be dragged along in the wake of whatever happened to gold itself.[155]

As both Machlup's and Coombs's comments suggest, the decision to forgo any backing for the SDR simply shifted the issue to the attributes the SDR had to be given to make it acceptable to national financial officials. In the end, acceptance could not be left to chance, and an "acceptance obligation"— a kind of international legal tender requirement—had to be negotiated. Just as national legal tender statutes normally require creditors to accept the national currency in discharge of debts,[156] so too the First Amendment to the Articles required acceptance of the SDR.[157]

The acceptance requirement could not be unqualified. Potential creditors were simply not willing to accept SDRs in unlimited amounts. The need to limit the acceptance requirement (unlike a true legal tender provision in national law) speaks volumes about the limits of technocratic planning in the international monetary system. Gold and foreign exchange "just grew" as reserve assets, but the SDR required complex legal provisions to make it viable.

To understand why there should be reluctance to accept the new asset, it must be borne in mind that SDRs would not be used directly by deficit countries but rather, like gold, would be used to obtain foreign exchange for market intervention. Thus, the creditor country which accepted SDRs from a debtor country would have to give up convertible currency.[158] The convertible currency provided would normally be dollars since most countries then held their foreign exchange reserves in dollars. But SDRs were unlikely to be considered as attractive as an equivalent number of dollars to the creditor central bank, if for no other reason than that the SDR was untried and there could be no private market for it.[159] A quantitative limit was

155. Coombs, pp. 190–91. See also Coombs' reference in his preface to the fading of the "initial bright hope of paper gold' in the form of the SDR." Ibid. p. x.
156. Arthur Nussbaum, *Money in the Law* (1939), pp. 37–42.
157. Article XXV, Sections 4 and 5(a), *first*.
158. The requirement that the currencies provided be "convertible in fact" was written into the Articles. See Article XXV, Section 4, *first*. The term was defined in Article XXXII(b), *first*. See discussion in Joseph Gold, *Special Drawing Rights: Chracter and Use*, 2d ed. IMF Pamphlet Series no. 13 (1970), pp. 36–47; Gold, *The Fund's Concepts of Convertibility*, IMF Pamphlet Series no. 14 (1971), pp. 30–32, 37–53.
159. SDRs could be held only by official institutions. See discussion p. 160.

therefore placed on the acceptance obligation. A participant[160] was not obliged to accept SDRs beyond twice its net cumulative allocation from the Fund—that is, its obligation to accept ceased once its holdings reached 300 percent of that allocation.[161]

A more subtle limitation on the acceptance requirement was provided by the designation mechanism. This mechanism specified which creditor country must provide the convertible currency. Even with an agreed acceptance limit, it was assumed that no country in balance-of-payments difficulty would welcome being in the position of having to provide valuable foreign exchange reserves in return for an asset of uncertain value such as the SDR. Therefore, the designation mechanism was a system of guidance by the Fund to assure that an unwilling transferee was in a strong enough position for the acceptance obligation to be reasonably imposed. The designation mechanism thus modified the acceptance obligation, but it can also be viewed as an enforcement device for that obligation because any participant failing to respond to a designation could lose its right to use the SDRs it already held.[162]

From the standpoint of the institutional development of the Fund, it was significant that the guidance was to be provided by the Fund, which in view of the detail and complexity of the guidance issues could have meant, as a practical matter, that the Fund staff would play a crucial role. But this rather considerable discretion was to be exercised in the light of various general principles. A participant was to be subject to designation "if its balance of payments and gross reserve position is sufficiently strong, but this will not preclude the possibility that a participant with a strong reserve position will be designated even though it has a moderate balance of payments deficit."[163] A modifying harmonization principle was that designation should "promote over time a balanced distribution of holdings of special drawing rights" among designated participants.[164]

This last concept of a "balanced distribution," however, could have many meanings. Differences in views on its meaning could be resolved only by limiting the designation rules to the "first basic period"—which was to be

160. The term "participant" rather than member is used because a Fund member was not required to participate in the SDR system. Article XXIII, Section 1, *first*. In fact, ten members did not at first become participants. J. J. Polak, *Thoughts on an International Monetary Fund Based Fully on the SDR*, IMF Pamphlet Series no. 28 (1979), p. 12. By April 1980 all 140 Fund members had become participants. *IMF Annual Report* 1980, p. 90.
161. Article XXV, Section 4, *first*. Participants' freedom to hold SDRs above the obligatory limit was of potential significance for their reserve use. Ibid. The articles speak of "*net* cumulative allocation," but the word "net" will remain redundant until such time as previously allocated SDRs are canceled. Article XXXII(a), *first*. See Walter Habermeier, *Operations and Transactions in SDRs: The First Basic Period*, IMF Pamphlet Series no. 17 (1973), p. 3, n. 4. Hence the word "net" will be omitted from the text in a compromise favoring simplicity over legal completeness.
162. Article XXIX, Section 2, *first*. See discussion of this "sanction" in Gold, *Selected Essays*, pp. 166–67.
163. Article XXV, Section 5(a)(i), *first*.
164. Ibid.

the five years following the first allocation of SDRs. After the first basic period, power was delegated to the Fund to adopt new designation rules.[165] During the first basic period participants whose reserve and balance-of-payments position was such that they were "subject to designation" were to be designated "for such amounts as will promote over time equality in the ratios of the participants' holdings of special drawing rights in excess of their net cumulative allocations to their official holdings of gold and foreign exchange."[166] In short, the Fund was to strive for equality among strong currency countries in their ratio of "excess SDR holdings" (that is, holdings in excess of allocations) to other official reserves.[167] Moreover, once equality had been achieved, then participants were to be designated "in proportion to their official holdings of gold and foreign exchange."

These rather technical designation principles reflected the widespread view that acceptance of SDRs might be painful and therefore that the pain should be spread equally. The provision for the promotion of equality "over time" further illustrates this skeptical view of the attractiveness of the SDR. In the case of a formerly deficit country that had been using its allocated SDRs but had subsequently improved its balance of payments and therefore became subject to designation for the first time, the "over time" limitation would protect it from being designated in all transactions until such time as equality in ratios with all other participants subject to designation was achieved. The pain of catching up with the SDR excess holding levels of other creditor countries would be reduced by being spread over time.[168]

Even these general principles were sufficiently indefinite that the Fund staff would necessarily be granted a good deal of discretion, as a consequence of the complexities resulting from the need to designate participants for various technical reasons,[169] as well as from various voluntary transactions among participants that tended to drive the SDR excess holdings ratios away from, rather than toward, equality.[170] To channel the Fund staff's discretion, a "designation plan" was provided for in the Fund's Rules and Regulations. This plan, to be approved by the Executive Board each quarter, would specify the participants subject to designation in the quarter and the amount for which they were designated. Although this plan would necessarily be phrased in terms of maximum amounts to be certain that it would not have to be

165. Article XXV, Section 5(c), *first*. The Executive Board decided, as a result of a 1972 review, that no new designation rules should be adopted. Habermeier, p. 20.
166. Schedule F, *first*.
167. This shorthand calculus is only roughly accurate. Of the various types of official reserves, only "gold and foreign exchange" are included, and positions in the Fund and GAB creditor positions were not considered.
168. See de Vries, *IMF 1966–1971*, 1:238–40. See also Habermeier, pp. 19–21.
169. See Article XXV, Section 5(a)(ii) and (iii), *first*. Such additional complexities included "reconstitution," a concept discussed pp. 163–64, below.
170. De Vries, *IMF 1966–1971*, 1:240.

amended in the quarter,[171] it nonetheless permitted the Executive Board to take decisions on a quarterly basis guiding the staff's exercise of discretion.

The question of what country would have to accept a transfer of SDRs had a logical counterpart in the question of the circumstances under which a participant might use its SDRs. Here, however, the SDR planners faced a dilemma. On the one hand, given the expectation that the SDR would be an unattractive asset, limitations on use were called for to prevent participants from trying to unload their SDRs as soon as possible. Obviously, if a substantial number of participants were to use their SDRs to acquire gold or foreign exchange in order to alter the composition of their reserves (rather than to acquire foreign exchange to support their exchange rate), the SDR experiment would fail. In short, the SDR scheme could be expected to work only if a balance-of-payments "need" requirement were included.

On the other hand, any need requirement was also a threat to the success of the SDR, and in two ways. A need requirement might qualify the unconditional nature of the SDR and thereby make it more like conditional Fund credit of the conventional sort. Thus, the SDR might not even be treated as an international reserve and therefore could not take its place with gold and foreign exchange, much less replace them. From the standpoint of SDR proponents such as the United States (though, as we shall see, not from the standpoint of France and to a lesser extent other SDR detractors), anything that rendered the SDR more like credit and less like an unconditional asset, would mortgage its future. Moreover, any limitation on permissible uses might render the SDR less attractive as an asset and therefore make creditor countries even less willing to accept SDRs, since those countries would have more difficulty in getting rid of them in the future (in contrast to gold and foreign exchange reserves, which could be freely used without legal impediment).

The challenge for the First Amendment draftsmen was therefore somehow to blend a need requirement with assurance of unencumbered use. Legal imagination was required to achieve, or at least to pay homage to, these contradictory objectives. The legal device adopted was to declare that a participant would be "expected" to use SDRs only in case of balance-of-payments need but to avoid making this need requirement a legal obligation and indeed to make SDR use by any participant legally unchallengeable at the time of use. Only after use could the need question be raised.[172]

To be more specific, the need requirement was articulated in the Articles as an expectation. Except for a limited number of specified SDR transac-

---

171. Ibid. 1:237.
172. The model for this legal technique was the treatment of unauthorized changes in par value in the original Articles of Agreement. Gold, *Selected Essays*, p. 166, and see chap. 4, above.

tions,[173] "a participant will be *expected* to use its special drawing rights only to meet balance of payments needs or in the light of developments in its official holdings of gold, foreign exchange, and special drawing rights, and its reserve position in the Fund, and not for the sole purpose of changing the composition of the foregoing as between special drawing rights and the total of gold, foreign exchange, and reserve position in the Fund."[174] However, use of the SDR was specifically made unchallengeable. Indeed, even though the transfer of an SDR from one holder to another became legally effective only upon the recording of the transfer on the books of the Fund, the Fund was not empowered to refuse to record a transfer even if made in violation of the need expectation. Nonetheless, any transfer would be subject to a later investigation, which could be initiated only by the Fund—that is, by a vote of the Executive Directors. However, if a participant was found to have used SDRs without fulfilling the need "expectation," then the Fund could suspend its right to use SDRs acquired thereafter.[175]

Rules requiring monetary authorities to accept SDRs and limiting those authorities' power to dispose of them were clearly not adequate to launch the SDR on a successful career as a reserve asset. More important would be the SDR's underlying financial characteristics. If the SDR was economically attractive to monetary authorities, the acceptance and use rules would be largely superfluous; if not, acceptance and use rules could not induce countries to vote for SDR allocations and countries might be led to ignore the rules.

The SDR's underlying characteristics can usefully be discussed under three headings: (1) valuation, (2) interest, and (3) limits on use. Valuation, which refers to changes in principal value, and interest together make up what are sometimes called the yield characteristics. If international reserves were held for investment alone, only the yield characteristics would be relevant (since there was essentialy no default risk with SDRs, apart perhaps from a total collapse of the Fund). But reserves are held to be used. Restrictions on use (of which there were a number beyond the need requirement already examined) would tend to make SDRs less attractive than gold and reserve currencies.

173. The technical transactions exempted from the need requirement were listed in Article XXV, Section 3(c), *first*. One of these Section 3(c) exemptions, however, was not at all technical. Transfers by agreement between transferor and transferee could be made without regard to need where the transferor held more SDRs, and the transferee fewer SDRs, than their respective cumulative allocation and therefore the transaction would "bring the holdings of special drawing rights by both participants closer to their net cumulative allocations."
174. Article XXV, Section 3(a), *first*. (Emphasis supplied.)
175. Article XXIX, Section 2(b), *first*.

Valuation

One of the most crucial decisions was to give the SDR a gold value guarantee. One SDR was to "be equivalent to 0.888 671 gram of fine gold."[176] This provision was included in large part at the insistence of the United States, which wanted "a first-class asset that would, like the dollar, be good as gold."[177] The significance of tying the SDR to gold was somewhat obscured by the fact that the U.S. dollar was, at its official par value, precisely equal in value to the SDR, and therefore it was common to think of one SDR as being equal to one dollar. But the significance of the gold value guarantee became apparent when the dollar was devalued against gold in late 1971. That devaluation had the effect of raising the dollar price of gold from $35 per ounce to $38 per ounce. Correspondingly one SDR became worth $1.08571.[178]

The use of the term "guarantee" with respect to gold value, though common terminology,[179] was also somewhat misleading. No country and certainly not the Fund actually guaranteed the value of the SDR. Indeed, SDRs, like gold but unlike foreign exchange, were not a liability of any country. What the gold value provision did was to determine the parity at which the SDR and the "currency convertible in fact" provided by the transferee would exchange. That parity was, subject to the "equal value" principle discussed below, the ratio of the value of one SDR and one unit of the currency, each at its gold par.

The transfer was not necessarily at parity. The reason illustrates some of the practical complexities involved in creating a new reserve asset. Since the transferee might choose the "currency convertible in fact," the transferee would have an economic incentive to choose a currency trading at a discount from parity with the transferee's own currency (though presumably still within the Bretton Woods exchange rate margins) and thereby provide the requisite currency at a lower cost than if some currency trading at parity or at a premium were chosen.[180] Therefore, the First Amendment provided that the exchange rates used should be "such that a participant using special drawing rights shall receive the same value whatever currencies might be provided and whichever participants provide those currencies."[181]

The technique used to carry out this "equal value" principle was one that was convenient under the Bretton Woods system but that had to be abandoned later when the system collapsed and generalized floating began. The technique was to treat the SDR as exchanging with the U.S. dollar at the

176. Article XXI, Section 2, *first*.
177. Cohen, p. 135.
178. *IMF Annual Report* 1972, pp. 2, 64.
179. See e.g. de Vries, *IMF 1966–1971*, 1:187.
180. The transferee might provide its own currency so long as it was "convertible in fact."
181. Article XXV, Section 8(a), *first*.

latter's par value and then to use the "representative rate for spot delivery" of the currency provided as the relevant rate between those two currencies.[182] The transferee was to provide the number of units of currency that would equal the dollar equivalent of the number of SDRs transferred.[183] Before the 1971 devaluation of the dollar, the calculation was simplified because, as just noted, one SDR equaled one U.S. dollar at par. Moreover, treating the U.S. dollar as exchanging at par was appropriate under the Bretton Woods system in view of the fact that the U.S. practice of not intervening in exchange markets left the dollar a passive and convenient center for comparison of both parities and exchange rates of all other currencies and in view of the U.S commitment to buy and sell gold at the U.S. par of $35 per ounce (albeit with a slight charge).

Interest

In view of the SDR's gold value guarantee, the decision to pay interest on the SDR made it, in the words of the German central banker Otmar Emminger, "something like an interest-bearing gold certificate."[184] Interest was to be paid in additional SDRs. Not all SDR holdings drew interest. Rather only holdings in excess of allocations did so. And the payment of interest was financed by a charge on participants holding fewer SDRs than allocated, to the extent of the deficit. Thus, ignoring the costs of Fund administration, the SDR system was a closed one, with SDRs being created costlessly at the time of initial allocation and with net users paying net acquirers.

The question of the appropriate rate of interest for the SDR was at the time and has remained an issue of some consequence. Since the SDR's ratio to gold was fixed (much like gold and silver under the bimetallic standard) and was specified in the not easily changed Articles of Agreement, a potentially serious Gresham's law problem could arise.[185] If the SDR interest rate were too low, gold would be held in reserves and SDRs would be offered in the market (albeit the restricted market afforded by the Articles). On the other hand, the SDR interest rate could, in principle at least, be set so high that monetary authorities would prefer to sell gold from reserves rather than to use their SDRs. And especially during the period of the 1960s when the dollar price of gold still was regarded as inviolate, the Gresham's law problem (or the "composition of reserves problem," as it was often called in this context) was complicated by the de facto fixed ratio between gold (and the

---

182. Rule O-3, as adopted on September 18, 1969, reprinted in de Vries, *IMF 1966–1971* 2:187.
183. Gold, *Special Drawing Rights* (1970), p. 53.
184. Otmar Emminger, "International Monetary Reform," address in Montreal, Canada, 11 September 1967, quoted in Solomon, p. 142.
185. See generally Robert Z. Aliber, "Gresham's Law, Asset Preferences, and the Demand for International Reserves," *Quarterly Journal of Economics* 81(1967):628–38, and the discussion of Gresham's Law, pp. 20–21.

SDR) and the dollar. Thus, the interest rate settled on could determine not merely the future of the SDR but also that of gold and the dollar as reserve assets.

The interest level chosen, 1½ percent (which was also the level of the charge imposed on net use), was relatively low compared to rates available on liquid dollar deposits and short-term securities, the normal form in which foreign exchange was held by monetary authorities. The interest rate on U.S. three-month Treasury bills, for example, averaged 5.3 percent in 1968. On the other hand, gold bore no interest at all. Nor did the gold tranche reserves of members.[186] There does not appear to have been any explicit rationale for the level chosen.[187]

Limitations on Use

In considering the attractiveness of the SDR for monetary authorities and possible Gresham's law problems, one cannot look at valuation and interest rate alone. Equally important were the many limitations on the use of the SDR that were not present for gold and the dollar. Aside from the need requirement, the use of the SDR was limited by the fact that the number of potential holders was strictly limited. The private sector could not then, and still cannot, hold SDRs. Indeed, only participants in the SDR facility and the Fund itself could, under the Articles, hold SDRs. In addition, the Fund by a qualified majority of 85 percent of the total voting party could permit nonmember countries, nonparticipating members, and "institutions that perform functions of a central bank for more than one member" (e.g. the Bank for International Settlements) to hold and use SDRs,[188] but even this list is severely restricted in comparison with gold and foreign exchange.

Not only do these limitations restrict the possible use of SDRs, but among potential holders the types of transactions were severely confined by the provision that, even when SDRs were transferred by agreement rather than designation, they had to be used to obtain an equivalent amount of currency. Although the provision on its face states that a "participant, in agreement with another participant, *may* use its special drawing rights . . . to obtain an equivalent amount of . . . currency,"[189] this provision has been interpreted to mean that no other type of SDR transaction is permitted. J. J. Polak, then the Fund's economic counselor, gave the following examples of forbidden

186. Remuneration was paid on super gold tranche positions. Article V, Section 9, *second*. For U.S. interest rates, see *Economic Report of the President* 1970, table C-55, pp. 242–43.
187. However, some flexibility was gained by the provision for varying the interest rate within narrow limits by a majority vote of the Executive Board. Article XXVI, Section 3, *first*, and Article V, Section 9(a), *first*.
188. Article XXIII, Section 3, *first*. See Rule D-4, adopted on 18 September 1969, reprinted in de Vries, *IMF 1966–1971*, 2:173. See further discussion of the "qualified holders" issue, p. 278, below.
189. Article XXV, Section 2(b)(i) and (ii), *first*. (Emphasis supplied.)

transactions: "A participant cannot give foreign aid to another participant in SDRs, or lend SDRs to it, or pledge its SDRs as security for a loan."[190]

In order to offset to the extent possible the effect on the SDR's utility of these severe restrictions on the number of holders and on permissible types of transactions, the First Amendment draftsmen were at pains to expand the use of SDRs in transactions between participants and the Fund. For example, the Fund was empowered to accept SDRs in repurchases of a member's currency from the Fund[191] and in payment of all charges (which includes the interest component on drawings of currency).[192] Although these powers to use SDRs were intended to enhance the acceptability of the SDR, and although they were exercised by participants (indeed, more than one-half of all charges were paid, and more than one-quarter of all repurchases effected, in SDRs during the 1970–72 period),[193] the exercise of these powers was ambiguous. Since repurchases and payments of charges in SDRs were not subject to the need requirement, there were convenient devices for participants to change the composition of their reserves by lightening their SDR holdings. The artificial character of a reserve asset that was for use only as a reserve asset and not for other purposes could not be easily remedied by these kinds of technical devices.[194]

The SDR as a Credit Instrument

The SDR has been discussed above as a reserve asset, since that was the intention of its proponents, and its reserve asset role (however modest) has come to be accepted over the years. Yet the SDR negotiations were in fact dominated by a dispute over the extent to which the new instrument should be an asset or a credit mechanism. France, and to a lesser extent some other European countries, resisted attempts to eliminate the credit aspect of the SDR. Indeed, France, fearing that the SDR might come to challenge gold as a reserve asset, reserved its position at the final Stockholm negotiating

---

190. Polak, *Reflections*, pp. 6–7. As Joseph Gold has observed, the currency obtained for SDRs could be used for these purposes, *Special Drawing Rights* (1970), p. 29, but of course the need requirement would normally limit any such efforts to use SDRs indirectly to engage in the transactions Polak lists. See discussion of later expansion of permissible transactions, pp. 276–78, below.

191. Repurchases typically occur because a member has previously drawn from the Fund. See discussion pp. 106–8, above. The Articles required the Fund to accept SDRs in compulsory repurchases, Article XXV, Section 7(b)(i), *first*, and authorized it to do so in other repurchases, Article XXV, Section 7(c)(ii), *first*. The Executive Board exercised this authority fully. Decision of 18 December 1969, *IMF Annual Report* 1970, pp. 176–77.

192. Ibid.; and see Article XXV, Section 7(c)(i), *first*, and Article V, Section 8, *first*. SDRs were also used to pay the expenses of the Fund's SDR account, Article XXV, Section 7(g), *first*; and the Fund could use SDRs in various transactions with participants, Article XXV, Section 7(d), (e), and (f), *first*.

193. Habermeier, pp. 29–30.

194. A further Fund-related use, the payment of gold subscriptions in SDRs, was left out of the First Amendment because of French objections. De Vries, *IMF 1966–1971*, 1:173.

meeting even after winning vital concessions, including the right of a member to opt out of the SDR mechanism entirely. France, nevertheless, eventually ratified the First Amendment and thereafter participated in SDR allocations.[195]

A number of concessions were made to the credit view of the SDR. The most important was the name, Special *Drawing* Right, which was chosen to stress the analogy to conventional Fund drawing rights. Other concessions involved the use of a deliberately ambiguous language calculated to gloss over the asset versus credit issue.[196] SDRs were "allocated," not "created" or "drawn" as might be appropriate if they were either purely assets or solely a credit device. They were "used," not sold. And all reference to "assets," or owned "reserves" or the like that had appeared in various preliminary documents was avoided.

This choice of language illustrates the important legal point that in drafting legal documents within a diplomatic context, precision is not always preferred to ambiguity. Indeed, the particular legal challenge, brilliantly discharged by the Fund staff,[197] was to draft a rather precise legal document using bland words like "use" that carried no diplomatic freight from earlier disagreements. Such an approach "enabled the proponents of divergent views to insist that their opinions had prevailed."[198] The Americans were able to point to the absence of any words smacking of credit. But the French finance minister Michel Debré was able to proclaim:

> These rights do not and cannot establish a new currency designed to replace gold. If such were the purport of the agreement, it is quite clear that France would not sign it. The plan provides for the possible extending of credit facilities.[199]

Compromise was made easier, however, by the fact that even those countries, such as the United States, that favored emphasizing the asset character of the SDR thought some safeguards were necessary "against the possibility that a participant would simply pay out the SDR received in allocation, and

195. Ibid. 1:173–76. The French-U.S. dispute is central to any historical analysis of the SDR negotiations. See references in footnote 123, above.
196. See Joseph Gold, *Special Drawing Rights: The Role of Language*, IMF Pamphlet Series no. 15 (1971) (hereafter cited Gold, *SDRs: Role of Language*); and Machlup, *Remaking the International Monetary System*, pp. 9–10. See also the discussion of the abandonment at French insistence of the term "reserve" drawing rights in favor of "special" drawing rights in Solomon, p. 139.
197. De Vries, *IMF 1966–1971*, 1:154.
198. Gold, *SDRs: Role of Language*, p. 2. See discussion in Machlup, *Remaking the International Monetary System*, pp. 8–12.
199. IMF, *Summary Proceedings of the Twenty-Second Annual Meeting of the Board of Governors* (1967), p. 67. This statement was made at the time the outline was completed in September 1967.

then abstain from further transactions."[200] But any requirement that a participant reestablish its SDR position at some specified time after use conveyed an image of credit use and repayment.

In the end the primary focus of the asset-versus-credit issue was what became known as *reconstitution*. This term was consciously chosen to avoid a word like "repayment" or even "repurchase," both of which would have a credit connotation. Yet the larger the proportion of used SDRs that had to be reconstituted, and the more promptly the reconstitution had to occur, the more the credit aspect would be perceived as significant. Indeed, because of the reconstitution rules, Debré was able to say that "rules of repayment," though "generous," nonetheless existed and were "categorical."[201]

In one sense, Debré was wrong. If an SDR had to be repaid to the Fund from which it was allocated, then the SDR would disappear from circulation, and reserves of member countries—one measure of liquidity—would contract. Reconstitution, on the other hand, merely refers to transactions in which prior users reacquire SDRs, which they do either from the Fund (assuming that the Fund holds a sufficient number as a result of prior transactions with participants) or by providing currency convertible in fact to some present holder of SDRs specified by the Fund.[202] Thus, the act of reconstitution in no way reduces reserves held by member countries.[203]

Negotiations of the reconstitution provision raised difficult policy and drafting problems; at one time five different formulas were under consideration.[204] Given the basic decision to state the reconstitution principle in highly specific rules, the final choice was between a harmonization principle advanced by the Italians and a net average use principle favored by the French. The term "harmonization" referred to harmonization in use of various kinds of reserve assets; participants using SDRs would be required from time to time "to reconstitute their outstanding special drawing rights to the extent necessary to restore the reserve position that would have obtained if they had used their special drawing rights in the same proportion as their total reserves."[205] The French concept, which in the end gained precedence, regulated the maximum use of SDRs weighted over time. As finally agreed, the reconstitution provision required a participant, beginning after the participant had received its first allocation, to conduct its SDR transactions so

---

200. U.S. Treasury, "Main Features of Special Drawing Rights Facility," reprinted in *Special Drawing Rights in the International Monetary Fund*, Hearings before the Senate Committee on Foreign Relations, 90th Cong., 2d Sess. (1968), p. 22. See also Gold, *Special Drawing Rights* (1970).
201. IMF, *Summary Proceedings*, p. 68.
202. Schedule G: 1(a)(iv), *first*.
203. This paragraph draws on Machlup, *Remaking the International Monetary System*, pp. 87–88.
204. De Vries, *IMF 1966–1971*, 1:152.
205. Ibid. 1:156.

that "the average of its total daily holdings of special drawing rights over the most recent five-year period will be not less than thirty percent of the average of its daily net cumulative allocation of special drawing rights over the same period."[206]

Although the reconstitution provisions formed a "barnacle" that SDR proponents would later seek to remove in order to enhance the prestige of the SDR as a reserve asset, these provisions were quite modest in their impact.[207] Allocated SDRs did not have to be reconstituted, but rather only those used. And a country that used no more than 70 percent of the SDRs allocated to it could ignore the average net use rule entirely. Moreover, the averaging of use over the entire five-year period, including the portion of the period prior to any use, delayed the bite of the reconstitution provision.[208]

Although the French net average use principle thus triumphed, agreement was reached only by reliance on two interesting legal devices. First, lip service was paid to the Italian harmonization principle by the admonition that participants also "pay due regard to the desirability of pursuing over time a balanced relationship" between their SDR holdings and their other reserve holdings.[209] This language appears purely precatory in view of its extreme generality in contrast to the arithmetic precision of the net use formula.[210] Nevertheless, the technique of giving proponents of the losing position some language, even while extracting substantive teeth from that language, revealed its virtue in resolving the issue and left its traces on the face of the First Amendment.

A second legal device, suggested by the Fund's general counsel,[211] that permitted resolution of the reconstitution dispute was to limit the net average use principle to the first basic period of five years, permitting a change in the reconstitution rules thereafter by Fund decision (that is, without the need for formal amendment of the Articles, with all the complexity and delay that the amendment process would engender).[212]

The Mechanics of SDR Creation

A good deal of time in the drafting of the First Amendment was given to what might seem to an outside observer to be mechanical matters. How would SDRs be issued? And what would happen if a participant dropped

---

206. Schedule G: 1(a)(i), *first*. The French had sought a figure of 50 percent over four years rather than the 30 percent over five years finally agreed. Strange, *International Monetary Relations*, pp. 250–51.

207. See Polak, *Reflections*, pp. 17–19. See discussion p. 279, below.

208. The five-year period was a rolling one, in which the duty to reconstitute arose at the end of each calendar quarter with respect to the preceding five years. Schedule G: 1(a)(i), *first*.

209. Schedule G: 1(b), *first*.

210. Gold, *Special Drawing Rights* (1970), p. 70 ("drafted more as a desideratum").

211. De Vries, *IMF 1966–1971*, 1:158.

212. Article XXV, Section 6(b), *first*.

out of the scheme or if the SDR arrangement should at some distant day be wound up entirely? Two quite separate motivations led to extensive consideration of these issues. One was high policy, notably concern about the degree of world liquidity. The second was a more narrowly legal concern about future contingencies.

The policy question was how to avoid, in a scheme designed to supplement world reserves, introducing entirely too much liquidity. Against the background of the worldwide inflation experienced in the 1970s, avoidance of excessive liquidity appears even more clearly to be a central issue for the future of the international monetary system. But at the time, the issue revolved about a policy difference, perhaps even a political difference, between the United States and major European countries over the U.S. balance of payments. The United States viewed the creation of SDRs as making possible the return to U.S. payments balance without provoking severe difficulties for other countries that would no longer be able to rely on the U.S. deficit as a source of reserves. But to the Europeans, and especially to the French, it was essential that the U.S. deficit cease before SDRs were allocated, lest the SDRs simply add to the flow of liquidity from a continuing U.S. deficit. The timing of the first SDR allocation became as important to the debate as its amount.

From one point of view, strongly supported by certain American economists, the SDRs faced a chicken-and-egg problem. According to this view, which focused on the capital items in the balance-of-payments accounts, the U.S. outflow was generated by the demand of the rest of the world for U.S. dollars, both by the foreign private sector for use in transactions and by foreign official institutions as reserves.[213] At least with respect to the foreign official institutions' demand, the creation of a new source of reserves would reduce the demand for U.S. dollars and thereby reduce the U.S. balance-of-payments deficit.

From a more political point of view, the debate over the conditions determining the timing of the first allocation of SDRs was a contest of strength in which the French under de Gaulle sought to end what they regarded as the special privileges of the United States as a reserve currency country. Appealing to the desire of their European Economic Community partners for unity in the negotiations, the French were able to play a political role in the SDR negotiations far beyond what the financial importance of the franc would suggest.[214]

In the end the French were not successful in making the elimination of the U.S. payments deficit a condition of the activation of the SDR scheme.

213. Emile Despres, Charles P. Kindleberger, and Walter S. Salant, "The Dollar and World Liquidity," *The Economist*, 5 February 1966, pp. 526–29; Robert Z. Aliber, *The International Money Game*, 3d ed. (1979), pp. 37–41.
214. See generally Cohen.

But the procedures were so designed as to give the European Economic Community a veto over the timing and amount of any SDR allocation. After a proposal by the Managing Director and approval of that proposal by the Managing Board, any allocation of SDRs would have to be approved by the Board of Governors by an 85 percent majority of the total voting power of participants.[215] Since the European Economic Community members then had 16.47 percent of the total voting power,[216] they could by voting together effectively block any particular allocation.

These procedural rules were supplemented by substantive criteria to be met in SDR allocation decisions. The Fund was to "seek to meet the long-term global need, as and when it arises, to supplement existing reserve assets in such a manner as will promote the attainment of its purposes and will avoid economic stagnation and deflation as well as excess demand and inflation in the world."[217] The key phrase in this counsel of perfection is "global need." The decision to allocate is not to be made on the basis of liquidity problems of any particular member or class of members. Rather the notion that there exists something known as "global liquidity" that can be both measured and controlled is to be central to the decision whether and how much to allocate.[218]

In the context of the SDR negotiations, the "global need" criterion is best seen as agreement that the rate of SDR creation and rate of the U.S. balance-of-payments deficit should be interdependent. But taking a longer view, especially given the 1978 decision to allocate additional SDRs at a time of historically high and even accelerating inflation, coupled with a large U.S. deficit, the "global need" criterion is revealed to generate a minimum, and certainly no maximum, in global liquidity.[219]

The extensive provisions on termination of participation by a member (Article XXX) and on liquidation of the special drawing account (Article XXXI) had less to do with high policy or political disagreement than with the need to reduce the SDR agreement to tidy language. Here a major role must be accorded to lawyers' natural desire to deal with all contingencies— a proclivity which Keynes in his final Bretton Woods speech had derided:

> I want [a lawyer] to tell me how to do what *I* think sensible, and, above all, to devise means by which it will be lawful for me to go on being sensible in unforeseen conditions some years hence. Too often lawyers busy themselves to make common sense illegal. . . . Not so our

215. Article XXIV, Section 4, *first*. See discussion of procedures in Gold, *Special Drawing Rights* (1970), pp. 19–23.
216. Ibid. p. 22.
217. Article XXIV, Section 1(a), *first*.
218. The "global need" criterion was emphasized by making it a "special consideration" in the first decision to allocate. Article XXIV, Section 1(b), *first*.
219. See discussion pp. 280–81.

lawyers here in Bretton Woods. . . . I have only one complaint against them. . . . I wish that they had not covered so large a part of our birth certificate with such very detailed provisions for our burial service, hymns, and lessons, and all.[220]

Even the Fund's general counsel at the time of the SDR negotiations has wryly noted that the "parturition of the facility was complicated by much concentration on its demise and on the less serious but still melancholy event of the withdrawal of a participant."[221]

Still, it is worth noting that at least the liquidation issue stemmed in part from the decision not to back the SDR. If outstanding SDRs were backed by equal amounts of other claims in the hands of the Fund, then liquidation could simply take the form of exchanging the backing assets against SDRs. But without backing, a default by a participant, either upon its withdrawal or upon liquidation of the facility, would require some system of priority at such time as the SDR system might finally be wound up. Hence the drafting of the First Amendment required the same kind of legal analysis that traditionally marks fields such as commercial and bankruptcy law.

The essence of the solution was to provide for a set-off of accounts between a withdrawing participant and the Fund (with the Fund paying the participant for its holdings of SDRs and the participant paying the Fund an amount equal to its cumulative allocation). In short, the withdrawing participant would have to pay for any net use of SDRs. In the event of liquidation a similar set-off would occur between the Fund and all participants: any shortfall resulting from default by a participant would be handled, under a specified order of redemption, so that the burden of default would be distributed proportionally to each participant's cumulative allocation. The goal was to assure that a participant would not bear a larger share of any default because of its willingness to accept SDRs.[222]

One final mechanical aspect that must be understood to follow the language of the First Amendment and some of the subsequent developments treated in later chapters is that the Fund established two accounts, the General Account and the Special Drawing Account. The General Account was the account in which were conducted the conventional transactions of the Fund—drawings, subscriptions and the like—of the kind that had preceded the First Amendment. The Special Drawing Account, as the name implied, was reserved for SDR transactions. This accounting device, which responded to the decision to lodge SDR creations in the Fund rather than in a new Fund

220. *Proceedings and Documents of the United Nations Monetary and Financial Conference, Bretton Woods, New Hampshire, July 1–22, 1944* (1948), 1:1109–10 (hereafter cited *Bretton Woods Proceedings*).
221. Gold, *Special Drawing Rights* (1970), p. 54.
222. The rules are spelled out in Articles XXX and XXXI and Schedules H and I of the First Amendment and are analyzed and compared with the rules under the original Bretton Woods agreement in Gold, *Special Drawing Rights* (1970), pp. 54–56.

affiliate (by analogy to the affiliates of the World Bank such as the International Development Association), was less simple than might appear. For example, because of the use of SDRs in General Account transactions, such as repurchase of currency and payment of charges, the General Account regularly held a substantial volume of SDRs.[223]

Fund Reform

In agreeing to the Special Drawing Rights amendments, European members successfully insisted on a series of other amendments to the Articles of Agreement. Although it was conventional to refer to these additional amendments under the rubric of Fund "reform" to distinguish them from the SDR amendments, they were in fact relatively minor in substance.[224] Moreover, unlike the 1976 Second Amendment, the so-called reform did not result in any comprehensive redrafting of the Articles. The SDR provisions having been hung onto the end of the Articles, the reform amendments involved merely a limited redrafting of a relatively small number of the original Articles.[225]

Several of the reform amendments were closely related to the SDR amendments. Just as the European Community countries had successfully demanded an effective veto on SDR allocations by requiring an 85 percent majority of the total voting power for Board of Governors approval of a Managing Director allocation proposal,[226] so too the First Amendment required the same special majority for quota enlargements and for certain technical issues in connection with such enlargements.[227] The justification was that both SDR allocations and quota enlargements involved increases in liquidity and therefore should be governed by the same voting principles.[228] The same relation between SDR allocation and other Fund sources of liquidity was the basis for an amendment prohibiting the Fund from developing any new forms of unconditional facilities. Thus, the interpretive techniques used prior to the First Amendment to make gold tranche drawings de facto unconditional would be off limits thereafter.[229]

Other reform amendments were of minor importance. Several merely made de jure that which had been achieved de facto through interpretation.

223. Ibid. pp. 81–83; Habermeier, pp. 26–32; and see generally Polak, *Thoughts on an IMF.*
224. De Vries, *IMF 1966–1971,* 1:253.
225. See "Executive Directors' First Amendment Report," annex A, in de Vries, *IMF 1966–1971,* 2:74–94 for the text of the changes to the Articles. On the style of amendment, see Gold, *Selected Essays,* pp. 128–47.
226. See discussion p. 166.
227. Article III, Sections 2 and 4(c), *first.* See de Vries, *IMF 1966–1971,* 1:254–55.
228. Joseph Gold, *Voting and Decisions in the International Monetary Fund* (1972), pp. 132–37, 141–47.
229. See discussion of the interpretation regarding the gold tranche, pp. 118–19, above. On the First Amendment's exclusion of such techniques, see Gold, *Reform,* pp. 30–32, and Gold, *Conditionality,* pp. 9–10.

The unconditionality on gold tranche drawings and the authorization of conditionality policies for credit tranche drawings have already been mentioned.[230] And a number of other changes dealt with various technical questions involving charges, repurchase, and the like.[231]

One amendment of some theoretical legal interest provided for appeals: decisions of the Executive Board formally interpreting the Articles could be appealed to a Committee on Interpretation of the Board of Governors.[232] But since Fund interpretations are rare and there have been no appeals, the committee has not been established. A Fund internal judicial system remains, at best, a possible institutional development for the future.

III. JURISDICTION

The legal concept of jurisdiction provides one perspective on the role of the Fund under the Bretton Woods system. Just as the permissible reach of a court's or a legislature's authority can be thought of as its jurisdiction, so the power of the Fund to impose its will and to shape events depends upon international understandings as to the scope of the Fund's jurisdiction. The Fund's incapacity to interfere with economic policies of a member country (other than through conditionality policies)[233] rests on a variety of legal concepts and explicit provisions in the Articles, notably the concept of national sovereignty and the concomitant principle that the Fund's powers include only those expressly granted by the Articles plus those that may reasonably be implied from the express powers.[234]

Another kind of jurisdictional question has not so much to do with the jurisdiction of the Fund vis-à-vis national governments as with its jurisdiction at the international organization level. What is the jurisdiction of the Fund compared to that of other international monetary bodies such as the Bank for International Settlements and the Group of Ten? The limitations on Fund jurisdiction stemming from the existence of these other organizations derive not from strictly legal considerations but rather from the understandings and presuppositions that grew up in the postwar period. The present role of competing organizations stems as much from the accidents of history as from any clearly defined concepts defining the roles of the competing organizations.[235] What is significant is that against the theme, often detectable in discussions concerning the Fund, that the Fund was not merely a universal

230. See pp. 118–22, above; Gold, *Conditionality*, pp. 8–9.
231. See generally Gold, *Reform*.
232. Article XVIII(b), *first*. See Gold, *Interpretation by the Fund*, pp. 64–68.
233. See discussion pp. 120–27.
234. See discussion of inherent and implied powers of international organizations in *Legal Advisers and International Organizations*, ed. H. C. L. Merillat (1966), pp. 14–17.
235. See e.g. Erin E. Jacobsson, *A Life for Sound Money: Per Jacobsson, His Biography* (1979), pp. 189–204.

organization but also the exclusive international monetary organization, runs another historical theme: namely, that other organizations have played an important role in the development of the international monetary system.

Bank for International Settlements

At the Bretton Woods conference a resolution was passed calling for liquidation of the BIS "at the earliest possible moment."[236] In large measure this resolution was motivated by charges of BIS collaboration with Nazi Germany. The notion that there would be little role for the BIS once the Fund came into existence also played a role, especially because it was assumed that the transfer of power from central banks to national treasuries that had begun in the interwar period had now been completed.[237] But central banks, which owned the BIS and therefore would have had to take the necessary action to liquidate it, preferred to see it continue, especially because they valued the opportunities provided by their regular monthly meetings in Basle.[238] Moreover, the legal incapacity of the German central bank, a BIS shareholder, to take the steps necessary to its liquidation during the occupation period immediately following the war, helped to keep the BIS alive.[239]

The BIS was essentially a European institution. The only non-European participant, the United States, had participated on a limited basis prior to World War II, and the U.S. Treasury was especially hostile to the BIS at the end of the war.[240] In view of this purely European sponsorship, the BIS did not appear to present a challenge to the Fund as the principal universal monetary organization.

Although nearly all major currencies, other than the U.S. dollar, were inconvertible after World War II and most trade therefore had to be carried on under bilateral trade and payment agreements, the initiative toward multilateralization of payments was first taken in Europe on a regional basis without any leadership from the Fund.[241] The European regional approach was stimulated by the American insistence that Europeans should organize themselves to plan the efficient use of Marshall Plan funds. And the Fund gave emphasis to this development by deciding in 1948 that countries obtaining dollar aid from the U.S. European Recovery Program "should request

236. *Bretton Woods Proceedings*, 1:939.
237. Henry H. Schloss, *The Bank for International Settlements* (1958), pp. 118–20. On the central banks and treasuries in the interwar period, see pp. 53–54, above.
238. Schloss, pp. 91–92, 121; Jacobsson, pp. 191–92.
239. G. Guindey, *Mythes et réalités de la crise monétaire internationale* (1973), p. 25.
240. Roger Auboin, *The Bank for International Settlements, 1930–1955*, Princeton Essays in International Finance no. 22 (1955), p. 17; Schloss, p. 120; Jacobsson, pp. 186–87.
241. A similar pattern developed on the trade side with a regional attack being launched in Europe on existing quantitative trade restrictions without assistance from the embryo General Agreement on Tariffs and Trade. See Kenneth W. Dam, *The GATT: Law and International Economic Organization* (1970), pp. 157–61.

the purchase of United States dollars from the Fund only in exceptional or unforeseen cases."[242]

The Fund's isolation from these regional monetary developments was increased when the BIS rather than the Fund became the agent for carrying out the functions of clearing agent under the first intra-European payments agreements. Although the first draft of the first of these payments agreements had provided that the Fund would be the clearing agent, the Fund was unaccountably not represented at the crucial Paris meeting in October 1947. The offer of the BIS, which was represented, to undertake the clearing agent function was accepted.[243]

As the original annual intra-European payments agreements—which were essentialy a network of bilateral payments agreements—evolved into a multilateral clearing system in 1950 under the European Payments Union (EPU), the role of the BIS in European monetary matters had become well established.[244] In addition, the creation of the Organization for European Economic Cooperation, which was the umbrella organization for the EPU, was the first step toward European integration; hence European economic integration was seen from the outset as having an important monetary dimension. The success of the EPU in leading to general external convertibility of many European currencies in 1958 created the basis for the three interrelated beliefs that were to influence international monetary developments in the 1960s and 1970s: first, progress in the monetary sphere required close cooperation among the major developed countries and could not be left to a universal organization with many less-developed country members, such as the IMF; second, one major instrument for that cooperation would be the BIS not only because of its restricted membership but also because of the confidentiality of its methods; and third, in addition to cooperation among the major developed countries, there was room for more formal organization along purely European lines.[245]

The 1960s saw a great development in the role of international monetary institutions other than the Fund. By 1969 it was possible for the Fund's general counsel to include in the official Fund history a section entitled "The

242. *IMF Annual Report* 1948, p. 74
243. On the "accidental" absence of the Fund from the Paris meeting, see Horsefield, *IMF 1945–1965*, 1:212–15, and Margaret G. de Vries, "The Fund and the EPU," in ibid. 2:323–24.
244. On the intra-European payments arrangements, including the EPU, see ibid. 2:317–31; Peter Coffey and John R. Presley, *European Monetary Integration* (1971), pp. 13–23; William Diebold, Jr., *Trade and Payments in Western Europe* (1952), pp. 3–149, 409–15; Raymond F. Mikesell, *Foreign Exchange in the Postwar World* (1954), pp. 100–135; Raymond F. Mikesell, *The Emerging Pattern of International Payments*, Princeton Essays in International Finance no. 18 (1954); Robert Triffin, *Europe and the Money Muddle: From Bilateralism to Near-Convertibility, 1947–1956* (1957), pp. 161–208; Yeager, pp. 407–40; and the Annual Reports of the Bank for International Settlements beginning with the *18th Annual Report* (1948).
245. See discussion of the European Monetary System, pp. 328–36.

Organization in the World," in which the place of the Fund as the "central but not the sole monetary institution" was analyzed.[246]

The major developments of the 1960s in this non-Fund institutional growth have already been mentioned. The negotiation of the General Arrangements to Borrow gave rise to the Group of Ten.[247] The weakness of the dollar at the outset of the 1960s led to swap arrangements, which were negotiated through the BIS.[248] Multilateral rescues of weak currencies in the 1960s gave the BIS a broader and renewed mission, its more technical clearing agent functions under the EPU having evaporated with the movement to external convertibility of the major European currencies. No longer would the BIS be seen, in the words of Susan Strange, as "a piece of historical detritus that happened to be of continuing professional and social convenience to central bankers, and which had been fortuitously protected from total decay and desuetude by its financial independence as an operating bank."[249] And the Gold Pool was an informal offshoot of the BIS.[250]

Group of Ten

Despite its expanding functions, the BIS remained essentially a central bankers' club. Its importance was bound to depend on the role of central banks in exchange and gold market intervention. Since responsibility for the planning of major changes in the international monetary system would inevitably be in the hands of treasuries within national governments, the Group of Ten, which was deemed more appropriate than the BIS as a meeting place for treasury officials, was to prove also more important. And it was the liquidity discussions leading to the SDR that lifted the Group of Ten from a journalistic phrase to a formal organization, albeit one without an international secretariat.

The Group of Ten, meeting usually at the deputies level, discussed various proposals for the reform of the system, one of which involved a new asset (the Collective Reserve Unit or "CRU") that would have been created by agreement among the Group of Ten countries rather than within the Fund.[251] But the Ten could not agree upon the CRU. In the end, political pressure from less developed countries and the efforts of the Fund Managing Director led to at least tacit agreement that any new reserve asset would be not only created within the Fund but allocated to all its members.[252] Nonetheless, the

---

246. Joseph Gold, "Constitutional Development," p. 518.
247. See discussion p. 149.
248. See discussion p. 150.
249. Strange, *International Monetary Relations*, p. 37.
250. See discussion p. 137.
251. *Statement by Ministers of the Group of Ten and Annex prepared by their Deputies*, (1964), Annex paras. 38–42, p. 12. See discussion in J. Dewey Daane, "The Evolving International Monetary Mechanism: The Report of the Group of Ten," *American Economic Review* 55(1965):150, 154–56.
252. De Vries, *IMF 1966–1971*, 1:82–96.

Group of Ten continued to provide a principal forum for liquidity discussions, and a report of the G-10 Study Group, the Ossola report, was a crucial document in the development of the SDR concept.[253] The G-10 deputies began to meet jointly with the Fund's Executive Directors.[254] The Group of Ten came to look more like a forum for reaching decisions on its members' policy positions on Fund issues than a separate organization.[255]

The process by which the SDR was agreed upon thus led to the conception of the Group of Ten as a caucus on Fund matters. The practice of G-10 ministers of meeting on the eve of the IMF annual meeting confirmed this view. The reputation of the Group of Ten as a privileged group of already advantaged countries operating in some loose sense within the Fund itself gave rise in the early 1970s to an offsetting caucus of less developed countries, the Group of Twenty-Four.[256] The Fund's then Managing Director Pierre-Paul Schweitzer described the origin of the Group of Twenty-Four, including his own role, after he left the Fund:

> A considerable amount of bad will was created amongst those outside the Group of Ten who then formed (I must say with my wholehearted support) a competing group, called the Group of Twenty-Four, which was an emanation of the so-called Seventy-Seven (who are, as you know, more than one hundred!). They were twenty-four because three continents were represented by eight members each. They became very active and they took their job very, very seriously. They created a special degree of cooperation between the nine Executive Directors who represent the developing countries, with the final result that in the Fund there is now much more unanimity of views between these nine Directors than amongst those who represent the Group of Ten, including the Common Market![257]

The Group of Ten thus came to be seen as a developed-country caucus. So long as it met, however, its existence evoked still another model for the organization of international monetary affairs that was competitive with the model of the Fund as an intergovernmental organ. Like the BIS, the Group of Ten was a forum for meetings of leading national monetary officials. Though the memberships of both the BIS and the Group of Ten were somewhat large, they together provided the framework for a key currency approach to international monetary affairs. Though the Williams key currency approach had not commended itself to the Roosevelt administration

---

253. Group of Ten, *Report of the Study Group on the Creation of Reserve Assets*. Report to the Deputies of the Group of Ten (1 August 1965).
254. De Vries, *IMF 1966–1971*, 1:104–6; Cohen, pp. 113–18.
255. The chronology set forth in de Vries, *IMF 1966–1971*, 1:190–205, is a helpful guide to the various meetings and reports leading to the First Amendment.
256. Gold, *Selected Essays*, p. 17.
257. Pierre-Paul Schweitzer, "Political Aspects of Managing the International Monetary System," *International Affairs* 52(1976):216.

postwar planners,[258] it was logically an alternative to a large-scale international organization with a professional and largely independent civil service. Consequently, the continued existence of the Group of Ten provided the possibility for an alternative institutional approach to some of the key issues of international monetary policy.

258. See discussion p. 73.

SIX

The Collapse of Bretton Woods and Its Legal Aftermath

Not all of the principal characteristics of the Bretton Woods system could have been deduced from the Bretton Woods agreement. Although the Articles of Agreement called for an adjustable pegged exchange-rate system, the attitudes toward the conditions under which the peg would be adjusted and the mechanism for adjustment varied through the Bretton Woods period. The fact that the Bretton Woods system would be a gold exchange standard with two principal reserve currencies, sterling and the dollar, could hardly have been divined from the text. Even the dollar's central role was only dimly visible in the seemingly precise language.

Far from determining the shape of the Bretton Woods system, the Articles of Agreement simply reflected the end-of-war understanding of the probable shape of that system. To be sure, the Articles established a financial institution and set forth some regulatory goals—principally, pegged exchange rates and the absence of exchange controls on current transactions. To a large extent those goals were achieved, certainly among developed countries, not least because of the eventual success of the Fund as a balance-of-payments financing institution. But the Bretton Woods system did not survive. In 1971, just a few years after the creation of the SDR, the system collapsed. By 1973 a new system based on floating rates took its place.

I. Steps in the Decline of the Bretton Woods System

Although this book is not the place for a comprehensive analysis, it is nevertheless important, particularly for an understanding of the legal and institutional changes that accompanied the transition to the post-1973 system, to trace the decline of the Bretton Woods system. The key developments involved precisely those aspects of the system that were not reduced to legal language in the Articles—the manner in which the adjustable peg feature would operate and the role of reserve currencies.

Adjusting the Peg

If the requirement of a "fundamental disequilibrium" as a condition precedent to a change in par value had any meaning at all,[1] it surely was to limit the number of such changes. Yet the problem turned out to be that there were too few, not too many, peg adjustments. After major devaluations of many currencies in the wake of the 30 percent devaluation of sterling in September 1949, there were few parity changes in the developed world until the 1967 devaluation of sterling. The principal exceptions were the devaluation of the French franc in 1957–58 and the relatively small 5 percent revaluations of the German mark and the Dutch guilder in 1961.[2] And it is generally conceded today that the 1967 sterling devaluation was far too long delayed, both for the British economy and for the smooth working of the international monetary system.[3]

Even after 1967 there were few exchange rate changes. President de Gaulle vetoed a 1968 devaluation of the French franc that his government not only favored but had actually negotiated with other major countries.[4] The effect

1. See discussion at pp. 90–92.
2. J. Keith Horsefield, *The International Monetary Fund, 1945–1965* (1969) 2:96–111; *BIS 28th Report* 1958, pp. 174–75; *BIS 29th Report* 1959, pp. 184–85; *BIS 31st Report* 1961, pp. 146–47.
3. See e.g. Charles A. Coombs, *The Arena of International Finance* (1976), pp. 150–51. See also Samuel Brittan, *Steering the Economy* (1971 ed.), pp. 363–66, 446–47; Harry G. Johnson, "The Sterling Crisis of 1967 and the Gold Rush of 1968," *Nebraska Journal of Economics and Business* 7(Autumn 1968):13–15.
4. Andreas F. Lowenfeld, *The International Monetary System* (1977), pp. 115–22; Gerald M. Meier, *Problems of a World Monetary Order* (1974), pp. 62–71.

was to postpone the devaluation until August the following year. The German mark was reluctantly and belatedly revalued later in 1969.[5]

One of the principal effects of these delays in parity changes was a great increase in private capital flows. As the need for parity changes grew, private capital would flow from weak currencies to strong currencies, thereby increasing the pressure for parity adjustments. But these capital flows were considered to be "disequilibrating" by national monetary authorities, who responded in many cases by new forms of capital controls, and, in some cases, by new controls on trade flows to attempt to stave off devaluation.[6] Although the Articles permitted capital controls, and trade restrictions were governed by the General Agreement on Tariffs and Trade, the resulting proliferation of controls on international economic activity could hardly be regarded as in the direction of the multilateral freedom of trade and payments that had become one of the principal goals of postwar international economic organization.

In addition to the hesitancy to undertake needed par value adjustments, the Bretton Woods period was marked by a pronounced preference for devaluations by weak currencies over revaluations by strong currencies. This is seen perhaps somewhat less clearly in the developed world, where one can point to the 1961 revaluation of the mark, than in the less developed world where devaluations were widespread and revaluations unknown.[7] Surplus countries viewed exchange rate adjustments as the duty of deficit countries and undertook revaluations only with the greatest reluctance. This attitude fit the received view from the interwar period that departures from existing par values were the fault of the devaluing countries. Indeed, the root theory of the Fund as a balance-of-payments financing institution was generally interpreted as implying that all exchange market support for existing currencies would be undertaken by the deficit country through purchase of its own currency and a corresponding sale of international reserves. Domestic economic policy adjustments necessary to avoid exchange rate crises were also viewed as primarily the obligation of the deficit countries.

The manner by which the peg was adjusted changed late in the Bretton Woods period. Although Canada had floated its currency from 1950 to 1962,[8] most exchange rate changes were made by discrete changes in par values

5. On the French and German devaluations, see Margaret Garritsen de Vries, *The International Monetary Fund 1966–1971* (1976), 1:449–64.
6. Ibid. 1:496–500; Andrew Crockett, *International Money: Issues and Analysis* (1977), pp. 154, 159–62. On the various types of restrictions actually imposed, see the Fund's *Annual Report on Exchange Restrictions* for the relevant years.
7. IMF Executive Directors, *The Role of Exchange Rates in the Adjustment of International Payments* (1970), chap. 3(d), pp. 37–39, reprinted in de Vries, *IMF 1966–1971*, 2:273–330.
8. See discussion pp. 129–30. In 1948 France had maintained a floating rate as part of a multiple exchange rate system. See discussion pp. 131–32.

until 1969, when Germany's first step in the revaluation of the mark was to allow it to float outside the margins around the existing par value. The floating period lasted only a month and was followed by the declaration of a new par value, which reflected a 9.29 percent revaluation.[9] In 1970, Canada again permitted its dollar to float but with the stated intention to return to maintenance of market rates within the margins around a par value (which might be a new par value), though without any indication of when that might occur.[10] And in May 1971, Germany and the Netherlands notified the Fund that they were ceasing to intervene to maintain exchange rate margins, with a declaration of an intention to return to the Bretton Woods par-value rule similar to that of Canada.[11] None of the three countries had abandoned floating when, in August 1971, the United States removed the cornerstone of the Bretton Woods system by floating the dollar. These moves by Canada, Germany and the Netherlands nevertheless had given new respectability to the idea of floating rates as a desirable measure, at least in arriving at a new par value under a pegged rate system.

The Gold Exchange Standard

The analysis of the interwar period in chapter 3 suggests that the undue emphasis placed on the shortcomings of floating rates tended to obscure, in the understanding of the generation of officials who planned the Bretton Woods system, the peculiar weaknesses of a gold exchange standard.[12] Yet it was such a standard that the Bretton Woods agreement created, however much the text of that agreement may have obscured this fundamental fact.

Under a gold exchange standard several questions must be answered, at least implicitly by the actions of the principal countries. First, what currencies will be held by other countries as reserves? The answer at the end of World War II was that two currencies, sterling and the dollar, would perform that function.

Second, what would be the convertibility obligations of the reserve currency countries? Here the answer was that neither currency would be officially convertible by private holders into other assets, such as gold. Indeed, foreign exchange and gold transactions by private parties in Britain would be for many years the subject of elaborate exchange controls.[13] But monetary authorities would be able to convert their currency holdings into other reserve assets by demand on the national monetary authorities in Britain as well as

9. De Vries, *IMF 1966–1971*, 1:458–62.
10. Ibid. 1:476–82; A. F. W. Plumptre, *Three Decades of Decision: Canada and the World Monetary System, 1944–75* (1977), pp. 219–22.
11. De Vries *IMF 1966–1971*, 1:522–24.
12. See discussion pp. 64–69.
13. "The U.K. exchange control: a short history," *Bank of England Quarterly Bulletin* 7(1967):251–60.

the United States. In the case of sterling, the conditions for such demands were not often tested because of the practice of selling sterling in the exchange markets rather than presenting it directly to the Bank of England. But in the case of the United States, the commitment to sell gold at $35 per ounce to foreign official institutions was not only an available convertibility mechanism but an essential element of the Bretton Woods system in the sense that with its removal the system collapsed.

A third question, and even more fundamental though the answer is more elusive, is how a reserve currency country keeps its currency sufficiently scarce that other countries choose to continue holding it. If official holders of a reserve currency lose confidence in it, then they may seek alternative holdings. The two principal options are, first, another reserve currency and, second, gold. Resort to both options had undermined sterling in the late 1920s and early 1930s and had destroyed the interwar gold exchange standard.[14]

The elusiveness of the answer to this third question lies in the lack of consensus among any of the three key domestic groups whose interaction results in the economic policies of the moment—politicians, officials, and economists. A necessary, though perhaps over the long run not a sufficient, condition of the requisite confidence in a reserve currency is that the domestic economy of the reserve currency country be stable. But the conditions of such stability, and even the definition of such stability (e.g., the relative importance of price stability versus growth) are the very heart of domestic politics in the reserve currency countries. And disagreements over the role of fiscal, monetary, incomes, regulatory, and other economic policies are pervasive and probably unresolvable simply by reasoned analysis and research because they are so deeply rooted in domestic political struggles. This is not the place to discuss these underlying questions of economics and economic policymaking, but in tracing the decline of the two Bretton Woods reserve currencies, occasional references to domestic economic policies in Britain and the United States will be necessary.[15]

Sterling as a Reserve Currency

Understanding of the postwar role of sterling as a reserve currency requires some grasp of the significance of the sterling area. Sterling was not a world-wide reserve currency but rather a reserve currency for a set of countries, mostly Commonwealth members and former British colonies, that held sterling as reserves but that in most cases came to hold dollars as well. Outside the sterling area, countries held dollars but seldom held sterling. Thus, even

---

14. See discussion pp. 64–69.
15. On economic policymaking in practice, see George P. Shultz and Kenneth W. Dam, *Economic Policy Beyond the Headlines* (1977).

from the beginning of the postwar period, sterling can be considered a regional reserve currency in contrast to the dollar. The region was, of course, defined more by history than geography, and sterling area countries were widely dispersed.

sterling area (margin note)

The sterling area dates back to the 1931 departure of Britain from the gold standard. At that time a number of countries devalued with Britain. Those countries became known as the sterling area to differentiate them from the Continental countries, known as the gold bloc, that did not devalue but rather remained on the gold standard.[16] The sterling area countries thereafter pegged their exchange rates on sterling and maintained their reserves in sterling. Outside this area, sterling was no longer held as reserves in significant quantities even by those countries that chose to peg their exchange rates on sterling.[17]

In typically British fashion the sterling area was simply a name given to a set of voluntary practices. But it took on legal significance in 1939. With the advent of World War II, Britain adopted an elaborate exchange control system that differentiated sharply between sterling area and other countries. The central concept was a "ring fence surrounding the sterling area as a whole, within which payments were free."[18] Within the sterling area, which had now shed most of its non-Commonwealth members, all members abandoned their own exchange controls in favor of a common set of controls administered from London. Members kept their reserves in sterling and in the form of claims on London institutions; transfers could then be made freely in London both between Britain and any member as well as between any two members of the sterling area.[19] Payments outside the sterling area, on the other hand, were subject to rigorous exchange control, and to the extent permitted, were made from London.[20]

Regional Cooperation (margin note)

The purpose of the sterling area exchange control system was to marshal the resources of the Commonwealth for the war, but the system continued in place long after the war.[21] In large part, the extension of the exchange controls was required by the vast wartime growth of British liabilities to members of the sterling area. In comparison to total external liabilities, in sterling and foreign currencies, of £542 million prior to the war, sterling

16. BIS, *The Sterling Area* (1953), pp. 13–16. See also discussion p. 75, above.
17. Benjamin J. Cohen, *The Future of Sterling as an International Currency* (1971), pp. 69–70.
18. Fred Hirsch, *Money International*, rev. ed. (1969), p. 484.
19. For convenience of exposition the term "sterling area member" is used here to refer to members of the sterling area other than Britain. Other formulations frequently used include "RSA" (Rest of Sterling Area), "Overseas Sterling Area members" and in the exchange control legislation, "Scheduled Territories."
20. Bank of England, "Sterling as an International Currency," *Committee on the Working of the Monetary System: Principal Memoranda of Evidence* (1960), vol. 1, part 1, Memorandum no. 7, paras. 9–10, p. 16 (hereafter cited Radcliffe Committee Memoranda).
21. "U.K. exchange control," p. 245 and passim.

liabilities reached £3,688 million by the end of 1945, of which £2,454 million involved sterling holdings by sterling area members.[22] These "sterling balances," which included a wide variety of relatively short-term official liabilities, not including liabilities of private institutions located in Britain, far exceeded British gold and foreign exchange reserves. Whereas British gold and dollar reserves before World War II slightly exceeded liabilities ($2.9 billion to $2.8 billion in 1938), sterling liabilities now far exceeded reserves ($15.7 billion to $2.2 billion in 1947).[23] In short, Britain emerged from the war with a deficit in its *net* international reserves.

The original White plan had proposed that sterling balances be absorbed by the Fund.[24] No solution was reached in the Bretton Woods agreement, but drastic reduction of the sterling balances remained a major U.S. concern in negotiation of the Anglo-American Financial Agreement in late 1945. The U.S. motive was that if its Lend-Lease claims on Britain were to be forgiven as part of a general postwar economic settlement, the sterling area suppliers of wartime Britain should share in the loss. The British, following an official policy (sharply criticized by Keynes) of what Moggridge has called "defensive drift," resisted the American proposals.[25]

With the continued exchange control arrangements after the war, the sterling area operated as a zone of systematic discrimination against the U.S. dollar. The effect of the system was to limit transactions that might require payments in dollars in order to protect the British reserve position and, with it, freedom of payments within the sterling area.[26]

22. *Reserves and Liabilities 1931 to 1945*, Cmd. 8354 (1951), tables 3 and 4, pp. 5–6. The postwar figures represent the sterling area as defined 31 December 1950, when some non-Commonwealth countries had already ceased to be members. The Bank of England estimated sterling balances of all countries then members of the sterling area as £3 billion out of a sterling total of £3.7 billion in 1945. Radcliffe Committee Memoranda, p. 16.
23. Robert Triffin, *Gold and the Dollar Crisis*, rev. ed. (1961), p. 61, table 13. See *Reserves and Liabilities*, pp. 3–6 for estimates in pounds sterling. See also R. S. Sayers, *Financial Policy 1939–45* (1956), pp. 438–40, and appendix 1, pp. 496–503.
24. Horsefield, *IMF 1945–1965*, 3:54–60; D. E. Moggridge, "From War to Peace—The Sterling Balances," *The Banker* 122(1972):1034.
25. Ibid. pp. 1034–35. For British policies and for the development of Keynes's views, from support of the early White proposal to advocacy of temporary postwar blocking of "all wartime sterling balances" to a program combining funding, cancellation, and "limited, phased release," see ibid. p. 1034, and D. E. Moggridge, "From War to Peace—How Much Overseas Assistance?" *The Banker* 122(1972):1165–67, and "New Light on Post-war Plans," *The Banker* 122(1972):341–42. See also Richard N. Gardner, *Sterling-Dollar Diplomacy* (1969), pp. 204–6, 234; *Selected Papers of Will Clayton*, ed. Fredrick J. Dobney (1971), pp. 146–51, 158. For the British view, see Sayers, *Financial Policy* chap. 14, "The Shadow of Debt, 1944–45. I: The Defence of Sterling," pp. 438–64, and pp. 474–75, 483–86. For a creditor view of cancellation of sterling balances, see the case of Egypt, in Judd Polk, *Sterling: Its Meaning in World Finance* (1956), pp. 66–69.
26. Radcliffe Committee Memoranda, p. 113; Cohen, *Future of Sterling*, pp. 79–84; Gardner Patterson, *Discrimination in International Trade: The Policy Issues 1945–1965* (1966), pp. 67–75.

The difficulties of a reserve center with a deficit in net reserves were compounded by a steady loss in the importance of sterling compared to dollars and other currencies. Sterling had been preeminent as a transactions currency before the First World War. At that time, according to one estimate, well over 60 percent of world trade involved contracts denominated and settled in sterling.[27] At the end of World War II this figure was still about 50 percent.[28] Thereafter, the decline of sterling accelerated, and by 1967 sterling was the currency for at most about 30 percent, and perhaps considerably less, of world transactions.[29] Moreover, sterling gradually lost its importance as an intervention currency as more countries switched from pegging their exchange rates on the pound to pegging on the dollar. With the 1949 devaluation of the pound, many of the non-Commonwealth countries that in the 1930s had pegged on the pound also elected to devalue, usually by the same percentage as sterling, but not even all sterling area countries followed sterling's 1967 devaluation.[30]

The attempt to defend sterling's reserve role, it was believed, required Britain to avoid devaluation by all economic policy means available. British economic policy was dominated during the pre-1967 decade by the tug-of-war between policies aimed at increasing growth and policies aimed at defending sterling, with first one set of policies and then the other gaining ground.[31] Controls on international trade and payments were retained and strengthened, even after the movement to external convertibility in 1958, in an effort to shore up the British reserve position.[32]

The 1967 devaluation coincided with an increase in the rate of diversification out of sterling by official holders.[33] Sterling had long been falling as a percentage of world foreign exchange reserves. Whereas official holdings of sterling had exceeded those of dollars by $14.9 billion to $6.9 billion in 1945, dollar holdings had come to exceed sterling holdings by 1952 and the gap between dollar and sterling holdings thereafter grew steadily.[34] Although

27. David Williams, "The Evolution of the Sterling System," in *Essays in Money and Banking in Honour of R. S. Sayers*, ed. C. R. Whittlesey and J. S. G. Wilson (1968), p. 268.
28. Ibid. p. 294; W. M. Clarke, *The City in the World Economy* (1965), p. 211.
29. See discussion in Cohen, *Future of Sterling*, pp. 70–76. See also "Financing World Trade" in "British Banking 1966: A Survey by The Economist," *The Economist*, 18 June 1966, pp. x–xiv.
30. Cohen, *Future of Sterling*, pp. 74–75, 191–95.
31. See generally Brittan; Leland B. Yeager, *International Monetary Relations: Theory, History and Policy*, 2d ed. (1976), pp. 450–59.
32. One of the principal measures was an import surcharge of 15 percent imposed on imports in 1964, reduced to 10 percent in 1965 and finally lifted late in 1966. *BIS 36th Report 1966*, p. 95; *BIS 37th Report 1967*, p. 93; Cohen, *Future of Sterling*, pp. 176–77. Controls on various kinds of payments by British residents were continued. IMF, *Eighteenth Annual Report on Exchange Restrictions* (1967), pp. 662–65.
33. On diversification out of sterling, see Cohen, *Future of Sterling*, pp. 76–78.
34. Robert Triffin, *Europe and the Money Muddle* (1957), p. 270, table 22.

holdings of sterling by members of the sterling area nevertheless grew temporarily in absolute terms, that growth stopped in the mid-1950s and in the mid-1960s it began to decline slowly. This decline was masked for a time by an increase in the holdings by other countries, largely as a part of efforts by developed countries outside the sterling area to support sterling.[35]

Even more ominous than the modest decline in sterling area holdings of sterling was the rapid growth, beginning in the early 1960s, in sterling area holdings of gold and dollars in reserves.[36] This process of investing incremental reserves in gold and dollar assets rather than in sterling heralded the end of sterling's role as a major reserve currency. But it was the absolute decline in sterling balances beginning in the mid-1960s that produced the most immediate problems for the international monetary system because Britain did not have sufficient gold and dollar reserves to meet a substantial and sustained decline in those balances. In 1966, British reserves ran about £2 billion, but external liabilities of the British government, including local authorities, were about £7 billion.[37] Under these circumstances, the process of sterling balance liquidation could have become increasingly rapid as holders of sterling came to fear imminent devaluation.

The 1966 Basle agreement, a response to this problem, was a multilateral effort to finance what was then regarded as a temporary fluctuation in the level of sterling balances. The principal countries associated with the Bank for International Settlements agreed to make swap facilities available to the Bank of England on the condition that they would not be available to finance British payments deficits.[38] Thus, the purpose was to offset fluctuations, not to provide a means of financing permanent reduction in sterling balances.

The 1967 devaluation, however, accelerated the liquidation of sterling balances by sterling area countries. In the second quarter of 1968, holdings of sterling by official institutions in the sterling area fell by £230 million.[39] To deal with what appeared to be possibly the beginning of a run on sterling in spite of a large IMF drawing, a new Basle facility was established.[40]

This time, however, the Basle arrangements were not limited to the provision of financing by the twelve developed countries taking part. Rather, the financing was accompanied by a series of formal bilateral agreements

---

35. Cohen, *Future of Sterling*, pp. 92–93, table 5.3. See also graph in Hirsch, *Money International*, p. 495.
36. Susan Strange, *Sterling and British Policy* (1971), pp. 76–77, charts 3.A and 3.B.
37. Ibid. p. 264, chart 8.A. Short-term liabilities of the central government to official holders were lower but still in excess of reserves. Ibid. p. 261, table 8.I. See also Cohen, *Future of Sterling*, pp. 92–93, table 5.3.
38. H.M. Treasury, *The Basle Facility and the Sterling Area*, Cmnd. 3787 (1968), p. 3; *BIS 37th Report* 1967, p. 170.
39. H.M. Treasury, *The Basle Facility*, p. 4.
40. Strange, *Sterling and British Policy*, pp. 74–75, 86–87; *BIS 39th Report* 1969, pp. 115–18; Milton Gilbert, *Quest for World Monetary Order* (1980), p. 71.

between Britain and each sterling area member. The commitments in these agreements limiting each member's ability to diversify out of sterling may be regarded as a conversion of short-term sterling holdings into long-term holdings. In short, the 1968 Basle agreements were a form of funding of sterling liabilities. They were also designed to prevent diversification out of sterling that took the form of investing incremental reserves in gold and dollars.

The sterling area countries guaranteed to maintain an agreed minimum proportion of their reserves in sterling. This proportion differed from member to member, reflecting their sterling holdings at the time of the agreement. The British government in turn agreed to guarantee the U.S. dollar value of the agreed holdings of sterling in excess of 10 percent of the member's total reserves. Thus, 10 percent of the member's reserves would remain unguaranteed sterling, while 90 percent of their reserves would be in the form of guaranteed sterling, nonsterling currencies, or gold.[41] The effect of the exchange guarantee was thus to put the sterling area members roughly in the same position, so far as the principal value of the guaranteed proportion was concerned, as if they had switched from sterling to dollars. As sterling's dollar value fell, the amount of sterling owed would rise.

The exchange guarantee and minimum sterling proportion commitments were mostly for three years with provision for a two-year extension by agreement, though some were for five years.[42] These commitments thus lapsed in 1973, at the end of the five years. Yet even before 1973 an important feature of the sterling area, the freedom of capital movements within the area, had been compromised by British capital export controls. In 1972 in expectation of its entry into the Common Market, Britain introduced a system of exchange controls that treated sterling area members and other countries by and large alike.[43] As Professor Pressnell has argued, "This [change] reduced the once world-wide sterling area to a few islands (Britain and the Isle of Man, the Channel Isles and Ireland), later joined by the Rock of Gibraltar."[44] Moreover, the floating of the British pound in June 1972 led many sterling area countries to abandon the peg of their currencies on the pound and led a number to peg on the dollar, thereby reducing the role of sterling as an intervention currency.[45]

41. H.M. Treasury, *The Basle Facility*, p. 6; Susan Strange, *International Monetary Relations* (1976), pp. 158–59. Minimum Sterling Proportions varied widely, e.g. 89 percent for Hong Kong and 40 percent for Australia, and could also be renegotiated. Ibid. pp. 162–64, 174.
42. H.M. Treasury, *The Basle Facility*, p. 6.
43. *IMF Annual Report* 1972, p. 39; L. S. Pressnell, "The End of the Sterling Area," *Three Banks Review*, no. 121 (March 1979), p. 3.
44. Ibid.
45. Yeager, p. 467; *IMF Annual Report* 1973, p. 47.

But if the sterling area was outdated as a concept, the sterling balances remained and a number of countries still held a high proportion of reserves in sterling. Indeed, by end of 1974, sterling liabilities to official institutions in the old sterling area had grown to £3.7 billion from only £2.8 billion in 1971.[46] Thus, sterling retained a reserve currency role but one of much smaller relative importance than the dollar and even of the German mark, which began to evolve toward reserve currency status in the late 1970s.[47]

The Dollar as a Reserve Currency

Until the 1950s, if one looked only to total holdings in international reserves sterling might have appeared to be more important than the dollar. The dollar was nonetheless the principal reserve currency after 1945 because of the regional character of sterling and because of the dominant position of the United States in the immediate postwar economy. By the mid-1950s, the dominance of the dollar was clear. But the dollar shortage period was short-lived, and by 1960 speculation against the dollar had already started. The 1960s were a decade of slow but steady retreat for the dollar as the world's principal currency.

The weakness of the dollar was a grave threat to the Bretton Woods system. Not only was the dollar payments deficit the principal source of liquidity in the system, a circumstance that was only imperfectly dealt with by the creation of the SDR, but the dollar was the world's principal intervention currency. And by the 1960s it had undoubtedly replaced sterling as the world's principal transactions currency. That a country whose currency was so dominant should be suffering persistent balance-of-payments problems and should also be pursuing inflationary domestic policies—in part as a result of the failure to finance the Vietnam war out of taxation—was profoundly disturbing to defenders of the Bretton Woods system.

Economic trends threatened the U.S. commitment to sell gold at $35 per ounce. The Gold Pool was the first attempt to protect U.S. gold holdings.[48] For its first three years, 1962–65, the pool was sometimes in the market as a buyer and sometimes as a seller of gold, but on balance it bought gold. But from early 1966 to its abandonment in 1968 the pool was a net seller of gold and thus could only slow, but not arrest, the leakage of gold from the U.S. Treasury. During this period the private demand for gold was such that any increased official holdings of gold by other countries could only be met by

46. Z. Res and G. Zis, "The Basle Agreement: An Exercise in Monetary Mismanagement," *The Banker* 125(1975):1270–71.
47. See discussion pp. 316–18.
48. See discussion of the Gold Pool, pp. 137–38.

U.S. stocks, which had fallen from $22.9 billion in 1957 to less than $11 billion early in 1968.[49]

The 1968 adoption of the two-tier system can thus be viewed as an attempt to increase gold production, and to moderate private demand, by allowing the market price to rise.[50] But whether it actually reduced private demand is doubtful because it could also be interpreted as the first step in the abandonment of the official $35 price; thus it may have raised expectations as to the probable future price of gold.

One of the effects of the weakness of the dollar in the 1960s was a growth in capital controls. At first these controls were imposed by the United States in an attempt to stem what was interpreted as a private outflow of dollars. In 1964 an interest equalization tax was imposed on the acquisition of foreign securities in order to make them more expensive to U.S. purchasers. In 1965 a voluntary program restricting the growth of foreign investment by U.S. corporations was adopted, and this program was strengthened and made mandatory in 1968. A parallel program restricting credit extensions to foreign borrowers was begun in 1965 and tightened in 1968.[51] In addition, in an attempt to affect the trade balance, the United States adopted a variety of inefficient trade policies, including a "gold budget" limiting offshore defense procurement and military "offset agreements" with Germany and Great Britain designed to increase U.S. military hardware exports.[52]

By 1970 the continuation of the U.S. $35 per ounce gold commitment had become a matter of widespread anxiety, especially as the incoming Nixon administration had adopted a "benign neglect" policy under which the international monetary problem was viewed essentially as a matter of other countries' exchange rate and trade restrictions policies.[53] Meanwhile, the earlier capital controls were increasingly seen not merely as a failure but as one that had weakened the U.S. international economic position. The controls had effectively eliminated New York as an international financial center, exporting to London and other European financial centers both the international lending and the international borrowing function. And they gave a powerful impetus to the growth of the Eurodollar market which, rightly or wrongly, was viewed as a threat to any regime of fixed exchange rates.[54]

49. *BIS 42d Report* 1972, pp. 16–19. A potential additional source of gold was sporadic sales by the Soviet Union.
50. See discussion of the two-tier system, pp. 138–42.
51. On these U.S. capital controls, see Shultz and Dam, p. 111; Yeager, pp. 572–74; and the relevant issues of the IMF's *Annual Report on Exchange Restrictions*.
52. On the offset agreements, see Strange, *International Monetary Relations*, pp. 270–75; Gregory F. Treverton, *The Dollar Drain and American Forces in Germany* (1978), pp. 10–13, 32–34, 40.
53. On the origin and content of this policy, see Hendrik S. Houthakker, "The Breakdown of Bretton Woods," in *Economic Advice and Executive Policy*, ed. Werner Sichel (1978), pp. 50–56.
54. On the Eurodollar market see discussion pp. 293–96.

Meanwhile, the net reserve position of the United States continued to worsen. By the end of 1970, gold holdings were only $11.1 billion. Total external liabilities had risen to $47.0 billion, of which $23.3 billion were claims held by official institutions. External liabilities continued to mount rapidly. Between the end of December 1970 and the end of June 1971, total external liabilities increased by $7.8 billion. And, ominously, private holders were diversifying out of dollars; in the same six-month period, private holdings by foreigners of dollars fell by nearly $3 billion.[55]

The United States attempted to stem the tide by making it clear that requests to convert dollars into gold at the Federal Reserve Bank of New York, though legally possible, would be viewed as an unfriendly act.[56] This diplomatic stance kept U.S. gold holdings largely intact but could not relieve the ever growing negative balance in the U.S. international reserve position. As Italian central banker Guido Carli later observed, "the fiction of dollar convertibility" had been "stretched beyond the limits of credibility."[57]

On 12 August 1971, the British sought to cover a portion of their dollar holdings by requesting the Federal Reserve to make a swap drawing on the Bank of England, a drawing that took place on Friday, 13 August, in the amount of $750 million. To the top U.S. decisionmakers the British request was the beginning of a run on the U.S. gold bank. The British move led directly to the decision, taken that weekend at Camp David and announced on Sunday, 15 August, to close the U.S. gold window.[58]

The Legality of the U.S. Gold Window Decision

This decision, which was part of a larger package of Camp David decisions, including a controversial 10 percent import surcharge,[59] raised a complicated legal issue. If the United States had been prepared to support its exchange rate through exchange market transactions, then the legal issue would not have arisen because the United States would merely have been substituting one method for another of complying with the requirements of Article IV, Section 4(b) concerning the maintenance of exchange market transactions for

55. See table 2, p. 145, above, and IMF, *International Financial Statistics* (1973 Supplement), p. 449.
56. Houthakker, p. 55.
57. Guido Carli, "Perspectives on the Evolution of the International Monetary System," *Journal of Monetary Economics* 4(1978):409.
58. The significance of the British action to the U.S. decision has been contested. Compare Robert Solomon, *The International Monetary System* (1977), p. 185, and Coombs, pp. 217–18 with Houthakker, p. 58, and Martin Mayer, *The Fate of the Dollar* (1980), pp. 186–88.
59. The decisions were announced in a speech by President Nixon on 15 August 1971. See *Public Papers of the Presidents of the United States. Richard Nixon . . . 1971* (1972), pp. 886–90. The import surcharge was imposed by Proclamation 4074, Federal Register, vol. 36 (1971), pp. 15724–26.

its currency within the margins on either side of parity.[60] But since the United States sought a depreciation of the dollar vis-à-vis other currencies, and since other countries did not intend to revalue unilaterally, the United States was inevitably in violation both of that provision and of Article VIII, Section 4.[61]

The latter section, which is part of the article establishing convertibility obligations, requires a member to convert balances of its own currency held by another member either into gold or into the currency of the member making the request. It requires, in short, what later became known as asset settlement. But the United States was stating flatly that it would not provide gold. Moreover, it did not even attempt to maintain foreign currency balances in sufficient quantity to substitute the currency of members seeking conversion. Indeed, even if it had had the foreign currencies, it would not have been willing to provide them at the existing parity precisely because it sought some new parity.

A number of points can be advanced in support of the U.S. position, some of them at least quasi-legal and some of them of considerably broader significance. First, it is not at all clear that any foreign government actually made any effort to request conversion of its dollar balances into its own currency; on the contrary, many continued to build up dollar balances as a consequence of their own exchange market intervention as they resisted any exchange rate change. One can plausibly argue that in the absence of any demand there can be no violation for failure to meet the demand.

More generally, the United States was entitled to one 10 percent devaluation merely for the asking under the 10 percent "free bite" clause of Article IV, Section 5(c)(i), which provides that the Fund shall raise no objection to a change in par values that does not exceed 10 percent of the initial par value. To be sure, the United States did not initially attempt such unilateral devaluation, for one reason because U.S. officials believed, not without justification, that other countries would simply devalue by an equal amount— leaving existing parities unchanged. To attempt to change market exchange rates without the acquiescence of foreign governments could simply have led to intervention at cross-purposes as the United States sold dollars to force a depreciation of the dollar and as foreign governments bought dollars precisely to prevent such a depreciation.

The United States had other reasons, however, for seeking to avoid a devaluation, which under the Bretton Woods rules could only be accomplished by increasing the price of gold in terms of dollars. The United States believed that the international monetary system should be fundamentally reformed to place more of the responsibility for adjustment on surplus countries. A corollary of this view was that surplus countries should discharge

60. See discussion, pp. 93–94.
61. Joseph Gold, *Legal and Institutional Aspects of the International Monetary System: Selected Essays* (1979), p. 557 (hereafter cited Gold, *Selected Essays*).

that responsibility by revaluing. Moreover, to devalue would have increased the role of gold in the international monetary system, contrary to U.S. views of the direction that reform should take. And under U.S. domestic legislation, a devaluation would have required congressional approval of an increase in the price of gold.[62] Congressional approval could not be assumed without the groundwork being laid by events and by extensive executive-legislative consultations. For the U.S. president to have declared a devaluation and then to have been rebuffed by the Congress through a rejection of gold price legislation might have been politically unattractive domestically and potentially disastrous for the international monetary system.

II. THE SMITHSONIAN AGREEMENT AND ITS IMPLEMENTATION

The months of 1971 following the August 15 decisions were spent negotiating a realignment of exchange rates and the contribution to those changes that each country would make in terms of the balance of devaluations and revaluations.[63] Prompt negotiation of an exchange rate realignment was impeded by the U.S. position that a much greater change in rates was required than Europeans and, especially, the Japanese seemed prepared to accept. Furthermore, the devaluation-revaluation issue was as important to other countries as it was to the United States. A country that revalued would have to reduce the price of gold in terms of its own currency, a result that was not likely to be popular in countries such as France where private ownership of gold was widespread. Moreover, its central bank would have to show a capital loss on dollars that it held. The same accounting result would also follow if the United States devalued but at least in that case, the wound would not be self-inflicted.

The Fund staff, by this time identifying its interests with the fortunes of the SDR as a reserve asset, was concerned that any reduction of the official price of gold in any important currency would impinge on the popularity of the SDR as a reserve holding. This paradoxical result would flow from the decision, embodied in the First Amendment, to tie the value of the SDR to that of a fixed quantity of gold.[64] With the interest rate set at the comparatively low rate of 1½ percent per annum,[65] any decision that would tend

---

62. The Bretton Woods Agreements Act, ch. 339, §5, 59 Stat. 514 (1945), prohibited any change in the par value of the U.S. dollar without congressional authorization.
63. The story of the negotiations leading to the December 1971 Smithsonian agreement has been told a number of times from several points of view and hence need not be recounted here. See e.g. Henry Kissinger, *White House Years* (1979), pp. 954–62; de Vries, *IMF 1966–1971*, 1:531–56; Solomon, pp. 188–209; Strange, *International Monetary Relations*, pp. 336–44; Mayer, pp. 189–203; Gilbert, pp. 159–63.
64. Article XXI, Section 2, *first*. See discussion p. 158, above.
65. Article XXVI, Section 3, *first*.

to reduce the principal value of the SDR in terms of major currencies would tend to reduce its acceptability as a reserve asset to some holders.

A breakthrough in the post–Camp David negotiations occurred at a U.S.-French meeting at the Azores, 13–14 December 1971, where Presidents Nixon and Pompidou agreed that the United States would devalue in terms of gold. Indeed, they agreed on the extent of the U.S. devaluation against the franc.

From the Azores it was a short step to the Smithsonian Institution in Washington, D.C., where on 17–18 December a realignment of exchange rates among the Group of Ten countries was agreed upon. The United States devalued by 7.89 percent, implying an official gold price of $38 per ounce. The French left the gold price unchanged in terms of francs. The Germans, whose mark had been floating, agreed on a revaluation, by 13.58 percent, of the dollar parity that had been in effect before the commencement of floating in May 1971—an amount that equaled an appreciation of the mark in terms of gold of 4.61 percent. And the Japanese, who had stopped intervening in support of their old dollar parity a few weeks after Camp David, agreed to establish a new yen-dollar parity involving a 16.88 percent appreciation of the yen above the old parity and a 7.66 percent appreciation in terms of gold.[66]

It is worth noting that since the United States did not reintroduce convertibility into gold, the increased gold price became, so far as the United States was concerned, largely a numeraire for calculating parities with other currencies. The new price of $38 per ounce became, in the phrase of the time, the price at which the United States did *not* buy or sell gold.

One striking aspect of the Smithsonian agreement was that it was negotiated at a Group of Ten meeting; the Managing Director of the IMF was the only Fund official present. The impression that when important monetary issues were to be decided the Fund would play a minor role was cemented in national officials' minds. But the Fund was depreciated as an institution for legal reasons as well. Most obviously, the United States still did not accept its convertibility obligation under Article VIII, Section 4; thus the entire structure of the Articles was no longer squarely placed on its Bretton Woods foundation. Indeed, the Fund was faced with major difficulties in even giving legal effect to the agreements reached at the Smithsonian.

One problem was that although the United States had agreed to raise the official price of gold, the executive branch had no authority to do so and, in

66. *IMF Annual Report* 1972, p. 38 (table 13). The other Group of Ten countries also revalued vis-à-vis the dollar with the exception of Canada, which continued to allow its dollar to float. Sweden and Italy revalued in terms of the U.S. dollar, but because the revaluation was small they actually devalued in terms of gold. Ibid. For the text of the Smithsonian Communiqué, see *International Financial News Survey* 23(1971):417–18 (hereafter cited Smithsonian Communiqué).

the event, did not receive congressional approval until March 1972.[67] Hence, it was in no position to communicate a new par value to the Fund. Moreover, several other countries also had to secure domestic legislative approval before they could communicate new par values; and the Fund was consequently unable to approve nonexistent new par values. In the interim these various countries could not maintain their currencies within the margins envisaged by the Articles because those were margins on either side of official parities, which were calculated by the ratios of any two currencies' official par values.[68]

Another problem was that the Group of Ten had decided at the Smithsonian that "pending agreement on longer-term monetary reforms," the G-10 members would observe 2¼ percent rather than the Bretton Woods 1 percent margins.[69] Any member allowing the market rate of its currency to diverge by more than 1 percent from parity with the dollar would nevertheless be in violation of the Articles.

To meet these twin problems, the Fund's Executive Board, on the same date as the Group of Ten's Smithsonian agreement, adopted a decision entitled "Central Rates and Wider Margins: A Temporary Regime."[70] The decision sought a legal basis in the Articles by referring to members' undertaking under Article IV, Section 4(a), to "collaborate with the Fund to promote exchange stability, to maintain orderly exchange arrangements with other members, and to avoid competitive exchange alterations." Although the Fund's general counsel heralded this "outstanding example of the use" of the provision, he nevertheless conceded that the two principal features of the decision were "incompatible with certain provisions of the Articles."[71] The theory of the decision, stated in its preamble, was that it would "enable members to observe the purposes of the Fund to the maximum extent possible during the temporary period preceding the resumption of effective par values with appropriate margins in accordance with the Articles."[72]

One notable aspect of the decision was that it introduced a new term, "central rates," to refer to rates communicated prior to U.S. congressional action on the U.S. increase in the price of gold. The decision assumed that after Congress acted, new par values would be communicated by all members changing the value of their currencies in terms of gold. Once a central rate had been communicated, it functioned exactly like a par value (albeit with wider margins around resulting parities). In this sense, the Smithsonian agreement and its accompanying Fund decision reestablished a pegged rate system. Yet the very term "central rates" suggested more flexibility than the

---

67. Par Value Modification Act, P.L. 92-268, 86 Stat. 116 (1972).
68. De Vries, *IMF 1966–1971*, 1:557.
69. Smithsonian Communiqué, para. 4, p. 418.
70. Decision of 18 December 1971, *IMF Annual Report* 1972, p. 85.
71. Gold, *Selected Essays*, p. 559.
72. Preamble, Decision of 18 December 1971, *IMF Annual Report* 1972, p. 85.

term "par values," especially in the new, albeit purportedly "temporary," regime of wider margins. Indeed, no time limit was placed on the replacement of central rates by par values, and some members continued to maintain par values well past U.S. congressional action and the establishment by the United States on 8 May 1972 of a new par value for the dollar.[73]

Another innovation imported by the decision was that central rates, unlike par values, did not have to be stated in terms of gold or of the 1944 gold content of the U.S. dollar as required by Article IV, Section 1. Rather it could be "communicated in gold, units of special drawing rights, or another member's currency." Three factors appear to have motivated this formulation. The first, reflected in the reference to "another member's currency," was that it would be a source of confusion to have central rates expressed legally in terms of a $35 per ounce dollar at the same time that the markets referred to it in terms of a $38 per ounce dollar. The second was the view that the contemplated reform of the system would downgrade the role of gold, and the possibility of expressing future par values in terms of SDRs or other currencies was one step in that direction.

A third motivation had especial relevance for the future. It was that the step away from gold could also be one moving the SDR toward stage center of the system.[74] The Executive Board decided in February 1972 that thenceforth all Fund accounts should be "summarized" in SDRs.[75] Thereafter, the Fund's public reports stated not merely its Special Drawing Account but also its General Account in SDRs.[76] Here one sees a Fund staff and Executive Board policy, which would be pursued repeatedly in the future, to elevate by small, often technical steps the public prominence of the SDR.

III. Generalized Floating

The revival of the pegged rate system in the Smithsonian arrangements was short-lived. The United Kingdom floated the pound sterling in June 1972. Sterling depreciated promptly about 6 percent and by the end of 1972 was trading about 10 percent below its Smithsonian parity.[77] Then, in early 1973, the U.S. dollar weakened seriously in the exchange markets. The Swiss authorities elected to allow the Swiss franc to float upward, rather than intervening in support of the dollar, which would have required a large

73. Gold, *Selected Essays*, p. 561. *IMF Annual Report* 1972, p. 39. For another kind of decision arising out of the unusual post-Smithsonian legal situation, see Decision of 4 January 1972, replaced, once the United States had adopted a new par value on 8 May 1972, by Decision of 8 May 1972, ibid. pp. 87–89.
74. See discussion of the decision in Gold, *Selected Essays*, pp. 560–62.
75. Decision of 25 February 1972, *IMF Annual Report* 1972, pp. 90–91. The Board of Governors approved on 20 March 1972. Ibid. p. 90, n. 17.
76. See e.g. *IMF Annual Report* 1973, pp. 112–17.
77. *IMF Annual Report* 1973, p. 5, chart 2.

increase in the Swiss money supply as Swiss francs were in effect printed to provide the francs to buy dollars in the exchange markets. The Swiss franc promptly went to a 6 percent premium over its former parity.[78]

In the first ten days of February 1973, foreign intervention in support of the dollar approached $10 billion.[79] On February 12 the U.S. secretary of the treasury announced that Congress would be asked to authorize a 10 percent devaluation of the dollar in terms of SDRs.[80] The Japanese reacted by floating the yen, which then appreciated by 5 percent on top of the 11.1 percent revaluation against the dollar that was the counterpart of the U.S. 10 percent devaluation. In addition, Italy floated the lira, and Britain continued to allow the pound to float.[81]

After a short respite, sales of dollars on exchange markets remained so great, with European intervention reaching $3.6 billion on 1 March 1973,[82] that exchange markets were finally closed in major European countries and Japan for a two-week period beginning the following day. The United States confirmed its intention to continue to refrain from supporting the value of the dollar in the exchange markets. The European Economic Community Council of Finance Ministers in turn announced the intention of the Community's member countries to float jointly against the dollar. Specifically, Germany (which at the same time revalued by 3 percent), France, the Netherlands, Belgium, Luxemburg, and Denmark agreed to maintain exchange rates against one another within a margin of 2¼ percent, but at the same time not to make any attempt to maintain their exchange rates against the dollar within the Smithsonian 2¼ margins around their dollar parity.[83]

From an international monetary viewpoint one could see the joint float as merely a decision by Germany to float against the dollar, with the other countries pegging their currencies on the German mark to form a mark area. However, the dictates of European integration required that the decision be presented as a European Economic Community initiative. It was announced, for example, that the other EEC members would "associate themselves as soon as possible with the decision,"[84] which meant that the lira and the pound (and with it, the Irish punt, which was then pegged on the pound) would, for the time being, continue to float not merely against the dollar but also against the currencies of other EEC members.

78. Ibid. p. 5.
79. Ibid.
80. U.S. Treasury, *Annual Report of the Secretary of the Treasury on the State of the Finances 1973*, p. 407. This change implied an increase in the price of gold to $42.22.
81. *BIS 43d Report*, 1973, pp. 24–25.
82. Coombs, p. 229.
83. *BIS 43d Report*, 1973, p. 25; "Press Communiqué of the EEC Council of Finance Ministers, March 12, in Brussels," *IMF Survey* 2(1973):88.
84. Ibid.

The joint float, viewed from the countries inside the float, was a continuation of the EEC snake arrangement arising out of the Smithsonian arrangements. In March 1972 the EEC members announced that, in aid of their goal of monetary union, they would maintain their market exchange rates vis-à-vis one another within margins only one-half as great as those countenanced by the Smithsonian temporary regime of wider margins.[85] The EEC rates then fluctuated against one another within the narrower "snake," which in turn floated up and down inside the Smithsonian "tunnel."[86] But the snake in the tunnel and indeed the tunnel itself were too confining for sterling, which had been floating since June 1972, and for the lira, which began floating in February 1973. Later the snake membership was to change, with France dropping out in January 1974.[87]

Whatever the European political purposes served by the joint float, it was in fact the beginning of generalized floating. This became indelibly clear with the French 1974 decision and with the tendency of the strong currencies in the resulting mark zone to revalue whenever the snake arrangements threatened to be too constraining for its members.[88] The principal legal and institutional issues raised by the move to generalized floating may be grouped under several interrelated questions. First, what were to be the rules on intervention within this floating system? Second, what was to happen to the SDR, and in particular its valuation, under a floating regime? Third, what, if any, relevance would liquidity issues have in a floating regime?[89]

Intervention in a Floating System

In the March 1973 Group of Ten meetings that took place during the closure of the exchange markets, the question arose as to the extent to which the joint float should be "clean"—that is, whether the snake should find its own dollar level without exchange market intervention.[90] The incompatibility

---

85. Decision of 18 December 1971, *IMF Annual Report 1972*, pp. 85–87.
86. On the European goal of monetary union, see generally *European Monetary Unification*, ed. Lawrence B. Krause and Walter S. Salant (1973); Richard W. Edwards, Jr., "The European Exchange Rate Arrangement Called the 'Snake,' " *University of Toledo Law Review* 10(1978):47, 49–50. One can think of the snake as being the maximum divergence between the snake currencies, in which case the snake could be narrower than 2¼ percent. See Günter Wittich and Masaki Shiratori, "The Snake in the Tunnel," *Finance and Development* 10(June 1973):11–12.
87. Sweden and Norway were associated countries in the snake arrangements at various times. France, having left the arrangement in January 1974, rejoined it briefly from July 1975 to March 1976. "The European System of Narrower Exchange Rate Margins," *Monthly Report of the Deutsche Bundesbank*, January 1976, pp. 22, 23–25; Edwards, "The Snake," pp. 69–72.
88. Edwards, "The Snake," pp. 69–72.
89. Other kinds of legal issues arose with the move to generalized floating. See, for example, the November 1973 decision amending the December 1971 "central rates and wider margins" decision. Decision of 7 November 1973, *IMF Annual Report 1974*, pp. 103–5. See the explanation in Joseph Gold, *Floating Currencies, Gold, and SDRs: Some Recent Legal Developments*, IMF Pamphlet Series no. 19 (1976), pp. 25–27.
90. Coombs, p. 230.

between the U.S. preference for clean floating (far more strongly held in the Treasury than in the Federal Reserve) and the European preference for extensive intervention was papered over by an agreement "in principle that official intervention in exchange markets may be useful at appropriate times to facilitate the maintenance of orderly conditions, keeping in mind also the desirability of encouraging reflows of speculative movements of funds."[91] The next sentence in the agreement made clear, however, that—maintenance of intrasnake currency relationships apart—the amount and timing of intervention was a question for the intervening government. The only obligation would be to consult the country whose currency was used for intervention, which meant essentially that the European members of the Group of Ten felt free to manage exchange rates so long as the United States was kept informed: "Each nation stated that it will be prepared to intervene at its initiative in its own market, when necessary and desirable, acting in a flexible manner in the light of market conditions and in close consultation with the authorities of the nation whose currency may be bought or sold."[92]

Each side could thus pursue its preference. The Europeans and Japanese could intervene when their floats took them too far from their targets, while the United States could remain passive, as it had been under the Bretton Woods system. As Robert Solomon observed, "It was a philosophical, as well as a political, question whether the dollar was also floating."[93]

Despite this affirmation on the European side of the virtues of managed floating, virtues that were repeatedly espoused, exchange rates were unprecedentedly volatile after the March 1973 move to generalized floating. By July 1973 the mark had appreciated against the dollar by 30 percent from the February level.[94] Various European countries then intervened more energetically, and the United States began limited intervention.[95] Yet there followed, within the space of a year, three swings in the mark-dollar rate in which the dollar alternately strengthened and weakened against the mark.[96] It was widely presumed, perhaps inappropriately, that cyclical behavior of particular bilateral exchange rates was undesirable.[97]

Meanwhile, concern arose in the United States that some countries might continue to maintain an inappropriate rate, especially an undervalued exchange rate as an aid to exports, by what was characterized as "dirty floating."

Dirty float

91. "Press Communiqué of the Ministerial Meeting of the Group of 10 and the European Economic Community, March 16, in Paris," *IMF Survey* 2(1973):88–89.
92. Ibid.
93. Solomon, p. 234.
94. Coombs, p. 231.
95. *BIS 44th Report*, 1974, p. 29.
96. Ibid. pp. 27–32; Paula A. Tosini, *Leaning Against the Wind: A Standard for Managed Floating*, Princeton Essays in International Finance, no. 126 (1977), p. 5, fig. 2.
97. Harry G. Johnson, "World Inflation and the International Monetary System," *Three Banks Review*, no. 107 (September 1975), pp. 3, 11–13. The need to explain these wide exchange rate swings set off an explosion of theoretical writing explaining that exchange rates move in response

Interest thus grew in devising a set of rules that might achieve either or both
of two objectives: (1) limit unnecessary or undesirable fluctuations arising
from floating; and (2) regulate intervention that might cause a supposedly
floating rate to be persistently undervalued.[98] These two goals are, it should
be noted, potentially inconsistent. Damping down cycles would require extensive intervention; preventing undervalued rates would require significant
limits on intervention. Rules that would be more than pious restatements of
objectives would have to be phrased in terms of the amount and timing of
intervention and hence might stand in the way, at any particular time, of
achieving one objective or the other.

The reform negotiations within the Committee of Twenty (C-20), to be
discussed in the next chapter, provided the occasion for the negotiation of
a set of rules on floating and intervention.[99] Since it was envisaged that the
reformed system would be a par value system, with floating rates adopted
only by a limited number of countries and only in particular situations
authorized by the Fund and subject to its surveillance,[100] the rules no doubt
took a somewhat different form than they would have taken if they had been
negotiated in a context where the long-run system had been envisaged as one
of generalized floating. Yet when the reform negotiations broke down, these
rules were adopted as Guidelines for the Management of Floating Exchange
Rates.[101] These Guidelines were not fully mandatory because the Executive
Board decision, taken under the collaboration undertaking of Article IV,
Section 4(a), simply called on members to "use their best endeavors to observe
the guidelines."[102] The Fund believed that the Guidelines had to be subject
to this collaboration undertaking because the Fund was unable to authorize
floating in view of the fact that the Fund articles then envisaged only a par
value system.[103]

The Guidelines can best be understood against the background of two
contradictions. The first is that although governments tend to consider themselves wiser than exchange markets about the inherent value of their currency,
they have been notoriously unsuccessful in predicting future exchange rate
changes. That is, they have not proved capable of determining consistently

---

not merely to different rates of inflation but also, as in any asset market, to changes in expectations. See especially papers by Richard N. Cooper, Rudiger Dornbusch, Jacob A. Frenkel,
and Michael Mussa, *Scandinavian Journal of Economics* 78, no. 2 (1976).
98. Tosini, pp. 24–25.
99. See pp. 239–43.
100. "Outline of Reform. June 14, 1974," para. 13, in IMF, *International Monetary Reform.
Documents of the Committee of Twenty* (1974), p. 12 (hereafter cited C-20 Documents).
101. "Guidelines for the Management of Floating Exchange Rates," *IMF Annual Report* 1974,
pp. 112–16 (hereafter cited Guidelines).
102. Decision of 13 June 1974, *IMF Annual Report* 1974, p. 112.
103. Guidelines, Introduction, p. 112; Gold, *Selected Essays*, p. 37.

whether today's exchange rate movements will be extended or reversed tomorrow. In 1978, Artus and Crockett concluded that "[m]arket forces may not always be 'right,' but the experience of the past decade indicates clearly that they have been right more often than the authorities."[104]

The second and related contradiction is that even though governments have not been both willing and able to maintain a par value in the 1970s, most major governments have held strong views as to the appropriateness of their exchange rate at any particular time. Hence, they frequently pursue active policies designed to change the rate or to prevent it from changing. Indeed, the level of intervention since the commencement of generalized floating in 1973 has been as great and perhaps greater than during the par value period prior to 1971.[105]

The first guideline did not limit intervention at all but rather stated that a member "should" intervene "to prevent or moderate sharp and disruptive fluctuations from day to day and from week to week." As this guideline implies, governments did not appear to have doubts about their ability to perceive situations where fluctuations are short-term and will be promptly reversed. Nor did they seem to doubt their ability to engage in what are often called "smoothing operations" in order to eliminate most of such short-term reversible swings. Finally, the desirability of smoothing out short-term swings was widely assumed in official circles, as reflected by the use of the pejorative term "disruptive." The Guidelines thus strongly encouraged smoothing operations by the precatory "should," though they did not mandate such operations, perhaps because the United States continued after 1973 to resist any extensive undertakings to intervene in support of the dollar. However, the essence of the first guideline was restated in the Rambouillet declaration at the first summit meeting of the Five (the United States, Germany, Japan, Britain, and France) in November 1975. There it was agreed that "monetary authorities will act to counter disorderly market conditions or erratic fluctuations in exchange rates."[106]

---

104. Jacques R. Artus and Andrew D. Crockett, *Floating Exchange Rates and the Need for Surveillance*, Princeton Essays in International Finance no. 127 (1978), pp. 27–28. See discussion pp. 198, 262, below.
105. See generally Weir M. Brown, *World Afloat: National Policies Ruling the Waves*, Princeton Essays in International Finance no. 116 (1976); W. Ethier and A. I. Bloomfield, "The Reference Rate Proposal and Recent Experience," *Banca Nazionale del Lavoro Quarterly Review*, no. 26 (September 1978), pp. 218–21; Donald S. Kemp, "The U.S. Dollar in International Markets: Mid-1970 to Mid-1976," *Federal Reserve Bank of St. Louis Review* 58(August 1976):7–9, 14; "Some Observations on Floating," Morgan Guaranty Trust Company, *World Financial Markets* (October 1973), pp. 4–8 (hereafter cited *World Financial Markets*). See also the semiannual reports on "Treasury and Federal Reserve Foreign Exchange Operations" published in the *Federal Reserve Bank of New York Quarterly Review*.
106. Guidelines, p. 113; *IMF Survey* 4(1975):350.

The second guideline dealt with what are sometimes called "medium-term fluctuations." Under it a member might "act, through intervention or otherwise, to moderate movements in the exchange value of its currency from month to month and quarter to quarter, and is encouraged to do so, if necessary, where factors recognized to be temporary are at work." However, a member "should not normally act aggressively with respect to the exchange value of its currency (i.e., should not so act as to depress that value when it is falling, or to enhance that value when it is rising)." The second guideline, by encouraging intervention to offset market movements but discouraging intervention that would accelerate or extend market movements, embodied what has come to be known as the "leaning against the wind" principle.[107]

The rationale for this guideline is less clear than for the first one. The assumption that the monetary authorities know more than the market is less justified the longer the time perspective, since the main thing that a government may know but the market may not is its own (or possibly another government's) intention with respect to future economic policies. In short, governments have the power to fool the market by making unanticipated changes in policy. But no government is likely to be certain what its own economic policies will be more than a few months into the future, and the market may indeed be a better judge of a government's ability to follow a particular policy over an extended period of time than are the monetary authorities who make the intervention decisions. Richard Cooper has argued that the leaning-against-the-wind strategy (which he calls the "smoothing and braking stategy") is justified by the possibility that although governments "do not know what the equilibrium exchange rate over any time period is, [the strategy] allows for the likelihood that the 'market' does not know either."[108]

A number of governments have pursued leaning-against-the-wind intervention policies. For example, the German Bundesbank in its 1974 annual report stated that its policy had been to attempt "to moderate excessive fluctuations in the Deutsche Mark rate vis-à-vis the U.S. dollar over extended periods of time."[109] At the same time, other countries may have leaned against an exchange market wind before which they would have been better advised to bend.[110] Nevertheless, if one believes that governments need not be encouraged to intervene to resist exchange rate changes but are rather too prone

107. Guidelines, p. 113; Tosini, p. 7.
108. Richard N. Cooper, "IMF Surveillance Over Exchange Rates," in *The New International Monetary System*, ed. Robert A. Mundell and Jacques J. Polak (1977), p. 77. Compare the views in Artus and Crockett, note 104, above, and Thomas D. Willett, "Alternative Approaches to International Surveillance of Exchange-Rate Policies," in *Managed Exchange-Rate Flexibility: The Recent Experience*, Federal Reserve Bank of Boston Series no. 20 (1978), pp. 154–55.
109. *Report of the Deutsche Bundesbank for the Year 1974*, p. 60.
110. See the discussion of the evidence on this point in Ethier and Bloomfield, "Reference Rate," pp. 219–21.

to do so, then the second guideline has the virtue of restraining aggressive intervention—that is, intervention that would accelerate an exchange rate change.

Guideline 3, by providing an exception to the rule against aggressive intervention, served to subject such intervention to some international regulation. It did so by requiring that a member choosing to intervene aggressively should adopt a "target zone of rates" and should consult with the Fund. The consultation was to encompass not merely the target zone but also "its adaptation to changing circumstances."[111] The adaptation question is particularly significant; though target zones, reference rates and the like have been widely advocated,[112] it is also widely recognized that any such scheme that fails to provide some means for changing a target zone or reference rate in response to new circumstances will be as vulnerable to short-term capital movements as was the par value system.[113]

The target zone approach, which was developed in some detail in the Guidelines and the appended official commentary, does not appear to have been adopted by many, if indeed any, countries.[114] Nonetheless, the approach is still available under the later 1977 surveillance decision, which replaced the Guidelines and which provides for ongoing Fund surveillance of exchange rate policies.[115] In any event, the Guidelines have historical importance as the first attempt to develop a set of rules for a floating system comparable to the Bretton Woods rules for a par value system.

The Guidelines had the further distinction of constituting a clear international agreement on the proposition that other national policies were analogous to intervention in their effects on exchange rates and therefore warranted comparable international regulation. In addition to intervention in both forward and spot markets, the Guidelines applied to "official foreign borrowing or lending, capital restrictions, separate capital exchange markets, various types of fiscal intervention, and also monetary or interest rate policies" so long as any of these measures had been adopted for balance-of-payments purposes.[116] Thus, the Guidelines appeared to have rendered improper the adoption of capital restrictions that had an effect analogous to aggressive exchange market intervention, even though the Articles of Agreement then in effect did not apply to capital restrictions.

---

111. Guidelines, p. 113.
112. Ethier and Bloomfield, "Reference Rate," pp. 211–32; Wilfred Ethier and A. I. Bloomfield, *Managing the Managed Float*, Princeton Essays in International Finance no. 112 (1975); John Williamson, *The Failure of World Monetary Reform, 1971–74* (1977), pp. 185–96; and compare Willett, pp. 152–54.
113. Raymond F. Mikesell and Henry N. Goldstein, *Rules for a Floating-Rate Regime*, Princeton Essays in International Finance no. 109 (1975), pp. 19, 21.
114. Ethier and Bloomfield, "Reference Rate," p. 221.
115. See pp. 259–67.
116. Guidelines, p. 115.

Valuation and Interest Rate of the SDR

Since the SDR was not traded in any market, its value had to be determined by the Fund. That in turn meant, in view of the enormous indirect purchasing power of the SDR when exchanged for currencies, that the valuation principles would have to be spelled out in precise written rules. The First Amendment had valued the SDR as equivalent to 0.888 671 gram of fine gold, which was equal to the par value of the U.S. dollar at the time.[117] It was therefore natural for the Fund, in Rule O-3, to treat one SDR as equivalent to one dollar. Under the equal value principle previously discussed, the value of the SDR in any currency other than the dollar was therefore calculated by using the current market exchange rate (the "representative rate" in the language of Rule O-3) of that currency with the dollar.[118]

The devaluations of the dollar in 1971 and 1973 did not affect the convenience of computing the value of the SDR in any currency via that currency's exchange rate with the dollar. However, it did become necessary to use a factor other than unity to arrive at the SDR value in terms of the dollar in view of the fact that one U.S. dollar was no longer worth one SDR. This result followed ineluctably from the fact that the U.S. devaluation took the form of a change in the price of gold while the SDR remained directly linked in the Articles to gold.

Once generalized floating began, however, a depreciation of the dollar against, say, the German mark did not result in a depreciation of the value of U.S. holdings of SDRs because under Rule O-3, the dollar was treated as being always at par. Moreover, as the dollar depreciated, even assuming that the mark remained at its par value, German holdings of the SDR would decline in value because of the necessity of using the dollar-mark exchange rate to determine the value of those German holdings. Thus, under generalized floating, the value of the SDR was inextricably tied to the fate of the dollar.[119] The capital gains or losses experienced on the SDR and on the dollar would be exactly equal (at least so long as par value changes were not made in response to exchange market changes). This was hardly a valuation rule likely to encourage countries to hold the SDR in preference to dollars in view of the 1½ percent SDR interest rate, which was far below that available on reserve holdings denominated in dollars (for example, U.S. Treasury bills).

One solution that was considered but soon abandoned was to substitute a stronger currency than the U.S. dollar to play the dollar's role. If the strongest currency could at all times be chosen, the effect would have been to give the SDR a capital value that would not have fallen in terms of any

---

117. Article XXI, Section 2, *first*; de Vries, *IMF 1966–1971*, 2:187.
118. See p. 158.
119. Gold, *Floating Currencies: Recent Legal Developments*, p. 10.

currency and would have risen in terms of most currencies. But there was no natural substitute for the dollar. And if the determination were to be made retrospectively in terms of the strongest currency over any time period, the future course of the SDR's capital value would have been hard to predict and perhaps even erratic.

Consequently, the decision was taken to use a basket of currencies in place of the dollar. Rule O-3 was amended to create a "standard basket" of sixteen currencies.[120] The basket was composed of $0.40 (U.S.), 0.38 D.M., 0.44 FF, 26.0 yen, and specified sums in the twelve remaining basket currencies.[121] Each of the fifteen non-U.S. currencies was then converted each day to an equivalent amount in U.S. dollars, and the sixteen amounts—now expressed in U.S. dollars—were summed to give a value for the entire basket in U.S. dollars. The SDR basket then having been valued in U.S. dollars, the basket could be valued in any other currency, using the same principle as used in Rule O-3 prior to amendment, namely, to use the current market exchange rate between the dollar and that currency. This value of the basket, calculated each day, thus became the value for that day for the SDR. Although the basket was changed in 1978 in order to substitute the Saudi Arabian riyal and the Iranian rial for the Danish krone and the South African rand (as well as to modify the relative weights of the sixteen currencies) and to provide for automatic adjustment of currencies and weights in the future, the principles of SDR valuation were not changed until 1980.[122]

Although a number of other solutions were canvassed in the C-20 reform negotiations, which were going forward at the same time that the SDR valuation problem was plaguing the Fund, the only solution that could be used effectively during a period of generalized floating was the standard basket method actually adopted. Because it was based exclusively on market exchange rates, the standard basket gave a unique value for the SDR, without any element of judgment, under a system where all currencies were floating, or a system where all currencies were maintaining par values, or any intermediate system. Any solution that was dependent on par values as an integral part of its formula, even to the extent of judging which of two currencies

120. Decisions of 13 June and 1 July 1974, *IMF Annual Report 1974*, pp. 116–18.
121. On the choice of currencies and the relative weight accorded to each, see Joseph Gold, *SDRs, Gold, and Currencies: Third Survey of New Legal Developments*, IMF Pamphlet Series no. 26 (1979), pp. 2, 4 (hereafter cited *Third Survey*). The sum of the contents of the basket was based, approximately, on a measure of the U.S. "commercial and financial role in the world" for the dollar and, for the other fifteen currencies, on members' proportional shares in world exports. These percentage weights were then converted into amounts of currency calculated on the basis of exchange rates for the three months ending 27 June 1974, adjusted to provide for continuity with previous SDR value.
122. Ibid. pp. 2–3; Gold, *Floating Currencies: Recent Legal Developments*, pp. 13–14; Decisions of 31 March and 30 June 1978, *IMF Annual Report 1978*, pp. 129–31. See *IMF Survey* 9(1980):297, 325–27, and discussion pp. 310–12, below, on the change in the number of currencies in the basket, effective 1 January 1981.

was maintaining its par value and which was not, introduced an element of judgment.[123]

A further difficulty with any method that relied on par values or central rates was that, after the commencement of generalized floating, par value changes were made for reasons that had nothing to do with any effort to change the country's exchange rate with the world at large. For example, some countries would declare new par values or central rates in order to "catch up" with an exchange market change that had already occurred. Similarly, changes in par values within the European snake might reflect attempts to alter relationships within the snake without affecting the relation of the snake itself to outside currencies.[124]

The main objection to the standard basket method was one that troubled primarily advocates of the SDR as the central reserve asset in the reformed international monetary system. The unfortunate fact was that the standard basket method gave one value to the SDR as numeraire and another value to the SDR as reserve asset. The fear was that the discrepancy between its numeraire and "transactions" value would cause undue confusion to those seeking to understand the SDR, and indeed that the SDR might be made to seem unduly artificial.

When, for example, a country announced a new par value and did so in SDRs, the SDR functioned as a numeraire, and that par value implied a reciprocal value of the SDR in terms of that currency. For example, if the par value of the Ruritanian franc were declared to be 0.5 SDR, that declaration implied a value of the SDR of 2.0 Ruritanian francs. Yet if Ruritania held one million SDRs as reserve assets, the value of those reserve holdings might be quite different from two million Ruritanian francs, and this would be so whether or not Ruritania kept its franc at par through exchange market intervention. Indeed, even if the value of the SDR temporarily were 2.0 Ruritanian francs, it might increase or decrease the next day as the result of an appreciation or depreciation of one of the sixteen currencies in the basket. For example, if the French franc were to weaken vis-à-vis all other currencies, then the value of the basket would decrease, and Ruritania's holdings of SDRs would be worth less than before. Similarly, Ruritania would receive less in foreign currency if it sought to use its SDRs. This would be true whether those SDRs were valued in Ruritanian francs or in any other currency (except French francs).

In the end, even those who favored an enhanced role for the SDR decided that they would simply have to put up with the dual valuation of the SDR in order to be able to use a valuation method that would work under conditions of generalized floating. Yet it is worth looking briefly at one of the

123. J. J. Polak, *Valuation and Rate of Interest of the SDR*, IMF Pamphlet Series no. 18 (1974), pp. 16–17.
124. Ibid.

other proposed valuation methods for the light it throws on the closely related issue of the SDR interest rate. Because the attractiveness of the SDR as a reserve asset depends heavily on its effective yield (that is, interest plus change in capital value) in comparison with the effective yield of other forms of reserve assets, the decision on how the capital value would be determined could not be taken separately from the decision on interest rates.

Central banks were not necessarily indifferent, however, between the two components of effective yield. Although within their domestic political systems central banks were not profit-maximizing institutions, many particularly feared capital losses, which showed on their books. Indeed, central banks suffering such capital losses might, under their domestic regulatory systems, have to seek legislation or treasury approval to make them good. Thus, central banks might not be indifferent between the two components in the sense that they did not necessarily view an additional 1 percent interest return as fully offsetting a 1 percent decrease in the SDR's capital value.

In the C-20 discussions these considerations were reflected in widespread interest in a "strong" SDR—that is, an SDR whose capital value would tend to appreciate against most currencies. Since the standard basket would produce an SDR that tended to track the capital value of the average of the principal currencies, one option became an "asymmetrical basket." Such a basket would be composed of the same currencies as those included in the standard basket, but when any currency devalued or floated downward, the number of units of that currency in the basket would increase. No change would be made for revaluation or floating upward, hence the "asymmetry" of the proposal. Thus, the basket would have a tendency to appreciate against the average of currencies in the basket. Moreover, no country holding SDRs in its reserves would suffer a loss on those holdings through the exchange rate movements of any other country.[125]

The asymmetrical basket would not work, however, in the very circumstances in which its merits were being considered. Since all major currencies were floating independently or as a block or were pegged on a floating currency, the Fund could not value the SDR without making what might well be a politically sensitive judgment. For example, on a day when the snake currencies were strong and the dollar weak, it would be necessary for the Fund technicians making the calculation to judge whether the snake was appreciating or the dollar depreciating, or both. In the last of these three cases the relative degree of appreciation and depreciation would have to be specified. The necessity for judgment arose from the very rule that produced a strong SDR—namely, that depreciations would result in an expansion of

125. Ibid. pp. 13–14. The statement in the text would not hold under certain conditions. For example, a depreciation within par value margins by another country could cause a minor loss of value in SDR holdings.

the number of units of a depreciating currency in the basket but no adjustment would be made in the case of appreciations.

Even a variant called the adjustable basket, in which appreciation and depreciation were treated comparably (that is, units of a currency decreased in the event of appreciation as well as increasing for depreciations) could not work if all currencies were floating. When there were no currencies at par to provide a ready point of reference, only a subjective judgment could determine which currencies were appreciating and which were depreciating. Without knowing which currencies were appreciating, for example, one could not apply the rule reducing a currency's units in the basket.[126]

One option intended to create a strong SDR included the concept of valuing the SDR in terms of a basket of commodities rather than currencies. This option was rejected quite early in the deliberations, in part on the ground that it could lead to a wide difference in the relative strengths of the SDR and alternative reserve assets. It was also attacked on the ground that it was a form of price indexation and therefore would be a precedent for such indexation of the economy generally—a practice that some people viewed as inflationary.[127]

As a consequence of using the standard basket rather than some form of price index (or gold), the capital value of the SDR in terms of domestic price levels has fallen sharply since 1974. For example, between 1974 and 1978, an index of the SDR's hypothetical purchasing power (using 1969 as a base of 1.0) fell from 0.857 to 0.699 in the United States and from 0.608 to 0.416 in Germany.[128] Of course, the U.S. dollar, the principal rival of the SDR, like other currencies also failed to maintain its purchasing power during this period.

In view of the standard basket's failure to produce a stronger SDR than the average of currencies, it was taken for granted that the interest rate of the SDR should be raised. This was particularly necessary, it was believed, because market interest rates in the member countries were much higher than they had been when the original 1½ percent rate was agreed upon. Moreover, the assumption, appropriate when the SDR was tied to gold and revaluations were rare, that the SDR would be strong in terms of currencies was now outmoded.

The principal decision to be made was whether the interest rate should be specified in advance or based on some average of market interest rates. In view of the growing volatility of interest rates and the desirability of some

126. The adjustable basket as well as a fourth option, the par value approach, apparently received little support. On the four options see C-20 Documents, annex 9, pp. 43–45; Polak, *Valuation of SDR*, pp. 12–16; Crockett, *International Money*, pp. 123–28; Williamson, pp. 131–43.
127. Polak, *Valuation of SDR*, p. 12.
128. Ugo Sacchetti, "The SDR: Ten Years of Experience," *Banca Nazionale del Lavoro Quarterly Review*, no. 131 (December 1979), p. 397, table 1.

objective determinants for the rate, the decision was taken that unless the Executive Directors could specify otherwise at the end of each six-month period, a formula based on the market rate would be used for the ensuing six months. Even if subjective determinations by the Executive Board were deemed appropriate, they could not always be taken easily in view of the requirement that decisions on the rate of interest be taken by 75 percent of the total voting power.[129]

In view of the fact that the SDR valuation rule necessarily tended to provide, *ex ante*, a more stable valuation for the SDR than the value of any of the sixteen currencies whose values were averaged together under the standard basket approach, it was decided that a "security discount" should be applied to the market averages. In retrospect the notion of a security discount appears less compelling than it did at the time. Indeed, the argument for a security discount was a misapplication of portfolio theory. Although an asset with a more stable principal value might well command a lower interest rate, there were alternative ways for a central bank to acquire most of the stability provided by the SDR. It could in principle acquire government securities denominated in each of the currencies constituting the SDR basket and thus create a "homegrown" SDR basket. Although securities could not in practice be acquired for all sixteen currencies in the basket, either because they did not exist or because the issuing country would resist any move toward its own currency becoming a reserve currency, it would nonetheless be possible for a central bank to acquire much of the SDR's stability by acquiring assets denominated in just a few of the most important of the SDR basket currencies.[130]

A further decision, perhaps not thought important at the time, based the market average on only five of the sixteen currencies in the standard basket; the rate was to be based on a weighted average of the U.S., German, U.K., French, and Japanese short-term interest rates. Because the exchange rates of those five currencies have generally been stronger than the exchange rates of the other eleven, and interest rates are generally lower in stronger currency countries, the SDR interest rate proved to be relatively low compared to what it would have been if more of the sixteen had been included.[131]

More threatening for the SDR's future, however, was the formula adopted to relate the SDR rate to the calculated average rate. That formula made the security discount larger than could possibly be justified even if the security discount theory had been fully valid. For example, at the outset the rate

129. See Article XXVI, Section 3, *first*, tying SDR interest rates in excess of 2 percent to the rate of remuneration, which could only be changed by a vote of three-quarters of the total voting power under Article V, Section 9, *first*.
130. J. J. Polak, "The SDR as a Basket of Currencies," *IMF Staff Papers* 26(1979):646–47 (1979).
131. *World Financial Markets*, September 1979, pp. 7–8. See also Polak, "SDR as a Basket of Currencies," pp. 644–45.

yielded by the formula was only 5 percent while market interest rates were 9 percent.[132] In part, this aspect of the formula stemmed from a coalescence of interest between the United States, which sought to protect the reserve currency status of the dollar from the competition of the SDR, and debtor countries, which expected to be net users of their SDRs and hence preferred to pay lower rates of interest on that net use.[133]

The formula also resulted in a growing absolute gap between the SDR and market rate as the market rate rose. Under the formula, when the market rate was below 9 percent, the SDR rate was to be 5 percent minus three-fifths of the difference between the market rate and 9 percent; but when the market rate was higher than 11 percent, the rate was to be 5 percent plus three-fifths of the difference between the market rate and 11 percent.[134] When the market rate was between 9 and 11 percent, the SDR rate would still only be 5 percent.[135] This formula was changed in 1976 so that, unless the Executive Directors decided otherwise, the SDR rate would be 60 percent of the weighted average of the five countries' market rates.[136]

Nevertheless, the combination of the valuation and interest rate principles embodied in Fund decisions produced a situation in which "the effective yield on the official SDR [was] impaired both by weak capital valuation and by weak interest return."[137] Between January 1975 and August 1979, the SDR produced an effective dollar yield of 5.6 percent compared to 7.4 percent to holders of U.S. dollar deposits and 10.2 percent on German mark deposits.[138] These considerations led to proposals for further increases in SDR rates in terms of market rates.[139] Whether even the 100 percent formula

132. The first six months interest rate of 5 percent was the result of an Executive Board decision rather than the application of a formula. However, under the formula a 5 percent rate implied average market rates of at least 9 percent. Decision of 13 June 1974, *IMF Annual Report* 1974, pp. 118–19. See Polak, *Valuation of SDR*, pp. 20–21.
133. Crockett, *International Money*, p. 127.
134. Decision of 13 June 1974, para. (b), *IMF Annual Report* 1974, p. 118.
135. Polak, *Valuation of SDR*, p. 20.
136. Decision of 30 June 1976, *IMF Annual Report* 1976, p. 118. Under both the old and new formulas, the SDR rate was to be rounded to the nearest one-quarter percent. The market rates averaged remained those of the U.S., Germany, U.K., France, and Japan. From January 1979 the SDR rate was increased from 60 to 80 percent of the market rate, and in 1981 the Executive Board proposed to raise it to 100 percent. Decision of 25 October 1978, *IMF Annual Report* 1979, pp. 128 and 66; *IMF Survey* 10(1981):19. In 1980 it was decided to round interest rates to the nearest one-eighth percent. *IMF Survey* 9(1980):326.
137. *World Financial Markets*, September 1979, p. 8.
138. Ibid. p. 7, table 3. The yields are nominal (rather than being adjusted for changing price levels), reflect exchange rate changes as well as interest, and assume investment in three month Eurocurrency deposits.
139. See note 136 above; see also Polak, "SDR as a Basket of Currencies," pp. 646–49. In 1980 further amendments (effective 1 January 1981) were introduced to increase flexibility, including quarterly fixing of the interest rate. *IMF Survey* 9(1980):326–27. See discussion p. 279, below.

proposed for 1981 will be adequate, especially as long as it is tied to a five-country base, remains to be seen.

Liquidity in a Floating World

Economists had long pointed out that under a floating system, international reserves would not be needed. But this proposition assumed an absolutely free float by each country independent of every other country. This was not at all the pattern that emerged. Many countries actively managed their exchange rate through market intervention and all countries intervened at least occasionally, with the previously noted result that intervention did not decline after the transition from the Bretton Woods par value system to a generalized floating system.

The wide variety of exchange rate systems made liquidity needs even harder to calculate. For example, the snake arrangements required intervention in the currencies of the members to keep the snake together as well as intervention in the dollar in order to manage the exchange rates between snake members and the dollar. Moreover, many currencies were pegged to other currencies and had to intervene in those currencies to maintain the peg. As of 30 June 1975, only eleven Fund member currencies were floating independently.[140]

One of the most startling developments of the period following approval of the SDR mechanism in the First Amendment has been the unprecedentedly rapid growth in world liquidity. Table 3 tells the story.

Of the 102 billion SDR increase in reserves in the period between year-ends 1968 and 1974, all but 8 billion SDR was accounted for by increases in official holdings of foreign exchange. Gold holdings (valued at the official price) had actually decreased, and SDRs, even with the completion of the allocations in the first official period, constituted only about 5 percent of reserves, roughly comparable to the value of reserve positions in the Fund.

Although the vast increase in foreign exchange holdings is associated in many minds with the onset of generalized floating, the increases in the first half of the 1970s can be attributed with at least equal justice to an attempt to preserve the fixed exchange rate feature of the Bretton Woods system and, in particular, to the resistance by the principal reserve currency countries to an appreciation of their currencies against the dollar. For example, a large percentage increase in foreign exchange had already taken place in 1970, and the largest percentage increase—the second largest in absolute terms—was experienced in 1971 (see table 3). These increases simply reflected the massive purchases of dollars, particularly by Germany and Japan, as the industrial and more developed countries sought to check the rise in their exchange rates

140. *IMF Annual Report 1975*, p. 24 (table 9). Other countries were pegged on the French franc, Spanish peseta, South African rand, and on a composite of currencies. Ibid.

208

Table 3
Official Reserves, 1960–78
(in billions of SDRs and percent [cols. 5 and 7])

	1. Gold	2. SDRs	3. Reserve positions in Fund	4. Foreign exchange	5. Rate of increase: foreign exchange (percent)	6. Total	7. Rate of increase: total (percent)
1960	37.7	—	3.6	19.9	—	61.2	—
1965	41.5	—	5.4	25.4	—	72.3	—
1966	40.7	—	6.4	26.1	2.8	73.2	1.2
1967	39.4	—	5.7	29.3	12.3	74.4	1.6
1968	38.7	—	6.5	32.5	10.9	77.8	4.6
1969	38.9	—	6.7	33.0	1.5	78.7	1.2
1970	37.0	3.1	7.7	45.4	37.6	93.2	18.4
1971	35.9	5.9	6.4	75.0	65.2	123.2	32.2
1972	35.6	8.7	6.3	95.9	27.9	146.5	19.0
1973	35.6	8.8	6.2	101.8	6.2	152.4	4.0
1974	35.6	8.9	8.8	126.3	24.1	179.6	17.8
1975	35.5	8.8	12.6	136.9	8.4	193.8	7.9
1976	35.3	8.7	17.7	159.8	16.7	221.5	14.3
1977	35.4	8.1	18.1	200.1	25.2	261.7	18.1
1978	35.7	8.1	14.8	220.8	10.3	279.4	6.8

Source: *IMF Annual Reports* for the following years: 1976, table 11, p. 34; 1979, table 14, p. 47. All figures are year-end. Gold is valued at SDR 35 per fine ounce in all years.

Table 4
Distribution of Reserves, 1960–78
(in billions of SDRs)

	1960	1968	1969	1970	1971	1972	1973	1974	1975	1976	1977	1978
United States	19.4	12.2	14.2	14.5	12.1	12.1	11.9	13.1	13.6	15.8	16.0	15.0
United Kingdom	5.1	2.4	2.5	2.8	8.1	5.2	5.4	5.7	4.7	3.6	17.3	13.1
Germany	7.0	9.9	7.1	13.6	17.2	21.9	27.5	26.5	26.5	30.0	32.7	41.4
Japan	1.9	2.9	3.7	4.8	14.1	16.9	10.2	11.0	10.9	14.3	19.1	25.7
Other industrial countries	15.1	24.7	24.7	30.1	37.3	41.4	41.0	41.6	48.4	49.8	54.4	65.2
More developed primary producing countries	3.7	7.3	7.6	8.5	12.1	19.4	19.9	17.3	15.3	15.8	15.9	20.0
Less developed countries	9.6	14.1	15.7	18.9	22.3	29.7	36.6	64.3	74.3	92.3	106.3	99.0
Major oil exporting	2.5	3.1	4.0	5.2	8.0	10.3	12.4	38.4	48.3	56.1	62.2	46.2
Non-oil	7.1	11.0	11.7	13.7	14.3	19.4	24.2	25.9	26.1	36.1	44.2	52.8
Total	61.8	73.5	75.5	93.2	123.2	146.5	152.6	179.5	193.8	221.6	261.7	279.4

Source: *IMF Annual Reports* for the following years: 1971, table 6, p. 28; 1973, table 14, p. 40; 1976, table 12, p. 35; 1979, table 18, p. 57. Figures from 1974 on are taken from the 1979 report and differ slightly from those appearing in the 1976 report. All figures are year-end.

Table 5
U.S. Liabilities to Selected Countries, 1968–78
(in billions of U.S. dollars)

	Germany	Japan	U.K.	Switzerland
1968	3.7	4.0	6.5	2.5
1969	2.5	4.5	11.8	2.6
1970	8.2	5.6	6.0	2.5
1971	12.4	16.0	7.8	4.5
1972	17.1	20.2	5.4	4.1
1973	25.1	11.5	6.6	4.9
1974	21.9	14.4	8.1	11.6
1975	21.1	13.5	7.3	10.2
1976	23.9	17.1	10.6	11.9
1977	28.0	22.1	23.1	14.6
1978	43.9	33.5	19.9	23.1

Source: IMF, *International Financial Statistics*, 1975, 1980. All figures are year-end.

(see table 4). Between year-ends 1969 and 1972, Germany and Japan alone acquired claims on the United States of about $30 billion, nearly half of the total increase of the foreign exchange holdings by all countries (compare tables 3 and 5). Until the late 1970s there was no comparable increase in liquidity.

The irony was thus that the attempt to hold on to the Bretton Woods fixity of exchange rates by intervention had the consequence of a massive increase in liquidity and made the SDR essentially irrelevant from the standpoint of the absolute amount of liquidity. This is a subject to which further attention will be given below; but surely one can say that, because of the way it was handled, the move to generalized floating "solved" the liquidity problem more by generating the liquidity than by reducing the need for it.[141]

141. For a discussion of the relevance of liquidity in a floating system, see the contributions of Gottfried Haberler and Herbert T. Grubel and the comments of Robert Triffin and Fritz Machlup under the title "How Important Is Control over International Reserves?" in *The New International Monetary System*, ed. Mundell and Polak, pp. 111–82.

SEVEN

Reform and the Committee of Twenty

When the British and Americans were negotiating the outlines of what became the Bretton Woods agreement, they did not think of themselves primarily as reforming the international monetary system. In keeping with the notion of a postwar family of international organizations to maintain the peace, the Fund was only one of a number of organizations concerned with economic matters. Even the Bretton Woods conference was also devoted to agreement on an International Bank for Reconstruction and Development (now the World Bank). Insofar as the Bretton Woods conferees negotiated about the monetary system, as opposed to the Fund simply as a balance-of-payments financing institution, their principal focus was on purging the system of aberrations that cropped up in the interwar period. The emphasis was on eliminating fluctuating rates, competitive depreciation, and exchange controls on current payments.

To the extent that the Bretton Woods agreement represented reform, it was reform of a highly conservative character—a return to an idealized past, though not all the way to the pre-1914 gold standard. Yet it was surely reform in the sense that the Bretton Woods architects did not intend to allow the system to evolve by itself. As previous chapters have shown, they rather overestimated their powers, especially since the Bretton Woods agreement did not deal with some of the crucial aspects of the post-1945 system, such as the role of reserve currencies and intervention arrangements.

The Bretton Woods agreement represented reform in another sense, too. The text was ambitious, even architectonic, and it substituted written rules, indeed legal formulations, for practice and implicit understandings. It is striking that the prime impetus for this rule-drafting, even legalistic approach came from the Anglo-Saxons, whose own private law had evolved primarily by judicial decision.

The moving force in providing the detailed rules was no doubt the United States, which provided the lawyers for drafting the Articles of Agreement. The United States had already established a reputation, as a result of its role in the formation of the League of Nations, for promoting comprehensive reform with a strong bias toward new international institutions. Another instance was the World War II planning exercise, conducted more by the State Department than the Treasury, for the United Nations and its special-ized agencies. In the 1950s the U.S. advocacy of a European defense com-munity, an ambitious attempt to create an international military force right down to vessels manned by seamen of various nationalities, is a later instance.[1] This bias toward large-scale, complex reform, if manifested only to a lesser extent in the First Amendment negotiations leading to the SDR, played a dominant role in the Committee of Twenty (C-20) effort from 1972 to 1974.

The First Amendment was, in one sense, an example of ambitious reform. Indeed, it represented the very antithesis of an evolutionary approach to change in the international monetary system. But as will become clearer in later chapters, the SDR, thought to be so revolutionary a concept at the time of the First Amendment, remained very much a detail on the great body of convention, practice and ad hoc arrangements that constituted the actual international monetary system. Indeed, as we have seen in the preceding chapter, that system changed far more radically in the twenty-month period from Camp David to the onset of generalized floating, than it did through the introduction of the SDR.

The major reform document to be analyzed in this chapter will be the 1974 Outline of Reform. The negotiations leading to the Outline produced very little actual change, though the Outline did lead indirectly to the Second Amendment to the Articles of Agreement. Conditions differed from those

1. See e.g. *Department of State Bulletin*, 26(1952):364–65, 367, 932.

that had shaped Bretton Woods and the First Amendment. The Bretton Woods planners were writing, at least so far as constitutional documents were concerned, on a tabula rasa. They found no built-in bureaucratic impediment, in the form of a Fund staff, to thoroughgoing reform. The First Amendment was concerned almost entirely with adding something substantive to the Articles, rather than with eliminating existing rules and institutions. In fact international bureaucratic incentives favored change; the Fund staff quickly came to see the SDR as an instrument for enhancing the role of the Fund.

Certainly conditions were not favorable for thoroughgoing reform in the C-20 negotiations. The Fund was in place, and so were the Articles of Agreement. The Fund staff could be expected to oppose changes that would downgrade the Fund's importance, and amendment of the Articles would in any event be a cumbersome and time-consuming exercise. The existence of the Fund, with a membership of more than one hundred countries, plus the precedent of the Fund's central role in the drafting of the First Amendment, made any attempt to negotiate reform within a small group of key countries unrealistic. On the other hand, the underlying system was evolving very rapidly even as the C-20 was meeting. It was clear that there could be no going back to the Bretton Woods system as such, even though the difficulties of returning from generalized floating to a par value system were not widely perceived at the time.

Even though the C-20 reform exercise was a diplomatic failure, it is worth discussing in detail for several reasons. First, given the propensities of the participants in the present international institutional arrangements, and particularly in the United States, to make efforts periodically to substitute reform for evolution, a new reform initiative in the next decade or so seems likely. Indeed, the mini-reform effort begun in 1979 to introduce a substitution account was founded directly on the C-20 analysis of such an arrangement. Second, the work by national and Fund staffs in the C-20 effort reveals much about the evolutionary process that had shaped the international monetary system up to that time. Read as history, the C-20 documents, even to the comparatively minor extent to which they have been published, provide a major source of insight into the breakdown of the Bretton Woods system and the transition to generalized floating.

I. Reform Studies Preceding the C-20

The first tentative steps toward reform of the exchange rate mechanism were taken in the Executive Directors' discussions leading to their 1970 report,

The Role of Exchange Rates in the Adjustment of International Payments.[2] The
stimulus for the report was in part the growing dissatisfaction with the
mechanics of exchange rate adjustments following sterling's belated 1967
devaluation[3] and the failure of a late 1968 Group of Ten meeting in Bonn to
arrive at an agreement concerning the timing and amount of a French franc
devaluation. Another stimulus was increasing concern with the growing volume of short-term capital movements that seemed to threaten the foundations
of the par value system.[4] But an equally important motivation for undertaking
the study was the fear that if the Fund did not grab hold of the issue, the
initiative might pass to the Group of Ten or conceivably to some ad hoc
institution. The G-10 had already played an important role in the First
Amendment creating the SDR, and the British Chancellor of the Exchequer
had called for a "new international monetary conference" on the pattern of
Bretton Woods.[5]

The report that was the product of a year and one-half of Fund discussions
was a distinctly conservative and modest document. The status quo was
endorsed with very limited exceptions: "the basic principles of the Bretton
Woods system are sound and should be maintained and strengthened."[6] De-
cisively rejected were three major changes: "fluctuating exchange rates,"
"substantially wider margins," and "a regime under which parities would be
adjusted at fixed intervals on the basis of some predetermined formula
which would be applied automatically."[7] The last of these possible innovations, known under the rubric of "crawling pegs" and "sliding parities," had
in fact received considerable support from the U.S., German, and Italian
Executive Directors, but they abandoned their advocacy of such a system.
Three reasons may have motivated that abandonment: opposition from other
Executive Directors, the desire of the European members to coordinate their
positions on monetary issues, and the European desire to bind their currencies
more closely together in what was to become the snake arrangement.[8]

The report did, however, leave open the possibility of eventual change in
three specific directions. On the first, "the prompt adjustment of parities in
appropriate cases," the Board set forth without endorsement a concrete, albeit
modest proposal:

2. Published as a separate document by the Fund in 1970 (hereafter cited IMF, *1970 Exchange
Rate Report*) and reprinted in Margaret Garritsen de Vries, *The International Monetary Fund
1966–1971* (1976), 2:273–330.
3. See discussion pp. 182–84.
4. On the French franc incident see Andreas F. Lowenfeld, *The International Monetary System*
(1977), pp. 119–22, and de Vries, *IMF 1966–1971*, 1:449–54. On short-term capital movements,
see ibid. 1:496–500.
5. Quoted ibid. 1:500–501.
6. IMF, *1970 Exchange Rate Report*, p. 67.
7. Ibid. p. 69.
8. De Vries, *IMF 1966–1971*, 1:511–15. On the snake, see discussion pp. 193–94.

[I]n order to facilitate small and gradual changes in parity as disequilibria develop and to avoid unnecessary delays in adjustment that may occur for various reasons, the Articles of Agreement might be amended to allow members to make changes in their parities without the concurrence of the Fund as long as such changes did not exceed, say, 3 per cent in any twelve-month period nor a cumulative amount of, say, 10 per cent in any five-year period.[9]

A second possible change involved a "slight," as opposed to the rejected "substantial," widening of margins. The third envisaged "temporary deviations from par value obligations."[10] All three possibilities were relegated to further study, and at the ensuing 1970 annual meeting the speeches of governors made it clear that no changes would be approved. Perhaps the decisive reason was that the changes could not be made without amendment of the Articles.[11] The travail involved in the First Amendment had sated the taste for the amendment-drafting process.

Events changed all that. Only about fifteen months later, in the wake of the Camp David decision and the diplomatic turmoil of the autumn of 1971, the Group of Ten ministers agreed at the Smithsonian in December that

> discussions should be promptly undertaken, particularly in the framework of the International Monetary Fund, to consider reform of the international monetary system over the longer term. It was agreed that attention should be directed to the appropriate monetary means and division of responsibilities for defending stable exchange rates and for insuring a proper degree of convertibility of the system; to the proper role of gold, of reserve currencies, and of special drawing rights in the operation of the system; to the appropriate volume of liquidity; to re-examination of the permissible margins of fluctuation around established exchange rates and other means of establishing a suitable degree of flexibility; and to other measures dealing with movements of liquid capital.[12]

This was an agenda for action that dwarfed in ambition even the range of ideas rejected in the 1970 report.

Meanwhile the Fund machinery had already been cranked up to undertake another study. In part in response to President Nixon's call in his 15 August speech for "necessary reforms to set up an urgently needed new international monetary system,"[13] the Board of Governors had approved a study resolution at the 1971 annual meeting. This resolution called on the Executive Directors

9. IMF, *1970 Exchange Rate Report*, pp. 71, 73.
10. Ibid. p. 71.
11. De Vries, *IMF 1966–1971*, 1:515–16.
12. Smithsonian Press Communiqué, para. 7, reprinted in *International Financial News Survey* 23(1971):418.
13. *Public Papers of the Presidents of the United States: Richard Nixon . . . 1971* (1972), p. 889.

to "study all aspects of the international monetary system" and "to make reports" on measures "for the improvement or reform" of that system.[14] Again, as in the case of the 1969 study, an incentive for pushing ahead with a Fund study was the fear that the reform initiative would pass to the Group of Ten.[15]

The Executive Board did not, however, provide an adequate forum for negotiation, for reasons that will be explored below in connection with the formation of the Committee of Twenty. The key point is that the result of eleven months of labor on a 1972 report, completed shortly before the 1972 annual meeting, was a document that set forth differing national views without any significant degree of compromise. Successive paragraphs tended to read "One view is . . . Another view is . . ." or "One approach would be . . . Under a second approach . . . Under a third approach. . . ."[16]

The movement toward reform had consequently still not been launched in any political sense by the time of the 1972 annual meeting. Nonetheless, the 1972 reform report formulated a number of issues that were to dominate subsequent discussions.[17] And for those informed enough to read between the lines to see which countries supported the various "views" and "approaches," the front lines of the subsequent negotiations could already be perceived.

II. FORMATION AND FAILURE OF THE C-20

Even before the 1972 reform study had been concluded, a decision was taken to create a new framework for the next stage of reform discussions. Although a sufficient ground for that decision would have been the fact that the Executive Board was proving to be an inadequate forum for negotiating major change in the international monetary system, the stimulus for the creation of the new forum, the Committee of Twenty, was somewhat more complex.

What the United States found inadequate in the Executive Board was the negotiating framework. The reasons were diverse. In the first place, the Executive Directors were not sufficiently high-ranking in their own governments to be able to gain support for the compromises necessary to reach agreement. The important issues would not be merely technical but would be political in the sense that various nations' wealth, income, and prestige would be at stake and indeed some of the issues might even play a role in domestic politics. Aside from their relatively low rank in their own govern-

14. Resolution No. 26–9, *IMF Annual Report* 1972, p. 36.
15. Joseph Gold, *Legal and Institutional Aspects of the International Monetary System: Selected Essays* (1979), p. 258 (hereafter cited Gold, *Selected Essays*).
16. IMF, *Reform of the International Monetary System: A Report by the Executive Directors to the Board of Governors* (1972), pp. 34, 38–39 (hereafter cited IMF, *1972 Reform Report*).
17. For a review of the treatment of those issues in the *1972 Reform Report*, see John Williamson, *The Failure of World Monetary Reform, 1971–74* (1977), pp. 60–67.

ments, the Executive Directors resided in Washington as a result of the Bretton Woods decision that the Executive Board should be in "continuous session,"[18] and therefore they were not always in intimate touch with the latest currents of thought and influence in their own governments.

A second factor motivating the U.S. opposition to the Executive Board as a forum was the feeling that the Executive Directors were too closely associated with the Fund staff to give full consideration to proposals that could attenuate the influence of the Fund. The Executive Directors not only lived in Washington, where the Fund was located, but they maintained offices at the Fund's headquarters and in some cases felt themselves more officials of the Fund than of their own governments. This was likely to be particularly the case for those directors, and they were a majority, who represented constituencies composed of more than one member. Use of the Board of Governors as the forum was not a live alternative. The governors were usually finance ministers or central bank governors and hence could meet only irregularly. The question was who could meet more often to narrow options and prenegotiate issues; only the Executive Directors existed for that function. In any event, the Board of Governors was too large a body, with one governor for each of the more than one hundred members, to constitute an effective working committee.

Finally, the United States believed that if the Executive Board were the reform forum, then the Fund staff would inevitably provide the secretariat function and the preparatory work and background studies might be biased toward solutions that were agreeable to the Fund staff and that enhanced the role of the Fund.[19] It must be added that although this concern with the Fund staff's role was appropriate during a period when "all options," including the survival of the Fund at least in its existing form, were open, the U.S. position also reflected some dissatisfaction with the Fund's Managing Director, whose reappointment to a third term the United States successfully opposed in 1972.[20]

The U.S. desire for a non-Fund forum enjoyed some support among other developed countries. But the less-developed countries strongly favored a Fund-based forum. They considered the Group of Ten to be an exclusive "rich man's club," and they had resented the Group of Ten's Smithsonian agreement from which they had been excluded.[21]

A compromise forum was therefore sought. The shared goal became a forum that was related to the Fund but that would nevertheless function at

18. See discussion p. 112.
19. On the perceived resistance of the IMF staff to reform, see Richard N. Cooper, "Prolegomena to the Choice of an International Monetary System," *International Organization* 24(1975):93. For a summary of the arguments against a Fund-based forum, see Gold, *Selected Essays*, p. 231.
20. Robert Solomon, *The International Monetary System, 1945–1976* (1977), p. 225; Williamson, pp. 66–67; Martin Mayer, *The Fate of the Dollar* (1980), p. 194.
21. Gold, *Selected Essays*, p. 261.

a higher level than the Executive Directors, that would be composed of political level officials from home governments, and that would have some organ other than the Fund staff to provide secretariat functions. On the other hand, the new forum would have to give the less-developed world as much representation as they had in the Fund. In the end, it became a requirement of universal agreement on the forum issue that representation in the new forum would have to be based on some existing model.

Out of this bundle of political requirements came the Committee of Twenty, based directly on the Executive Board's twenty-constituency model, with a political-level Deputies group to provide the option-narrowing, pre-negotiation function, and with a Bureau to provide the secretariat function. The C-20 was, in legal theory, a committee of the Board of Governors; hence, as part of the Fund structure, its creation did not constitute a disavowal of the Fund. It was established by the Board of Governors as an "ad hoc Committee of the Board of Governors on Reform of the International Monetary System and Related Issues."[22]

The membership of the Committee was, as its popular name conveys, exactly twenty; each member and constituency entitled to appoint an Executive Director was empowered to appoint one member of the Committee. Although the composition of its membership was in a sense a historical accident, the Executive Board twenty-member model had the political virtue of providing nine seats to the less-developed world while at the same time assuring the developed members that they would not be outnumbered as they were in United Nations organs. Fewer seats for the less developed countries might have meant that the reform exercise would never have gotten off the ground, while fewer for the developed countries, who would be providing the bulk of the resources and bearing the bulk of the responsibility, might have removed any hope that the C-20 could become more than a debating society.[23]

Each member could in turn appoint two associates, thereby allowing single-member constituencies a solution to the problem faced by some, especially the United States, of how to make room for participation by an independent central bank governor who might be a person of some influence in local political councils (in the U.S. case, Arthur Burns). The two associates rule also permitted multimember constituencies an opportunity for participation by nationals of more than one of their members, thereby possibly facilitating eventual political compromise.

A Deputies group was established by the same Board of Governors' resolution that created the Committee itself. Each member of the Committee could appoint two deputies, and Fund Executive Directors were also entitled

22. Resolution No. 27-10, *IMF Annual Report* 1972, p. 92.
23. Gold, *Selected Essays*, pp. 262–63.

to participate in the Deputies' meetings, as were two members of the Fund staff. In addition, each Committee member could appoint five advisers, who, though not entitled to speak, tended to make a meeting of the Deputies look more like a parliament than a working committee. Still, those accredited to Deputies' meetings were less numerous than those accredited to Bretton Woods.[24] And, most important, the Deputies themselves were high-ranking, broadly experienced national officials generally just below the ministerial level, who knew the issues and were experienced at political compromise. From the standpoint of the organization of international decisionmaking, the important fact was that the Deputies were part and parcel of the forum compromise and as such considered a threat to the Executive Director's traditional role.

Another important element of the compromise on the forum issue was the creation of a five-man Bureau to carry out the secretariat function in lieu of the Fund staff. The Bureau was headed by the Chairman of the Deputies, Jeremy Morse, who had been a high Bank of England official. Its other four members, who were Vice-Chairmen of the Deputies and had also been active in monetary matters, worked on a full-time basis with Morse in offices at the Bank of England. Their experience made them more than merely highly qualified technicians. One, Alexandre Kafka, a Brazilian, was an economist. and prominent Fund Executive Director.[25] Another, Robert Solomon, who had been a U.S. Federal Reserve official playing an important role in drafting the U.S. reform proposal that formed the basis for much of the C-20's work, has described the function of the Bureau members as follows:

> While we all regarded ourselves as international officials rather than national representatives, we were expected to, and did, try to see that the positions of the countries with which we were associated were clearly formulated and reflected in the evolving vision of a reformed system. At times the influence went the other way; each of us on occasion tried to influence the deputies of his country or group to alter or adopt positions that were more conducive to a successful reform effort.[26]

The Bureau thus gave the C-20's intellectual preparation some distance from the Fund staff. But the Fund was in no way excluded from the C-20 exercise. Aside from the participation of the Managing Director in C-20 meetings and the participation of Executive Directors and of two Fund staff

24. Williamson, p. 68. This list is not exhaustive; there were also, for example, observers—with a right to speak—from six international organizations. See also attendance lists in IMF, *International Monetary Reform: Documents of the Committee of Twenty* (1974), pp. 244–53 (hereafter cited C-20 Documents).
25. See e.g. Alexandre Kafka, "The International Monetary System in Transition—Parts I and II," *Virginia Journal of International Law* 13(1972):135–57, 539–52, and *The IMF: The Second Coming?* Princeton Essays in International Finance no. 94 (1972).
26. Solomon, p. 237.

members in meetings of the Deputies, the Fund staff was able to make its views known to all participants and to influence the Bureau's work through the circulation of documents.[27]

The main instrument of the Bureau was the preparation of drafts of what eventually evolved into the Outline of Reform, including alternative draft language on issues to be resolved and commentary on those issues. The First Outline of Reform, published at the time of the 1973 annual meeting in Nairobi, Kenya, was actually only one of a series of drafts.[28]

The Nairobi meeting was a turning point in the reform exercise. One year had already elapsed since the formation of the C-20 and nearly two years since the Smithsonian. The First Outline, when examined closely, served only to underline the extent of profound disagreement on the principal issues. Indeed, despite the extensive and elaborate language, little had been agreed beyond the somewhat ambiguous statement that the reformed system would be "based on stable but adjustable par values."[29] This phrase, agreed originally between French finance minister Giscard d'Estaing and U.S. treasury secretary Shultz and endorsed by the C-20 in March 1973, was taken by other delegates to mean an adjustable peg system despite an additional sentence in the March C-20 communiqué recognizing that "floating rates could provide a useful technique in particular situations."[30] The dominant attitude at Nairobi was one of gloom at the prospects for agreement, and despite a call for an accelerated work program to complete the Outline by July 1974,[31] little was accomplished thereafter beyond the generation of many documents.

By the time the oil crisis in the winter of 1973–74 had given rise to a new set of fears about the difficulties of meeting the developed oil-importing countries' resulting balance-of-payments difficulties and of "recycling" the oil-exporting countries' mounting surpluses, it became apparent that the C-20 exercise would not lead to a new international monetary charter. Indeed, the notion of an adjustable peg system came to look increasingly utopian as the period of generalized floating lengthened and as the oil crisis made the time for a return to par values retreat into the distant future.

Consequently, at the January 1974 C-20 meeting, a decisive procedural decision was taken: that priority in the C-20 deliberations would be given to reform measures that could be implemented soon. The implication was that broad-gauged reform did not have to be agreed on fully because it could not in any event be implemented in the immediate future. As a natural outgrowth of that decision, the final Outline, published in June 1974, de-

---

27. Resolution No. 27-10, *IMF Annual Report 1972*, pp. 92–93.
28. The text of the First Outline was published in *IMF Survey* 2(1973):305–8.
29. First Outline, *IMF Survey* 2(1973):306.
30. C-20 Documents, p. 215. See Solomon, pp. 248–49, on his understanding of the origin of these phrases.
31. Report to the Board of Governors by Chairman of Committee of Twenty (24 September 1973), C-20 Documents, pp. 227, 228.

scribes a "Reformed System," not as a constitution for future adoption, even at some distant unspecified time, but rather merely as an outline that "records the outcome of the Committee's discussion of international monetary reform and indicates the general direction in which the Committee believes that the system could evolve in the future."[32] Bureau member Solomon has offered the following explanation of this subtle transition from reform to evolution:

> When the deputies met in Washington on March 27–29, [1974], they debated the usefulness of bringing forth a "vision" of a reformed system, given the uncertainties as to the duration of the interim period characterized by widespread floating and mammoth surpluses of the oil-exporting countries. The majority supported [U.S. treasury undersecretary] Paul Volcker's position that such a vision—incorporated in an Outline of Reform—should be put before the world as a guide to an evolutionary reform of the system.[33]

The Outline papers over many disagreements as to the shape of the "Reformed System." For some areas of disagreement, Annexes were published "to record the state of the discussion in those areas, and to provide illustrative schemes and operational detail."[34] The Outline also contained a Part II, entitled "Immediate Steps," which the Committee agreed should be taken immediately, to govern the "interim period" and "to begin an evolutionary process of reform."[35] Because the C-20 negotiations involved a wide range of issues, some of considerable complexity, an understanding of the outcome as embodied in the Outline of Reform requires an issue-by-issue analysis.

III. ADJUSTMENT AND THE EXCHANGE RATE MECHANISM

In addition to the failure to involve policy-level national officials in the process, one reason for the inability of the Executive Directors to make any progress toward resolution of the reform issues was the absence of a reform initiative from any of the principal countries. The Bretton Woods negotiations, in contrast, had been based on two coherent plans, the Keynes and White plans. Despite all of the talk from the U.S. side about the need for thoroughgoing reform, the Camp David decisions had not been preceded by any planning about the successor to the Bretton Woods system. Moreover, U.S. attention until the time of the Smithsonian agreement had been focused on obtaining a realignment of exchange rates. Nor was there any sign of

32. C-20 Documents, p. 7.
33. Solomon, p. 262.
34. C-20 Documents, p. 7.
35. Ibid. pp. 18–19. Among these steps were the adoption of the standard basket method of valuation of the SDR (see pp. 201–2 above) and the Guidelines for Floating already discussed (see chapter 6), ibid. pp. 20–21.

comprehensive planning on the European side, which in any event would have been difficult because of the practice of coordinating positions within the European Economic Community as part of the emerging plans for a European monetary system.

The speech by U.S. treasury secretary Shultz at the IMF annual meeting in September 1972 consequently came not simply as a surprise but as a relief.[36] The existence of a U.S. plan meant that there would be something to which policy-level officials from other countries could react. The U.S. plan remained the only comprehensive plan on the C-20 table. Indeed, the United States was the only country to work out a full statement of its negotiating position. Marcus Fleming, a high-level Fund official actively involved in the C-20 process, commented on the shortcomings of national preparation for the C-20 exercise:

> Very few of the major countries established coherent national positions over the whole range of these [reform] issues, and only one of them, the United States, brought out a fairly comprehensive statement of its position. Even that was not comparable in clarity and precision to the Keynes and White plans of former days. The Europeans handicapped themselves by trying to agree issue by issue on a joint EEC position. The less developed countries made great efforts to agree on a common program of reform through the Group of Twenty-Four, but this agreement was inevitably confined to a few isolated matters of common interest, such as the nature of the link between SDR creation and development finance.[37]

Reserve Indicators

The core of the U.S. proposal concerned an objective reserve indicator approach to the questions of what country had the burden of adjusting to payments imbalances and when adjustment actions should be taken.[38] The plan was a reaction to the widely held view that the adjustment system was inadequate. As Henry Wallich observed at the time, the proposition that the adjustment system worked poorly provided "a welcome note of universal agreement,"[39] but there was widespread controversy about how the system should be improved.

The U.S. plan naturally responded to the U.S. view that the prime problem was an asymmetry—namely, that deficit countries alone bore the burden

36. IMF, *Summary Proceedings of the Twenty-seventh Annual Meeting of the Board of Governors, 1972*, pp. 34–44.

37. J. Marcus Fleming, *Reflections on the International Monetary Reform*, Princeton Essays in International Finance no. 107 (1974).

38. The U.S. proposal, in the form in which it had been worked out by November 1972, is reprinted in *Economic Report of the President 1973*, pp. 160–74 (hereafter cited U.S. Proposal).

39. Henry C. Wallich, "The Monetary Crisis of 1971—The Lessons To Be Learned," Per Jacobsson Lecture 1972, in Henry C. Wallich, C. J. Morse, and I. G. Patel, *The Monetary Crisis of 1971—The Lessons To Be Learned* (1972), p. 12.

of adjustment under the Bretton Woods system and that a reformed system should place the burden equally on surplus and deficit countries. What was meant by the language of asymmetry was that a surplus country that did not choose to revalue did not have to do so as long as it was willing to intervene in exchange markets and acquire foreign exchange.[40] In the context of the times, a reference to this asymmetry implied that Germany and Japan, the leading surplus countries, did not have to adjust so long as they were willing to continue to acquire dollars in exchange markets. In the U.S. view, this asymmetry made impossible any return to a U.S. convertibility obligation so long as the United States would have to settle in reserve assets imbalances attributable to the policies of the surplus countries. Moreover, it encouraged surplus countries to keep their currencies undervalued in order to maintain the competitiveness of their export industries. This in turn reinforced existing payments disequilibria and created political pressures within deficit countries for protectionist legislation in defense of domestic industries facing competition from exporting industries in the surplus countries.[41]

At least as important in the U.S. view was the fact that the willingness of the surplus countries to continue to acquire dollars through intervention to prevent an appreciation of their currencies would deprive the United States of the control over its own exchange rate enjoyed by other countries. This difference in control over, and relative flexibility of, exchange rates within a par value system was a further asymmetry, which became the basis for the U.S. proposal for a multicurrency intervention system (to be discussed separately below). The Europeans pointed to a quite separate asymmetry, which became the basis for their objections to the U.S. plan and for their arguments favoring asset settlement (also discussed separately below). The U.S. proposal on adjustment and the exchange rate regime was sufficiently complicated and raised such difficult issues that the subject warrants separate treatment from the multicurrency and asset settlement issues, however closely linked those issues would inevitably be in any reform of the international monetary system.

The U.S. reserve indicator proposal originally had something of a hidden agenda underlying it. Therefore, although it is possible to find intellectual precursors for both objective indicators and a reserve-based system in this or that article or proposal,[42] its immediate origin is worth describing briefly. Using reserves as a mandatory indicator compelling exchange rate changes

40. On the concept of asymmetry, see Marina v. N. Whitman, *Reflections of Interdependence* (1979), pp. 213–54; Richard N. Cooper, "Eurodollars, Reserve Dollars, and Asymmetries in the International Monetary System," *Journal of International Economics* 2(1972):325–44.
41. George P. Shultz and Kenneth W. Dam, *Economic Policy Beyond the Headlines* (1977), pp. 113–14.
42. See Trevor G. Underwood, "Analysis of Proposals for Using Objective Indicators as a Guide to Exchange Rate Changes," *IMF Staff Papers* 20(1973):100–17, for a review of some earlier proposals in which objective indicators and/or reserves played a role.

was proposed to later treasury secretary Shultz by economist Milton Friedman when Shultz was still director of the Office of Management and Budget.[43] After Shultz became treasury secretary in June 1972, he made the Friedman proposal the basis for U.S. planning, and Friedman played a role in the drafting of Shultz's 1972 Fund annual meeting speech.

Friedman was a leading and highly articulate advocate of floating exchange rates,[44] who was nevertheless politically realistic enough to appreciate that the world was not then prepared to accept a floating system. But a system involving margins around a reserve norm (by analogy to the Bretton Woods margins around exchange rate parities) and requiring exchange rate changes whenever the reserve margin was crossed, would engender more frequent exchange rate changes. The narrower the reserve band defined by the margins, the more frequent the rate changes would be. Indeed, at the limit, an infinitesimally narrow reserve band would imply the absence of any possible intervention and hence a de facto system of floating exchange rates.

The U.S. proposal, while clearly directed toward imposing an adjustment burden on surplus countries, can thus also be viewed as a transitional system toward a floating exchange rate system. But it was not so presented. One reason was that in September 1972, more than half a year before the onset of generalized floating, a floating system was still regarded as unthinkable by nearly all finance ministers and central bank governors. A second reason was that there was not sufficient support for a floating system within the U.S. government, particularly in view of strong opposition to floating from Federal Reserve chairman Arthur Burns, to make outright advocacy of floating a feasible negotiating strategy. But, as described below, the United States did argue that individual countries should be able to choose to float within an overall par value framework.

The U.S. proposal closely linked the concept of objective criteria with that of a central role for reserves in signaling the need for adjustment (which, under the U.S. plan, might or might not take the form of an exchange rate change). The two concepts were, however, easily separable, as quickly became clear when the issue was discussed in the C-20. Objective indicators need not involve reserves at all and, reciprocally, it would be possible to agree that reserves would be the crucial criterion in any exchange rate decision taken, for example, within some Fund deliberative process. Nevertheless, the U.S. plan treated the two concepts as reinforcing each other. Linking the two would not only create a superstructure of substantive rules but also

43. The proposal was made in a dinner meeting held in Shultz's OMB office on 22 May 1972. Also in attendance were Arthur Laffer, then OMB economist, and the author, then OMB assistant director for national security and international affairs.
44. See e.g. Milton Friedman, "The Case for Flexible Exchange Rates," in his *Essays in Positive Economics* (1953), pp. 157–203, and his contributions to Milton Friedman and Robert V. Roosa, *The Balance of Payments: Free versus Fixed Exchange Rates* (1967).

establish what could be viewed as a legal system for applying those substantive rules. The U.S. plan and, even more, the European reaction can thus usefully be viewed from this jurisprudential perspective.

The United States favored objective criteria over either the existing principle of national discretion or a system in which the Fund would be given authority to require exchange rate changes. According to the U.S. proposal, objective indicators were "essential on grounds of efficacy and equity." National discretion would not work because "[a]djustment decisions are frequently difficult for any government, and there is a tendency to postpone and avoid such decisions until long after the time when adjustment policies should have been adopted." Delegation of authority to the Fund would not work because "international groups are reluctant to deal promptly with difficult and politically sensitive adjustment questions."[45] The Executive Board, for example, was a committee, and a committee would rarely be able to agree to force unpleasant action on one of its members.

The U.S. plan called for international agreement on an initial reserve base level, called the "norm," for each country as well as a trend line for that norm over time. Countries with reserves below the norm would be subject to a different set of rules from those with reserves above the norm. Below the norm would be a low point, which would represent a "minimum level ordinarily necessary to maintain confidence and to guard against extreme emergencies."[46] When reserves fell below the low point for a period of time, adjustment action, including if necessary devaluation, would be required; if such action were not forthcoming, the member would be subject to international sanctions. A country could make small devaluations at any time and larger devaluations normally only when reserves were below a lower warning point, located between the norm and the low point.[47] The purpose of these rules would be, first, to assure that countries would not repeat Britain's persistent failure to devalue and, second, to permit more exchange rate flexibility through small devaluations while at the same time precluding large competitive devaluations.

The heart of the U.S. plan, however, concerned the responsibilities of countries with reserves above the norm—by which was envisioned persistent surplus countries like Germany and Japan. Corresponding to the deficit country's lower point would be, on the upside, an outer point. When reserves rose above the outer point, adjustment action would be mandatory, including if necessary revaluation; if adjustment action was not forthcoming, sanctions could be imposed. The role of the upper warning point, placed between the norm and the outer point, was less precise. The U.S. plan suggested that that point, in addition to triggering a Fund review of the country's policies,

45. U.S. Proposal, para. 12, p. 163.
46. Ibid. para. 24(a), p. 167.
47. Ibid.

might coincide with a "convertibility point." Above the convertibility point, surplus countries could no longer acquire "primary reserve assets" (that is, gold, SDRs, and claims on the Fund) and would have to hold any additional reserves in reserve currencies.[48] The convertibility point would thus provide protection to the United States, especially if it should once again assume a convertibility obligation, from the consequences of any decision of a country with large dollar holdings to convert those holdings into primary reserve assets.

A key element of the U.S. plan was what became known as the floating option. In addition to being entitled to let its currency float temporarily to a new parity, a country would be able to elect to float its currency indefinitely, subject to compliance with internationally agreed standards that would "assure the consistency of its actions with the basic requirements of a cooperative order. These standards would relate, for example, to movements in its reserves, its intervention policies, elimination of controls on the inward flow of capital, avoidance of restrictive trade controls imposed for balance-of-payments purposes and elimination of any existing extraordinary balance-of-payments measures."[49] One sees here the intellectual origins of the 1974 Guidelines for Floating, though the U.S. proposal was in fact much more ambitious than the Guidelines proved to be.[50]

Secretary Shultz's IMF speech had given at least some people the impression that the U.S. proposal envisaged that the indicators would operate automatically much like a rule of law.[51] According to this reading, a reserve indicator might by itself require an exchange rate change. Many other countries reacted strongly against such "automaticity" in an area that had previously been left to national discretion and that was regarded as so economically complex and politically charged as to require the exercise of the most mature and informed judgment. One rhetorical phrase often used was that computers should not determine exchange rates.

Two issues were actually involved. In addition to the automaticity question, a second issue was what adjustment action would be required even assuming automatic operation of a reserve indicator. The Shultz speech suggested that a country would have its choice of adjustment measures: "Increasing the provision of concessionary aid on an untied basis, reduction of tariffs and other trade barriers, and elimination of obstacles to outward investment could, in specific circumstances at the option of the nation concerned, provide supplementary or alternative means."[52] At the same time,

48. Ibid. para. 24(c)–(e), pp. 167–69.
49. Ibid. para. 28(c), p. 170.
50. See discussion of the Guidelines, pp. 196–99, above.
51. IMF, *Summary Proceedings 1972*, pp. 39–41.
52. Ibid. p. 41.

this very language implied that if the "alternative means" did not work, then an exchange rate change would be required.

If the United States implicitly proposed in the Shultz speech that the indicators act automatically, it quickly retreated from that position. By November its position was that reserve indicators would create a "strong presumption" but could be "overridden" in "exceptional cases."[53] This position, too, was rejected by most other countries. Most European countries argued that reserve indicators should have at most the role of triggering consultations. Such a limited use of reserve indicators would, of course, rob them of any substantive effect since bilateral consultations could be held at any time and since it was not clear how Fund consultations would add any pressure on surplus countries to adjust. To meet this objection, the notion of Fund "assessment" based on reserve indicators was developed. The issue then became what the role of reserve indicators would be within the assessment process. Based on the continuing discussion of this central issue, the Bureau developed two alternatives.

Under either alternative, the assessment process would involve consideration of a wide variety of economic and policy factors.[54] However, under the first alternative, which corresponded to the U.S. position, a country would be expected to take action to correct the imbalance if its reserves had risen or fallen beyond defined reserve indicator points and had remained there for a specified period of time, unless there had been a contrary movement in the country's basic balance of payments or unless the Executive Board decided on other grounds that such action was unwarranted. This alternative also envisaged the application at a specified later time of certain graduated pressures (a subject discussed at greater length below), unless the Executive Board decided that such pressures were unwarranted. The thrust of this alternative was thus that pressures would in the end automatically be applied to force exchange rate adjustment unless the Executive Board in the assessment process decided otherwise.

Under the second alternative, which was supported by most other countries, even after a trigger point was reached the Executive Board would have to decide affirmatively to call on the member to take action, and thereafter would have to decide whether the member had failed to take adequate action and, if so, whether and when graduated pressures should begin to apply. In addition to this requirement of three separate affirmative decisions, the second alternative appeared to call for the decision to be taken on policy, if not indeed diplomatic, grounds, rather than on any basis that could be classified as juridical. The question of the capacity in which the Executive Board would act was not squarely faced. Rather it was a fair assumption from the nature

---

53. U.S. Proposal, para. 11, p. 163.
54. For discussion of the U.S. plan, and reactions to it, see Solomon, pp. 225–28, 241–44.

of the Board that at least the single constituency Directors would be acting under instruction from national governments and hence that any decision to apply pressures would be likely to be a high-level diplomatic decision.

The U.S. objection to the second alternative was that, under such circumstances, the Executive Board would be unlikely to vote to apply pressures to any powerful country. But other countries believed that domestic polities would not be willing to submit to the determination of their exchange rate by any international set of rules based on quantitative data, even if the data gave rise only to a presumption and the possibility remained of the presumption being overridden. (By hypothesis, if pressures were applied the presumption would not have been overridden.)

In one sense the issue raised the same question of rules versus discretion in the design of international institutions that had led Keynes to observe that "[p]erhaps the most difficult question to determine is how much to decide by rule and how much to leave to discretion."[55] But whereas Keynes had treated discretion as being delegated to "central management," the second alternative before the C-20 delegated discretion to a body that was for these major issues more a meeting of Fund members than a group of independent experts applying a body of hard evidence and objective criteria. Of course, it might be possible, as the Board passed on more and more cases, that a sense of precedent and a tradition of objectivity might develop, much as it had developed in applying the conditionality principle in connection with borrowing from the Fund. But there was a major difference. Those who sought Fund financing, in addition to being in most instances smaller countries without their own Executive Director, were often in the position of suppliants. In contrast, the reserve indicators' main impact, if they were to be successful, would be on the leading surplus countries.

The differences between the two alternatives were never fully bridged. Departing from the second alternative's principle that the Executive Board had to vote affirmatively to call for adjustment action, the Outline of Reform moved slightly in the direction of the first alternative by rather vacuously stating that "normally" assessment "would be expected to lead to appropriate adjustment action."[56] And no agreement at all was reached on the method of "activation" of pressures.[57]

In addition to these procedural issues, two other classes of issues were raised by the U.S. reserve indicator proposal. One had to do with how reserves should be measured, and the second with the kinds of pressures that might be applied. A brief review of these complex issues not only sheds light

55. J. Keith Horsefield, *The International Monetary Fund 1945–1965* (1969), 3:6. See Joseph Gold, *The Rule of Law in the International Monetary Fund*, IMF Pamphlet Series no. 32 (1980), pp. 33–34, and discussion pp. 78–79, above.
56. Outline of Reform, para. 10, C-20 Documents, p. 11.
57. Outline of Reform, annex 2, ibid. p. 28.

on the international monetary system in the form to which it had evolved by the time of the C-20 discussions, but also shows how difficult it would be to draft any international agreement that could have any force of law in compelling adjustment action by reluctant members.

Measurement of Reserves

The measurement of international reserves had long raised statistical issues, but data issues rarely engender major policy differences of concern to finance ministers. However, once it became a possibility that exchange rate changes and the application of international pressures might turn on the measurement of reserves, a number of ambiguities and conceptual issues took on major significance.

What constituted reserves, for example, was not an easy question. Though foreign exchange held by governmental bodies might in general be recognized as reserves, should one also consider the large increases in foreign exchange holdings of oil-exporting countries as reserves? To do so within the context of a reserve indicator system might involve repeated revaluation of oil exporters' currencies, even though the foreign exchange might actually represent a financial investment by an oil-exporting country unable to absorb imports sufficiently rapidly to balance its payments.

Another kind of problem involved the foreign exchange holdings of commercial banks. Although one might exclude all such holdings on the ground that they were usually not held as a source of future support for the exchange rate but rather constituted working balances and investment accounts for private sector institutions, there was also a suspicion that some surplus countries might be inclined to "hide" reserves in commercial banks in order to avoid taking adjustment action. In any event, the extent to which commercial banks as opposed to governmental institutions held foreign exchange out of motivations normally associated with reserves differed from country to country, creating issues of equitable application of the reserve indicator scheme if only officially held foreign exchange was included. And yet to include privately held foreign exchange might lead to private banks' commercial transactions triggering mandatory adjustment action.

More significant issues than the definition of reserves involved the way in which reserve amounts were to be calculated. Although the U.S. proposal had envisioned measuring the *stock* of reserves, Italy proposed that the indicator be based on the *flow* of reserves.[58] Conceptually there was little difference between the flow of reserves and the balance of payments. Indeed,

---

58. Williamson, p. 101. Williamson argues that the U.S. language was ambiguous in places and therefore lent itself to the interpretation that the United States would accept a flow indicator. Ibid. p. 103. In fact, the U.S. government was split on the issue with the Treasury favoring a stock indicator and the Federal Reserve a flow indicator. Given Treasury control over the negotiations, the Treasury view prevailed. See Shultz and Dam, pp. 123–26.

there was considerable European support for substituting the basic balance for a reserve indicator or at least supplementing any reserve indicator with a basic balance indicator.[59]

The principal argument against a stock indicator was that it measured primarily the past, since it was simply the cumulative result of past reserve flows. A partial answer was that the rule should require a further movement in reserves in the same direction as the cumulative result of past flows to trigger adjustment. Perhaps a more telling point was that a stock indicator might prove inflationary. No country was prepared to say that its present reserve level was more than adequate. Thus, the total of reserve norms to which members individually were likely to agree would surely exceed the present global total of reserves. Consequently, such a system might tend indirectly toward a massive increase in world liquidity, perhaps by creation of a large volume of SDRs, and hence might lead to worldwide inflation.

A flow indicator had its own problems. To differentiate it from a balance-of-payments indicator, its advocates proposed that a flow indicator would begin to "run" once reserve acquisition (or loss) reached some initial rate and would then run until accumulation (or decumulation) of reserves stopped. The indicator might begin to run again once a new substantial movement in reserves occurred. Such a scheme might, through a "ratchet effect," allow a country to accumulate excessive stores of reserves so long as it did so in a series of discrete increases.[60] Thus, both the stock and flow approaches might be useful to trigger adjustment, or at least assessment of the need for adjustment, but the flow indicator would be unlikely to achieve the objective of maintaining a reasonable distribution of reserves among countries.

Under either a stock or flow indicator, it would be necessary to decide whether to measure reserves gross or net. This issue is easier to understand in a stock indicator context. The question was whether to deduct foreign liabilities of official institutions from foreign assets in calculating reserves. In the case of the United States the difference was enormous because though it held substantial reserve assets, its official liabilities were so great that on a net basis, U.S. reserves would be less than zero. The anomaly of negative reserves could be avoided, however, by measuring reserves on a net basis from some initial gross reserve norm. Thus, the U.S. norm would be a positive number but a net reserve basis could be used for calculating the U.S. position at any time.[61]

59. "The traditional definition of the basic balance includes current account, long-term capital, and certain government capital transactions. It deliberately excludes short-term capital. It usually excludes net errors and omissions." Report of Technical Group on Indicators, para. 32, C-20 Documents, p. 59.
60. Report of Technical Group on Adjustment, paras. 13–15, C-20 Documents, p. 144.
61. Ibid. para. 24, p. 146. See also Solomon, p. 261.

The U.S. argument that a gross reserve indicator would allow greater "elasticity" in the system by permitting global reserve growth through expansion of U.S. liabilities did not set well with some other countries. They took the U.S. argument as a species of special pleading seeking to exempt the United States from the rigors of its own reserve-based system.[62] So long as U.S. deficits were financed by an increase in U.S. liabilities rather than a running down of U.S. reserve assets, a gross reserve indicator would not signal any need for U.S. adjustment.

The net system, on the other hand, had serious practical difficulties, most notably that few countries published net reserve data. Moreover, there were conceptual problems about whose liabilities members' deposits in the Eurocurrency market should be. Should they be treated as liabilities of the country where the deposit was made or of the country in whose currency the deposit was denominated?[63]

The very complexity of these issues concerning the measurement of reserves sheds light on the institutional ambition of the U.S. plan. Moreover, these issues were closely related to similarly complex issues in a number of other closely linked areas of C-20 negotiation, especially settlement and multicurrency intervention. In comparison to any eventual document resolving these kinds of issues, the Bretton Woods agreement would surely prove to have been a simple document.

IV. SANCTIONS AND PRESSURES

Crucial to any objective indicator system, however much watered down by assessment procedures it might be, would be the associated system of sanctions. In this particular area a good deal of progress was made in understanding how a system of sanctions might be structured in a decentralized world without a central sovereign to impose them. Though, like most of the C-20 work, this analysis came to naught, it is nonetheless of critical significance not simply to a lawyer but to anyone who envisions the development and elaboration of international rules governing the conduct of nation states.

The Fund's system of sanctions was primitive if viewed only from a legalistic perspective. Indeed, it was "a policy of the Articles to limit, or to make it possible to limit, the impress of illegality on the action or inaction of members."[64] The assumption was that any sanction for violation of the Articles or Fund decisions should be avoided if at all possible, if for no other reason than that any such sanction was likely to be ignored, with a consequent decline in the credibility of the Fund. In addition, as the Fund's general counsel commented in 1974, the "Executive Board has become reluctant to

62. Solomon, p. 261.
63. Report of Technical Group on Adjustment, paras. 23, 25–30, C-20 Documents, pp. 146–48.
64. Gold, *Selected Essays*, p. 184.

apply remedies because of the strong reactions they provoke against the organization and other members and because a remedy applied against one country may be a precedent for similar action against one's own country."[65] Past practice did not mean that Fund rules were ostentatiously flouted with any regularity. It did mean, however, that the Fund's hierarchy of sanctions (of which the principal one was ineligibility to use Fund resources)[66] was not likely to be effective in making surplus countries regularly conform to a reserve indicator mechanism signaling a revaluation of their currencies, especially where such a revaluation would do substantial harm to export industries.

In order to avoid the connotation of illegality, which was thought distasteful to sovereign states, the C-20 discussion centered on the concept of pressures. The term "pressures" was not, however, merely diplomatic language for "sanctions." It also conveyed the important notion that certain measures might move a powerful country in a desirable direction even before that country was actually required to take any specific step. A surplus country, not yet required to revalue under a reserve indicator scheme, might be induced to do so by a tax or other financial burden that made the surplus country decide that, on balance, revaluation was in its own interest. Indeed, the application of a Fund pressure might itself engender further pressures from the market; for example, the application of a tax might be interpreted by the market as a signal that revaluation (devaluation) was near and hence short-term capital flows into (out of) the country might suffice to bring about an exchange rate change.[67] Thus, the central notion was that pressures that were not regarded as sanctions for any violation might paradoxically be just what was needed to "contribute to the most fundamental necessity of an effective international monetary order, a process of adjustment that would really work."[68]

The concept of pressures received a major boost in the C-20 negotiations when France, the country most opposed to the U.S. reserve indicator scheme, nevertheless suggested at one point that a system of graduated pressures might be devised in which excess reserves would have to be paid into a special account that would bear a negative interest rate.[69] This pressure would be graduated in the sense that the larger the excess holdings, the higher would be the penalty rate. The purpose of this French initiative seems to have been to suggest an alternative to the U.S. proposal of a convertibility point, past which a creditor country could not force a reserve currency country to convert liabilities into primary reserve assets. Not only did the

65. Ibid. pp. 215–16.
66. On Fund sanctions, see ibid. pp. 148–81, 184–85.
67. Report of Technical Group on Adjustment, para. 54, C-20 Documents, p. 153.
68. Gold, *Selected Essays*, p. 216.
69. Williamson, p. 111; Solomon, p. 253.

specific sanction win support but the notion of pressures being "graduated" gained general acceptance.

As with many of the ideas supposedly conceived in the C-20 negotiations, the negative charge on excess reserves can be traced to the Keynes plan, which would have imposed charges both on positive and negative balances of bancor. R. F. Harrod then commented that the proposal was a "paradox, to pay interest on your deposit as well as your overdraft."[70] But thirty years later, divorced from the abstruse concept of bancor, the notion of paying a charge on excess as well as borrowed reserves quickly gained acceptance.

The C-20 negotiations on pressures thus did not revolve about their desirability but rather about several specific issues. One issue, which was at base the same as that of the degree of automatism in the reserve indicator system, was what action would be necessary, and by what body, to "activate" pressures. Here the dilemma was that countries were reluctant to bear pressures triggered by an abstract indicator system, but at the same time were skeptical about the willingness of the Executive Board to activate severe pressures, judging by its past practice of avoiding sanctions. Some delegations argued, unconvincingly, that the dilemma could be resolved by requiring that pressures be activated only by political-level Fund organs, such as the Board of Governors or an intermediate-level Council.

The second issue concerning pressures, and the one on which the highest policy-level attention was focused, was whether to impose trade restrictions on persistent surplus countries that failed to take adequate adjustment action. The principal argument against trade pressures was that the Fund, as a monetary institution, should not become involved in trade matters. Yet this argument represented a triumph of form over substance because the only sanction against surplus countries in the Articles of Agreement, the scarce currency clause, permitting discriminatory exchange restrictions in narrowly limited circumstances, in effect authorized discriminatory trade restrictions.[71] The fact that it had never been used as a sanction was paradoxically asserted as a ground against its use as a pressure. This argument overlooked the fact that the failure to apply the clause arose out of an early interpretation to the effect that it could only be applied if the Executive Board reached an adverse judgment on the policies of the country in question,[72] which was precisely the judgment that would not have to be made if it were to be used as a pressure.

Perhaps a more serious reason for opposing trade pressures was the fear that they would only be used against unpopular countries (a fear that was

---

70. Keynes plan, paras. 16, 17(3) and (5), in Horsefield, *IMF 1945–1965*, 3:6–7; R. F. Harrod, *The Life of John Maynard Keynes* (1951), p. 542. See pp. 81–83, above.
71. See discussion of the scarce currency clause, pp. 108–10, above, and see Article VII, Section 3(b), *original*.
72. Gold, *Selected Essays*, p. 209; Horsefield, *IMF 1945–1965*, 1:193.

justified in the early 1970s when discriminatory trade action against Japan was widely discussed). Still more cogent a ground for avoiding trade pressures was the possibility that use of such pressures could set off a trade war, which could be more harmful to the international economy than persistent balance-of-payments surpluses. Nonetheless, the opposition to trade pressures failed to come to grips with the central point that the motivation for the failure of a surplus country to revalue was likely to be a desire to support its export industries; hence, trade restrictions were a peculiarly appropriate counter-pressure on a surplus country to offset the internal political pressure on its government from its export industries. In any case, part of the opposition to trade sanctions was concern that they might be made mandatory on the importing countries. Since trade restrictions were at least as likely to harm the importing country as the exporting country, opposition to requiring, as opposed to merely permitting, trade restrictions was soundly based.

The third issue concerning pressures was discussed largely at the technical level, in view of the absence of any likely agreement on the reserve indicator proposal as a whole. This issue concerned the kinds of pressures that might be added to the Fund arsenal. Here the degree of technical level agreement was remarkable. The First Outline of Reform contains an Annex listing pressures that "could be applied."[73]

For surplus countries the Annex listed in addition to the previously mentioned mandatory deposit in an excess reserve account and a negative charge on excess reserves, the possibility of the withholding of SDR allocations, a Fund report on the external position and policies of the surplus country and, finally, discriminatory trade and other current account restrictions. In keeping with the resistance to trade pressures such restrictions were characterized as "the most extreme form of pressure."[74] For deficit countries the Annex listed a charge on reserve deficiencies (possibly graduated with respect to the size and duration of the shortfall), an increased charge on Fund borrowings, restriction on access to Fund resources, withholding of SDR allocations, and a report on the deficit country's external position and policies.

Most of these sanctions were only an extension of existing Fund powers. The Fund already had the power, never in fact utilized, to publish "a report made to a member regarding its monetary or economic conditions and developments which directly tend to produce a serious disequilibrium in the international balance of payments of members."[75] Similarly, the possible restriction on access to Fund resources was actually "an extreme form of conditionality on drawings from the Fund."[76] One of the most interesting

---

73. C-20 Documents, p. 28.
74. Annex 2, A(v), C-20 Documents, p. 29. See also the discussion of these pressures on surplus countries in Report of Technical Group on Adjustment, paras. 58–62, ibid. p. 154.
75. Article XII, Section 8, *original* and *first*.
76. Report of Technical Group on Adjustment, para. 66, C-20 Documents, p. 155.

pressures discussed in the Technical Group on Adjustment, which did not command enough assent to be included in the Annex, was that "the international community could in appropriate cases place limitations on official borrowing or officially induced borrowing by countries in deficit."[77] It may be that if concern over excessive liquidity arising from commercial bank borrowing should continue to mount, this pressure might once again be the subject of discussion.[78]

The very richness of the menu of pressures available to the Fund became a source of concern. The Italian delegation pointed to the necessity for the selected Fund body (whether the Executive Board, the Council, or the Board of Governors) not only to choose the particular pressures to be applied but also their intensity and perhaps to increase certain pressures over time. It argued that decision on pressures would thus place an impossible institutional burden on a decision-making system that would have to operate essentially by consensus. The Italian delegation therefore urged adoption of a single and easily graduated pressure, such as a progressive charge on reserve accruals.[79]

In the end agreement on sanctions was unnecessary due to the failure of the more basic reserve indicator negotiations. The Outline of Reform did make clear, however, that pressures would be "available" to the Fund rather than being imposed automatically. And the Outline did confirm the symmetry principle of "graduated pressures to be applied to countries in large and persistent imbalance, whether surplus or deficit."[80] In view of this confirmation in principle and the high degree of technical-level agreement, it was disappointing to those seeking a greater use of legal techniques in international organization that the subsequent Second Amendment ignored the question of pressures. Indeed, the Second Amendment left in the otherwise extensively altered Articles the now-antiquated scarce-currency provision albeit in modified form.[81] Despite what might be taken by the uninformed as an attempt to breathe life into a wrongly slighted sanction, "[n]othing in the discussion of the amended Article VII . . . suggested that the scarce currency clause was likely to be invoked in the future."[82]

V. ASSET SETTLEMENT AND SUBSTITUTION

If the principal U.S. demand in the C-20 negotiations was that a reformed system require persistent surplus countries to adjust, the principal European demand was that the reformed system force adjustment by the United States,

77. Ibid. para. 67, p. 155.
78. See discussion of international commercial bank lending and liquidity, p. 293–96.
79. Report of Technical Group on Adjustment, paras. 69–72, C-20 Documents, pp. 155–56.
80. Outline of Reform, para. 10, C-20 Documents, p. 11.
81. Article VII, Sections 2–5, *second*.
82. Gold, *Selected Essays*, p. 216.

a persistent deficit country enjoying what were regarded as the special privileges of a reserve currency country. These reciprocal demands were the
counterparts of the U.S. and European conception of the dominant asymmetries of the Bretton Woods system. Those asymmetries were, respectively,
the freedom of surplus countries from the constraints on deficit countries and
the exceptional capacity of a reserve currency country to settle deficits with
its own liabilities. The latter asymmetry had now been exacerbated by the
closing of the gold window, which was equivalent to a declaration by the
United States that thenceforth it would settle only in liabilities and virtually
never in primary reserve assets.

The European demand that the United States too settle in reserve assets
was encapsulated in the phrase "asset settlement," which had first been used
in the 1972 Reform Report.[83] The United States could not object outright
to the principle of asset settlement, though it continued to prefer bilateral
convertibility as under Bretton Woods. Under bilateral convertibility, it
would be up to each creditor country to determine whether, and to what
extent, to present dollar balances to the United States for conversion into
primary reserve assets.[84] In contrast to bilateral convertibility, the concept
of asset settlement implied prompt conversion of any dollar balances into
primary reserve assets, thereby putting the dollar on the same basis as currencies that had no reserve status. Asset settlement, in its pure form, was
thus also a restraint on surplus countries since they would not be able to
elect to hold reserves in dollars. Asset settlement coupled with SDR creation
to provide liquidity had a severe elegance that attracted many people. One
Fund official captured the appeal in saying that the "SDRs would ensure that
there were enough reserves, asset settlement that there were not too many."[85]

The United States did not oppose asset settlement in principle but tied
its acceptance to a number of conditions. One was that agreement would
first have to be reached on its reserve indicator proposal (on the ground that
the United States could not settle in reserve assets so long as surplus countries
unjustifiably accumulated, in the form of excessive dollar exchange, claims
on U.S. reserve assets).

The United States also made two arguments that in effect conditioned its
support for asset settlement. First, even though asset settlement might be
appropriate for future deficits, it would be an unsupportable burden with
respect to past deficits represented by the large "overhang" of dollar claims
held by foreign governments. In response to this concern, the possibility of

83. IMF, *1972 Reform Report*, pp. 33–40.
84. Solomon, p. 252. On bilateral convertibility versus asset settlement, see Fleming, pp. 4–5.
85. Fleming, p. 5. On the differing approaches to asset settlement, see Joseph Gold, "Substitution in the International Monetary System," *Case Western Reserve Journal of International Law*
12(1980):289–91.

a substitution account was advanced. The core idea was that SDRs could be substituted for existing dollar holdings via the Fund as intermediary.

Second, the United States argued that asset settlement should in any event be voluntary for the creditor country because of the useful role that reserve currencies played in providing elasticity to the system and in giving other countries freedom over the composition of their reserves. Since it bore on the future of reserve currencies, this aspect of the U.S. position on asset settlement was intimately related to the future of other reserve assets, most particularly the SDR and gold, and hence will be discussed separately below. For the present it may simply be noted that the principal response to the U.S. elasticity argument was that credit facilities through the Fund or bilateral swap arrangements were a preferable form of elasticity.

The logically obvious alternative to the idea of a Fund substitution mechanism—namely, the funding of short-term U.S. liabilities into long-term obligations that could not be converted into reserve assets until maturity—did not receive serious consideration in the C-20. The first reason was that funding seemed to be regarded, no doubt wrongly, as an inherently bilateral activity resting on agreement between debtor and creditor and the C-20 was by its history and composition oriented toward collective solutions. A second, and more important, reason was that funding of dollar holdings was equivalent to a reduction in reserves, and no country regarded its reserves as excessive.[86] Long-term currency assets cannot be directly used in exchange market transactions. Indeed, even if additional SDRs were created to leave total liquidity where it had been prior to funding, individual countries, particularly the less-developed countries, tended to prefer to hold dollars, especially in view of the lower interest rate on SDRs compared to dollars.

The implication of this preference for dollars was that, even under a Fund substitution arrangement, other countries would not be willing to accept SDRs in exchange for the entire amount of the dollar overhang. Though the United States was prepared to accept a voluntary once-for-all substitution through the Fund of the entire overhang into SDRs (with future deficits subject to bilateral convertibility as under the Bretton Woods system),[87] this position was unacceptable to the less-developed countries, which preferred to have discretion as to the extent and rate at which they would exchange dollar balances for SDRs. At least some sovereignty over the composition of reserve holdings thus became a sine qua non of any agreement on asset settlement and, more generally, on U.S. resumption of convertibility.

With respect to future U.S. deficits, two competing asset settlement systems were discussed, a "more mandatory" system and an "on demand" system.[88] In the former, members would have to present new balances for

86. Solomon, p. 252.
87. Ibid.; Williamson, p. 152.
88. Outline of Reform, annexes 5 and 6, C-20 Documents, pp. 37–41.

conversion, and in the latter members would have an option whether to do so. But even under the more mandatory system, the obligation would be imposed only on those countries that chose to become members of the "settlement group."[89] It was apparently anticipated that, at a minimum, many less-developed and oil-producing countries would not join the settlement group. Thus, the desire of members for control over the composition of their own reserves was squarely in conflict with the principle of full asset settlement.

In view of the failure of the C-20 negotiations, the lasting value of the debate on asset settlement lies in the discussion of a Fund substitution facility, in which old dollars would have been exchanged for new SDRs, since the interest in such a facility was to recur again at the end of the 1970s. The purpose of a substitution facility would have been to permit the United States to adopt asset settlement while at the same time protecting it from the conversion of the overhang. If countries could demand conversion of the overhang, then the United States would be likely to face at some point in the future a demand for conversion exceeding its holdings of primary reserve assets and would have to suspend convertibility once again.

Much of the debate over substitution involved whether the substitution should be once-for-all or whether, on the contrary, it should be a continuing facility in which a country could at any time present dollars for SDRs. The United States feared that the latter type of facility would have perverse effects since it would lead to substitution only when the dollar was weak. The latter danger was lessened to some extent by agreement that the facility would be one-way only. That is, no country would be able to present SDRs for dollars, and thereby be able to speculate directly by going back and forth between dollars and SDRs through the facility.[90]

The substitution negotiations did not come to a head. What the outcome would have been is difficult to know, especially because less-developed countries suspected that a substitution account would not only force them into low-yielding SDRs but also would stand in the way of the transfer of resources to them through a "link." India, for example, argued that the creation of SDRs as part of the establishment of the substitution facility would satiate the world's desire for additional SDRs and therefore foreign assistance schemes based on transfer of new SDRs to less-developed countries would have no chance of acceptance.[91]

Moreover, in view of the continued growth of official Eurodollar deposits and the rapid growth of the oil-exporting countries' dollar balances, it was

89. Report of Technical Group on Intervention and Settlement, para. 45, C-20 Documents, pp. 125–26.
90. For a fuller discussion, see Williamson, pp. 152–53. See also Gold, "Substitution," pp. 292–93.
91. Williamson, pp. 146, 152; see also Solomon, pp. 245–46, and Gold, "Substitution," p. 293.

not at all clear that many countries actually wanted to be placed in the position of having to seek asset settlement for their own dollar holdings.[92] With the decline of interest in asset settlement, the interest in a substitution facility collapsed.

Because the substitution negotiations did not come to a head, the most difficult issues involving a substitution facility were not comprehensively discussed. Those were, first, the interest rate the United States would pay to the Fund and that the Fund would pay on SDRs to users of the facility, and second, the allocation of the currency risk (that is, who would bear the risk of U.S. devaluation as between the United States, the Fund, and the holders of the newly created SDRs). These were the issues that were to emerge as central when the substitution concept received a new lease on life at the end of the 1970s.[93]

One by-product of the asset settlement and substitution negotiations warrants note. Since the United States favored the greatest freedom from full asset settlement, it was forced to find some substitute concept to deal with the problem that a major continued role for reserve currencies would mean that there would be no effective control over growth in international liquidity. The United States therefore proposed that the Fund should exercise "surveillance" over the total volume of foreign exchange reserves.[94] This idea found its way into an Annex of the Outline of Reform, which stated that agreement had been reached on the "principle that the aggregate volume of official currency holdings should be kept under international surveillance and management."[95] Moreover, Part II of the Outline prescribed as one of the "immediate steps" in the "interim period" that the "Fund will exercise surveillance of the adjustment process." From there it was a fairly short step to inclusion of the surveillance concept in the Second Amendment and the subsequent adoption of surveillance procedures.[96]

VI. Multicurrency Intervention

From the standpoint of legislation of monetary rules, one of the most interesting aspects of the C-20 negotiations was the discussion of multicurrency intervention (MCI). Had an MCI arrangement been adopted, it would have been a major piece of international legal engineering. Such a scheme assumed, however, a par value system, and so the MCI discussions did not come to any final resolution.

92. Williamson, pp. 154–57.
93. See discussion pp. 313–14, below.
94. Williamson, p. 155.
95. Outline of Reform, annex 5, C-20 Documents, p. 37.
96. Ibid. para. 34, p. 19. See discussion pp. 259–67, below.

The United States launched the discussion, perhaps as much for dialectical purposes as out of any desire to see an MCI system adopted. The MCI discussion served to underscore what the United States regarded as a further asymmetry in the system. Under the Bretton Woods system the United States had had only half as much flexibility for market exchange rate variation within the Bretton Woods margins as other countries. The reason for this anomaly lay in the role of the U.S. dollar as the principal intervention currency.

The Bretton Woods agreement did not recognize any special intervention role for the dollar. Each member was prohibited from permitting spot exchange rates between its currency and the currency of each other member from diverging more than 1 percent from parity.[97] When the principal European currencies adopted nonresident convertibility in 1958, it became clear that the market exchange rate of two non-U.S. currencies pegged on the dollar, one strong and one weak, might diverge from their cross-parity by more than 1 percent. For example, if the German mark were at the ceiling against the dollar and the French franc were at the dollar floor, then the mark and franc market exchange rates would diverge by 2 percent from their cross-parity.

The Fund chose in 1959 to validate such a divergence by an exceptional decision rather than to adhere to the letter of the Fund Articles, which would have meant that members pegging on the dollar would have had to limit the divergence of their market exchange rates against the dollar to a mere ½ percent from parity. The Fund decision, rather dubiously based on the power of the Executive Board to approve multiple currency practices, provided that a 2 percent divergence in rates would be accepted "whenever such rates result from the maintenance of margins of no more than 1 percent from parity for a convertible . . . currency."[98]

Many of the developed country members chose not to take full advantage of this flexibility and voluntarily limited their currencies' fluctuations to ¾ percent against the U.S. dollar.[99] Nevertheless, the end result was that the dollar could fluctuate only one-half as much against any other currency as that currency could fluctuate against a third currency. Indeed, under the 1959 decision, a currency (say, in the sterling area) pegging on some secondary intervention currency (sterling) was allowed to maintain a 1 percent margin against its secondary intervention currency.[100] This provision permitted, at least as a matter of arithmetic, a further range of flexibility for members pegging on secondary intervention currencies. Two such currencies pegged

97. Article IV, Sections 3(i) and 4(b), *original*. See discussion of margins, pp. 93–94, above.
98. Decision of 24 July 1959, *IMF Annual Report* 1960, p. 31. See Gold, *Selected Essays*, pp. 552–54.
99. Decision of 24 July 1959, *IMF Annual Report* 1960, p. 31.
100. Ibid., and see Gold, *Selected Essays*, p. 554.

against different secondary intervention currencies could thus depart from their cross-parity by up to 4 percent.

When the Smithsonian regime of 2¼ percent margins was adopted, the 1959 decision was rewritten to permit deviation of up to 4½ percent from parity, where it resulted from fluctuations up to 2¼ percent from parity with an intervention currency. The Smithsonian rules thereby perpetuated the existing asymmetry. And this decision continued to accord the additional 1 percent margins for those pegging on secondary intervention currencies. [101]

Shortly thereafter, however, the European Economic Community adopted its snake system, under which the members maintained narrower margins than the Smithsonian 2¼ percent margins among one another. Moreover, they did so not by choosing one snake member's currency as their internal intervention currency but rather by each member intervening in the currency of each other member whenever the rate of divergence between the two currencies would otherwise exceed 2¼ percent. In effect, the snake margins were thus only half the Smithsonian margins, although the snake as a whole might move up or down in the Smithsonian tunnel as the snake currencies strengthened or weakened against the dollar. [102] Thus was born the world's first multicurrency intervention system, and the snake became a model for the C-20 MCI discussions. Indeed, the EEC system was somewhat more complicated than a C-20 MCI system would have had to be because the snake currencies had to maintain the level of the snake against the dollar through intervention by snake members in dollars.

The MCI idea received a remarkable degree of support. France supported it, and many other countries gave it either lukewarm support or at least did not oppose it openly. And it received active support from at least some Fund staff members. J. Marcus Fleming of the Fund staff argued, for example, that an MCI system would not only establish symmetry between the dollar and other currencies but would also reinforce asset settlement because, at least in the snake version, balances of other members' currencies were settled immediately. He also saw an MCI system as providing a framework where the dollar could float while other members maintained pegged exchange rates *inter sese*. [103] Moreover, one aspect of considerable attraction to the Fund staff was the possibility that the SDR might be used in the MCI mechanism.

Whether intervention took place in currencies or SDRs, it was envisaged that not all Fund members would participate in the MCI system. To include all members, at least in the currency (as opposed to the SDR) alternative,

101. Decision of 18 December 1971, *IMF Annual Report* 1972, pp. 85–87. See also Decision of 7 November 1973, *IMF Annual Report* 1974, pp. 103–5, adapting the 1971 decision for situations where the intervention currency was floating.
102. "The European System of Narrower Exchange Rate Margins," *Monthly Report of the Deutsche Bundesbank* 28(January 1976):23; Richard W. Edwards, Jr., "The European Exchange Rate Arrangement Called the 'Snake,'" *University of Toledo Law Review* 10(1978):49–50.
103. Fleming, p. 8. On the latter point, see also Williamson, p. 80.

would be unwieldy and perhaps impossible because exchange markets did not exist for all currencies in all markets. Indeed, with some exceptions involving the snake and secondary intervention currencies, the only active private foreign exchange market in any given country would normally be the dollar market. Without a private party on the other side of a central bank intervention transaction, such intervention could not take place within a local exchange market. Consequently, it was assumed that the MCI group would encompass some ten to twenty members,[104] and other members would peg on one or more of the MCI group.

Each MCI group member's central bank would agree to intervene in each other member's currency at the margin. One of the characteristics of such a system would be that if one member's currency was at the margin vis-à-vis a second currency, then so would be the second against the first. Thus, an important policy issue was which of the two countries should intervene. The United States favored ceiling rather than floor intervention; that is, intervention should be the responsibility of the strong currency country, though it would normally act as agent for the weak currency or at least would promptly present balances of the weak currency acquired in the intervention process for settlement in primary reserve assets. Ceiling intervention would be a reversal of normal Bretton Woods floor intervention practice, where it was the weak currency country that intervened. (When the dollar was weak, however, it was the strong currency country that intervened to prevent its own rate from appreciating because the dollar was passive.)

A country practicing floor intervention used international reserves, and indeed that was the principal purpose of such reserves. When those reserves were gone and none could be borrowed, devaluation was the only alternative. But a country engaged in ceiling intervention could continue to do so indefinitely because it used its own currency, which it could create for the purpose. The price of ceiling intervention, of course, would be an increase in the money supply of the ceiling country and thereby what was often called "imported inflation." For a ceiling country to continue to intervene indefinitely under an MCI system in the face of a possible devaluation by the floor country would surely depend upon the allocation of the currency risk. One of the key issues under an MCI system was therefore which country would make the decision to stop intervention and how the risk of parity change would be allocated.[105]

Advocates of using the SDR rather than currencies in an MCI system had to confront the fact that, since SDRs could not be privately held, there was no market in SDRs in which any country could intervene. (Though the prohibition on private SDR ownership did not extend to claims denominated

104. Report of Technical Group on Intervention and Settlement, paras. 12–22, C-20 Documents, pp. 116–19.
105. Ibid. paras. 23–26, pp. 119–20.

in SDRs, there was also no existing market in SDR-denominated claims.) Transactions between central banks would be reserve transactions but would not have any direct, one-to-one influence on market exchange rates. However, with some ingenuity, a system was sketched by SDR advocates in which commercial banks would act as intermediaries between central banks without the commercial banks ever actually holding SDRs. The need to provide the commercial banks with a financial incentive to provide this arbitrage function would have required some complication of the basic margin arrangement. Even under this scheme, however, it was not clear that the arbitrage system would work effectively in maintaining currency rates within the prescribed margins.

Perhaps the biggest barrier to adoption of an SDR-based MCI system was that it would work well only if the par value system of SDR valuation were adopted. Under any other system the SDR's value would not be directly and unambiguously translatable into a currency value. Yet at the very time that an MCI system was being discussed, the advent of generalized floating was pushing the C-20 conferees toward a basket system of SDR valuation.[106]

In the end the C-20 Outline of Reform went no further than agreement that "it would be desirable that the system of exchange margins and intervention should be more symmetrical than that which existed in practice under the Bretton Woods system."[107] An Annex was attached containing "possible operational provisions with illustrative schemes" for a currency-based and SDR-based MCI system.[108]

VII. The Dollar, Gold, and the SDR

The future of the three major reserve assets—reserve currencies, gold, and the SDR—was at the heart of the C-20 negotiations. The C-20 discussions about reserve indicators, asset settlement, and a substitution facility can readily be seen, at least in retrospect, to be an elaborate negotiation over the future of the dollar. These negotiations led to no conclusion because, with the advent of generalized floating and the likelihood that it would continue as a result of the 1973–74 oil crisis, neither the United States nor for that matter the major European countries were prepared to take a step into the unknown by relegating the dollar to a subsidiary, limited role in the world's reserve asset and intervention system. At best the C-20 conferees could agree on the abstract principle, as stated in the Outline of Reform, that the "role of . . . reserve currencies will be reduced."[109]

106. On SDR intervention, see ibid. paras. 35–41, pp. 122–25. On SDR valuation, see discussion pp. 200–207, above.
107. Outline of Reform, para. 12, C-20 Documents, p. 12.
108. Ibid. annex 3, pp. 30–33.
109. Ibid. para. 24, p. 15.

The SDR

The agreement on reducing the role of reserve currencies was less a judgment against the dollar than one in favor of the SDR:

> The SDR will become the principal reserve asset and the role of gold and of reserve currencies will be reduced. The SDR will also be the numeraire in terms of which par values will be expressed.[110]

The proposition that the SDR should become the principal reserve asset was accepted with astonishing ease.[111] As early as the 1971 Fund annual meeting, British finance minister Barber advocated making the SDR the numeraire of the international monetary system.[112] At the 1972 annual meeting U.S. treasury secretary Shultz assented to that proposition.[113] By January 1973 the United States was supporting increased reliance on the SDR as the primary source of world reserve growth over time and envisaging a much reduced but continuing role for foreign exchange. From there it was no more than an editorial decision for the United States to support the proposition that the SDR should become the principal reserve asset, as agreed in the Outline of Reform.

What accounts for the easy and early agreement on the promotion of the SDR to first rank among reserve assets? The answer is not self-evident in view of the widespread skepticism with which finance ministry officials and especially central bankers viewed the SDR. One may, however, surmise the existence of the following constellation of interests among the four principal participants in the reform negotiations. The United States found enhancement of the SDR easy to support at a time when most of its proposals were being met with hostility by the other participants. Whether the SDR would indeed become the principal reserve asset would depend on future events and more deep-seated attitudes whatever language was used in the Outline of Reform, and meantime support of the SDR was an outward-looking gesture toward international cooperation. The Europeans, with the partial exception of France, which wanted the SDR to share the limelight with gold, found support for the SDR an additional weapon in their fight against what looked after 1971 increasingly like a dollar standard in practice, whatever was written on paper. The less-developed countries supported the SDR because they viewed it as the best vehicle for forging a link between reserve creation and development aid. And the Fund staff favored the SDR because whatever promoted the SDR enhanced the role of the Fund, a role that with

110. Ibid.
111. This proposition was agreed upon on 27 March 1973, at the first meeting of the Committee of Twenty after their organizational meeting. See Communiqué, C-20 Documents, p. 215.
112. IMF, *Summary Proceedings of the Twenty-sixth Annual Meeting of the Board of Governors, 1971*, pp. 32–35.
113. IMF, *Summary Proceedings 1972*, p. 38.

the onset of generalized floating appeared none too secure. Moreover, all of the principal countries in the C-20 negotiations felt considerable pressure to find some issue on which they could agree. Diplomacy abhors a vacuum.

Agreement on the steps to be taken to elevate the SDR to the status of principal reserve asset was somewhat more difficult. But with Giscard rather than de Gaulle and Debré in power in France, it was not difficult to agree that the barnacles that had been placed on the SDR with regard to reconstitution, need, and so forth should be reconsidered and that new uses for the SDR within the Fund structure should be studied.[114] Indeed, one of the "immediate steps" agreed upon for the "interim period" was that the Executive Board should prepare draft amendments "to introduce improvements in the . . . characteristics of and rules governing the use of the SDR."[115] These amendments were subsequently adopted as part of the Second Amendment of the Articles.[116]

More difficult was any agreement over the size of future SDR allocations, which surely would have to grow from the existing 5.7 percent of total international reserves[117] if the SDR were to become the principal reserve asset in anything but name. But the obstacles in the way of such agreement were formidable. Already the perception was spreading that the explosion of dollar holdings in the early 1970s had produced a situation in which there was too much liquidity.[118] Though the oil crisis raised questions in some quarters about the adequacy of the existing level of liquidity, there was no enthusiasm for an immediate increase in the volume of SDRs outstanding. Moreover, in the absence of any precise agreement on asset settlement and on a substitution account, there was no reason to believe that the volume of foreign exchange in international reserves would not continue to grow rapidly. Finally, any need for additional liquidity that could be furnished by additional SDRs depended on what was done about the price of gold, an issue to be discussed below.

In the event, only general, pious statements on the relation of SDR creation to the desirable level of global liquidity could be agreed upon:

> As part of the better international management of global liquidity, the Fund will allocate and cancel SDRs so as to ensure that the volume of global reserves is adequate and is consistent with the proper functioning of the adjustment and settlement systems. In the assessment of global reserve needs and the decision-making process for SDR allocation and cancellation the Fund will continue to follow the existing principles as

114. Outline of Reform, para. 27, C-20 Documents, p. 16.
115. Ibid. para. 41, p. 22.
116. See discussion pp. 200–207.
117. *IMF Annual Report* 1974, table 12, p. 34 (figure for end of first quarter, 1974).
118. See discussion in Report of Technical Group on Global Liquidity and Consolidation, paras. 4–8, C-20 Documents, pp. 163–66.

set out in the Articles of Agreement. However, it is agreed that the methods of assessing global reserve needs must remain the subject of study, and it has been suggested that they may need to give additional emphasis to a number of economic factors.[119]

If agreement on the SDR as the principal reserve asset was thus somewhat hollow, the C-20 did achieve the objective of making the SDR the numeraire, as seen in the previous chapter. And as also discussed there, the issue of the valuation of the SDR was resolved.[120]

Gold

Much less success was enjoyed in the C-20 on gold issues, although those issues were to be resolved not long after the Outline of Reform was published. But the C-20 negotiations were marked by a sharp disagreement between France and South Africa, both of which wanted gold to retain an important role, and the United States, which wanted the role of gold to diminish. Most European countries were prepared to accept a reduced role for gold but were not prepared to push for it.

The resulting discussion centered on two related issues. The first was what should happen to the official price of gold, which remained 35 SDR per ounce (equal to $42.22 after the 1973 devaluation of the dollar). With the market price over $100 per ounce much of the time during the C-20 proceedings,[121] gold held by members in reserves was effectively immobilized. Since it was worth more, as measured by a market standard, than a signatory to the two-tier arrangement was permitted to sell it for in the private market,[122] and more than the price at which any two Fund members could exchange it among themselves, a central bank was led by the economic principal of Gresham's law to keep the higher-valued gold in its reserves and hence out of circulation and to use instead lower-valued foreign exchange or SDRs. The effect of Gresham's law can easily be seen by putting oneself in the place of a central banker. Such an official would be loath to give up gold at $42.22 per ounce so long as he had the alternative of using SDRs or reserve currencies when, perhaps only a few years hence, he might lawfully receive twice as much or more than that amount for the gold. Hence, if gold were to be used by members, the official price of gold would have to be increased.

An alternative solution would be to abolish the official price of gold and to permit members to transfer gold among themselves at whatever price they could agree upon, which would presumably be at or close to the private

119. Outline of Reform, para. 25, ibid. p. 15. See also ibid. para. 37(a) and annex 8, pp. 20, 43.
120. See discussion pp. 200–207.
121. See graph of gold prices, *BIS 44th Report* 1974, p. 126.
122. See discussion of two-tier gold arrangement and premium sales and purchases, pp. 135–42.

market price. In that event, gold and reserve currencies would be equally valuable, and Gresham's law would not operate to immobilize gold.

A second, and related, issue was whether the right of members to trade in gold in private markets should be expanded. Under the two-tier system at least half the Fund members had bound themselves, albeit outside the legal framework of the Fund, not to sell any gold reserves in the private market.[123] When the original signatories to the two-tier system terminated it on 13 November 1973,[124] that action effectively resolved the issue of market-priced sales in the market and relieved to some extent the immobilization of gold. But members still could not buy gold because of the rule in the Articles prohibiting purchase at a premium, and some countries would be loath to sell gold when their currencies were weak if they could not reacquire it when their currencies strengthened.

Resolution of these issues was not achieved in the C-20. The Outline of Reform went no further than to list three alternatives. The first was that "monetary authorities, including the Fund, would be free to sell, but not to buy, gold in the market at the market price"; however, "they would not undertake transactions with each other at a price different from the official price, which would be retained and would not be subject to a uniform increase." This first alternative would have preserved the status quo, but the members would have been committing themselves never to increase the official price in the future. Under the second alternative "the official price of gold would be abolished and monetary authorities, including the Fund, would be free to deal in gold with one another on a voluntary basis and at mutually acceptable prices, and to sell gold in the market." The third alternative would have gone even further by "authorizing monetary authorities also to buy gold in the market."[125]

Although the C-20 did not resolve these issues, it did agree to agree. The Executive Board was asked to prepare amendments to the Articles on gold,[126] and, as detailed in the next chapter, agreement was reached in the next few years, primarily as a result of high-level U.S.-French negotiations.

VIII. Capital Controls

A side issue in the C-20 negotiations involved the possibility of changing the Fund's rules on capital controls. U.S. authorities believed that the distinction in the Articles between current and capital controls, under which Article VIII countries could impose capital controls but not current controls, was

---

123. See discussion pp. 140–41.
124. *BIS 44th Report* 1974, pp. 124–25; Gold, *Selected Essays*, p. 222.
125. Outline of Reform, para. 28, C-20 Documents, pp. 16–17.
126. Ibid. para. 41(e), p. 22.

irrational. Most European countries, on the other hand, supported the distinction.

The difference was in part one of interest, in part one of ideology, and in part simply a by-product of differences on other issues. The United States was still a major capital exporting country, and the 1960s had been a period in which some European countries had felt themselves threatened by U.S. investment. But this self-interest difference, related more to long-term investment than short-term capital flows, was already being overtaken by the shifting fortunes of U.S. and European economies and, in any event, was perhaps less important than the ideological differences.

To most U.S. officials economic efficiency arguments for freer trade in goods logically carried over to freer trade in money. But to many European officials the purpose of international economic relations was trade in goods, and since capital flows could affect the exchange rate at which goods traded, those flows should be controlled. In large part, European attitudes favoring control of capital flows were a mental carryover from the Bretton Woods system where short-term capital flows tended to be regarded as "disequilibrating." This view was illustrated by the establishment by the C-20 in March 1973, at the very time when the move to generalized floating was occurring, of a technical group to "define and analyse the sources of disequilibrating capital flows and the technical problems involved in the use of measures to influence them . . . and of measures to finance them or offset them."[127]

As managed floating became the prevailing system, it took only a slight adjustment of view for Europeans to regard short-term capital flows as threats to the exchange rate that they would prefer to maintain for the benefit of their export industries. It was precisely this European focus on controlling capital flows to improve a surplus country's exchange rate in aid of its export goals to which the United States objected. From the U.S. perspective, capital controls were being used to avoid currency appreciations that should occur.

As is often the case in diplomatic negotiations, the capital controls issue was handled by giving each side the language it sought. How the two sets of contradictory language were to be made consistent was left to the future. One paragraph, under the heading "Controls," espoused the U.S. point of view:

> Countries will not use controls over capital transactions for the purpose of maintaining inappropriate exchange rates or, more generally, of avoiding appropriate adjustment action. Insofar as countries use capital controls, they should avoid an excessive degree of administrative restriction which could damage trade and beneficial capital flows and should not retain controls longer than needed.[128]

127. Report of Technical Group on Disequilibrating Capital Flows, para. 1, ibid. p. 78.
128. Outline of Reform, para. 15, ibid. p. 12.

In contrast, an entirely separate paragraph, under the heading "Disequili-brating Capital Flows," openly advocated controls:

> Countries will cooperate in actions designed to limit disequilibrating capital flows and in arrangements to finance and offset them. Actions that countries might choose to adopt could include . . . the use of ad-ministrative controls, including dual exchange markets and fiscal incentives.[129]

The latter paragraph went on to suggest "improved consultation in the Fund on actions designed to limit disequilibrating capital flows."

Although in one sense the debate on capital controls was a stand-off, the state of the debate nevertheless marked a considerable change in opinion from the Bretton Woods period when it was assumed, certainly by Keynes, that capital controls were inevitable and indeed desirable.[130] When the Executive Directors reached the crucial surveillance decision in 1977, they were able to agree that the introduction of restrictions on capital flows might indicate the need for adjustment.[131]

IX. THE LINK

Another area in which no agreement was reached in the C-20 was the question of a possible link between reserve creation and development assistance. The outspoken opposition of the United States and, to a lesser extent, Germany prevented this issue from ever advancing beyond technical discussions, though it seems likely that both of those countries would have eventually agreed to some kind of link if they had been satisfied with the reform package. The less-developed members had made the link their primary condition for any reform agreement.

Another reason for the absence of any agreement had to do with the kind of link favored by the Group of Twenty-Four, the less-developed country caucus. That group had concluded that "their interests would best be served by an increase in their share of SDRs by means of direct country allocations by the International Monetary Fund, to be used for development purposes."[132] The underlying idea was that less-developed country members would receive a disproportionately large SDR allocation and would then be able to transfer them to developed countries to pay for imports. The effect would be the same as a resource transfer through traditional development assistance pro-grams, but it was hoped that a link mechanism would bypass developed

129. Ibid. para. 17, p. 13.
130. See discussion pp. 80, 98–99.
131. Decision of 29 April 1979, and "Surveillance over Exchange Rate Policies," para. 2, *IMF Annual Report* 1977, pp. 107–8. See discussion of the surveillance decision, pp. 259–67, below.
132. Report of Technical Group on the SDR/Aid Link and Related Proposals, para. 3, C-20 Documents, p. 95.

country legislatures that were increasingly skeptical of assistance programs. Although other kinds of link arrangements were considered, including allocations of SDRs to development finance institutions and allocation to all members under the existing quota-based formula followed by transfer of SDRs from developed countries to finance institutions,[133] all of the schemes required additional allocations of SDRs to provide any resource transfer. Yet the large increase in liquidity stemming from the growth of foreign exchange reserves and the possibility, indeed probability, of an increase in liquidity from a revaluation of gold holdings both augured poorly for new SDR allocations. Recognizing that allocations were unlikely, the less-developed country C-20 members did not push hard for agreement on the link.[134]

Finally, the support of some developed country members for a link was doubtless rather lukewarm. Such support cost them little so long as no actual resource transfer was in prospect. Moreover, some developed country officials were concerned that, whatever might be agreed as to the need to base SDR allocations on global liquidity needs, an SDR-aid link would inevitably lead through the international political process to excessive SDR allocations and hence to worsening world inflation. A further fear was that the use of SDRs for aid purposes would undermine confidence in what was still a fledgling asset.[135] For these reasons, the link discussions did not even approach resolution in the C-20 discussions. Moreover, as will be seen in the next chapter, in the negotiations leading to the Second Amendment, less-developed country members changed their strategy away from an SDR-aid link toward other methods of resource transfer through the Fund.[136]

Nevertheless, the very discussion in the C-20 of development needs led to some changes in Fund lending practice. The C-20 agreed that a new "extended Fund facility" should be created "under which developing countries would receive longer-term balance of payments finance."[137] Such a facility, which was essentially a three-year stand-by arrangement, was in fact created by the Executive Board in September 1974.[138] Other measures of a

---

133. Ibid. paras. 9–12, p. 101.
134. Gold, referring to a Group of Twenty-Four meeting in January 1975 (somewhat after the 1974 conclusion of the C-20 negotiations), quotes the comment of some Group deputies that "even a handsome percentage of zero is still zero." *Selected Essays*, p. 488.
135. For a review of the arguments for and against a link, see e.g. Report of Technical Group on the SDR/Aid Link and Related Proposals, paras. 5–8, C-20 Documents, pp. 96–101; Harry G. Johnson, "The Link That Chains," *Foreign Policy*, no. 8 (Fall 1972), p. 119; Williamson, pp. 143–47. See also the debate between Peter Bauer and Lord Kahn: Peter Bauer, "Inflation, SDRs and Aid," *Lloyds Bank Review*, no. 109 (July 1973), pp. 31–35, and "The SDR Link Scheme—A Comment," ibid. no. 111 (January 1974), pp. 42–43; Lord Kahn, "SDRs and Aid," ibid. no. 110 (October 1973), pp. 1–18.
136. See discussion pp. 271–73.
137. Outline of Reform, paras. 30, 39, C-20 Documents, pp. 18, 21. See discussion of extended facility and other new facilities, pp. 284–89, above.
138. Decision of 13 September 1974, *IMF Annual Report 1975*, pp. 88–90. See Gold, *Selected Essays*, p. 53.

more general nature that nonetheless benefited less-developed members included creation of an oil facility,[139] liberalization of the compensatory financing facility,[140] and an increase in quotas.[141] Furthermore, the C-20 recommended as an "immediate step" the creation of a joint Fund and World Bank committee on the various issues that had underlain the link discussion.[142] The resulting Joint Ministerial Committee of the World Bank and the Fund on the Transfer of Real Resources to Developing Countries, less cumbersomely known as the Development Committee, has not proved to be an influential body.

X. INSTITUTIONAL CHANGE IN THE FUND

The same reasons that motivated the United States to urge that the reform negotiations be taken out of the hands of the Executive Board and placed in a more political body such as the C-20 also led the United States to advocate a reform of the Fund's decision-making machinery. U.S. treasury secretary Shultz argued in his 1972 Fund annual meeting speech that in the reformed system "[i]nternational decision making will not be credible or effective unless it is carried out by representatives who clearly carry a high stature and influence in the councils of their own governments."[143] The C-20 had proved to be a congenial forum for its developed country representatives, and the United States sought to build on the C-20's precedent. What the United States wanted was an ongoing Council midway between the Board of Governors and the Executive Board. Like Keynes's original concept of the Executive Board, the Council would be composed of policy-level officials of national governments who were active in their own national decisionmaking and who would travel to a common meeting ground perhaps three or four times a year rather than being in "continuous session."[144]

Although there was some opposition to the Council, especially from the less-developed countries, the decision not to create a Deputies group for the Council helped to protect the role of the Executive Board and thereby to dampen opposition.[145] Moreover, the absence of any Bureau protected the interests of the Fund staff. Consequently, the C-20 was able to arrive at agreement on a Council patterned on the C-20 itself:

139. Decision of 13 June 1974, *IMF Annual Report* 1974, pp. 122–24.
140. Decision of 24 December 1975, *IMF Annual Report* 1976, pp. 52–54; Louis M. Goreux, *Compensatory Financing Facility*, IMF Pamphlet Series no. 34 (1980), p. 2.
141. Board of Governors Resolution of 22 March 1976, *IMF Annual Report* 1976, pp. 103–11.
142. Outline of Reform, para. 39, C-20 Documents, p. 21.
143. *IMF Summary Proceedings 1972*, p. 42.
144. See discussion pp. 111–12. See Gold, *Selected Essays*, pp. 15–16, 250.
145. On the compromises involved in negotiating the Council, see Gold, *Selected Essays*, pp. 261–82.

A permanent and representative Council, with one member appointed from each Fund constituency, will be established. The Council will meet regularly, three or four times a year as required, and will have the necessary decision-making powers to supervise the management and adaptation of the monetary system, to oversee the continuing operation of the adjustment process, and to deal with sudden disturbances which might threaten the system.[146]

Moreover, the C-20 recommended that the Council be established "as soon as practicable" by amendment of the Articles.[147]

Although the Second Amendment authorized the creation of a Council,[148] a more fateful step turned out to be the recommendation by the C-20 at its final meeting of a successor organization, the Interim Committee of the Board of Governors on the International Monetary System, which was to have "an advisory role in those areas in which the Council . . . will have decision-making powers."[149] The Interim Committee, patterned directly on the C-20, though like the proposed Council in being without Deputies and without a Bureau, was successful in reaching agreement on the Second Amendment at Jamaica in January 1976. On the strength of that success, it has remained in existence. The remarkable fact is that the Interim Committee, explicitly designed to be a temporary body, continues to meet as a major policy body, while the permanent Council has never been created.[150] *Ce n'est que le provisoire qui dure!*

146. Outline of Reform, para. 31, C-20 Documents, p. 18.
147. Ibid. paras. 33, 41(a), pp. 19, 22.
148. Article XII, Section 1, and Schedule D, *second.*
149. Communiqué of 13 June 1974, C-20 Documents, p. 222. The Interim Committee was created by a Board of Governors resolution in October 1974. Resolution of 2 October 1974, *IMF Summary Proceedings 1974*, pp. 364–67.
150. For an analysis of the reasons for the failure to create the Council, see Joseph Gold, "The Fund's Interim Committee—an Assessment," *Finance and Development* 16(September 1979):32–33.

EIGHT

The
Jamaica
Agreement

The most important conclusion of the Committee of Twenty was that the Executive Board should prepare draft amendments to the Articles of Agreement.[1] The Interim Committee, created in the image of the C-20, was given a broad mandate which included the consideration of such amendments.[2]

The initial conception was that the amendments would be limited to the subjects listed by the C-20. In the end, the Second Amendment encompassed a thoroughgoing revision of the Articles as a whole. In this respect, the Second Amendment differed fundamentally from the First Amendment, which beyond adding the SDR provisions was limited to inserting minor "reform" changes.

1. Outline of Reform, para. 41, IMF, *International Monetary Reform. Documents of the Committee of Twenty* (1974), p. 22 (hereafter cited C-20 Documents).
2. Board of Governors Resolution No. 29-8 (2 October 1974), IMF, *Summary Proceedings of the Twenty-ninth Annual Meeting of the Board of Governors 1974*, p. 366.

The Jamaica Agreement

As initially envisaged, the Second Amendment was intended merely to adjust the Articles to make them seaworthy for a floating "interim period" pending adoption of the "reformed system" based on stable but adjustable par values outlined by the C-20. But it gradually became clear that generalized floating was likely to remain the dominant system for a long time, particularly in view of the high and widely divergent inflation rates in the principal developed countries, and in view of an increasingly militant pro-floating ideology propounded by the United States under treasury secretary William Simon (1974–77). The notion thus gained ground that the amendments should place the Fund in a position to function for an indefinite period of time.[3]

The conception evolved, after agreement began to be reached within the Interim Committee on some key points, that the Second Amendment might be drafted in such a way as to permit a movement toward a regime resembling the C-20's "reformed system," including a return to par values, without any further amendment of the Articles. The device to be used was provision for specified changes by the vote of a high proportion of the membership but without any amendment of the Articles.[4] Under this "enabling powers" technique, a special majority of 85 percent of the total voting power[5] would, for example, permit a veto by the United States, which under the quota increase agreed upon concurrently with the Second Amendment would retain 19.96 percent of the total voting power.[6] Similarly, it would permit a veto by the European Economic Community members acting jointly, or by the less-developed countries as a group,[7] and thus constitute a requirement of essential unanimity by the various interest groupings. Nevertheless, an enabling power subject to such qualified majority vote would permit a prompt change in one aspect of the international monetary system without the time-consuming process of amendment of the Articles. Moreover, the Fund staff used the opportunity offered by the Second Amendment to revise many provisions of the Articles to bring the text up to date with interpretations of the existing Articles that had already been reached within the regular

3. Joseph Gold, *Legal and Institutional Aspects of the International Monetary System: Selected Essays* (1979), p. 126 (hereafter cited Gold, *Selected Essays*).
4. On the concept of enabling powers, see Joseph Gold, *The Second Amendment of the Fund's Articles of Agreement*, IMF Pamphlet Series no. 25 (1978), pp. 16–18. See also Gold, *The Rule of Law in the International Monetary Fund*, IMF Pamphlet Series no. 32 (1980).
5. All special majorities involve a percentage of the total voting power rather than simply of the votes cast. For simplicity, the reference to total voting power has been omitted in subsequent discussion of special majorities.
6. National Advisory Council on International Monetary and Financial Policies, *Special Report to the President and to the Congress on Amendment of the Articles of Agreement of the International Monetary Fund and on an Increase in Quotas in the International Monetary Fund*, p. 32, House Document No. 94-447, 94th Cong., 2d Sess. (1976).
7. Gold, *Selected Essays*, p. 21.

Fund processes by the Executive Directors.[8] The changes wrought by the Second Amendment consequently far transcended the limited scope of those envisaged as "immediate steps" in the C-20's Outline of Reform.

An illustration of a key weakness of the enabling powers technique is the provision on establishment of a Council.[9] Though the Second Amendment provided for the creation of a Council upon approval by 85 percent of the total voting power,[10] the Council has never come into effect. In part, the failure of the Council to appear upon the institutional scene can be explained by continuing satisfaction with the work of the still extant Interim Committee. But the example of the Council also lays bare the ambiguity of the concept of enabling powers. An enabling power exercisable by an 85 percent vote may simply stand as evidence that when the Second Amendment was negotiated, there was both extensive support for and strong concerted opposition to the measure in question. The existence of the enabling power thus may mean no more than that the opponents were prepared to give the supporters the symbol of victory in the shape of a provision in the Articles but to withhold the reality by retaining an effective veto power.

In the case of the Council, the continuing opposition of some less-developed countries raises the question whether the *Interim* Committee may not become permanent and the supposedly permanent Council remain in embryo, even though these same countries have no greater representation in the Interim Committee than in the Council. There are, of course, differences between the Interim Committee and the Council. The Interim Committee cannot act but can only propose action, though recommendations of the Interim Committee are likely to be implemented. The Council would be more of an institutional threat to the Executive Board. The Council, unlike the Interim Committee, which does not vote at all, could use weighted voting (though voting in the Board is rare).[11]

Since amendments "to introduce improvements in the General Account and in the characteristics of and rules governing the use of the SDR"[12] were not controversial in principle, however complex they might prove to be when the actual drafting began, the core of the controversy in the Interim Committee revolved around two issues, the exchange rate regime and the role of gold. Here the two chief protagonists, the United States and France, initially took diametrically opposed positions, and each seemed intent on blocking any global settlement on the terms of a Second Amendment unless its conditions were met. To some the pitting of the pro-floating, anti-gold views of

8. Gold, *Second Amendment*, pp. 11–12.
9. See discussion pp. 251–52.
10. Article XII, Section 1, and Schedule D, *second*.
11. On the Council versus the Interim Committee, see Gold, *Selected Essays*, pp. 279–82. See also Gold, "The Structure of the Fund," *Finance and Development* 16(June 1979):13–15.
12. Outline of Reform, para. 41, C-20 Documents, p. 22.

the United States and the anti-floating, pro-gold views of France took on the dimensions of a theological dispute.[13]

A crucial decision in the negotiations process was consequently the decision to end "the battledore and shuttlecock of proposals" by informally delegating the exchange rate issues to bilateral U.S.-French negotiations.[14] The result was a bilateral negotiation of the principal features of the Second Amendment, not unlike the U.S.-British negotiation of the Bretton Woods agreement. As in the Bretton Woods case, the other countries were prepared to abide by the central conclusions of the bilateral negotiations.[15] In the case of the Second Amendment, the Fund general counsel was available to rationalize the language of the U.S.-French agreement with the text and usage of the rest of the articles.[16] And, unlike the Bretton Woods case, the U.S.-French negotiations concerned only a portion of the text and the remainder had to be agreed upon in a broader procedural context. Nevertheless, the key exchange rate and gold provisions of the Second Amendment can only be understood against the background of U.S. and French attitudes.

I. THE EXCHANGE RATE REGIME

In these U.S.-French bilateral negotiations conducted in the autumn of 1975, the United States in general carried the day on the exchange rate issues and France on the gold issues. However, there were compromises on both subjects. In the exchange rate provisions, for example, the United States was successful in legalizing floating, but the French won acceptance of a procedure for a return to par values.

On one transcending principle the U.S. and French representatives were apparently of one mind. That was the principle that stability of domestic economies must precede stability of exchange rates. The notion was that stable exchange rates depended more upon orderly underlying conditions in domestic economies than upon any international commitments to maintain stable exchange rates.[17] In short, exchange stability cannot be imposed by international agreement when national economies are suffering from instability and inflation. This "Copernican revolution" in international monetary

13. Tom de Vries, "Jamaica, or the Non-Reform of the International Monetary System," *Foreign Affairs* 54(1976):589.
14. Gold, *Selected Essays*, p. 126.
15. Martin Mayer, *The Fate of the Dollar* (1980), pp. 238–40; Andreas F. Lowenfeld, *The International Monetary System* (1977), pp. 203–6.
16. T. de Vries, "Jamaica," p. 589; Robert Solomon, *The International Monetary System, 1945–1976* (1977), p. 310.
17. The principle is stated in several different ways in Article IV, Section 1, *second*, and was heavily emphasized by both the U.S. and French governments. See J. J. Polak, "The Fund after Jamaica," *Finance and Development* 13(June 1976):8; Richard W. Edwards, Jr., "The Currency Exchange Rate Provisions of the Proposed Amended Articles of Agreement of the International Monetary Fund," *American Journal of International Law* 70(1976):734.

thinking turned the received wisdom from Bretton Woods on its head.[18] The conventional view embodied in the original Articles of Agreement was that only by maintaining a par value system could discipline be imposed upon profligate governments and the certainty be provided under which international trade might flourish.

It is relatively easy to see why the United States should have advocated adoption of the new principle. Its negotiating position at the time went far beyond support for floating exchange rates as a necessary evil in a time of high and divergent inflation rates and took on the burden of arguing the superiority of a floating system. To meet that burden, it had to face the widespread identification among officials, particularly central bankers, of floating rates with economic instability. This attitude may have been an illogical carry-over from the very different conditions of the interwar period,[19] but it was strongly held nonetheless. The U.S. rhetorical response was to maintain that what was needed was not a system of stable exchange rates but rather, as asserted by language it succeeded in inserting in the new Article IV, "a stable system of exchange rates." Floating rates could be stable, the United States argued, and indeed more stable than an adjustable peg system, where rate changes nevertheless took place and where repeated international exchange rate crises occurred. Thus, the principle that domestic stability must precede exchange stability fit nicely with the U.S. advocacy of floating as a "stable system."

France equally supported the primacy of domestic stability, though not because it favored floating (which it regarded as "a dangerous phenomenon that disturbs the world economic order")[20] but rather because it recognized that a return to par values would not be feasible until the principal developed countries brought their inflation rates down to a level which would make it possible to maintain a parity for an extended period. Where two economies were inflating at say two and four percent respectively, a parity between them might be practicable. But where the rates were 10 and 20 percent, the parity would soon become unrealistic and short-term capital flows would undermine official efforts to maintain it.

Thus, out of diametrically opposed motives, the United States and France could agree to reverse the hierarchy of economic policy values embodied in the Bretton Woods agreement. It is perhaps this emphasis upon abstract principles rather than on what was actually to be done that makes the new Article IV read, as one commentator has noted, "somewhat more like a press communiqué than a formal statement of legal obligations."[21]

18. Otmar Emminger, *On the Way to a New International Monetary Order* (1976), p. 13.
19. See discussion pp. 61–63.
20. Address of French finance minister Fourcade, IMF, *Summary Proceedings 1975*, p. 96.
21. Edwards, "Exchange Rate Provisions," p. 733.

On the level of general principles, the United States and France also found it possible to agree to insert in Article IV some restrictions on the conduct of surplus countries. Although, in common with other European countries, France had opposed in the C-20 discussions the use of objective indicators to force adjustment by surplus countries, it was more an aspirant to surplus-country status than a country that regularly enjoyed that status. France was thus prepared to accede to the principle that each member should "avoid manipulating exchange rates or the international monetary system in order to prevent effective balance of payments adjustment or to gain an unfair competitive advantage over the other members."[22] Whatever those words may come to mean, they referred, in the context of the negotiations, to the behavior attributed to major surplus countries (Japan and sometimes Germany) in maintaining artificially undervalued exchange rates through exchange market intervention, exchange controls, and even trade restrictions.

If France was prepared to accept floating *faute de mieux* for the moment, it was not prepared to bless it with specific language in the Articles. At the same time the United States insisted that no "implied judgment that floating [was] in any way a less desirable practice than the maintenance of a par value" should find an anchor in the terms of the Second Amendment.[23] This almost ideological disagreement over the desirability of floating led to curious language in the new Article IV. Under what has sometimes been called a freedom of choice principle, a member might adopt a par value system (so long as the par was not expressed in gold) or "other exchange arrangements of a member's choice."[24] This language underscores the great diversity of exchange arrangements maintained by various members at the time, a diversity so great that the draftsmen could not characterize the existing international monetary system beyond referring to it as "an international monetary system of the kind prevailing on January 1, 1976."[25]

Although the term "generalized floating" might suffice in general discussions to describe the relations between the dollar, the yen, and the snake currencies, that term did not do justice to the variety of formal exchange arrangements that had been adopted by individual countries since the Smithsonian. As of 30 June 1975, only eleven countries were floating independently (though they accounted for almost half of the trade of Fund members). Seven members, accounting for 23.2 percent of member trade, were floating jointly as part of the European snake arrangement. In contrast, fifty-four currencies

22. Article IV, Section 1(iii), *second*. See also Article IV, Section 4, and Schedule C:7, *second*, which apply to a future par value system.
23. Gold, *Selected Essays*, p. 34.
24. Article IV, Section 2(b), *second*. This provision also mentioned "cooperative arrangements by which members maintain the value of their currencies in relation to the value of the currency or currencies of other members." The European snake arrangements would be an example. See discussion pp. 193–94, above.
25. Article IV, Section 2(b), *second*.

were pegged to the U.S. dollar, thirteen to the French franc, ten to the pound sterling, and four to other currencies. Five members, mainly in Latin America, were pegged to the SDR, and fourteen were pegged to composites of currencies.[26]

The freedom of choice principle was vigorously attacked by many critics of the Jamaica agreement. A Dutch Alternate Executive Director of the Fund protested the "Non-Reform" of the system.[27] Similarly, the Bank for International Settlements commented officially that "the Fund has adapted itself to the world, instead of the other way around."[28] Robert Triffin thought Article IV "more worthy of a slapstick comedy than of a solemn treaty defining a new international monetary system."[29]

Surveillance

To compensate for the substantively laissez-faire Article IV, a provision was added under which the Fund was required to "exercise firm surveillance over the exchange rate policies of members, and [to] adopt specific principles for the guidance of all members with respect to those policies."[30] Fund members in turn were to "provide the Fund with the information necessary for such surveillance, and, when requested by the Fund, [to] consult with it on the member's exchange rate policies."[31] In short, procedures were in large measure substituted for substantive requirements and prohibitions. The surveillance procedures were envisaged by the Fund staff as safeguards so that "freedom of choice" would not mean "freedom of behavior."[32] To be sure, the "specific principles" were, as discussed below, somewhat more specific than the text of Article IV, but they were still sufficiently general for constraints on behavior to depend almost entirely on the surveillance procedures.

The surveillance requirement was implemented in two stages. First, a decision spelling out the requisite "specific principles" and establishing consultation procedures was adopted on 29 April 1977.[33] Then, consultations

---

26. *IMF Annual Report 1975*, p. 24, table 9. See also H. Robert Heller, "Choosing an Exchange Rate System," *Finance and Development* 14(June 1977):23–27, and *IMF Survey* 5(1976):35–39, 158–59.
27. T. de Vries, "Jamaica."
28. *BIS 46th Report 1976*, p. 118.
29. Robert Triffin, "Jamaica: 'Major Revision' or Fiasco?" in Edward M. Bernstein et al., *Reflections on Jamaica*, Princeton Essays in Internatinal Finance, no. 115 (1976), p. 47. See "Commentary" by Fred Hirsch in *Exchange Rate Flexibility*, ed. Jacob S. Dreyer et al. (1978), pp. 200–202.
30. Article IV, Section 3(b), *second*.
31. Ibid.
32. H. Johannes Witteveen, "The Emerging International Monetary System," *IMF Survey* 5(1976):180.
33. Decision of 29 April 1977, *IMF Annual Report 1977*, pp. 107–9 (hereafter cited First Surveillance Decision). See discussion of the decision in J. R. Artus and A. D. Crockett, "National Sovereignty and International Cooperation over Exchange Arrangements," *Case Western Reserve Journal of International Law* 12(1980):334–37.

were to be held with members at least annually, and the consultations were to result in decisions of the Executive Board.

The debate on the content of the surveillance decision centered, at least within the U.S. government, on the interplay between those two stages of implementation and throws interesting light on the nature of lawmaking within an international economic organization. The principal alternatives were characterized as the legislative and the common law approaches. Under the former, specific principles would be elaborated in the surveillance decision and then applied in the periodic country consultations. Under the common law approach, the principles would be developed over time in the consultations as experience and reflection permitted more specificity. The common law approach had been urged by U.S. treasury secretary Simon at the 1976 Fund annual meeting:

> The Fund should, in its surveillance of members' exchange rate policies, proceed by a careful and evolutionary approach. . . . Rather than adopting a sweeping, pre-conceived, rigid economic code, we need to construct, through a case-by-case approach, a common law based on case history. If we proceed in this manner, we will be able to delineate broad principles of behavior that can be elaborated on the basis of experience.[34]

Fund Managing Director Witteveen, in contrast, spoke of the then forthcoming surveillance decision as a "code of conduct."[35]

The analogy to legislative versus common law lawmaking in domestic legal systems was, of course, in the minds of those who debated these issues; but, since the debaters were largely officials and economists, the legal content of the distinction was left somewhat vague. How under the "common law" approach, for example, new principles derived from the consultations would be reduced to textual form was left entirely up in the air. Indeed, it is difficult in retrospect to determine which side won. The specific principles in the surveillance decision were not much more specific than those in the Articles of Agreement themselves, and yet, since the results of consultations are not made public, it is impossible to know whether those principles have been given any more definite content. Certainly unless consultations have produced new principles that then bind members in later consultations, nothing that a lawyer would recognize as a "common law" approach can be identified.

---

34. IMF, *Summary Proceedings 1976*, p. 96.
35. Ibid. p. 244. "In rejecting precise guidelines for IMF surveillance," Secretary Simon noted that the "Articles, after all, are meant to serve as an international constitution, not a commercial contract." Attempts to impose "detailed rules and formulas" would be inequitable, given the great differences between IMF members, and unrealistic in view of the absence of "the capability, the experience, or the knowledge to develop such a set of rules to be applied across a broad spectrum of individual national situations." Ibid. pp. 94–95. On the emergence of the idea of the code of conduct in international law, see François Rigaux, "Pour un autre ordre international," in Jacques Blanc and François Rigaux, *Droit économique II* (1979), pp. 364–77.

The lack of illuminating comment by Fund officials and governments, however, suggests that little or nothing of the "common law" approach is to be found in the consultation process and that the consultations do not represent, from a legal point of view, any substantial development from those already held by the Fund with members under Articles VIII and XIV.

Perhaps no more was intended by reference to the "common law" approach than that the Fund might someday add new surveillance principles or alter old ones when views had changed. The Fund's general counsel apparently took this more limited view in commenting that the "disproportion between principles and procedures in the decision reflects wariness about a detailed and abstract code on economic matters, and a preference for the evolution of principles as the result of experience."[36]

The 1977 surveillance decision replaced the Guidelines for Floating once the Second Amendment became effective on 1 April 1978.[37] The decision therefore covers some of the same ground as the Guidelines.[38] Yet since it applies even to members that purport to be pegging their currency to some external standard (another currency, the SDR, etc.), the surveillance decision applies more broadly than did the Guidelines.[39]

The surveillance decision sets forth three kinds of principles—"General Principles," "Principles for the Guidance of Members' Exchange Rate Policies" and "Principles of Fund Surveillance over Exchange Rate Policies." The general principles are limited almost entirely to gathering together principles already stated in Article IV.[40] Principles for the "Guidance of Members" are in part restatements of Article IV and in part adaptations of the Guidelines. In the restatement category is the language quoted above that prohibits "manipulating exchange rates or the international monetary system in order to prevent effective balance of payments adjustment or to gain an unfair competitive advantage over other members."[41] John H. Young, a Fund official directly concerned with the drafting of the decision, gave this language an illuminating interpretation:

> [It] in effect says that a country shall not have the "wrong" exchange rate, that is, a rate which overvalues or undervalues its currency. . . .
> The purpose of Fund surveillance is to reduce the economic costs and

---

36. Joseph Gold, *A Third Report on Some Recent Legal Developments in the International Monetary Fund*, World Association of Lawyers (1978), pp. 9–10.

37. Gold, *Second Amendment*, p. 27.

38. See discussion of the Guidelines pp. 196–99, above.

39. Gold, *Second Amendment*, p. 27.

40. John H. Young, "Surveillance over Exchange Rate Policies," *Finance and Development* 14(September 1977):17.

41. First Surveillance Decision, *IMF Annual Report* 1977, p. 108, and Article IV, Section 1(iii), *second*.

the international political frictions which result from a country having the wrong exchange rate over a significant period.[42]

Moreover, "in exercising surveillance the first question to settle is whether or not a member does or does not have the wrong exchange rate."[43]

Young's interpretation bears on the recurring question whether the Fund, or even the member in question, is in a position to determine the "right" rate, at least in a system not based on par values. A narrower position, suggested by Young's interpretation, is that the Fund can at best determine when a current rate is "wrong" (say, from evidence of persistent one-way intervention to support the current rate).[44] This view represents a rejection of the more ambitious role assumed by the Fund before the surveillance decision, when it frequently gave "advice to countries on what exchange rate [was] appropriate for them and what policies they should pursue in order to achieve it."[45] Young's interpretation is consistent with growing doubt, in both academic and banking circles, that finance ministries and central banks are both able to determine the correct rate and then make it effective through exchange market intervention. For example, informed commercial bankers, at least outside the United States, appear to be highly skeptical of central banks' intervention policies.[46]

A second principle addresses the related question of the desirability, whatever the general level of an exchange rate, of avoiding short-term fluctuations and especially what is often referred to as disorderly market conditions. It provides that "a member should intervene in the exchange market if necessary to counter disorderly conditions which may be characterized inter alia by disruptive short-term movements in the exchange value of its currency."[47] Although this principle implies that a member can know when exchange rate changes are a move away from rather than toward the "right" rate, the formulation adopted is actually somewhat less ambitious than that used in the Guidelines, where intervention was called for "as necessary to prevent or moderate sharp and disruptive fluctuations from day to day and from week

42. Young, "Surveillance," p. 18.
43. Ibid. p. 19. On differing definitions of "exchange rate," see Jacob Frenkel, "Discussion," *Managed Exchange-Rate Flexibility: The Recent Experience*, Federal Reserve Bank of Boston Conference Series no. 20 (1978), pp. 176–77.
44. See also discussion pp. 196–97. For views of a number of prominent officials and economists, see *The New International Monetary System*, ed. Robert A. Mundell and Jacques J. Polak (1977), pp. 104–7.
45. Statement by Fund Managing Director Witteveen, cited in ibid. p. 105.
46. Group of Thirty, *The Foreign Exchange Markets under Floating Rates* (1980). pp. 30–33. See also Karl Brunner, "Reflections on the State of International Monetary Policy," *Banca Nazionale del Lavoro Quarterly Review*, no. 131 (December 1979), p. 374. Frenkel notes that, contrary to intention, "in many cases the policies of intervention [of major central banks] did not contribute to increased stability." Frenkel, pp. 179–80.
47. First Surveillance Decision, *IMF Annual Report* 1977, p. 108.

to week in the exchange value of its currency."[48] The Guidelines would thus have required a country to take a view of the correct value of its currency over a period of weeks, whereas the second principle in the surveillance decision requires only a decision as to when market conditions are disorderly.[49]

Perhaps the second principle in the surveillance decision is intended to state no more than that pronounced fluctuations are bad without regard to the level of the rate. Such an interpretation would be consistent with the condemnation in the new Article IV of "erratic disruptions." What this term means is inherently uncertain. In response to a congressional written question, the U.S. Treasury could provide no better definition of "erratic fluctuation" and "disorderly markets" than the following:

> These are general terms which we have used to try to convey in a broad sense the type of situation which we feel could warrant exchange market intervention. In our view, the terms "erratic" and "disorderly," while not precisely defined or precisely definable in advance, are synonymous, in the sense that they are both meant to describe a situation in which the markets are not functioning properly. Put another way, it is in our view likely that erratic fluctuations would be characterized by disorderly market conditions. The issue is unavoidably and appropriately judgmental, and decisions must be taken on the basis of continuing surveillance and analysis of market developments.[50]

As this U.S. Treasury statement reveals, one of the problems of interpretation is that many official participants in exchange markets believe that although they cannot define a disorderly market, they know it when they see it. Some officials further believe that "smoothing" operations to offset short-term fluctuations are both feasible and useful.

The origin of the surveillance decision's provision on disorderly markets was the agreement of six major countries at the Rambouillet summit conference in November 1975 to "act to counter disorderly conditions or erratic fluctuations in exchange rates."[51] There, too, no definition had been arrived at, but a procedural consequence was daily consultations on exchange rate movements and intervention:

---

48. Guidelines for the Management of Floating Exchange Rates, *IMF Annual Report* 1974, p. 113. See discussion of this Guideline p. 197.
49. See Young, "Surveillance," p. 18. A third principle calls for members to "take into account" the interests of "countries in whose currencies they intervene."
50. Letter from William E. Simon to Henry S. Reuss, dated 3 February 1976, printed in Hearing before the Subcommittee on International Economics of the Joint Economic Committee, *The IMF Gold Agreement*, 94th Cong., 1st Sess. (1976), p. 84. See also discussion in Frenkel, pp. 176–77.
51. *IMF Survey* 4(1975):350.

The daily telephonic exchanges of the "snake" members about market conditions and interventions were extended to include the United States, as well as Canada, Japan and Switzerland, and provision was made for periodical consultations between both Finance Ministers and their Deputies. Beyond that, judgement as to whether the market is disorderly or rate movements erratic, together with any decision on intervention or other corrective action, is left up to each country. Such judgements are often uncertain and in any case the United States has made it clear that the agreement does not signify any basic change in its policy of limited intervention. This is another way of saying that in the US view fundamental market forces comprise a much wider range of factors—notably capital movements—than in the eyes of many European countries for which the word "fundamental" refers primarily to the current balance of payments.[52]

The third set of principles—those concerning "Fund Surveillance over Exchange Rate Policies"—reflects a further leaning toward the narrower view that at most the Fund can know when a rate is clearly "wrong" and not necessarily when it is right. Most of the indicia to which the Fund is to look in the surveillance mechanism involve actions by a member that could constitute the "manipulation" of its own rate:

> In its surveillance of the observance by members of the principles set forth above, the Fund shall consider the following developments as among those which might indicate the need for discussion with a member:
>
> (i) protracted large-scale intervention in one direction in the exchange market;
>
> (ii) an unsustainable level of official or quasi-official borrowing, or excessive and prolonged short-term official or quasi-official lending, for balance of payments purposes;
>
> (iii) (a) the introduction, substantial intensification, or prolonged maintenance, for balance of payments purposes, of restrictions on, or incentives for, current transactions or payments, or
>
>   (b) the introduction or substantial modification for balance of payments purposes of restrictions on, or incentives for, the inflow or outflow of capital;
>
> (iv) the pursuit, for balance of payments purposes, of monetary and other domestic financial policies that provide abnormal encouragement or discouragement to capital flows; and
>
> (v) behavior of the exchange rate that appears to be unrelated to underlying economic and financial conditions including factors affecting competitiveness and long-term capital movements.[53]

---

52. *BIS 46th Report* 1976, p. 117.
53. First Surveillance Decision, *IMF Annual Report* 1977, pp. 108–9.

Only the last of these criteria does not involve actions of the member. That criterion is formulated in terms of the "behavior of the exchange rate," largely to emphasize that a rate could be wrong even though it has not moved if, again to quote Young, its lack of movement is "out of line with developments in the long-run determinants of the exchange rate, for example, relative rates of inflation among countries."[54]

Thus, the surveillance decision as a whole represents a backing away from the view that officials are better able than the market to determine the correct exchange rate for a currency. In this respect, the surveillance decision represents a movement toward the pro-market views held by the United States. Treasury secretary William Simon forcefully spelled out the U.S. position in June 1976 before a congressional committee, equating the opposing view with the fixed rate philosophy underlying Bretton Woods:

> Fund surveillance of members' policies should not be aimed at trying to calculate a zone, or target, or right rate for individual currencies toward which exchange rate policies should be directed. Such an approach is, in my view, inconsistent with the new article IV, and is neither conceptually sound nor technically feasible. It suffers from the same basic flaw as the par value system—it assumes that we know, or can determine, what should be at least approximately the equilibrium rate for each currency. It is, in attenuated form, a throwback to Bretton Woods, a fixed rate psychology, a search for fundamental equilibrium. Even in theory there is no single right rate in a world of large capital flows in which inflation rates, domestic objectives, monetary and fiscal policies, to name but a few influences, not only differ among countries but can change rather rapidly.
>
> The technical difficulties of calculating a proper exchange rate zone or right rate are so formidable as to render this approach impractical as a guide to policy. The approach assumes that we can compare one country's inflation rate against other countries', and thereby determine what its exchange rate should be. There are problems of obtaining the right indices—knowing what weights and base periods to use; problems of obtaining proper data—which are inadequate in most countries; and problems of measuring price and income elasticities. Perhaps more importantly, these calculations look only at the impact of merchandise trade on exchange rates, and pay no account to capital movements, which loom so large in determining the exchange rates of so many currencies. With the present state of the art, such attempts on the part of monetary authorities to calculate the right rate and then use the results as a basis for exchange rate policy are tantamount to a daily renegotiation of a par value system on the basis of limited and inadequate data underpinned

54. Young, "Surveillance," p. 18. Young points out that the members' actions referred to in the surveillance document "were to be regarded as 'pointers' indicating the need for discussions, rather than treated as conclusive evidence of inappropriate exchange rate policies." Ibid. See also Frenkel, p. 178.

by flawed concepts. Moreover, the data used all relate to past periods, and are entirely backward-looking, whereas exchange rates are partly forward and partly backward looking, anticipating future economic and financial trends as well as recording past developments.[55]

The procedural framework for application of the surveillance standard is annual consultations with each member country. Since members were already consulting annually with the Fund, either mandatorily under Article XIV or voluntarily under Article VIII, and the new surveillance provisions were to "comprehend" these other consultations in an annual consultation with each member,[56] one of the principal procedural effects of the decision was to broaden the scope of the consultations.[57] The scope was broadened by the requirement that the Fund's appraisal is to be based not only on the member's external policies but also on its domestic economic policies:

> This appraisal shall be made within the framework of a comprehensive analysis of the general economic situation and economic policy strategy of the member, and shall recognize that domestic as well as external policies can contribute to timely adjustment of the balance of payments. The appraisal shall take into account the extent to which the policies of the member, including its exchange rate policies, serve the objectives of the continuing development of the orderly underlying conditions that are necessary for financial stability, the promotion of sustained sound economic growth, and reasonable levels of employment.[58]

Any attempt under this language to second guess a member's domestic economic policies, and particularly their relation to "financial stability," "sound economic growth," and "reasonable levels of employment," is likely to be considered by some Fund members interference in their internal affairs. And, in view of the fact that social and political objectives are usually the driving force behind fiscal and monetary policies that lead to inflation, such

55. Statement of William E. Simon, *To Provide for Amendment of the Bretton Woods Agreements Act*, Hearings before the Subcommittee on International Trade, Investment and Monetary Policy of the Committee on Banking, Currency and Housing, House of Representatives, 94th Cong., 2d Sess. (1 June 1976), p. 11.
56. Procedures for Surveillance, para. II, First Surveillance Decision, *IMF Annual Report 1977*, p. 109. See also Gold, *Second Amendment*, pp. 28–29; Edwards, "Exchange Rate Provisions," pp. 739–42. Paragraph IV of the Procedures for Surveillance adds a procedure under which the Managing Director can initiate his own "discussion" with a member. These provisions were "supplemented" in 1979. Decision of 22 January 1979, *IMF Annual Report 1979*, p. 136.
57. A second procedural effect was that the "conclusions" reached will be "the legal equivalent of decisions of the Executive Board." No such decision was possible in Article VIII negotiations. Gold, *Second Amendment*, pp. 28–29. The decisions will not be published but will of course be well known to all parties concerned and constitute "the judgment of peers or the mobilization of shame." Joseph Gold, "Exchange Arrangements and International Law in an Age of Floating Currencies," in *American Society of International Law, Proceedings of the 73rd Annual Meeting* (1979), p. 8.
58. Principles of Fund Surveillance over Exchange Rate Policies, para. 3, First Surveillance Decision, *IMF Annual Report 1977*, p. 109.

members will be able to point to the provision in new Article IV that sur-veillance "shall respect the domestic social and political policies of mem-bers."[59]

The potential conflict is an important one. Reluctance to surrender sov-ereignty has limited the impact of surveillance, for if surveillance is to be effective, it must be concerned with domestic policies that generate inflation and thereby domestic economic instability. Indeed, it would be a denial of the fundamental shift in priorities between Bretton Woods and Jamaica, from exchange rate stability to domestic stability, to foreclose inquiry into domestic policies in the surveillance process. Yet an attempt through an international organization to influence such policies is likely to be fiercely resisted. In the past, the Fund has successfully used its conditionality policies, sometimes despite considerable resistance in the countries concerned, to negotiate lim-itations on public spending, borrowing requirements and money supply growth.[60] The carrot of Fund financial assistance is likely to be more influ-ential than the stick of Fund surveillance.

A Return to Par Values?

In return for acceding to the U.S. position on freedom of choice, France successfully insisted upon a procedure for returning to par values and on rules governing any future par value system. The United States refused, however, to agree to a simple majority vote for determining when the return to par values should occur. Rather that decision was made subject to an 85 percent special majority,[61] thereby giving the United States a veto.

Lest the U.S. government someday give way to international pressure to vote for a return to par values, the U.S. Treasury successfully won insertion of a clause that permits any member to float indefinitely notwithstanding a Fund vote to return to par values.[62] This double safeguard for a U.S. dollar float is further bolstered by a set of criteria to be observed in making a determination to return to par values. These criteria are apparently intended not merely to impede any hasty return but indeed to import some of the C-20 long-term Outline of Reform into the transition to par values. Specifically, the determination to return to par values must be made in the light of

59. Article IV, Section 3(b), *second*. On other difficulties in application of the surveillance de-cision, see Artus and Crockett, pp. 337–39.
60. See discussion pp. 124–26. See also Joseph Gold, *Conditionality*, IMF Pamphlet Series no. 31 (1979), pp. 22–25; *World Financial Markets*, December 1980, p. 6.
61. Article IV, Section 4, *second*. See a parallel provision in Article IV, Section 2(c), involving not par values but "general exchange arrangements." Joseph Gold has suggested that such arrangements might include a regime of central rates as opposed to true par values. Gold, "A Report on Certain Recent Legal Developments in the International Monetary Fund," *Vanderbilt Journal of Transnational Law* 9(1976):228.
62. No country is required to declare a par value even in connection with a general return to par values. Schedule C:2-3, *second*. See the parallel safeguard for floating in Article IV, Section 2(c), *second*.

the evolution of the international monetary system, with particular reference to sources of liquidity, and, in order to ensure the effective operation of a system of par values, to arrangements under which both members in surplus and members in deficit in their balances of payments take prompt, effective, and symmetrical action to achieve adjustment, as well as to arrangements for intervention and the treatment of imbalances.[63]

This recitation of the key concepts in the C-20 Outline of Reform—especially symmetry—appears, however, to be little more than pious rhetoric in view of the fact that the new par value system would be much like the Bretton Woods system.[64] Although par values are to be "stable but adjustable" as under the C-20 formulation,[65] reform of the par value regime goes little beyond the consensus already reached by the time of the Smithsonian agreement. Margins are to be the 4½ percent Smithsonian margins (rather than one percent as under Bretton Woods).[66] Par value changes are permitted not only to correct a fundamental disequilibrium, but also to prevent its emergence, but the concept of a fundamental disequilibrium is still central and still undefined.[67] Perhaps the most far-reaching change is that the "common denominator" for the new par value regime shall not be gold or a currency, which means almost certainly that it would have to be the SDR.[68]

Although these changes are significant, they might have been introduced (with the possible exception of the SDR "common denominator") even without the C-20 reform discussions. There are no provisions for reserve indicators or pressures and, a fortiori, nothing about multicurrency intervention or reducing the role of reserve currencies.[69] The details of the new par value scheme, largely ignoring as they do the C-20 discussions, may engender profound skepticism about the value of such a massive reform exercise. By the time of the Jamaica agreement it seemed so unlikely that a par value scheme would be introduced in the foreseeable future that it was apparently

63. Article IV, Section 4, *second.*
64. On differences between the Bretton Woods and Jamaica par value systems, see Joseph Gold, "The Fund Agreement in the Courts—XIII," *IMF Staff Papers* 25(1978):360–67.
65. Article IV, Section 4, *second.*
66. Schedule C:5, *second.* At the Smithsonian, 4½ percent margins were permitted only if they resulted from maintaining 2¼ percent margins against an intervention currency (that is, the dollar). See discussion pp. 191–92, above.
67. Schedule C:6 and 7, *second.*
68. Schedule C:1, *second,* provides that par values may be expressed "in terms of the special drawing right, or in terms of such other common denominator as is prescribed by the Fund" but the "common denominator shall not be gold or a currency."
69. The Report by the Executive Directors makes clear, however, that such reforms as multicurrency intervention could be adopted without further amendment. See e.g. IMF, *Proposed Second Amendment of the Articles of Agreement of the International Monetary Fund, Report by the Executive Directors to the Board of Governors* (1976), Part II:C.8, p. 14 (hereafter cited *Executive Board Second Amendment Report*).

worth no one's time to attempt to negotiate reforms that would never become operational. Certainly the United States, whose float was already doubly safeguarded, had little reason to worry about the shape of a distant and unlikely par value regime.

II. Reserve Assets

Despite the disdain of the draftsmen of the Bretton Woods agreement for the gold standard, they nevertheless gave gold a central role in the Articles. Certainly it was the numeraire for the Bretton Woods system. Par values were expressed in gold or the dollar, and even in the latter case they had to be expressed in terms of "the United States dollar of the weight and fineness in effect on July 1, 1944."[70] The requirement that subscriptions normally be 25 percent in gold made gold one of the principal assets of the Fund.[71] And in the international monetary system in practice, as opposed to that on paper, gold not only occupied the role of the principal reserve asset in the early postwar years but was replaced by the U.S. dollar only through persistent U.S. deficits, which were in later years interpreted by many as a sign of weakness rather than strength of the dollar as an international reserve. As for the SDR, it was created to supplement gold and reserve currencies, not to replace them.[72]

Gold

When it was decided in the C-20 negotiations, therefore, to elevate the SDR to the formal status of principal reserve asset, gold necessarily had to be formally demoted. What precisely to do with gold became a contentious issue. While it was simple enough, indeed largely symbolic, to transfer the numeraire function to the SDR, a good deal of national prestige turned on more material issues, such as the value to be placed on gold and the disposition to be made of the Fund's large holdings of gold.

On the doctrinal level, the most important factors were that the United States chose to crusade for the demonetization of gold whereas France chose to defend the older gold faith, and that many central bankers believed that it would be dangerous, perhaps impossible, to abolish gold's international reserve role. On a more material level, a key datum was that gold was trading,

70. Article IV, Section 1(a), *original*. See also the provision on maintenance of gold value in Article IV, Section 8, *original*. See discussion pp. 86, 97, above.
71. Article III, Section 3(b), *original*.
72. Article XXI, Section 1, *first*. See also J. Marcus Fleming, "The Bearing of the Supply of Other Reserves on the Need for Special Drawing Rights," pp. 321–27, 348–49, and Edward M. Bernstein, "Comments," pp. 350–52, in IMF, *International Reserves: Needs and Availability* (1970). See discussion of growth of foreign exchange, especially the dollar in international reserves, pp. 142–45, 207–10, above.

throughout the Second Amendment negotiations, for at least three times the official price.[73]

All sides sought to capture the value represented by the difference between the official and market prices. Less-developed countries saw the possibility of achieving through the possible capital gain over the official price a substitute for the SDR link schemes that had been debated in the C-20. Moreover, gold holdings were unevenly distributed among nations, certainly in absolute terms but also even as a proportion of each country's international reserves. Hence, attitudes toward gold were shaped in part by quite understandable financial motivations. Finally, the U.S. pressure on its European allies and Japan—as part of its diplomatic defense of the dollar throughout the 1960s— to avoid converting dollar reserves into gold had created what some chose to characterize as a moral commitment to those countries that had stayed loyal to the dollar and had foresworn additional gold holdings during the dollar's long trial.[74]

A few numbers summarize the relationships. At the end of May 1975, gold reserves of all Fund members, valued at the official price, totaled $44.6 billion (compared to $160.6 billion of foreign exchange reserves). Of that $44.6 billion, the United States held $12.0 billion, and five European countries (France, Germany, Italy, Switzerland, and the Netherlands) held in total another $19.1 billion. Japan, Canada, and the United Kingdom held less than $1 billion each. And less-developed non-oil-exporting countries, which preferred interest on dollars to the vaunted security of gold, held only $2.3 billion, or roughly 5 percent of the total. The distribution of foreign exchange was far different. Even the gold-holding countries (other than the United States) had substantial foreign exchange reserves, and the less-developed non-oil-exporting countries accounted for $24.4 billion, or about 15 percent of the total.[75] Meanwhile, the Fund held some 150 million ounces of gold, worth, at the official price, more than $6 billion.[76] Each of these gold values would have to be multiplied several times at least to reflect what the various countries then assumed, in view of the market price, was the gold's actual worth.

In this financial context the key issues became, first, how the diametrically opposed U.S. and French views on the future of gold in the system could be reconciled, and second, what should be done with the Fund's gold? The first issue was dealt with by diplomatic ambiguity, the second by an undiplomatic melon-cutting exercise.

---

73. *BIS 46th Report* 1976, p. 112.
74. See the testimony of former U.S. treasury secretary Fowler, who had been a Treasury official during most of the 1960s, in Hearings before the Subcommittee on International Economics of the Joint Economic Committee, *The IMF Gold Agreement*, 94th Cong., 1st Sess. (10 October 1975), pp. 5, 12.
75. Ibid. pp. 17–21 (exhibit C).
76. Ibid. pp. 13, 68.

The requirements for a successful resolution of the first issue were that the United States be given language pointing to an end to gold's role in the international monetary system and that France be given a reality which, if it did not preserve gold's role, nevertheless preserved the objective conditions in which gold might evolve back to the center of the system. In keeping with the U.S. goal, the formal attributes and uses of gold previously specified in the Articles were eliminated root and branch. Gold would no longer have any numeraire function. Members choosing to maintain par values were forbidden to base them on gold.[77] Subscriptions no longer had to be made partly in gold.[78] The gold tranche consequently became the reserve tranche.[79]

The substantive issues were more difficult. The U.S. goal was complete demonetization of gold, so that it could thenceforth be treated like any metal. The United States sought therefore an agreement to abolish the official price of gold, sale of much of the Fund's gold with the proceeds (at least to the extent of the capital gain) to be used for the benefit of less-developed countries, and some limitation on how much gold any country could acquire.

France, on the other hand, wanted to rescue gold from its current immobility and return it to the status of a usable reserve, which implied its valuation at a "market-related" price. The French also sought freedom for central banks to buy and not merely to sell gold, and, in view of the extensive private holdings of gold by French citizens, some protection of the market price from price-depressing sales of the Fund's gold.[80]

In order to keep some of the capital gain for the benefit of the larger developed countries and to avoid price-depressing sales, the French proposed "restitution" of the Fund's gold to members in proportion to their quotas. This proposal led to a compromise, adopted at the August 1975 meeting of the Interim Committee, providing for "[s]ale of one sixth of the Fund's gold (25 million ounces) for the benefit of developing countries . . . and restitution of one sixth of the Fund's gold to members."[81] The logic of restitution assumed that 25 million ounces of gold would be sold at the official price with each member purchasing an amount proportionate to its quota. Each country would thus enjoy a capital gain, if it later sold that gold at the market price, equal to the difference between the official and market prices. And, of course, the largest potential capital gain would go to the countries with the largest quotas.

As part of the compromise, the French agreed to the U.S. and less-developed country demand for sale of a second 25 million ounces of gold for

77. Article IV, Section 2(b), and Schedule C:1, *second.*
78. *Executive Board Second Amendment Report*, Part II:I, pp. 40–41. On future use of gold at the option of a member, see Article V, Section 12(d), *second.*
79. Article V, Section 3(b), *second*, and *Executive Board Second Amendment Report*, Part II:D:9, pp. 19–20.
80. For more detail on the U.S. and French positions, see Solomon, pp. 312–17.
81. *IMF Annual Report* 1976, p. 121.

the benefit of less-developed countries. One important effect of this agreement was that it served to defuse the demand for an SDR link.[82]

The dynamics of policy formation among the less-developed countries were such that those countries with the largest quotas, which tended of course to be the financially stronger ones, were successful in capturing a disproportionate share of the benefits from the sale of the second 25 million ounces. All 104 less-developed country members received collectively a share of the profits corresponding to their collective share (27.8 percent) in total Fund quotas. Each member then received by direct transfer a portion of this 27.8 percent share in proportion to the size of its quota. Thus the less-developed countries with the largest quotas benefited most from this distribution.[83] Only the remaining 72.2 percent of the profits on the second 25 million ounces would therefore be used solely for the benefit of poorer less-developed countries. The result was that the wealthier less-developed countries did not have to make any implied transfer for the benefit of their poorer confrères, although some in fact did so. And the resources available to the poorer less-developed countries were correspondingly smaller than if the entire second 25 million ounces had been sold for the benefit of those countries.[84]

An innovative legal device was used in connection with the second 25 million ounces. A Trust Fund was established to pay over the first 27.8 percentage of the profits directly to 104 less-developed countries, and to channel the remaining profits in the form of loans to the poorer less-developed countries.[85] Although one of the purposes of the creation of a Trust Fund was to help the Fund put the sales into operation before the Second Amendment became effective, the Trust Fund continued to be used for disbursements thereafter.[86] Trust funds had been used for various purposes by other

82. A number of measures, of which the trust fund was only one, that favored less-developed countries were treated as a "reform package" justifying abandonment of the demand for an SDR link. See Jahangir Amuzegar, "The North-South Dialogue: From Conflict to Compromise," *Foreign Affairs* 54(1976):552–54.
83. Schedule B:7(b), *second*. See Dhruba Gupta, "The Operation of the Trust Fund," *Finance and Development* 15(September 1978):37–38. The Interim Committee also agreed that the remaining 100 million ounces of Fund gold should be salable under "a range of broad enabling powers, exercisable with a high majority." *IMF Annual Report* 1975, p. 100. This provision was implemented in Article V, Sections 12(c)–(g), *second;* such sales were made subject to an 85 percent special majority and several new accounts were provided for the proceeds. See also Schedule B:7, *second*.
84. J. Carter Murphy, *The International Monetary System: Beyond the First Stage of Reform* (1979), p. 175. Six OPEC countries transferred their shares of the direct profits to the Trust Fund to increase its resources. Romania and Yugoslavia also contributed to the Trust Fund. *IMF Annual Report* 1980, p. 88.
85. Decision of 5 May 1976 and Instrument to Establish the Trust Fund, *IMF Annual Report* 1976, pp. 111–17. For the decision to terminate the Trust Fund, see *IMF Survey* 10(1981):10–13.
86. After the Second Amendment became effective, the Fund auctioned the gold directly though continuing to hold the receipts separately from the General Resources of the Fund. See Schedule B:7, *second; IMF Annual Report* 1978, p. 71. On the complicated arrangements used before the

international organizations,[87] but this was the first use by the IMF. Building on the general concept of a trust in Anglo-American law, the central concept was that the assets held by the trust fund, although legally owned by the IMF as trustee, were held solely for the benefit of less-developed countries. The profits remaining after the direct transfers of 27.8 percent of the profits to all 104 less-developed members were to be used for the benefit of some 61 less-developed members designated in the trust instrument. The assets of the Trust Fund were not to be commingled with general IMF assets and could only be used for the purposes specified in the trust instrument and for the benefit, through loans on concessional terms, of those 61 beneficial owners.[88]

The 61 countries, later reduced to 59 in the second two-year period, were those members with per capita incomes of less than SDR 300.[89] The Trust Fund, as a legal entity, was able to invest its funds to increase the sum available for such loans. Thus, the Trust Fund assets included as yet unsold gold, profits from sales of gold, earnings from investments, and interest income from loans.[90] Auctions began in 1976 and were completed over a four-year period. The total profits received came to $4.64 billion and by 30 April 1980 the Trust Fund's total assets equaled SDR 3.1 billion.[91]

One implicit purpose of the Fund gold auctions, at least from the viewpoint of the United States, was to attempt to phase gold out of the international monetary system by moving some of the Fund's gold into private hands. The United States endeavored to bolster any such effect by starting gold auctions from its own holdings.[92] So long as the Second Amendment (which eliminated the official price and hence the premium purchase prohibition) had not been ratified, Fund members were not able to buy at Fund gold auctions because the rule against premium purchases was still in effect (though there was some ambiguity about whether the Bank for International Settlements might buy

---

effective date to compensate for the lack of explicit authority under the existing Articles, see Joseph Gold, "Trust Funds in International Law: The Contribution of the International Monetary Fund to a Code of Principles," *American Journal of International Law* 72(1978):860. The authority relied on was the power to perform financial and technical services for members. Ibid. After final disbursement of Trust Fund loans and termination of the Trust Fund itself, the Fund proposed to transfer SDR 750 million of repayments of Trust Fund loans to the Subsidy Account for the benefit of less developed members. *IMF Survey* 10(1981):1, 9–13.
87. Gold, "Trust Funds," pp. 859–60.
88. Ibid. pp. 863–65; Instrument to Establish the Trust Fund, Section 1, para. 1, *IMF Annual Report* 1976, p. 112; Gupta, pp. 37–38.
89. Ernest Sturc, "The Trust Fund," *Finance and Development* 13(December 1976):31; *IMF Annual Report* 1979, p. 86.
90. *IMF Annual Report* 1979, pp. 170–71. On the operation of the Trust Fund, see ibid. pp. 86–87; Joseph Gold, *A Second Report on Some Recent Legal Developments in the International Monetary Fund* (1977), pp. 20–31; Gupta, p. 37.
91. *IMF Survey* 9(1980):145; *IMF Annual Report* 1980, p. 192, appendix VIII.
92. Treasury sales from official U.S. gold stock began in January 1975, *BIS 45th Report* 1975, p. 105. A further U.S. program began in 1978. *BIS 49th Report* 1979, p. 151. In 1979 the U.S. sold 412 tons of gold, as against 79 tons in 1978. *BIS 50th Report* 1980, p. 105.

on behalf of a member).[93] To assure that the effects of the gold sales would not be offset by central bank activities tending to enhance the role of gold, several measures were adopted. The first was a two-year agreement among the Group of Ten that "there be no action to peg the price of gold" and that "the total stock of gold now in the hands of the Fund and the monetary authorities of the Group of Ten will not be increased."[94]

Although the Group of Ten agreement appears to have been adhered to, it lapsed in 1978, and in view of the effectiveness of the Second Amendment, all members became free to acquire as much gold as they liked at the market price. Moreover, since Fund members were free even before the Second Amendment to sell gold at premium prices so long as they did not sell to members and after the Second Amendment could trade at the market price among themselves, and hence were free to value gold at a market-related price,[95] the aggregate value of gold reserves could increase greatly. France chose to use market values for its gold reserves as early as January 1975,[96] but most Fund members continued to use the old official price.[97] Furthermore, although the official price was abrogated by the Second Amendment, the Fund continues to use the old official price to value its own gold and members' holdings.[98] Even where a country does not revalue its gold to reflect the higher market price, its officials may very well conduct their economic policies on the basis of their own subjective valuation of the country's gold holdings.

A second measure was the provision in the Second Amendment requiring the Fund to be "guided in all its policies and decisions . . . by the objective of avoiding the management of the price, or the establishment of a fixed price, in the gold market."[99] However, this obligation is specifically restricted to operations and transactions under Article V, Section 12, which involves transactions in gold by the Fund. Thus, it does not prohibit members from entering into agreements among themselves to peg the price of gold. For

93. See exchange of correspondence between representative Reuss and treasury secretary Simon in Hearing before the Subcommittee on International Economics of the Joint Economic Committee, *The IMF Gold Agreement*, 94th Cong., 1st Sess. (1976), pp. 80–85.
94. This Group of Ten agreement was embodied in the Interim Committee's communiqué on its 31 August 1975 meeting. *IMF Annual Report 1976*, p. 121.
95. Joseph Gold, *Floating Currencies, SDRs, and Gold: Further Legal Developments*, IMF Pamphlet Series no. 22 (1977), p. 52.
96. Ibid.
97. Joseph Gold, *SDRs, Gold, and Currencies: Third Survey of New Legal Developments*, IMF Pamphlet Series no. 26 (1979), pp. 33–34 (hereafter cited Gold, *Third Survey*).
98. *IMF Annual Report 1980*, p. 81, and p. 181 (Accounting Practices). However, valuation of members' gold holdings at the old official price is for Fund "operational purposes," ibid. p. 81, whereas gold as a proportion of holdings of world reserve assets is now valued at "London market price," ibid. p. 59, table 14. For changes in the Fund's gold valuation practices, see Joseph Gold, *SDRs, Currencies, and Gold: Fourth Survey of New Legal Developments*, IMF Pamphlet Series no. 33 (1980), pp. 87–88 (hereafter cited Gold, *Fourth Survey*).
99. Article V, Section 12(a), *second*.

example, the Group of Ten or the Bank for International Settlements group of central banks could agree to peg the price of gold. Nor does the prohibition, strictly speaking, prevent the Fund from cooperating with members in connection with their gold-pegging operations so long as no Fund transactions under Article V, Section 12 are involved.[100]

The commitment to make the special drawing right the principal reserve asset, on the other hand, might be taken to imply a commitment to avoid actions, such as pegging the price, that would maintain the importance of gold as a reserve asset. Under the Second Amendment,

> Each member undertakes to collaborate with the Fund and with other members in order to ensure that the policies of the member with respect to reserve assets shall be consistent with the objectives of promoting better international surveillance of international liquidity and making the special drawing right the principal reserve asset in the international monetary system.[101]

The Fund's general counsel commented that this provision, though it does not mention gold specifically and although it is "written in Stressperanto, the language of laborious international compromise . . . means, among other things, that, in ways to be determined later, members will collaborate on a gradual reduction in the role of gold."[102] But such legal agreements are hardly likely to determine the role of gold in the international monetary system. That issue was thus left to the future.

Special Drawing Rights

The ease with which the agreement was achieved on making the SDR the principal reserve asset contrasts nicely with the meagerness of the Second Amendment's contribution to that result.[103] Indeed, the abrogation of an official price for gold has tended to have the effect of increasing the value of gold as a percentage of total reserves.[104] What the Second Amendment did accomplish was to give the SDR the function of unit of account, or numeraire, for the international monetary system. Beyond that, the Second Amendment's changes were largely limited to according the SDR a larger role in Fund transactions and to making it a potentially more attractive reserve asset.

The Second Amendment carried out explicitly the earlier decision to make the SDR the numeraire. Quotas are to be expressed in SDRs.[105] The value

---

100. See, however, more general language in Gold, *Third Survey*, p. 32.
101. Article VIII, Section 7, *second*. See also Article V, Section 12(a), *second*.
102. Gold, "Report on Recent Legal Developments," p. 234.
103. Article VIII, Section 7, *second*, requires each member "to collaborate" to make the SDR "the principal reserve asset." See also Article XXII, *second*.
104. See *BIS 48th Report* 1978, p. 133, concerning the impact of valuation changes on the reported value of gold reserves during the year, and p. 337, below.
105. Article III, Section 1, *second*.

of the Fund's assets in the account of the General Department are expressed in SDRs, and the value of currencies in the General Resources Account are to be "maintained in terms of the special drawing right."[106] Similarly, the SDR is no longer defined in terms of gold but, rather, as discussed in an earlier chapter, in terms of a basket of currencies. Thus, a particular currency is valued in terms of the SDR, whose value is in turn based on a basket of currencies.[107]

In order to give the SDR a larger role in Fund transactions, including those in the General Department and not just in the Special Drawing Rights Department, a number of changes were made.[108] For example, SDRs are henceforth to be used in payment of 25 percent of quota increases, thereby replacing gold in the subscription process.[109] A participant may purchase currencies of another member for SDRs, whereas previously gold was required.[110] And, using SDRs, the Fund may acquire from one participant currencies of another member.[111] Both of these kinds of Fund-participant transactions can take place by mutual agreement.[112] As a result of these changes as well as use of SDRs for other purposes, transfers of SDRs from the Fund to participants increased from SDR 495 million in financial year 1977 to SDR 1,513 million in 1980. Similarly, transfer of SDRs from participants to the Fund has increased, though the increase has been irregular.[113] To what extent these increase are due to the Second Amendment changes and to what extént due to a more persistent effort by members to get rid of SDRs when possible is unclear.

Probably more important than the changes with respect to Fund transactions were changes designed to eliminate some of the barnacles encrusted on the SDR as a financial instrument at the time of its creation in the First Amendment.[114] With respect to some of the remaining barnacles, the Second Amendment included an enabling power permitting their subsequent re-

106. Article V, Sections 10–11, *second*. A General Department replaced the earlier General Account, and a Special Drawing Rights Department replaced the Special Drawing Rights Account. See Articles XII and XXI, *second*. Provision was made for a number of accounts in the General Department, the principal account being the General Resources Account. See e.g. Article V, Section 12(f), *second*. On maintenance of value, see discussion pp. 104–5, above.
107. See discussion pp. 200–204. On future changes in the method of valuation, see Articles XV, Section 2, and XXI(a)(iii), *second*. See also discussion in *Executive Board Second Amendment Report*, p. 68.
108. See explanation of those two departments, note 106, above.
109. Article III, Section 3(a), *second*. The Board of Governors may prescribe the use of currencies rather than SDRs. Ibid.
110. Article V, Section 6(a), *second*.
111. Article V, Section 6(b), *second*.
112. See discussion of the theory of, and limitations on, these SDR transactions in *Executive Board Second Amendment Report*, Part II:D:17, p. 23. On the use of SDRs for replenishment, a transaction in which gold was usually used before the Second Amendment, see ibid. Part II:J, p. 50.
113. *IMF Annual Report* 1980, p. 92, table 28.
114. See discussion p. 164.

moval by a special majority. The Fund's general counsel observed that the enabling power technique was used in some instances because of "a division of opinion on whether some of the possible changes in characteristics or uses would strengthen or weaken the SDR."[115] He also hinted, however, that the enabling power technique may have been used in some instances because of powerful opposition to the change in question.[116] Under these circumstances the proponents won a constitutional base permitting later adoption of their proposal without the necessity of the lengthy amendment process, but the opponents retained an effective veto over adoption of the proposal so long as they remained of the same view. Hence, some of the SDR enabling powers "may be testimony also to differences of opinion about whether the SDR should be so attractive, and therefore so competitive with other reserve assets, as to create a strong inducement to hold SDRs instead of other assets."[117] Here again one sees the ambiguity observed in connection with the creation of the Council; an enabling power may be as much evidence of a deadlock as of resolution of an issue.[118]

Perhaps the most important immediate change was the authorization of transfers among participants by agreement. Previously transfers by agreement were permitted, except when specifically authorized by the Fund, only if SDRs were exchanged for the transferor's own currency, a kind of transaction that would be likely only where the transferor was a reserve currency country.[119] The Second Amendment provides for transfer by agreement without Fund authorization so long as an equivalent amount of currency is received (which henceforth need not be the currency of the transferor but may, for example, be the currency of the transferee).[120] It also eliminates the requirement of a balance-of-payments need for such transfers by agreement.[121] As an example of the result of these two changes, the United States was able to acquire a portfolio of foreign currencies without Fund approval as part of its 1 November 1978 package of measures to strengthen the dollar.[122]

The Second Amendment also authorizes the Executive Board, by a 70 percent majority, to permit SDR transfers by agreement among participants

---

115. Gold, *Second Amendment*, p. 24.
116. Ibid.
117. Ibid.
118. See discussion of the Council, p. 252.
119. See discussion pp. 158–59. The U.S. had obtained inclusion in the First Amendment of the provision authorizing transfers on the ground that, as it did not then intervene in the market to support its currency, it would not transfer SDRs to obtain other currencies. SDRs would thus only be useful to the U.S. as a means of redeeming U.S. dollars held by other participants. See Gold, *Second Amendment*, p. 23, and Article XXV, Section 2(b)(i), *first*.
120. Article XIX, Section 2(b), *second*. See explanation in *Executive Board Second Amendment Report*, Part III:Q:1(v), p. 69.
121. See discussion of the need requirement pp. 156–57. The need requirement remains for transactions by designation rather than agreement. Article XIX, Section 3, *second*.
122. SDRs were used by the United States to acquire SDR 600 million of German marks and SDR 500 million of Japanese yen. *IMF Annual Report* 1979, p. 68.

even though an equivalent amount of currency is not exchanged for the SDRs.[123] Using this authority, the Executive Board in late 1978 and early 1979 voted to permit transfer of SDRs "to settle a financial obligation," "to make a loan," and "to secure the performance of a financial obligation."[124] In addition, a fledgling secured-interest system has been established under which a pledge of SDRs as security for a financial obligation may be recorded on the books of the Fund.[125] The use of SDRs in forward operations and swaps has been approved.[126] Most recently, the use of SDRs in donations has been approved, after initial opposition from some developed countries who feared that approval of this kind of use of the SDR might lead in the long run to an SDR-aid link.[127]

The usefulness of SDRs remains severely limited by the fact that private parties cannot hold SDRs (though they may, to be sure, hold claims denominated in SDRs). The First Amendment permitted the Fund to "prescribe" as authorized SDR holders, by an 85 percent majority, "institutions that perform functions of a central bank for more than one member," and the Bank for International Settlements was approved in 1974.[128] But the BIS has never engaged in any SDR transactions.[129] The Second Amendment carries this enabling power further by permitting, again by an 85 percent majority, the Fund to approve "other official entities." Although eight additional holders have been approved—the East Caribbean Currency Authority (St. Kitts), the International Fund for Agricultural Development (Rome), the Nordic Investment Bank (Helsinki), the Swiss National Bank (Zurich), the Andean Reserve Fund (Bogota), the Arab Monetary Fund (Abu Dhabi), the World Bank, and its affiliate the International Development Association[130]—and the prescription of individual holders may be anticipated, the SDR will remain off-limits for the foreseeable future to the great bulk of potential public SDR holders, not to speak of private parties. In this respect the SDR differs fundamentally from its two principal reserve asset rivals, reserve currencies and gold, which are widely held in the private sector and therefore enjoy highly liquid markets.

123. Article XIX, Section 2(c), *second*. The Fund may prescribe certain "terms and conditions" for such "operations." Ibid.
124. Decisions of 28 December 1978 and Decision of 26 February 1979, *IMF Annual Report* 1979, pp. 130–34; Gold, *Fourth Survey*, pp. 5–7.
125. Decision of 26 February 1979, *IMF Annual Report* 1979, pp. 132–33; Gold, *Fourth Survey*, pp. 7–10.
126. Decisions of 28 November 1979, *IMF Annual Report* 1980, pp. 141–43; Gold, *Fourth Survey*, pp. 10–11.
127. Gold, *Fourth Survey*, p. 12; Decision of 5 March 1980, *IMF Annual Report* 1980, p. 143.
128. Article XXIII, Section 3(i), *first*; Decision of 26 November 1973, effective January 1974, *IMF Annual Report* 1974, pp. 105–8. See discussion pp. 160–61.
129. *IMF Annual Report* 1979, p. 67; ibid. 1980, p. 96.
130. *IMF Survey* 10(1981):6.

A different kind of change was the lowering of the special majority required to modify or eliminate the reconstitution requirement from 85 to 70 percent.[131] Reconstitution had been a concept insisted upon by France at the time of the First Amendment to make the SDR look more like credit and less like a reserve asset. A country using SDRs to acquire currency had in effect to "pay back" the implicit loan (though not necessarily to the provider of the original currency) by later reacquiring SDRs.[132] The Executive Board took advantage of this enabling power to reduce the percentage of SDRs that had to be held from 30 percent of its net cumulative allocation to 15 percent.[133] The theory behind the reduction of the reconstitution percentage was not merely to make the SDR look increasingly like a reserve asset but also to promote its actual use as such an asset. Such a change runs the risk, of course, of encouraging some members to get rid of newly allocated SDRs as soon as possible after they are received.

At least as important as the changes in the usability of the SDR has been the change in its interest rate. In the Second Amendment all limitations on the SDR rate of interest were removed and the actual rate was made subject to Executive Board determination by a 70 percent majority.[134] The interest rate was increased in 1979 from 60 to 80 percent of the weighted-average rate in the five largest quota countries; and in 1981 the Board proposed to raise it to 100 percent of the full market rate of the five currencies in the valuation basket.[135]

Despite all of these changes the SDR can hardly become the principal reserve asset so long as the amount of outstanding SDRs is only a tiny percentage of total reserve assets. The rapid growth of currency reserves from SDR 96 billion in 1972 to SDR 221 billion in 1978 swamped SDRs, which actually declined from SDR 8.7 to 8.1 billion in the period as a result of members' transactions with the Fund.[136] Moreover, the need to worry about an inadequate amount of liquidity declined sharply in the late 1970s as commercial banks became a major source of financing for deficit countries, especially less-developed countries. Countries could, and increasingly did, satisfy their demand for international reserves by the simple device of borrowing from commercial banks and redepositing the proceeds in the Euro-currency market, at a relatively minor cost measured by the difference

131. Article XIX, Section 6(b), *second.*
132. See discussion of the reconstitution requirement pp. 163–64. See Article XIX, Section 6 and Schedule G, *second.*
133. Decision of 25 October 1978, *IMF Annual Report* 1979, pp. 129–30; Gold, *Fourth Survey,* pp. 13–14, and see discussion of net use concept, pp. 163–64, above. The Interim Committee subsequently proposed elimination of the reconstitution requirement. *IMF Survey* 10(1981):19.
134. Article XX, Section 3, *second.* See explanation of the elimination of the prior limitation in *Executive Board Second Amendment Report,* Part II:Q:2(xiv), p. 72.
135. *IMF Annual Report* 1979, p. 66; *IMF Survey* 10(1981):19, 23. See also *IMF Survey* 9(1980):326–27, and discussion of the SDR interest rate, pp. 204–7, above.
136. *IMF Annual Report* 1979, p. 47, table 14.

between borrowing and lending rates.[137] That these are only gross reserves, rather than net reserves as would have been the case of new SDR allocations, does not alter the fact that the proceeds of commercial bank loans are available for use in exchange market intervention, the prime purpose of liquidity.

After the initial allocation of SDR 9.3 billion in the first basic period, 1970–72, there were no further allocations until 1979.[138] The second basic period was an " 'empty' period" as a result of the excess of liquidity. The SDR, created to cure a shortage of liquidity, had little role in a period of excess liquidity. After the Second Amendment, however, the command to make the SDR the principal reserve asset was in conflict with the original notion that the SDR was to be used only to supplement existing liquidity when it proved inadequate.

The Fund decided in 1978 to resume allocation of SDRs. The prime justification was the mandate in the Second Amendment to promote the SDR as the principal reserve asset. As the Managing Director noted in his proposal to make allocations in the third basic period, without such allocations the SDR "would continue its rapid decline as a proportion of reserves."[139] The basic argument advanced against the objection that additional SDR allocations would simply feed the excess supply of international liquidity, perhaps adding further to world inflation, was that the volume of reserves was largely demand, not supply, determined. Hence, newly allocated SDRs would largely substitute for commercial bank borrowing: "[W]ith a highly elastic supply of reserves available through international capital markets, a substantial part of any allocation of special drawing rights could be expected to substitute for increases in official holdings of foreign exchanges that would otherwise have taken place."[140] Besides, argued the Managing Director, SDR allocations were preferable to commercial bank borrowing because SDRs need not be refinanced periodically.[141]

On a more practical level, a substantial part of the SDR allocation actually agreed upon at the end of 1978, SDR 4 billion on 1 January of each of the successive years 1979 to 1981,[142] would be used simply to make the required 25 percent SDR subscriptions for the next round of quota increases. The decision in the 1978 seventh general quota review to increase quotas[143] raised them from SDR 39 billion to SDR 60 billion.[144] More than SDR 5 billion

137. *IMF Annual Report* 1979, p. 53.
138. *IMF Annual Reports* 1973, p. 34; ibid. 1979, p. 66. See report by the Managing Director (29 June 1977), *IMF Annual Report* 1977, pp. 110–11.
139. Proposal by the Managing Director (25 October 1978), *IMF Annual Report* 1979, p. 125.
140. Ibid.
141. Ibid.
142. Interim Committee Communiqué, para. 6 (24 September 1978), *IMF Annual Report* 1979, pp. 142–43; Board of Governors Resolution of 11 December 1978, ibid. pp. 127–28.
143. Report of the Executive Board, "Increases in Quotas of Fund Members—Seventh General Review," and Board of Governors Resolution of 11 December 1978, ibid. pp. 118–23.
144. Ibid. p. 62; *IMF Survey* 9(1980):377.

of the total allocation of SDR 12 billion would therefore flow into the Fund's General Resources Account. Thus, not all of the SDR allocation could be considered a net increase in international liquidity beyond the partly unconditional and partly conditional liquidity represented by total Fund quotas.

III. FUND MECHANICS

The Fund staff used the opportunity provided by the policy decisions involving exchange rates and reserve assets to make a number of more technical changes in the Articles of Agreement. These technical changes far transcended in number and complexity those made in the "reform" part of the First Amendment.[145] A single example will serve to illustrate the importance to the operation of the Fund of such technical changes.

Under the "mixed bag of currencies" approach adopted at Bretton Woods, and vigorously criticized by Keynes, a large portion of the Fund's assets was of no utility.[146] At first only the dollar was drawn in substantial quantities and even later, as more currencies became convertible, it nonetheless remained true that most of the currencies subscribed by members were of no utility because they could not be used in exchange market intervention and, in many cases, were not convertible into currencies that could be so used. Although the Fund sought to encourage members subscribing such unusable currencies to exchange them for currencies useful in intervention,[147] there was no legal basis for requiring them to do so. Indeed, since such an exchange would reduce the subscriber's foreign exchange reserves, the incentives to refuse to do so were strong, especially as an unusable currency was usually a sign of balance-of-payments difficulties.[148] Thus, the effective amount of liquidity available to members through the Fund was considerably smaller than the nominal amount.

The imbalance in rights and obligations created by the circumstance that so few currencies were usable created negotiating problems in connection with the increase of quotas. All members received increased rights to draw when quotas were increased; but with respect to that portion of their increased quota subscribed in their own currencies, members with inconvertible currencies or even members whose currencies did not bulk large in the mar-

---

145. See discussion pp. 168–69.
146. See discussion pp. 102–3.
147. Decision of 20 July 1962, *IMF Annual Report* 1962, p. 245, and ibid. pp. 36–41.
148. A member might obtain remuneration if the use of its currency created a reserve position, but the rate of remuneration was less than the market rate of interest on foreign exchange reserves. Gold quotes Shakespeare: "Remuneration! O! that's the Latin word for three farthings." Joseph Gold, *Use, Conversion, and Exchange of Currency under the Second Amendment of the Fund's Articles*, IMF Pamphlet Series no. 23 (1978), p. 125, n. 77. See also Gold, *Fourth Survey*, pp. 14–15.

ketplace took on little or no burden and did not effectively contribute to any increase in the Fund's overall resources.[149]

The Interim Committee decided that "because an important purpose of increases in quotas was strengthening the Fund's liquidity, arrangements should be made under which all the Fund's holdings of currency would be usable."[150] The technique adopted to achieve that objective was to impose an obligation on each member to exchange a "freely usable currency" for its own currency whenever another member purchased that currency from the Fund.[151]

This solution required a definition of a "freely usable currency." An important constraint on the formulation of that definition, and indeed a key consideration in choosing the words "freely usable," was that the United States adamantly opposed any suggestion that it should resume convertibility of the dollar into reserve assets. Having failed to obtain what it regarded as an adequate reform of the system in the C-20 exercise and still suffering from a deficit net reserve position, the United States objected to any language that could imply a duty to convert dollars into gold or to defend any particular rate through exchange market intervention. Hence, it considered any term or definition with the word "convertible" in it (including the previously used terms "convertible currency" or "currency convertible in fact") to be unacceptable.[152]

The definition of a freely usable currency raised a number of other issues having to do with the liquidity of the foreign exchange market. Even a currency not subject to any exchange restrictions might have such a thin market that a member required to provide it in exchange for its own currency might not be able to acquire it in the needed quantity without substantially affecting the market exchange rate. Similarly, the market for the "freely usable currency" should have enough liquidity that a member acquiring it, whether from the Fund initially or in exchange for some other currency drawn from the Fund, would be able to use it in defense of the drawing member's own exchange rate without concern for the impact on the issuer's exchange rate. The definition, though a "problem of great difficulty and

---

149. Gold, *Use of Currency*, p. 57.
150. Interim Committee communiqué, para. 5, *IMF Annual Report 1975*, p. 98.
151. Article V, Section 3(e)(i), *second*. If the purchased currency was already "freely usable," then the issuer of the currency had no obligation to provide some other currency that the purchaser might prefer, since the exchange markets would always be available, but the issuer could insist on a direct exchange in preference to a market transaction. Article V, Section 3(e)(iv), *second*. On this and related technical issues involving the exact extent of the obligation, see Gold, *Use of Currency*, pp. 68–83, 88–92, and Gold, *Second Amendment*, pp. 29–30.
152. Gold, *Use of Currency*, pp. 59–60. On U.S. views on convertibility in the drafting of the Second Amendment, see Joseph Gold, "Symmetry as a Legal Objective of the International Monetary System," *New York University Journal of International Law and Politics* 12(1980):452–53.

. . . one of the last to be resolved in the drafting of the Second Amendment,"[153] nonetheless has a deceptive simplicity:

A freely usable currency means a member's currency that the Fund determines (i) is, in fact, widely used to make payments for international transactions, and (ii) is widely traded in the principal exchange markets.[154]

By determining that only five currencies—the U.S. dollar, the German mark, the Japanese yen, the British pound sterling, and the French franc—were "freely usable,"[155] the Executive Board emphasized that a freely usable currency is not simply one unencumbered by exchange restrictions. Moreover, by including the U.S. dollar, it underscored the irrelevance of convertibility in view of the U.S. authorities' continued resistance to any mandatory conversion of the dollar into reserve assets.

The freely usable currency technique cannot deal, however, with the fact that many countries suffer from a long-term weakness in their balance of payments and in their reserve position. If the Fund were to sell such a country's currency, it would create further reserve problems for the country because of the requirement that the issuer provide the purchaser with a freely usable currency; the effect would be to worsen further the issuer's reserve position. This fact of economic life is recognized in the requirement that the Fund adopt "policies and procedures on the selection of currencies to be sold that take into account . . . the balance of payments and reserve position of members."[156] The Fund consequently adopts "operational budgets" stipulating what currencies it is prepared to sell.[157] At any one time substantially fewer than half of the currencies held by the Fund are likely to be considered strong enough to permit sale.[158] And many fewer are likely to be sold in fact.[159] It seems likely that many countries, particularly oil-importing less-developed countries, are likely to be more or less permanently in the position of not making an economic contribution to the Fund through their currency subscriptions. To this extent Keynes's criticism of the mixed-bag-of-currencies approach retains some validity even under the Second Amendment.

153. Gold, *Use of Currency*, p. 58.
154. Article XXX(f), *second*, and see Gold, *Rule of Law*, p. 55.
155. Decision of 31 March 1978, *IMF Annual Report 1978*, p. 127. See generally Gold, *Use of Currency*, pp. 55–68. The concept of "freely usable currency" also plays a role under the Second Amendment in connection with repurchases and with the SDR designation process. See Article V, Section 7(j), *second;* Article XIX, Section 4, *second;* and Gold, *Use of Currency*, pp. 77–86.
156. Article V, Section 3(d), *second*. The Fund is also required to take into account other factors specified in this subsection.
157. *IMF Annual Report 1978*, p. 68.
158. David S. Cutler, "The Liquidity of the International Monetary Fund," *Finance and Development* 16(June 1979):38; *IMF Annual Report 1980*, p. 81.
159. See e.g. *IMF Annual Report 1978*, p. 105, table I.12.

IV. CHANGE WITHOUT AMENDMENT:
THE FUND'S WINDOWS

The emphasis in the Second Amendment on enabling powers may make amendments of the Articles less important, if not indeed less frequent, in the future. In one vital sector of Fund activity, the Fund has transformed itself almost entirely without the benefit of amendments or even Second Amendment enabling powers. That sector is the Fund's role as a financial institution.

This development, accelerating in recent years, was largely preceded by the previously-traced growth of conditionality in the credit tranches and of the unconditional right to draw in the gold tranche.[160] From an institution providing essentially one kind of balance-of-payments facility—albeit graded in accessibility under the tranche policies concerning conditionality and made more effective through stand-by arrangements—the Fund has become a more complex financial institution through a proliferation of credit "windows." Each of these windows is a separate financing facility with, typically, its own declared purposes, terms, and charges.

The Extended Facility

The establishment by Executive Board decision of two special facilities, one for compensatory financing of export fluctuations (created in 1963 and liberalized in 1975) and the other for buffer stock financing (established in 1969), has already been mentioned.[161] These two facilities were thought of at the time as exceptions to general Fund policies to accommodate special needs of certain less-developed countries. The creation of the extended facility in 1974, however, was a harbinger of more profound change.[162]

The extended facility was essentially a longer-term stand-by arrangement than had previously been compatible with Fund practice. Stand-by arrangements had originally been limited to six months but later reached twelve months in duration.[163] Under the extended fund facility a period of three years became possible.[164] Such an extended stand-by arrangement could be entered into upon a determination that the solution to the member's balance-of-payments problem would require a longer period than the normal Fund stand-by period. The Executive Board decision postulated the need for a

160. See discussion pp. 118–19. As there explained, the de facto unconditional power to draw in the gold tranche was made a de jure right in the First Amendment. The gold tranche was renamed the reserve tranche in the Second Amendment. See discussion p. 271, above.
161. See discussion pp. 127–28, above. On recent developments with respect to the buffer stock facility, see Gold, *Third Report*, pp. 30–35, and with respect to the compensatory financing facility, see Louis M. Goreux, *Compensatory Financing Facility*, IMF Pamphlet Series no. 34 (1980).
162. Outline of Reform, paras. 30, 39, C-20 Documents, pp. 18, 21.
163. Gold, *Conditionality*, p. 17.
164. Decision of 13 September 1974, Part II, para. 3, *IMF Annual Report* 1975, p. 89.

longer period for (1) "an economy suffering serious payments imbalance relating to structural maladjustments in production and trade and where prices and cost distortions have been widespread" and for (2) "an economy characterized by slow growth and an inherently weak balance of payments position which prevents pursuit of an active development policy."[165] Although only the latter of these two clauses seems to have been drafted especially with less-developed countries in view, such countries have been in fact the sole users.[166] When in 1977 the United Kingdom and Italy sought stand-by arrangements exceeding twelve months in length, that goal was accomplished through ad hoc exceptions to the regular stand-by policies. Similar ad hoc exceptions followed for several less-developed country members.[167]

Such stand-by arrangements were not, however, entered into under the extended facility and therefore they did not benefit from other liberalizations accorded that facility. Previously amounts outstanding at any one time under a stand-by arrangement had been limited to 100 percent of quota, and drawings thereunder could not increase the Fund's holdings of a member's currency above 200 percent of quota. Under the new facility, however, purchases could reach 140 percent of quota and could increase the Fund's holdings to 265 percent of quota.[168] As in the case of the duration issue, the precedent of the extended facility led to exceeding of earlier guidelines in later conventional stand-by arrangements.[169]

The Oil Facilities

The use of an ad hoc facility to deal with a particular world economic development is exemplified by the 1974 oil facility. This facility was created in order to meet the increased need for balance-of-payments financing in the wake of the fourfold increase in the price of oil in the winter of 1973–74 (or, perhaps a Fund critic might say, in order to permit the Fund to compete with rapidly growing commercial bank lending to less-developed oil-importing countries). The Fund financed this facility by borrowing from oil-producing countries, a device that differed from the earlier General Arrange-

165. Decision of 13 September 1974, Part I, para. (ii), *IMF Annual Report 1975*, p. 88.
166. *IMF Annual Report 1977*, p. 53; ibid. 1978, p. 66; ibid. 1979, pp. 73–74; ibid. 1980, pp. 77–78.
167. Ibid. 1977, p. 52; ibid. 1978, p. 66.
168. In this and the following discussion the effect of so-called floating features of other facilities, such as the compensatory financing facility, will be ignored. See discussion, pp. 127–28, above, and Decision of 13 September 1974, Part II, para. 4, *IMF Annual Report 1975*, pp. 89–90.
169. See the Peruvian arrangement, *IMF Annual Report 1979*, p. 73. The extended facility also lengthened the period to complete repurchase to a maximum of eight years, which was further extended to ten years in December 1979. Decision of 13 September 1974, Part II, para. 5, *IMF Annual Report 1975*, p. 90, and Decision of 3 December 1979, *IMF Annual Report 1980*, p. 145. The extended facility also undoubtedly influenced the conditions of access under the 1977 supplementary financing facility, which was available only under arrangements of more than one year and for purchases beyond the first four credit tranches. Decision of 29 August 1977, *IMF Annual Report 1978*, pp. 112–15. See discussion pp. 287–88, below.

ments to Borrow in at least two ways. The oil facility was broader insofar as the GAB had been essentially a mutual assistance pact from which only Group of Ten members could benefit. On the other hand, the oil facility was seen as a one-time affair, unlike the GAB which has continued in force.[170]

Drawings under the 1974 oil facility, which were made by both developed and less-developed countries, bore special terms concerning repurchase and charges as well as its own specifications on maximum access, measured in part by the costs of oil imports in excess of the cost in 1972.[171] A second oil facility was arranged in 1975, with terms and conditions somewhat different from those in the 1974 facility.[172] Although the two oil facilities covered only a three-year period, they represented a significant proportion of Fund lending activity in those years, accounting for more than half of total drawings in 1975.[173]

A further and related type of ad hoc balance-of-payments financing device was not, strictly speaking, a facility at all. The Subsidy Account was, rather, a special account created to reduce the effective rate of charges on drawings under the 1975 oil facility. Such subsidies were available for the members determined to be "most seriously affected" by the oil price increase, and contributions to the account were made voluntarily by twenty-four other members plus Switzerland.[174]

Although the two oil facilities were ad hoc responses to a new problem, they can in retrospect be viewed as first steps in transforming the Fund as a financial institution from the Bretton Woods mutual insurance model, in which all members supply resources to be made available to those most in need of balance-of-payments financing, into a financial intermediary. As a financial intermediary the Fund would borrow from one set of parties to obtain the resources to lend to another set of parties, much as does a finance company or savings and loan association on the American domestic scene. In the case of the oil facilities the potential borrowers were limited to members,[175] but the lenders included not merely members but also the central banks of certain members, a territorial subdivision (Abu Dhabi) of a member

170. *IMF Annual Report* 1974, p. 53; ibid. 1975, p. 53. See David Williams, "Increasing the Resources of the Fund: Borrowing," *Finance and Development* 13(September 1976):22–23.
171. Decision of 13 June 1974, *IMF Annual Report* 1974, pp. 122–23.
172. Decision of 4 April 1975, *IMF Annual Report* 1975, p. 94. See also ibid. pp. 53–54.
173. See *IMF Survey* 7(1978):180, chart. For an illustration of differing charges depending upon the Fund window used, see ibid. p. 299, table.
174. Decision of 1 August 1975, *IMF Annual Report* 1976, pp. 98–99, and see ibid. 1978, pp. 75–76.
175. In 1977 the principle that only members could borrow was arguably stretched in the operation of the buffer stock facility, when the Fund approved financing of a sugar buffer stock "nationally owned but internationally controlled pursuant to the 1977 International Sugar Agreement." The stocks were under the control of the International Sugar Organization. Decision of 16 December 1977, *IMF Annual Report* 1978, pp. 128–29.

(United Arab Emirates), a nonmember country (Switzerland), and a non-member country central bank (Swiss National Bank).[176]

The Supplementary Financing Facility

The role of of the Fund as a financial intermediary was greatly expanded by the creation in 1977 of a supplementary financing facility. On the lending side the facility did not present much of a new departure, especially as any drawings had to be made under stand-by or extended arrangements. As the name of the facility implies, the amounts advanced were to be supplementary to other funds provided under such arrangements, with the new facility's distinctive role being to permit purchase beyond the credit tranches.[177] But on the borrowing side, the exclusive reliance for the supplementary financing facility on borrowing at market rates and particularly the special arrangements for making the resulting claims of the lender highly liquid marked a further step in the direction of making the Fund a financial intermediary.[178]

The interest rate paid by the Fund was designed to be a market rate. The rate for each six-month period was to be "the average of the daily yields during that period on actively traded U.S. Government securities, determined on the basis of a constant maturity of five years."[179] Indeed, it could be argued that this rate of interest was slightly above a market rate (ignoring any possible repayment risk) because, in view of the SDR's role as numeraire under the Second Amendment, the claim was denominated in SDRs. Ex ante, the value of a claim denominated in SDRs could be expected to be more stable than a dollar claim and therefore should require a lower rate of interest.[180] On the other hand, private banks could put together, for relatively small cost, a portfolio of foreign currency investments equivalent to the SDR

176. *IMF Annual Report* 1976, p. 91, table I.16.
177. For an explanation of the conditions of access to the supplementary financing facility, see Joseph Gold, *Financial Assistance by the International Monetary Fund: Law and Practice*, IMF Pamphlet Series no. 27 (1979), pp. 34–36.
178. Although the Fund's legal authority has been broad enough to encompass borrowing from any source so long as the member issuing the borrowed currency concurs, Article VII, Section 2(i), *original*, and Article VII, Section 1(i), *second*, the Fund limited its borrowing to official sources and, unlike the World Bank, did not borrow from the market. See Gold, *Financial Assistance*, pp. 42–44. In 1980, however, the Fund began to consider market financing. Interim Committee communiqué and statement by Managing Director J. de Larosière, *IMF Survey* 9(1980):305, 311.
179. Annex to Decision of 29 August 1977, para. 4(iii), *IMF Annual Report* 1978, p. 117.
180. An interesting aspect of denominating the lender's claim in SDRs is that if the Fund should decide to change the method of SDR valuation, the lender "shall have the option to require immediate repayment of all outstanding claims on the basis of the method of valuation in effect before the change." Ibid. para. 7(a), p. 117. Silard has referred to this provision under the rubric of the "repayable SDR." Stephen A. Silard, "The General Standard of International Value in Public International Law," in *American Society of International Law, Proceedings of the 73rd Annual Meeting* (1979), p. 20.

basket, and therefore lenders could not be expected to accept an SDR rate significantly below a market rate.[181]

The market principle had its counterpart on the lending side. Although the language of purchases and charges continued to be used, the "charge" was to "be equal to the rate of interest paid by the Fund from time to time" on its own borrowings plus a margin equal to "1/5 of 1 percent per annum for the first 3½ years after a purchase" and a somewhat greater percentage thereafter.[182] Thus, the Fund became an intermediary in the most literal sense, keeping what was functionally equivalent to a markup, but of course bearing the risk of default by a drawing member.[183] In 1980 a new Subsidy Account was created to reduce the interest cost of supplementary financing facility loans to low-income members. The resources of this Subsidy Account were to come from the proceeds of repayments of Trust Fund loans.[184]

The liquidity of the lender's claim on the Fund was assured by a new transfer provision. Although the Fund had concurred in transfers of claims on the Fund arising out of its borrowings under the General Arrangements to Borrow,[185] it now committed itself in advance to recognize and register transfers, including transfers by a party that was itself a transferee, and to pay interest to the registered transferees. Moreover, the GAB transfers had been exclusively to other members of the Group of Ten, but the new transfer provisions permitted transfer to parties that had not been lenders to the Fund.[186] The only restrictions were that the transfer be "for value agreed" (and thus not, for example, a foreign aid transaction) and that the transferee be a member, the central bank of a member "or any institution that performs functions of a central bank for more than one member" (for example, the Bank for International Settlements).[187] The only important right that cannot be transferred is a right to early repayment, which has been qualified in order, in the words of Joseph Gold, "to safeguard the Fund against the risk of being called upon to make an early repayment by confining the right to transferees unlikely to use it."[188]

A potentially important aspect of the transfer provisions is that they could lead to the development of a market in SDR claims.[189] The claim of a lender

181. See J. J. Polak, "The SDR as a Basket of Currencies," *IMF Staff Papers* 26(1979):647.
182. Decision of 2 September 1977, para. 1, *IMF Annual Report* 1978, pp. 118–19. In addition, a one-time service charge was imposed. Ibid. para. 4.
183. See, however, the qualification in ibid. para. 2.
184. Interim Committee communiqué, *IMF Survey* 9(1980):305–6; "Instrument Establishing the Supplementary Financing Facility Subsidy Account," *IMF Survey* 10(1981):10–13.
185. Williams, "Increasing Resources," p. 21.
186. Gold, *Third Report*, pp. 26–27.
187. Annex to Decision of 29 August 1977, para. 8, *IMF Annual Report* 1978, pp. 117–18. On the capacity of the Bank for International Settlements to be a transferee, see Gold, *Third Report*, p. 27.
188. Gold, *Third Report*, p. 28.
189. Ibid. pp. 28–29.

is *denominated in* SDRs but is not a claim *to* SDRs. Moreover, although the identity of "advance consent" transferees is restricted, the Fund retains the right to permit transfers to nonofficial holders who could not, under the rules pertaining to SDRs, hold SDRs themselves. Thus, the transfer provisions could be the vehicle for creating a private market in SDR-denominated claims or at least be a precedent illustrating a technique for doing so. This technique could partially circumvent the restriction on SDR holders in the present Articles, a restriction that could be eliminated only by amendment of the Articles. The importance of technical legal provisions for the future of the system is well illustrated by this example because the device of the SDR-denominated transferable claim may prove to be of transcendent importance to the future of the SDR in the international monetary system.[190]

V. Jamaica in the Light of the Outline of Reform

Even counting changes not included in the Second Amendment, such as the proliferation of Fund financing facilities, the reforms of the 1974–78 period fall far short of the broad vision of the long-term Outline of Reform. Indeed, not even all of the amendments of the Articles of Agreement recommended in that portion of the Outline of Reform devoted to "immediate steps" were adopted.

One amendment not adopted was the proposal "to give permanent force to the voluntary pledge . . . concerning trade or other current account measures for balance of payments purposes."[191] The "voluntary pledge" was an undertaking, parallel to a pledge by the twenty-four industrialized-country members of the Organization for Economic Cooperation and Development,[192] not to introduce such measures for a period of two years without a Fund finding that there was a balance-of-payments justification.[193] Even the two-year pledge never entered into effect because it failed to attract, in view of the opposition of less-developed members, the support of a 65 percent Fund majority in accordance with its terms.[194] A trade amendment would have constituted an important expansion of the jurisdiction of the Fund into the trade domain formerly reserved for the General Agreement on Tariffs and

190. See more generally on SDR-denominated claims, Silard, "General Standard," pp. 18–24; Gold, *Third Survey*, p. 9. See further discussion pp. 312–13, below.
191. Outline of Reform, para. 41(c), C-20 Documents, p. 22.
192. OECD agreement was reached May 30–31, 1974. *IMF Survey* 3(1974):170.
193. The "Declaration on Trade Measures" was set forth in an Appendix to the Outline of Reform, C-20 Documents, p. 23. See also para. 36 of the Outline, ibid. p. 20.
194. See remarks of Jeremy Morse, *IMF Survey* 3(1974):211–12.

Trade,[195] and at least some of the opposition to the voluntary pledge was due to "the traditional objection . . . to a merger of jurisdiction over trade and currency."[196]

A second area in which the Outline of Reform called for the drafting of amendments but none was forthcoming was a "substitution account."[197] Here the opposition of the United States plus the difficulty of negotiating the crucial technical details such as the allocation of the exchange rate risk foreclosed agreement on such an account. It was not until the United States swung around to tentative support for such an account in 1979 that discussions of the technical details could begin in earnest.[198]

The substitution account is nonetheless a good example of how reform ideas can lie fallow for some time and then leap to prominence once more when underlying economic and political conditions are ripe. Even the substitution account reform had to be abandoned, at least for the time being, when the dollar temporarily became a strong currency in the early spring of 1980. Since the best of forecasters cannot predict economic and political events more than a few weeks in advance with any regularity, it would be idle to attempt to predict what changes in the international monetary system the future may bring.

Yet it is possible to survey the kinds of proposals for change that are being discussed at the time this book is being written and that will be the burden of the final chapter. There, as in chapter 7, the framework for inquiry will be the way in which rules may be used to effect change or to retard it.

195. See Edgar Jones, "The Fund and the GATT," *Finance and Development* 9(September 1972):30; and Kenneth W. Dam, *The GATT: Law and International Economic Organization* (1970), pp. 152–57, for an analysis of the Fund's role relative to that of the GATT in trade matters under the original and First Amendment versions of the Articles. For later developments, see Frieder Roessler, "The Gatt Declaration on Trade Measures Taken for Balance-of-Payments Purposes," *Case Western Reserve Journal of International Law* 12(1980):383–403.
196. Joseph Gold, *Use of Currency*, p. 7.
197. Outline of Reform, para. 41(d), C-20 Documents, p. 22. See discussion of the C-20 consideration of a substitution facility, pp. 238–39, above. For proposals discussed but not adopted following the Outline of Reform, notably a Gold Substitution Account, see Joseph Gold, "Substitution in the International Monetary System," *Case Western Reserve Journal of International Law* 12(1980):295–302.
198. Gold, "Substitution," pp. 299–301, and see discussion pp. 313–14, below. The proposed amendment to "authorize the Fund to implement a link between development assistance and SDR allocation," Outline of Reform, para. 41(f), C-20 Documents, p. 22, was also not adopted, but the Trust Fund can be viewed as a substitute for such an SDR-aid link. See discussion pp. 272–73, above.

NINE

Prospects for Reform and Evolution

Changes in the international monetary system, whether by reform or evolution, are heavily influenced by political and economic developments. Those developments, by their nature, are difficult if not impossible to predict. Changes in the international monetary system are therefore also hard to foresee.

Only in retrospect can one detect a steady line of development from the gold standard to Bretton Woods to the current system. Even the international monetary events of a particular decade have seldom been anticipated by reigning opinion at the outset of that decade. Few would have predicted in 1910, the zenith of the international gold standard, that it would collapse four years later. In 1940 few would have foreseen that the Second World War would lead to a massive postwar planning exercise culminating in a scheme as ambitious as the Bretton Woods system and the International Monetary

Fund. The end of the dollar shortage and the onset of the "dollar problem" in the 1950s were not generally recognized until after they had occurred. And although informed observers in 1970 realized that the U.S. commitment to sell gold at $35 per ounce might soon be abrogated, few anticipated either the 1973 move to generalized floating or the fundamental alterations in the world oil market that emerged during the ensuing decade.

The reader of a book written at the beginning of the 1980s should therefore be extremely skeptical of any predictions as to what the decade may bring in the international monetary system. This chapter will attempt no more than to analyze the options for reform being discussed at the time this book is being written and to trace the implications of more evolutionary changes that appear to be taking place. Here, as in previous chapters, the emphasis will be on the role of rules in bringing about reform and in either institutionalizing or resisting evolutionary change.

In order to pursue this inquiry, however, it is first useful to review how fundamental transformations in the world economy in the 1970s have conditioned the outlook and therefore the potential for change in the 1980s. Although future political and economic events may fundamentally alter the international monetary environment in which the 1980s began, it is still necessary to take stock of the changes of the 1970s to gain any insight into the options for reform and the prospects for evolution in the coming decade.

I. THE NEW ENVIRONMENT

The fundamental change in the world oil market that burst upon the public consciousness with the fourfold increase in oil prices in the winter of 1973–74 had a number of consequences for the international monetary system even apart from its impact on the Committee of Twenty reform discussions and its role in preventing any retreat from generalized floating. The first was that the principal oil exporters would enjoy, for a time at least, large payments surpluses and, correspondingly, most of the rest of the world would have to live with payments deficits. Although many oil exporters were able to absorb a much higher volume of investment and imports than was at first anticipated, and although Germany and Japan continued for some time to be persistent surplus countries in the face of the new oil conditions, the fact of persistent surpluses and deficits undermined the assumption on which the Fund as a financial institution had been built. The Bretton Woods conception was that despite the immediate postwar payments strength of the United States, payments surpluses, and, particularly, deficits would be temporary. Under the mutual assistance model implicit in Bretton Woods, temporary deficits would be financed through the Fund by members temporarily in surplus and those countries in turn would enjoy the advantages of financing through the Fund whenever, in the ebb and flow of economic events, their turn came to cope with payments deficits.

The second consequence of the fundamental change in the world oil market was that the spectacular increases in liquidity that accompanied the collapse of the Bretton Woods system continued through much of the 1970s. Moreover, new liquidity increasingly took the new form of commercial bank lending to deficit countries. The earlier practice of providing liquidity through the Fund, either by its lending or by SDR creation, took a back seat. Even liquidity creation through purchase of dollars by surplus countries in resisting appreciation of their currencies became less important.[1]

The Role of Commercial Banks and Eurocurrency Markets

"Non–oil developing countries" came to look increasingly to commercial banks rather than the Fund or bilateral official sources for balance-of-payments financing. In the early 1970s, 65–70 percent of such countries' external debt was owed to official creditors and 30–35 percent to private creditors. By 1978 private creditors' share nearly equaled the share of official creditors. Moreover, the proportion of their total external debt owed to financial institutions and bondholders had climbed from just over 10 percent to 40 percent in the same period.[2] Moreover, the share of long-term external financing from financial institutions was rising steadily, from $4 billion in 1973 to $17.3 billion in 1979.[3] Official long-term external financing was also increasing, but most of the increase (from $5.5 billion to $11.4 billion) took place in the 1973–75 period. Thereafter, the volume of such financing rose more slowly, from $10.2 billion in 1976 to $15.9 billion in 1979 (see table 6).

Increased lending to less-developed countries by commercial banks was only one manifestation of a massive growth in international banking during the 1970s. The most publicized sector of that growth was the Eurocurrency market. Although foreign lending by domestic banks also increased, growth was more rapid in offshore banking, a term that refers to deposits and loans

1. *World Financial Markets*, December 1979, pp. 2–3; Robert Triffin, "The Future of the International Monetary System," *Banca Nazionale del Lavoro Quarterly Review*, no. 132 (March 1980), p. 48, table 4, and pp. 52–53, annex tables 1 and 2. Triffin estimates the increase in international lending 1976–78 at $463.5 billion, of which only 29 percent came from creation of monetary reserves (central bank and IMF sources), and 71 percent from the private market (foreign claims of commercial banks and international bonds). Ibid. p. 48.
2. *IMF Annual Report* 1979, p. 26, chart 13. Long-term loans from private financial institutions declined slightly in 1979, while short-term loans increased. Overall percentages remained basically unchanged. Ibid. 1980, pp. 31–33.
3. On the effects of increased dependence on private financing, see Charles Lipson, "The International Organization of Third World Debt" (paper prepared for delivery at the 1980 American Political Science Association Convention, Washington, D.C.; mimeo), pp. 18–20.

Table 6

Non–Oil Developing Countries: Net external borrowing, 1973–79
(in billions of U.S. dollars)

	1973	1974	1975	1976	1977	1978	1979
Long-term borrowing from official sources, net	5.5	9.6	11.4	10.2	12.4	13.3	15.9
Other long-term borrowing from nonresidents, net	6.6	10.2	14.7	17.6	15.8	25.1	23.4
From financial institutions	(4.0)	(8.6)	(9.2)	(10.9)	(15.6)	(19.3)	(17.3)
Through bond issues	(0.5)	(0.3)	(0.2)	(1.1)	(2.6)	(3.0)	(2.0)
Other sources	(2.1)	(1.3)	(5.3)	(5.6)	(−2.4)	(2.8)	(4.1)
Other	−1.1	5.1	6.1	5.7	−2.1	−0.6	5.2
Net external borrowing	11.0	24.9	32.2	33.5	26.1	37.8	44.5

Source: *IMF Annual Report* 1980, p. 32, table 10. The IMF includes in its category of "non–oil developing countries," a subgroup of twelve countries that are net exporters of oil but, unlike the main oil-exporting countries, show significant current account deficits. Ibid. p. 29.

denominated in currencies other than the currency of the country in which the bank is located. The offshore bank is often a branch or subsidiary of a banking corporation headquartered in the country in whose currency the transaction is denominated. A leading example would be branches of U.S. banks located in London accepting deposits and making loans in U.S. dollars.

The most important sector in offshore banking has been the Eurodollar market, in which transactions are denominated in dollars but take place outside the United States, whether or not conducted by branches of U.S. banks. The Eurodollar market is just one segment of the Eurocurrency market, or Euromarket. Although the prefix "Euro" reflects the European origin of offshore banking, the Eurocurrency market now typically refers to all offshore markets, including subdivisions such as the Asian dollar market, located in centers such as Singapore. Developments in offshore banking have given rise to various proposals that are separately discussed below.[4]

The rapid growth of commercial bank lending has had a number of effects on the composition of reserves and on the role of the Fund in providing liquidity. Commercial bank lending has been a major factor in the growth of foreign exchange holdings. Although such lending has been an important source of finance for balance-of-payments deficits, it is also true that many countries have found it prudent to borrow currencies and then redeposit them in the Eurocurrency market. Such transactions are used to increase gross reserves at relatively low cost—essentially the difference between Euromarket borrowing and lending rates. As a member of the U.S. Federal Reserve Board has noted, "Thanks to the Euromarkets, the holding of international reserves is not expensive. For countries that have debt outstanding in these markets, carrying reserves in the currency of that debt involves a cost of no more than the spread over LIBOR paid on that debt."[5] Not every country has, of course, the credit rating essential to such low-cost borrowing and some oil-importing less-developed countries have found commercial bank credits unavailable at any interest rate.

Although "no concrete evidence of a systematic causal relationship running from Euromarket growth to growth in international reserves" has been found,[6] the fact is that a large portion of official foreign exchange holdings

---

4. See discussion pp. 323–27. See also *BIS 50th Report* 1980, pp. 120–29.
5. Henry C. Wallich, "The World Monetary System after Postponement of the Substitution Account," address to the HWWA-Institut für Wirtschaftsforschung, Hamburg, Germany, 12 June 1980 (mimeo), p. 11. LIBOR is the London Interbank Offer Rate for short-term dollar deposits. See discussion of composition of reserves, pp. 316–18.
6. *IMF Annual Report* 1979, p. 53. See also IMF, *International Capital Markets: Recent Developments and Short-Term Prospects*, Occasional Paper no. 1 (1980), pp. 41–45. However, against the view that as "the dollar is the domestic currency in the United States, no . . . currency conversion takes place and Eurodollar flows do not potentially increase the amount of base money apart from differences in deposit reserve requirements," ibid. p. 42, cf. the comment of Henry C. Wallich: "For the United States, the reserve currency role has become a burden, in a world where the banking systems of foreign countries, as well as foreign branches of our own banks,

take the form of Euromarket deposits. At the end of 1979 identified official holdings of Eurocurrencies totaled SDR 64.0 billion out of total foreign exchange holdings of SDR 245.7 billion.[7] Euromarkets are particularly important for non-dollar foreign exchange holdings by official institutions. At the end of 1979, SDR 17.7 billion were held in the form of non-dollar Eurocurrency deposits, as against SDR 25 billion in official claims in specified currencies such as sterling, the mark, or the franc.[8]

The ready access of countries with payments imbalances to commercial bank lending tended in the late 1970s to displace Fund provision of liquidity. Interest and other terms equal, borrowers normally preferred to avoid submitting themselves to the conditionality policies of the Fund. And as spreads between commercial bank borrowing and lending rates became narrower in the late 1970s, falling from nearly 2 percent in the 1975–76 period to less than one percent in 1979, and as average maturities became longer (rising from just over 5 years in the 1975–76 period to nearly 10 years in early 1979),[9] less-developed countries increasingly preferred commercial banks. In 1978 and 1979, although the Fund continued to provide new balance-of-payments financing, repurchases rose above purchases, and the Fund was no longer a net source of liquidity to the international monetary system.[10] Only about 3 percent of less-developed-country financing was provided by the Fund in the 1974–79 period. The Fund's new Guidelines on Conditionality, issued in 1979, were intended to counteract this trend by softening conditionality requirements, largely confining them to "macroeconomic variables" and acknowledging the permissible "diversity of . . . institutional arrangements of members."[11]

---

can freely add to the world's supply of dollars." Wallich, "International Monetary Evolution," remarks at Columbia University, New York, 20 February 1980 (mimeo), p. 2.

7. *IMF Survey* 9(1980):166, table 1.

8. Ibid. Of the total official holdings of foreign exchange of SDR 245.7 billion, official claims on the U.S. accounted for SDR 108.4 billion and Eurodollar claims for SDR 46.3 billion. European Currency Units were introduced in 1979 and accounted for SDR 32.5 billion.

9. Statement by Henry C. Wallich, in Hearings before the Subcommittee on International Trade, Investment and Monetary Policy of the House Committee on Banking, Finance and Urban Affairs, *To Amend the Bretton Woods Agreement Act* . . . , 96th Cong., 2d Sess. (1980), p. 408, table 7. The figures refer to syndicated loans to nine non-oil developing countries and four Eastern European countries.

10. *IMF Survey* 10(1981):14, table 1. In part this imbalance in Fund transactions arose from particularly heavy repurchases, and in 1980 purchases again rose above repurchases. See also IMF, *International Capital Markets*, p. 21, for predictions of greater future reliance on the Fund, and *IMF Survey* 10(1981):13–14 for increased use of Fund resources.

11. Of the total net amount to be financed 1974–79 (1979 figures are estimates) of $182.3 billion, official sources provided 33 percent, IMF and related sources 3 percent, suppliers' credits 4 percent, and "all others, including commercial banks" 60 percent. *World Financial Markets*, December 1979, p. 3. See also *BIS 50th Report* 1980, p. 113; Guidelines on Conditionality, Decision of 2 March 1979, para. 9, *IMF Annual Report* 1979, p. 137, and ibid. pp. 62–63.

The Fund and Commercial Banks:
Competition and Collaboration

Repeated oil price increases in 1979 and 1980 gave rise to new concerns about the availability of liquidity, particularly to the oil-importing less-developed countries whose payments imbalances were expected to worsen significantly. The experience with the 1973–74 oil price increases raised the question whether the Fund would necessarily play an important role in financing the new imbalances. After the 1973–74 price increase, the surpluses of the oil-exporting countries were readily "recycled" to deficit countries largely through the commercial banking system, and those surpluses eventually nearly vanished, decreasing from $68 billion in 1974 to $6 billion in 1978.[12] Even though the oil-exporting countries' surpluses rose to an annual rate of about $100 billion in early 1980, commercial banks' outstanding external loans to non-bank borrowers increased even more rapidly (though, of course, far from all of the borrowers were monetary authorities).[13]

Although the new rounds of oil price increases thus created an opportunity for a major expansion of Fund financial activities, it became clear that the Fund would have to be aggressive in competing with the commercial banks for the new credit demands of oil-importing countries. Without some new institutional initiative, the Fund faced the possibility that, at least so long as it insisted on conditionality, it would be likely to be called upon primarily to bail out those less-developed countries that were already overextended and had therefore reached the limits of the willingness of commercial banks to continue to expand their outstanding loans. So far as the overall volume of lending to oil-importing countries as a class was concerned, the commercial banks were considered likely to be able to obtain the resources from the oil-exporting countries themselves, who deposited a large portion of their surpluses in the Eurocurrency market. Out of a total estimated current account surplus of $63 billion for OPEC nations in 1979, Eurocurrency deposits accounted for $31.2 billion of identified short-term investments of $40.9 billion.[14] Although the proportion of surpluses accounted for by such deposits in earlier years was smaller, surpluses may nonetheless find their way into the resources of commercial banks by other routes, such as by dollar deposits in the United States and sterling deposits in the United Kingdom.

If the Fund were to attempt to expand its lending role, it would also have to be aggressive in competing with the commercial banks for the necessary

---

12. Ibid. p. 15, table 5.
13. "International Bank Lending Expands, Outstanding Claims Exceed $1 Trillion," *IMF Survey* 8(1980):81, 88–90; *The Economist*, 22 March 1980, pp. 9, 15–16; *BIS 50th Report* 1980, pp. 100–101; *IMF Annual Report* 1980, p. 19, table 6. The total flow of Fund resources to member countries in the first ten months of 1980 was twice that of the comparable period in 1979. *IMF Survey* 9(1980):361. But net drawings remained small in relation to the rate of increase of commercial bank lending. *BIS 50th Report* 1980, pp. 85, 100–101.
14. *BIS 50th Report* 1980, pp. 100–101.

resources. Unlike the World Bank and many development banks, the Fund has no unpaid capital that it can call at times of increased need. In principle, Fund quotas could be increased, but, for reasons explored below, quota increases are neither as easy to negotiate nor as promising a source of Fund resources as in the past.[15] Hence the Fund would have to move further toward a financial intermediary model and away from its traditional mutual assistance model.[16]

The Fund might, for example, borrow from members. Because of the structure of world oil trade, however, the developed world as a whole has tended to be in balance-of-payments deficit at those times when the less-developed countries were most in need of balance-of-payments financing. Even Germany and Japan, the leading persistent surplus countries in the developed world during the preceding decade, were running current account deficits in 1979 and 1980.[17] Members in deficit are unlikely to favor large loans to the Fund for further lending to other members.

Therefore, as a practical matter, any major increase in Fund financing would require Fund borrowing either from surplus countries, especially oil-exporting countries, or from the market. To the extent that the Fund borrowed from the oil-exporting countries, it would be competing with the commercial banks for funds. To the extent that it borrowed from the market, it would be either competing with commercial banks for funds or actually borrowing from commercial banks themselves, directly or indirectly. In September 1980 the Interim Committee decided that the Fund "should make, as soon as possible, the necessary arrangements to enable [it] to borrow from various potential sources of financing, not excluding a possible recourse to the private markets if this were indispensable."[18]

Extensive borrowing by the Fund would require that the Fund pay market interest rates. This is obviously the case with borrowing from the market,

15. See discussion pp. 303–7. On World Bank capital provisions, see Articles of Agreement of the International Bank for Reconstruction and Development, Article II, Section 5, and Edward S. Mason and Robert E. Asher, *The World Bank since Bretton Woods* (1973), pp. 114–18.
16. See discussion of the Fund as a financial intermediary p. 286.
17. In 1979 Japan had a current account deficit of $8.6 billion and a basic balance-of-payments deficit (after net long-term capital outflows of $13 billion) of $21.6 billion (1978 surpluses had been $16.5 billion and $4.1 billion respectively). In the first quarter of 1980, the current account deficit was $6 billion, although other developments reduced the effect on the overall balance of payments.
  The 1979 German current account deficit was $5.8 billion, its first since 1965. In spite of a capital account surplus of $5.6 billion, net official monetary assets fell, as a result of other factors, by $2.4 billion for the year. In the first quarter of 1980 the current account deficit was $3 billion and the overall deficit $7.9 billion. *BIS 50th Report* 1980, pp. 91–93.
18. Interim Committee communiqué, *IMF Survey* 9(1980):305. In October 1980, Managing Director de Larosière predicted Fund borrowings of SDR 6–7 billion in 1981 alone, and indicated that the Fund would need to diversify its sources and terms of finance. Ibid. pp. 350–51. For discussion of the Fund's needs and options, see David Tonge, "IMF Debating How to Borrow," *Financial Times*, 26 November 1980.

but it is also true, as the experience with the Fund oil facilities and the supplementary financing facility demonstrates, that oil-exporting countries will insist on market rates. If the Fund must pay market rates, then the question is how the Fund could compete against commercial banks in the lending market while at the same time insisting on conditionality. The answer is that the Fund must either somehow subsidize interest rates or defer repayment longer than commercial banks are prepared to do. Unless the subsidy on interest rates is considerable, both techniques will probably have to be used.

The question therefore becomes, how can the Fund obtain the resources to subsidize interest rates? Existing quotas and quota enlargements could in principle provide such resources, but such use of quota-derived resources would be totally inconsistent with the mutual assistance notion that such resources are to be recouped through repurchase for possible use by those members that provided them initially. Thus, even if a way could be found to square such a use of quota-derived resources with the Articles, a change in the basic concept of the Fund would be required.

The Fund might solicit contributions from developed countries to provide the subsidy element. Such an approach was used in the 1974 and 1975 oil facilities. Another, and perhaps more likely, source of resources for subsidization would be the Fund's gold. It could, for example, be sold on the market and the difference between the old official price and the market price claimed as a profit available for subsidy. That approach was the essence of the Trust Fund but could be used directly under the Second Amendment, which authorized creation of a Special Disbursement Account to receive profits from additional gold sales.[19] The account could be used, for example, to provide resources for the General Resources Account or to provide "balance of payments assistance . . . on special terms to developing members in difficult circumstances."[20]

Although an expanded future financing role for the Fund thus implies competition between the Fund and commercial banks, they also collaborate in providing balance-of-payments financing. The increased balance-of-payments financing needs of oil-importing countries in the wake of the 1979–80 oil price increases have awakened interest in furthering such collaboration. Commercial banks may not be able to meet the perceived needs of all such countries, especially those facing large debt service requirements even prior to the oil price increases and those plagued with domestic instability in economic policies or in politics. Collaboration between commercial banks

19. Article V, Section 12(c) and (f), *second*. See discussion of the Trust Fund pp. 272–73, above.
20. Article V, Section 12(f), *second*. In providing such assistance "the Fund shall take into account the level of per capita income." Ibid. Resources in the Special Disbursement Account could also be transferred to the General Resources Account. Article V, Section 12(f)(i), *second*. See also the provisions on a possible Investment Account. Article XII, Section 6(f), *second*.

criteria
performance

and the Fund has thus far been, however, largely informal. The Fund has no clear authority under the Articles to engage in cofinancing with banks or, for that matter, with member countries.[21] The Fund consequently takes the position that it cannot enter into formal agreements with other lenders as to joint provision of resources. That does not mean, however, that other lenders cannot make their loans conditional upon, say, negotiation of a Fund stand-by arrangement. The existence of a Fund stand-by agreement thus serves as a "good housekeeping seal of approval" for the banks.[22] The effect is that commercial banks in such instances are able to piggyback on the Fund's conditionality practices because the performance criteria redound to the protection of the commercial banks as well as the Fund.[23] This is an important advantage to commercial banks because, even acting collectively, they have not been able to impose economic conditions on sovereign borrowers. A 1976 attempt to impose a stabilization program on Peru was widely regarded as a failure.[24]

The Fund also collaborates with commercial banks whenever a Fund member that has purchased currencies from the Fund is involved in rescheduling of its debts. At that point the Fund becomes a creditor and has a strong incentive, if only in order to protect its own position, to take an active role in the rescheduling negotiations.[25] But the Fund still operates at arm's length

21. Joseph Gold, *Financial Assistance by the International Monetary Fund: Law and Practice*, IMF Pamphlet Series no. 27 (1979), pp. 38–44. See, however, Victoria E. Marmorstein, "Responding to the Call for Order in International Finance: Cooperation between the International Monetary Fund and the Commercial Banks," *Virginia Journal of International Law* 18(1978):445–83. See also Jonathan David Aronson, *Money and Power: Banks and the World Monetary System* (1977), pp. 161–80.
22. For further discussion and examples, see Marmorstein, pp. 453–55; Aronson, pp. 166–70, 178. See also the papers by Barbara Stallings, John S. Odell, Jonathan David Aronson, and Charles Lipson in *Debt and the Less Developed Countries*, ed. Jonathan David Aronson (1979), pt. 3, "The Politics of International Debt Renegotiations," pp. 225–333.
23. Banks' loan contracts may include references to the Fund, either indirectly requiring compliance with conditions already imposed by the IMF in return for use of its resources or including default conditions that relate to the Fund. Fund approval of bank loans may appear informally or through inclusion of specific Fund-linked conditions. Joseph Gold, *Conditionality*, IMF Pamphlet Series no. 31 (1979), p. 40. On the possibility of private banks imposing IMF-type conditionality, "even in the absence of a binding contract," see Henry C. Wallich, "How Much Private Bank Lending Is Enough," printed in *International Banking Operations*, Hearings before the Subcommittee on Supervision, Regulation and Insurance of the House Committee on Banking, Finance and Urban Affairs, 95th Cong., 1st Sess., 23 and 24 March, 5 and 6 April, 1977, p. 914 (hereafter cited *International Banking Operations*). However, for an account of an unsuccessful attempt to do so, see n. 24.
24. Marmorstein, p. 454; Don Oberdorfer, "U.S. Banks Impose Conditions, Set $240 Million Loan for Peru," *Washington Post*, 29 August 1976, reprinted in *International Banking Operations*, pp. 921–22; Juan de Onis, "Peru Unable to Pay Its Creditors. . . ." *New York Times*, 17 December 1977. See also Barbara Stallings, "Peru and the U.S. Banks: Privatization of Financial Relations," in Aronson, *Debt and Less Developed Countries*, pp. 232–43. For the Fund's recipe for a "prudential" commercial bank role, see *IMF Survey* 9(1980):348–50.
25. Marmorstein, pp. 460–62; Lipson, pp. 30–32.

from the commercial banks, uniformly refusing, for example, to provide the banks with information on members from its own investigations and files.[26]

The distinction between competition and collaboration, though useful for analyzing what has happened in balance-of-payments financing of less-developed countries, does not fully explain the support that many developed country governments have given to the expansion of Fund financing facilities. These governments have sought an expanded Fund neither as a concession to any Parkinsonian tendency of the Fund to grow nor out of any desire to curb commercial bank lending. Rather they see the Fund as a device for financing problem countries that can no longer borrow commercially and as a means of imposing, through the Fund's conditionality policies, some discipline on those countries that also borrow from the banks. For these reasons the continued ability of the Fund to compete for resources can be regarded as important for both the poorer less-developed countries and the banks themselves, as it enables them to avoid political pressure to lend to the poorest risks and to share the benefits from borrowers' conditionality commitments to the Fund.

Legal Problems of Fund Borrowing

An important element in expanding the Fund's ability to borrow from official creditors, particularly the oil-exporting countries, involves legal steps to improve the quality of the lenders' claims. A number of steps in this direction have been taken, and others can be anticipated.

A key aspect of the quality of a claim is its transferability. The easier it is for a creditor to transfer a claim and the wider the circle of potential transferees, the more attractive the claim. The claims on the Fund of Group of Ten lenders under the General Arrangements to Borrow have improved in this manner over the years. In March 1979, for example, the transferability of those claims was improved retroactively.[27] Similarly, as outlined in the last chapter, transferability of claims was an important factor in enabling the Fund to borrow for the oil facilities and the supplementary financing facility.[28]

---

26. The Fund's Managing Director reiterated this principle, while urging voluntary disclosure of information by debtor countries, in October 1980, *IMF Survey* 9(1980):350. See also Marmorstein, pp. 470–79; Arthur F. Burns, "The Need for Order in International Finance," in *International Banking Operations*, pp. 862–67.

27. GAB claims were then given a degree of liquidity, similar to that for claims under the supplementary financing facility, in that transfers of claims for repayment to certain GAB participants and the Swiss National Bank were permitted. See n. 28 below. *IMF Annual Report* 1979, p. 78.

28. See discussion pp. 288–89. Under the supplementary financing facility lenders were permitted "to transfer their claims to any other lender, any Fund member, or certain other official entities at prices agreed between the transferor and transferee." No prior reference to the Fund was required. *IMF Annual Report* 1979, p. 78. See also Decision of 4 December 1978, ibid. p. 135, on transferability of claims under the oil facility.

The largest step that could be taken in this direction would be to allow transfer to nonofficial entities. Then private financial institutions could acquire claims on the Fund and the liquidity of those claims would be greatly enhanced. Consideration of such a step would raise the question, however, why the Fund should not borrow from the market in the first place.

One of the principal legal questions raised by borrowing from the market would involve the Fund's immunity from suit. It seems unlikely that private lenders would be willing to advance large amounts to the Fund if they had no access to a domestic legal system or to some alternative legal forum in the event of a legal dispute. The World Bank, which regularly borrows from the market, has waived its immunity from suit and hence the claims of private World Bank bondholders can be enforced in domestic courts.[29]

A related question involves the governing law to be applied in the event of any dispute, whatever the forum. In its borrowings from official lenders under the GAB and for the oil and supplementary financing facilities the Fund has attempted, apparently successfully, to preclude legal disputes by careful drafting of borrowing agreements. In addition, it has included within the GAB agreements a mutual interpretation clause under which any "question of interpretation . . . shall be settled to the mutual satisfaction of the Fund, the participant raising the question, and all other participants."[30] Such an approach attempts to circumvent the question of underlying law by appealing to the mediation of interested parties other than the Fund and the claimant. This is perhaps superior to the provisions of the oil and supplementary financing facilities, which provide that any dispute is to be settled to the mutual satisfaction of the lender and the Fund.[31] Such a clause would most likely be unsatisfactory to private lenders.

Any borrowing from the market would have to be approved by the issuer of the currency in which the loan proceeds were denominated,[32] just as is the case today when, for example, oil-exporting countries lend dollars to the Fund. A problem in this respect may arise from the fact that under current

29. For a statement of the extent of immunity, see the opinion of Judge Harold Leventhal in Broadbent v. Organization of American States, 628 *Federal Reporter* 2d, pp. 30–33 (1980). For the World Bank waiver of immunity, see Articles of Agreement of the International Bank for Reconstruction and Development, Article VII, Section 3, and cf. IMF Article IX, Section 3, *original* and *second*. See also Aron Broches, "International Legal Aspects of the Operations of the World Bank," in *Académie de Droit International, Recueil des Cours 1959*, 98, vol. 3 (1960):308–10. The Bank's Articles establish that it may be sued by individuals in any country in which it conducts operations; the right does not extend to member states or their agents, on the ground that members have access to other means of redress.
30. General Arrangements to Borrow, para. 20 (2 June 1978 version), *Selected Decisions of the International Monetary Fund, Supplement to the Eighth Issue* (1978), p. 58.
31. See paragraph 11 in model agreements, Annex to Decision of 13 June 1974, *IMF Annual Report* 1974, p. 126, and Annex to Decision of 29 August 1977, *IMF Annual Report* 1978, p. 118.
32. Article VII, Section 1(i), *second*. It should be noted that even though the claim against the Fund may be denominated in SDRs, the advance to the Fund is necessarily in one or more currencies.

rules the value of any currency held in the General Resources Account must be maintained in value.[33] Thus, not every member may wish to see its currency borrowed by the Fund because it might subsequently be required, in the event of a depreciation, to furnish the Fund additional amounts of its currency. Moreover, it seems inevitable that the Fund would have to comply with local law and regulations governing capital market issues. In the United States, for example, any public issue by the Fund would surely have to comply with the disclosure requirements of the Securities and Exchange Commission.[34]

Toward a New Concept of the Fund

Borrowing institution

If the Fund should come to rely increasingly on borrowing rather than on quotas for its resources, a new concept of the Fund as a financial institution is likely to emerge. The Fund would look more like a bank, with the quota contributions constituting the equity capital, but with its main resources derived from borrowing. A commercial bank borrows primarily through deposits, but the parallel remains.

Under the original conception, not only was the Fund a mutual assistance society with its capital forming a revolving fund, but a member's quota determined its access to the Fund's resources. A member could not make net drawings in excess of 25 percent of its quota in any twelve-month period. Nor could it make cumulative net drawings resulting in the Fund's holding the drawing member's currency in excess of 200 percent of quota, which implied that the maximum amount of drawings outstanding at any time would be 125 percent of quota.[35] Although these limits could be, and in the case of the 25 percent per annum limit frequently were, waived, the notion that the quota limited the maximum amount that could be drawn was fundamental to the original conception.[36] A traditional norm of 100 percent of quota was established as a policy limit on drawings.[37] In recent years, particularly since the Fund began borrowing to finance lending to less-developed countries, the limit on total drawings has been waived with increasing reg-

---

33. Article V, Section 11, *second*. See discussion of maintenance of value, p. 105, above.

34. From its inception the World Bank worked closely with the Securities and Exchange Commission to ensure that it did not infringe U.S. regulations. Mason and Asher, pp. 127, 129. Gold mentions as other legal issues "the extent to which banks can lend to a single borrower under domestic law, and the SDR as a unit of account under domestic law." Joseph Gold, *A Third Report on Some Recent Legal Developments in the International Monetary Fund* (1978), p. 25. On the latter issue, see Joseph Gold, *A Second Report on Some Recent Legal Developments in the International Monetary Fund* (1977), pp. 36–37, 47–48.

35. The 200 percent of quota would thus consist of 75 percent of quota originally contributed in the member's currency and 125 percent drawings. See discussion p. 108.

36. Joseph Gold, "New Directions in the Financial Activities of the International Monetary Fund," *International Lawyer* 14(1980):450–51.

37. See the reference to this policy norm in Report of the Executive Board to the Board of Governors, Increases in Quotas of Fund Members—Seventh General Review, para. 3, *IMF Annual Report* 1979, p. 119.

ularity. Outstanding drawings have in repeated instances become a multiple of the quota.

This movement away from a one-to-one correspondence between quotas and lending limits has been facilitated by the increasing number of Fund windows, which, when combined, permit total drawings far in excess of quota even without a special waiver.[38] By the late 1970s, several hard-pressed members were permitted to draw amounts two or three times their quota, and in September 1980 the Fund approved a stand-by arrangement authorizing Turkey to draw up to 625 percent of its quota. With the adoption of quota increases under the Seventh General Review in December 1980, the Fund set annual limits of 150 percent of quota (excluding uses under the compensatory and buffer stock facilities), or up to 450 percent over a three-year period, with a 600 percent limit on cumulative access.[39]

Since the quota determines voting power, the increasing attenuation of the correlation between the access of members to resources and the size of their quotas has moved the Fund further from the original mutual assistance model toward the banking model, especially when coupled with a parallel trend toward longer and longer repurchase periods.[40]

If the developments just reviewed mean that quotas will become largely a source of equity capital, having little or no influence on the capacity of members to borrow from the Fund, there remain the questions of who will control the policies of the Fund and who will contribute the resources. Under the original conception the quota controlled both questions and indeed linked the two issues formally, although the mixed-bag-of-currencies approach meant that the economic contribution of soft-currency countries was limited to their gold contribution. This latter aspect of the original model was, of course, modified in the provisions of the Second Amendment concerning the duty of members to provide a freely usable currency when its own currency is borrowed. But the Fund does not permit the borrowing of currencies with a weak balance-of-payments and reserve position.[41]

38. See discussion of the Fund's windows, pp. 284–89. See the special 140 percent limit in connection with the supplementary financing facility, Decision of 29 August 1977, para. 6(a), *IMF Annual Report 1978*, p. 113. For "leniency" under the extended facility, see terms and conditions of the 1980 $1.73 billion loan to Pakistan, David Dodwell, "The IMF Gives Pakistan a Fighting Chance," *Financial Times*, 5 December 1980.
39. Given the 50 percent increase in quotas, the 150 percent access was one-eighth greater in absolute terms than the 200 percent of quota which the Fund had approved in September 1980. *IMF Survey* 10(1981):17; Interim Committee communiqué, *IMF Survey* 9(1980):305, 177. Purchases up to 351 percent of quota had been authorized for Jamaica in June 1979 and up to 400 percent for Korea and Guyana in March and June 1980. *IMF Survey* 8(1979):193; *IMF Survey* 9(1980):92, 233.
40. On repurchase periods, see discussion pp. 284–85. In December 1979 the period for repurchase under the extended facility was increased from eight to ten years. *IMF Survey* 8(1979):381.
41. See discussions pp. 102–5 and p. 283.

The borrowing of currencies by the Fund circumvents any difficulties of this character. To the extent that the Fund borrows from members, the resources are provided by lending members. When these members are paid a market rate of interest and lend voluntarily, their provision of resources is obviously of a different kind from provision of resources through quota contributions. And under the Fund's weighted voting scheme only the latter determines voting power.

Recently the less-developed countries have demanded an increase in voting power unrelated to their economic contribution. In the complex negotiations constituting the sixth and seventh quota reviews, the question of voting power played a complicating role. Room had to be made for the growing power and contribution of the oil-exporting countries. Yet neither the United States, which wanted to maintain a veto power in special majority issues, nor the less-developed countries, which sought such a veto power collectively, were willing to cede any substantial voting percentage. More recently, the Group of Twenty-Four has demanded that less-developed countries, whose share of the voting power rose to about one-third after completion of the seventh enlargement, receive a substantial increase in quotas and voting power.[42]

These developments suggest that with the growing attenuation of the link between quotas and access to Fund resources may come a parallel attenuation of the link, inherent in weighted voting, between contribution of resources and voting power. One can only speculate about the implications of any movement away from the weighted voting principle. Two rather obvious implications, however, are that the Fund's willingness and ability to insist on conditionality would be likely to decline and that the Fund would become more concerned with development and relatively less with balance-of-payments financing as such.

Even without an increase in voting power, the effective influence of less-developed country members on Fund decisions may be expected to increase. The OPEC countries have frequently made common cause with less-developed countries on Fund matters. The strength of the OPEC members stems from their unparalleled capacity to provide the resources the Fund requires for major expansion. To be sure, the OPEC countries have often seemed willing to provide resources through the Fund for the benefit of less-developed members only when they received a market rate of interest.[43] Nevertheless,

---

42. Group of 24, Outline for a Program of Action on International Monetary Reform, IV B.8, *IMF Survey* 8(1979):322. The Group of 24 has proposed that the share of less developed countries in Fund quotas should rise from 33 to 45 percent. Communiqués of the Group of 24, *IMF Survey* 9(1980):136, 300. The seventh increase in quotas was finally approved late in 1980 by 128 out of 141 members, representing 75.62 percent of total Fund quotas. U.S. concurrence was delayed pending congressional approval. Ibid. p. 377.

43. See, however, the contributions of Saudi Arabia to the Subsidy Account, *IMF Annual Report* 1980, p. 90, table 27, and the transfer by six OPEC members to the Trust Fund, ibid. p. 88.

the availability of resources even at market rates can be crucial. It was, for example, important to the Fund and derivatively to the oil-importing less-developed countries in connection with the oil facilities. In the future, the potential alliance between OPEC and less-developed members might, for example, lead to arrangements in which the Fund's quota-derived resources (such as its gold) were used to bridge the interest rate gap between market rates paid to OPEC lenders and concessional rates received from less-developed member borrowers.[44]

The potential alliance between OPEC and less-developed countries has created, however, a new set of issues in the Fund. These issues arise from the willingness of some OPEC members to use the Fund forum to advance their political interests to a greater degree than has been typical in the past. The potential impact of political issues on the functioning of the Fund came to the forefront of attention when, in connection with a dispute concerning the presence of the Palestine Liberation Organization as an observer at the 1980 Fund annual meeting, two OPEC countries threatened to make further loans to the Fund conditional on the Organization's representative being seated.[45]

The main impact of any increase in influence of less-developed countries will almost certainly be to move the Fund somewhat in the direction of a development institution. The Fund has already become more involved in development concerns than it was under the original conception. The Development Committee that emerged from the Committee of Twenty deliberations was largely a symbol,[46] but the Trust Fund was much more focused on the special problems of poorer countries. Moreover, the longer repayment periods available recently from the newer of the Fund windows, as well as the tendency of the Fund to roll over drawings, reflect at least a tacit policy of contributing long-term resources in aid of development.

Meanwhile, the World Bank has moved, through a "structural adjustment" facility, in the direction of the Fund by an increasing emphasis on program lending, as opposed to lending on specific projects. By 1980, convergence of Fund and Bank approaches manifested itself in the Fund's $130 million loan to Guyana (equivalent to 400 percent of quota) for "structural reform" and increase in "domestic supply capabilities," which was described as "an approach that is being developed for Fund financial programs in close col-

[handwritten margin note: World Bank & IMF cooperation]

44. The September 1980 decision to grant China a quota of SDR 1,200 million, which will give it approximately three percent of the total voting power, may give additional weight to this alliance if China sees its interests in international monetary affairs as corresponding to those of less-developed countries generally. *IMF Survey* 9(1980):281. China's quota gives it 12,250 votes (Article XII, Section 5, *second*) which is almost twice the voting power of Saudi Arabia. *IMF Annual Report* 1980, p. 168.
45. "IMF Dispute over PLO," *Financial Times*, 5 September 1980; "IMF Delays Seeking Arab Loans," ibid. 6 September 1980.
46. See discussion of the Development Committee, p. 251.

laboration with the World Bank."[47] This convergence in interest of the two institutions potentially raises important issues concerning institutional cooperation and relative spheres of influence and responsibility.

All of these developments in the concept of the Fund and in its shifting role give new pertinence to a sly observation that is part of the oral tradition of the field: the prime mistake made at Bretton Woods, it is often said, was that the two institutions were misnamed—the Fund should have been called a bank, and the Bank a fund.

II. The Future of the SDR

In the previous chapter a sharp distinction was drawn between the role of the SDR as a unit of account and its role as a reserve asset. The Fund has obviously faced an uphill struggle in making the SDR the "principal reserve asset" as called for by the Second Amendment.[48] In contrast, the SDR has enjoyed a number of successes as a unit of account.

Unit of Account

It is useful to distinguish three major roles for the SDR as a unit of account. The first is as a currency peg, the second as a unit for official international organizations, and the third as a unit for private transactions. It is in the first area that the greatest substance is to be found for the SDR, because the decision of a country to denominate its currency as a certain number of SDRs causes that country to behave differently in exchange markets than it would have done had it chosen some other currency or a homemade basket of currencies. Although exchange market transactions are necessarily carried out in currencies, and in many cases largely in the dollar rather than the SDR, this use of the SDR is still significant. As of 30 June 1980, fifteen Fund members pegged their currencies on the SDR and twenty-one on other composite currency baskets of their own creation.[49] The fact that more countries prefer to construct their own currency baskets may reflect the interest that countries often manifest in damping the variability in their exchange rate with their principal trading partners. The SDR basket may be inappropriate for accomplishing this objective.

47. *IMF Survey* 9(1980):233, 245. See the statement of Robert S. McNamara, president of the World Bank, at the 1979 annual meetings of the Fund and Bank in Belgrade, *IMF Survey* 8(1979):328. See also E. Peter Wright, "World Bank Lending for Structural Adjustment," *Finance and Development* 17(September 1980):20–23. The Group of 24 has urged that the Bank's structural adjustment facility be kept distinct from the IMF, with "low conditionality." Communiqué of 24 April 1980, *IMF Survey* 9(1980):136.
48. See discussion pp. 244–46.
49. *IMF Annual Report* 1980, pp. 54–56, table 13. See also IMF, *Annual Report on Exchange Arrangements and Exchange Restrictions*, 1979, p. 6. For a discussion of other exchange arrangements, see pp. 258–59.

The adoption of the SDR by a number of regional and international organizations, mostly intergovernmental, and in a number of international conventions (such as the Convention on Carriage of Goods by Sea, 1978) has been well chronicled by Fund officials.[50] The fact remains, however, that most international organizations, even of an intergovernmental character, continue to use some other unit of account. The Fund's sister institution, the World Bank, continues to denominate its loans and its bond issues in currencies (though it recently began to value its capital stock in SDRs).[51] A uniform movement by official regional and international organizations toward the SDR as a unit of account may be an essential precondition for acceptance of the SDR, even for this limited function by the private sector.

Use by the private sector of the SDR as a unit of account has been noteworthy but insignificant quantitatively. Aside from the SDR's previously mentioned use in international conventions, its use in the private sector has been extremely limited. In one sense, this fact should come as no surprise. Despite the great interest expressed from time to time in the use of various "currency cocktails" for bonds and other financial instruments, these private composite units of account have never "caught on" with either buyers or sellers. The reason appears to be that private institutions can hedge currency risks, at least in the short term, by exchange market transactions. For longer-term commitments the matching of assets and liabilities by currency is another device. And for those individuals and firms that are located in a single country, assets and liabilities denominated in their own currency are not normally regarded as involving exchange risk.

Despite these hurdles, there have been examples of banks standing ready to accept deposits denominated in SDRs. SDR-denominated bond issues have been successfully floated.[52] And the Fund has attempted to promote use of SDR deposits through the demonstration effect of itself investing Trust Fund assets in SDR-denominated deposits with the Bank for International Settlements.[53]

---

50. Joseph Gold, *Floating Currencies, Gold, and SDRs: Some Recent Legal Developments*, IMF Pamphlet Series no. 19 (1976), pp. 45–48; Gold, *Floating Currencies, SDRs, and Gold: Further Legal Developments*, IMF Pamphlet Series no. 22 (1977), pp. 43–49; Gold, *SDRs, Gold, and Currencies: Third Survey of New Legal Developments*, IMF Pamphlet Series no. 26 (1979), pp. 19–24 (hereafter cited Gold, *Third Survey*); Gold, *SDRs, Currencies, and Gold: Fourth Survey of New Legal Developments*, IMF Pamphlet Series no. 33 (1980), pp. 20–39 (hereafter cited Gold, *Fourth Survey*); Stephen A. Silard, "Carriage of the SDR by Sea: The Unit of Account of the Hamburg Rules," *Journal of Maritime Law and Commerce* 10(1978):21–37; and successive Fund annual reports.
51. *World Bank Annual Report 1978*, appendix G, note B, p. 149.
52. Gold, *Floating Currencies* (1976), pp. 59–64, and references cited therein; for reservations on such use of SDRs see Gold, *Third Survey*, pp. 28–30; but cf. Gold, *Fourth Survey*, pp. 39–43; and proposals for a London market in SDR-denominated certificates of deposit, *IMF Survey* 10(1981):6. The volume of SDR-denominated deposits was estimated at $2.5 billion early in 1981. Peter Montagnon, "The New, Improved SDR," *Financial Times*, 8 January 1981.
53. *IMF Annual Report 1978*, p. 77, and Decision of 16 June 1978, ibid. pp. 132–33; *IMF Annual Report 1979*, p. 67; Gold, *Fourth Survey*, p. 41.

The SDR as a Reserve Asset

Even if the acceptance of the SDR as a unit of account were pervasive in intergovernmental circles and extended to the private sector, it would still not follow that the SDR would become the principal reserve asset. Although the Fund staff has used its influence in many ways to promote the SDR both as a unit of account and as a reserve asset, in keeping both with its institutional interest in enhancing the role of the Fund and with what the staff views as its mandate under the Second Amendment, the Fund's members have been much less enthusiastic.

The U.S. interest in the SDR has tended to ebb and flow with U.S. officials' judgment of the prospects for and desirability of the dollar's role as a reserve currency. Less-developed countries tend to welcome an expanded role for the SDR but only so long as that expanded role leads to a greater flow of resources to them; indeed, one prime motivation for supporting pro-SDR initiatives appears to be the hope that someday an SDR-aid link may yet be worked out. And many European countries, though generally supportive of the SDR, apparently continue to regard its role as less important than more basic monetary issues such as the exchange rate regime.

Even within particular governments, views on the SDR may differ sharply, depending upon the role of any particular official. For those officials whose role is predominantly in the IMF arena, the SDR represents internationalism and economic solidarity. But for many domestically oriented officials in finance ministries and central banks, the SDR is still "funny money"—a bureaucratic construct that is not necessarily of much practical use and that could become an instrument of inflation if the felt need to expand its role should lead to an accelerated growth of liquidity. These doubts about the SDR are even more widespread in private banking and business circles.

For all of the hesitations and reservations about the SDR, the constellation of interests favoring an expanded role for the SDR has in recent years led to some changes in Fund doctrines and to the invention of new institutional techniques. One of the most important changes in doctrine has been the revolution in the justification for new SDR allocations. As traced in the preceding chapter,[54] that justification now involves treating the SDR not as a supplement to existing reserve assets but as a substitute for such assets. It is based on a shift in attitudes toward the determinants of the volume of international reserves from a view that emphasizes the supply of reserves to one that emphasizes the demand for reserves. Only under a doctrine that assumes that the volume of reserves is determined essentially by demand have the proponents of the SDR been able to meet effectively both the legal objection that SDRs may be allocated only to meet a "long-term global need

54. See discussion p. 280.

. . . to supplement existing reserve assets"[55] and the economic objection that further allocations would be inflationary.

Some of the means of increasing the use of the SDR lie, as a practical matter, within the discretion of the Fund staff, even though the Executive Board must give its assent. An example is the policy of selling SDRs in preference to currencies when members draw on the Fund. In the fiscal year ended 30 April 1979, some 82 percent of all sales to members through the operational budget involved SDRs. The sale of SDRs in this manner is, of course, largely cosmetic, because nearly 90 percent of the SDRs purchased were promptly exchanged for currencies, mainly the U.S. dollar.[56]

Other steps to enhance the usability of the SDR have been quite technical in character, such as the previously discussed expansion in the kinds of possible transactions between members and in the number of "other holders."[57] But these kinds of steps are purely facilitative. It remains to be seen whether any significant economic use will be made of these legal opportunities.

The Basket Issue

Another kind of technical change of potentially great significance was the decision of the Executive Board in September 1980 to reduce the number of currencies in the SDR valuation basket from sixteen to five.[58] As previously noted, a basic anomaly was the existence of different currency baskets for determining the valuation and the interest rate of the SDR.[59] The valuation basket had been composed of sixteen currencies and the interest rate basket of only five currencies. Aside from the fact that the discrepancy was illogical and could lead to a stronger or weaker SDR than would be the case if the same basket were used, the use of sixteen currencies in the valuation basket was a deterrent to SDR-denominated transactions in several respects. Any bank that accepts an SDR-denominated deposit incurs an exchange risk, just as if it accepted a foreign currency-denominated deposit, because the SDR's value varies with the value of each currency in the basket. But whereas the currency exchange risk can be hedged by forward transactions in the exchange market, the SDR exchange risk cannot be hedged directly. More precisely, the SDR exchange risk can only be hedged by acquiring positions in each of the currencies that compose the basket. J. J. Polak spelled out the alternative techniques:

> One of the ways in which banks could cover themselves when they accepted, say, U.S. dollars from a depositor who wanted to establish

55. Article XVIII, Section 1, *second*.
56. *IMF Annual Report* 1979, p. 76.
57. See discussion pp. 276–79.
58. *IMF Survey* 9(1980):297, 325–27.
59. See more extensive discussion pp. 201–6.

a deposit denominated in SDRs would be to invest the whole amount of dollars in some suitable interest-earning dollar asset of a maturity corresponding to that of the deposit and to enter into contracts to purchase forward the amount of each of the 15 other currencies that, according to the basket, was contained in the amount of SDRs created as a deposit by the bank. Alternatively, they could buy the component currencies spot and invest these. Either technique gives banks a complete hedge for their SDR liabilities and net interest incomes, on the basis of which they can quote interest rates that they are prepared to pay on SDR deposits.[60]

Such techniques should be less costly with five than with sixteen currencies. Forward markets for the least used of the sixteen currencies were not sufficiently liquid for large transactions. Moreover, the practice of acquiring assets to offset foreign currency liabilities was not practicable on a routine basis for countries where there are few assets acquirable by foreigners and available in the requisite volume.[61]

An interesting difference of views within the Fund over the desirability of the change from a sixteen currency basket throws light on the problems of expanding the use of the SDR. When the valuation basket was changed in 1978 to substitute two new currencies and to change percentage weights, great efforts were made to emphasize the continuity between the earlier SDR and the post-1978 SDR, including provision for change at five-year intervals in accordance with a formula.[62] The reduction in the number of currencies in the basket, though technically not ultra vires since one decision of the Executive Board cannot deprive it of authority for the future, nevertheless could undercut the sense of continuity, predictability, and stability sought by the foregoing provisions of the 1978 decision. A basket that can be radically changed once can be radically changed again.

The view of the proponents of change was that it was more important to get the substantive aspects of the SDR right than it was to be punctiliously consistent with prior decisions. It was, of course, true that the value of the SDR did not change because of the alteration in the basket and that one could not predict the effect of the change in basket size on the value of the SDR in following periods (unless one could first predict future exchange rates).

Both the opponents and proponents of change offered the importance of enhancing the role of the SDR as their principal argument, but their paths to achieving that enhancement were different. The advocates of continuity

60. J. J. Polak, "The SDR as a Basket of Currencies," *IMF Staff Papers* 26(1979):631.
61. Ibid. p. 630, n. 10 and p. 637. See, however, ibid. p. 631, n. 12, and *BIS 40th Report* (1979), p. 168.
62. Decision of 31 March 1978, *IMF Annual Report* 1978, pp. 129–30. See discussion p. 201, above. The decision stated that the formula would apply "unless the Fund decides otherwise in connection with a revision" at the end of the five-year period.

emphasized the security of transactions and sought to assure that rule changes would not disappoint economic expectations. The advocates of reform held that rules should be changed whenever necessary to move toward an optimum institutional arrangement.

Which of the two approaches would do more to promote use of the SDR in the future, particularly in the private sector, was an important question. The view that continuity of rules is often a precondition to desirable change along evolutionary lines is well-known, and in most epochs dominant, in domestic private law. The notion that immediate changes in rules are the most direct path to an optimum result is more common to public law, particularly in this century. In the case of the SDR basket, the issue was narrower since proponents of both views had the same objective—using rules to reform the international monetary system through promotion of the SDR to a central place in the system.

SDR-Denominated Claims

The decision on improving the SDR valuation basket is only one illustration of a concern with increasing the volume of SDR-denominated claims. To the extent that official and private institutions can be encouraged to hold claims denominated in SDRs, the SDR will play a more important role in the international monetary and financial systems without the necessity of actually allocating any additional SDRs. In that way the inflation objection to allocation can be largely circumvented.

An SDR-denominated claim is a close substitute for an SDR and, unlike the SDR, can be held by private parties. Aside from the allocation question, the main difference is that with the SDR-denominated claim, the claim will normally be created and liquidated with a transfer of some currency. But the difference is not great because the principal use of an SDR is to obtain freely usable currency. Thus, to the extent that the SDR-denominated claim becomes widely held, the unit of account function may eventually merge with the asset function. Monetary authorities may come to hold their reserves in the form of SDR-denominated claims.

Since the Fund operates, as a result of the Second Amendment, entirely on an SDR unit-of-account basis, all claims on the Fund by its members are denominated in SDRs. The claims that arise from the reserve tranche and from the Fund's sale of a member's currency to another member are not transferable. But when the Fund borrows, the claim created is valued in SDRs and is transferable, to a greater or lesser degree as specified in the decision authorizing the borrowing and in the particular agreements with the lenders. In these circumstances the precedent has been created for the transfer among financial institutions of reserve assets denominated in SDRs. Indeed, one possible motivation for increasing the Fund's rate of borrowing is to put into the marketplace a greatly expanded amount of such claims. Transfers of SDR-denominated claims have not yet, however, become significant.

In connection with outstanding purchases, the Fund in turn has SDR-denominated claims on its members, which totaled over SDR 8.8 billion at the end of the 1980 fiscal year.[63] Although the Fund cannot transfer these claims, a repurchase obligation is an SDR-denominated liability from the standpoint of the member. Similarly, if other international and regional organizations adopt the SDR as the unit of account for their transactions, then SDR-denominated claims and liabilities will proliferate. To the extent that these claims are transferable, the basis for a market in such claims will have been laid.

The Substitution Account Issue

The resurgence of interest in a substitution account in 1979, after some years of quiescence, can best be understood in the light of the interest in encouraging the creation of SDR-denominated claims as a means of elevating the status of the SDR in the international monetary system. Although the same concern with finding some means of dealing with the "overhang" of U.S. dollars and the same interest in phasing reserve currencies out of the international monetary system that motivated earlier international discussions of such an account still played a role,[64] the future of the SDR was a prime consideration. Indeed, the Interim Committee went so far as to say, in the communiqué at the end of its March 1979 meeting, that "the purpose" of such an account would be "to take a further step toward making the SDR the principal reserve asset."[65] To be sure, the issuance of SDRs themselves in exchange for dollars would have been an even greater step in that direction, but SDR-denominated claims had technical advantages, not least that no new amendment of the Articles would be required to authorize the account. The substitution account would have generated a large volume of widely and easily transferable SDR-denominated claims, which would have been held by central banks and other official institutions as reserves. Moreover, these claims would have been used in a variety of ways to finance balance-of-payments deficits and to maintain the value of the holders' currencies.

In the end this renewed effort toward creation of a substitution account failed for the same reasons that the substitution account had not progressed beyond the discussion phase within the Committee of Twenty, namely, the difficulty of allocating the exchange and interest rate risks involved in such

---

63. *IMF Annual Report* 1980, p. 181.
64. Joseph Gold, "Substitution in the International Monetary System," *Case Western Reserve Journal of International Law*, 12(1980):302–5, 308–9. On earlier negotiations concerning such an account, see discussion pp. 238–39, 290, above.
65. Interim Committee Communiqué, 7 March 1979, *IMF Annual Report* 1979, p. 145. See Gold, "Substitution," pp. 313–14 for interpretation of this communiqué.

an account. Although the issuance of SDR-denominated claims against dollars and the investment by the account of its assets in U.S. government securities would be simple enough, some rather precise agreement was necessary to determine who would bear the loss if in the end those securities turned out not to be adequate to discharge the claims, say because of a depreciation of the U.S. dollar. A similar problem would arise with respect to interest payments because the account's receipts of interest on its investments might not be sufficient to meet interest payments on its liabilities.[66] Although as a practical matter the account might never be liquidated and therefore the question of who would be left holding an empty bag would probably never have to be faced directly, it would be difficult to negotiate a gigantic arrangement involving many billions of dollars (and SDRs) without some agreement on these issues. The same legal imperative can be observed in the elaborate provisions in the Articles for winding up the special drawing rights arrangement and the Fund itself.[67]

Those countries that held dollar reserves already bore, of course, an exchange risk with respect to their dollar holdings. Thus, they would be better off with an inherently diversified SDR claim and a moral commitment than they were with dollars alone (assuming that the substitution transactions would otherwise be attractive). But many European countries saw the substitution account as a way of taking international pressure off the United States to pursue the prudent fiscal and monetary policies that would be necessary to maintain the value of the dollar in exchange markets. When the time came for agreement at the crucial Hamburg meeting of the Interim Committee in April 1980, the bases for an agreement on the exchange risk and interest rate issues had not yet been constructed and the substitution account returned to the back burners of reform.[68] And so a principal means of generating large amounts of SDR-denominated claims came to naught.

III. The Future of Reserve Currencies

The failure of the substitution account negotiations raised anew the question whether the C-20 goal of phasing reserve currencies out of the international monetary system was realistic. And it gave new force to the widespread view

---

66. Ibid. pp. 323–24, and see pp. 319–23 on the difficulties of assuring the "attractiveness" of SDR-denominated claims. On the issues involved in any substitution account, see Dorothy Meadow Sobol, "A Substitution Account: Precedents and Issues," *Federal Reserve Bank of New York Quarterly Review* 4(Summer 1979):44–48; "Reserve diversification and the IMF substitution account," *World Financial Markets*, September 1979, pp. 9–14; Group of Thirty, *Towards a Less Unstable International Monetary System: Reserve Assets and a Substitution Account* (1980), pp. 6–12.
67. Articles XXIII–XXVII, *second*.
68. On the points agreed by the Executive Directors prior to the Hamburg meeting, see the press conference remarks of Managing Director de Larosière, *IMF Survey* 9(1980):133–36.

that a more likely development would be an evolution from a dollar-based system to a system with multiple reserve currencies.

Thus far, however, relatively little attention has been paid to two questions: first, what rules or changes in rules might accelerate or decelerate such an evolution, and, second, what rules might prevent a multiple reserve currency system from generating exchange rate instability. History shows that any multiple reserve system may suffer instability as reserve holders change from one asset to another. Switches between a reserve currency and gold were an obvious problem under the gold exchange standard, one indeed that brought the Bretton Woods system to an end. More to the point, switches between reserve currencies were a serious problem during the interwar years in the relations between sterling and the franc, on the one hand, and between sterling and the dollar, on the other.[69]

One crucial economic difference should, however, be borne in mind in considering these historical parallels. When the rate at which two reserve assets exchange is fixed, then a Gresham's law problems arises. Hence, when underlying values change, market transactions are likely to generate further stresses as holders seek to divest themselves of the less valuable asset at the fixed price. In a period of floating rates the necessary condition for the operation of Gresham's law is no longer present, and the change in the relative prices of the various reserve assets creates the conditions for a new equilibrium distribution of those assets. Of course, a floating rate system may generate its own instabilities in the form of wide swings in exchange rates between the principal reserve currencies, but at least the Gresham's law problem will have been avoided.

Another important difference between the present and the 1925–31 period, when the world experienced instability in the dollar-sterling-franc triangle, lies in the much greater degree of cooperation among central banks and particularly among governments. Cooperation then was limited to central banks and largely evaporated when the understanding between Benjamin Strong and Montagu Norman was ended by Strong's death in 1928. Still, not much comfort can be gained from intergovernmental cooperation. Despite the improved means of communication and transportation, such cooperation remains limited almost wholly to exchange market and off-market reserve transactions.

Such transactions are, however, largely means of dealing with symptoms, and the underlying stability required for exchange stability must come, as recognized in the negotiations leading up to the Jamaica agreement, from sound fiscal and monetary policies. Those domestic policies are determined in a domestic political framework. One searches in vain for important in-

---

69. See discussion p. 68. Related problems brought about the collapse of the bimetallic system. See discussion pp. 19–21.

stances, particularly in the United States, in which the fortunes of other countries or the goal of tranquility in exchange markets played an important role in the domestic political struggle over the budget, taxes, and interest rate policy. Nonetheless, an institutional basis for cooperation in support of a multiple reserve currency system exists.

The Path to a Multiple Reserve Currency System

Most discussion of the development of a multiple reserve system starts from the assumption that it will take the form of a diversification by reserve holders out of U.S. dollars. Yet during the 1970s the dollar constituted a remarkably stable portion of foreign exchange reserves in the face of a considerable decline in the U.S. economy's share of world output and trade.[70] The share of U.S. dollar holdings in total world reserves fluctuated between 75 and 80 percent throughout the decade,[71] although the dollar share fell significantly in 1979.[72]

This relative stability does not mean, however, that there was not significant diversification out of the dollar. On the one hand, increased holdings of dollars by some countries masked sales of dollars by others. Some of the countries least likely to want to diversify into other currencies—notably Germany and Japan, which themselves were then vigorously resisting any movement toward a multiple reserve currency system—acquired substantial holdings of dollars at various times in the 1970s through exchange market intervention as they sought to resist appreciation of their own currencies. Similarly, the OPEC countries continued to increase their holdings of dollar assets even while placing an increased percentage of their accretions to reserves in investments denominated in other currencies.[73] The bulk of reserve diversification out of the dollar has involved the oil-importing less-developed countries, but their actions have not greatly affected the share of the dollar in total foreign exchange reserves simply because those countries' share of such reserves is comparatively small. Thus, the continued large share of the U.S. dollar in world reserves largely reflects the fact that the Group of Ten countries have continued to maintain the vast bulk of their exchange reserves in dollars.[74]

70. *Economic Report of the President* 1980, p. 178. In 1979, dollars constituted 77 percent of foreign exchange holdings, but the U.S. accounted for only 35 percent of the OECD aggregate of gross national product and only 16 percent of total OECD foreign trade. *World Financial Markets*, September 1979, p. 6.
71. Ibid. September 1978, p. 8, and September 1979, p. 6. P. M. Oppenheimer, "International Monetary Arrangements: The Limits to Planning," Bank of England, Papers presented to the Panel of Academic Consultants, no. 8, July 1979, pp. 22–23.
72. *IMF Annual Report* 1980, pp. 61–64. For comparability adjustments must be made for swaps of dollars against ECUs in the European Monetary System. Ibid.
73. *World Financial Markets*, September 1978, p. 8.
74. Ibid. December 1979, p. 9. The United Kingdom, however, has diversified extensively. In August 1980, it was estimated that it held 30 percent or about $5 billion of its foreign exchange

The 1970s saw a growth in reserve holdings of the German mark and to a lesser degree of the Japanese yen and Swiss franc. To a large extent these increases merely offset a rapid decline in the position of sterling from 8 percent of foreign exchange reserves to less than 2 percent in 1978.[75] Nonetheless, the steady growth of the mark in world reserves was essentially unrelated to the running down of sterling balances and continued despite the outright hostility of German officials. By the end of 1978 the recorded mark holdings of foreign monetary authorities were estimated at more than 11 percent of total exchange reserves of such authorities.[76] About two-thirds was held in Euromark deposits.[77] Such mark holdings had risen more than sixfold in four years.[78]

This rapid emergence of the mark as a reserve currency does not necessarily indicate any immediate challenge to the dollar, at least so long as the German government resists a reserve currency role. The mark is still used as a transactions currency almost exclusively in German foreign trade, with 80 percent of exports but still only 40 to 50 percent of imports, invoiced in marks.[79] Moreover, the mark is held in reserves primarily by the less-developed countries and the smaller industrial countries.[80] The members of the Group of Ten, by continuing in most instances to observe the commitments made in 1971 in a short-term formal agreement not to hold reserves in the Eurodollar market, have in effect acceded to Germany's desire to avoid a reserve currency role by foreclosing a ready subterfuge.[81] A 1972 agreement between EEC central banks to hold each other's currencies solely to execute payments, except with explicit authorization, further limits the growth of the mark as a reserve currency.[82]

A number of events in 1979 and 1980, moreover, undermined the German government's resistance to the growth of the mark as a reserve currency. In

---

reserves in nondollar currencies. David Marsh, "OPEC Piles Up Sterling," *Financial Times*, 15 August 1980.

75. *IMF Annual Report* 1979, p. 55. These figures are derived from a sampling of seventy-six Fund members. See also *IMF Annual Report* 1980, p. 64, table 16. Sterling may be partially rehabilitated as a reserve currency through strength gained from North Sea oil. Samuel Brittan, "Oil Restores Sterling's Reserve Role," *Financial Times*, 11 December 1980.

76. "The Deutsche Mark as an International Investment Currency," *Monthly Report of the Deutsche Bundesbank* 31(November 1979):26.

77. *Report of the Deutsche Bundesbank for the Year 1979*, p. 56.

78. Bundesbank, "The Deutsche Mark," pp. 30–31. See also *World Financial Markets*, September 1979, p. 6; and *IMF Annual Report* 1980, p. 64, table 16.

79. Bundesbank, "The Deutsche Mark," p. 27.

80. Ibid. p. 31.

81. *IMF Annual Report* 1972, p. 16; Robert Solomon, *The International Monetary System 1945–1976* (1977), pp. 177–78. For factors limiting the effectiveness of the 1971 "self-denying ordinance," see David Marsh, "The Move Away from the Dollar," *Financial Times*, 7 March 1979. See also *IMF Annual Report* 1979, p. 53, on the renewal of the 1971 agreement.

82. Bundesbank, "The Deutsche Mark," p. 32.

the autumn of 1979 the U.S. government decided to accept responsibility for maintaining the exchange value of the dollar through exchange market intervention. This decision required it to acquire foreign currencies, and for this purpose it not only drew on German and Swiss swap lines but also sold a total of $2.29 billion of bonds denominated in German marks (so-called Carter bonds) in November 1979 and February 1980.[83] The result was that the United States acquired substantial holdings of German marks, which itself constituted an expansion in the mark's role as a reserve currency.[84]

Germany's transition, beginning in 1979, from a persistent surplus country to one suffering large current-account payments imbalances, also created a new situation, especially as the new payments deficit was coupled with a large budget deficit.[85] A DM 17.5 billion current account surplus in 1978 became a DM 10.5 billion deficit in 1979, and German central bank projections for the 1980 current account deficit ran as high as DM 25 billion.[86] The German budget deficit, which first emerged as a significant factor in the mid-1970s, grew to about 3½ percent of GNP in 1979.[87] In 1980 the German authorities decided to meet both the current account deficit and the budget problems by foreign borrowing, in part from foreign governments.[88] These borrowings generate claims by foreign governments on the German government. To the extent that these claims are short-term and liquid, they create foreign exchange reserves denominated in marks. Moreover, the increased intervention by members of the European monetary system in their own currencies contributed to a rise in mark holdings by European governments.[89]

Rules to Facilitate a
Multiple Reserve Currency System

In the light of developments such as these, which are paralleled to a lesser extent for the Japanese yen and the Swiss franc, many observers have come

83. Scott E. Pardee, "Treasury and Federal Reserve Foreign Exchange Operations," *Federal Reserve Bank of New York Quarterly Review*, 5(Spring 1980):37, 39; Francis Ghiles, " 'Carter Bond' Issue Attracts DM 4.6bn," *Financial Times*, 25 January 1980. As the dollar later strengthened and the mark weakened, the United States repaid mark borrowing under the German swap arrangements. Scott E. Pardee, "Treasury and Federal Reserve Foreign Exchange Operations: Interim Report," *Federal Reserve Bulletin*, 1980, p. 954.
84. Bundesbank, "The Deutsche Mark," p. 32.
85. *Bundesbank Annual Report 1979*, pp. 13, 15.
86. Ibid. p. 44; *Bundesbank Monthly Report* 32(August 1980):11; Jonathan Carr, "Bonn: The Uncertain Stride of a New Political Giant," *Financial Times*, 11 April 1980; *World Financial Markets*, May 1980, pp. 3–6.
87. *Bundesbank Annual Report 1979*, p. 15.
88. In March 1980, for example, the German government raised over DM 3 billion in direct and indirect loans from OPEC countries. *Bundesbank Monthly Report* 32(May 1980):13. See also ibid. 32(June 1980):6, 36; Carr, "Bonn."
89. "The European Monetary System," *Bundesbank Monthly Report* 31 (March 1979):15–16; *Bundesbank Annual Report 1979*, pp. 56, 59. On possible softening of opposition to a reserve currency role for the mark, see ibid. p. 56 and "How the New Reserve Centres See It," *The Economist*, 22 March 1980, p. 59. See also n. 74, above.

to "an abrupt recognition that the evolution of a multi-currency reserve system is today's reality, not an avoidable development that somehow can be deferred indefinitely."[90] This recognition has led to some interest in the kind of rules that might facilitate the smooth working of such a system, but so far attention has been focused on a single set of problems—how diversification out of the dollar may occur without depressing the dollar exchange rate to the point where a flight out of the dollar occurs and without creating unnecessarily wide swings in the dollar-mark exchange rate.

Until the collapse of negotiations over a substitution account in April 1980, such an account was viewed as the principal vehicle for accomplishing these objectives. But it is obvious that substitution can occur on a unilateral or bilateral basis in a variety of ways. Various off-market possibilities have been discussed. For example, the German government or Bundesbank could sell, for dollars, securities denominated in marks to official and indeed to private institutions on terms negotiated between the parties.[91]

The rationale for all such diversification schemes is that the foreign exchange market is not an adequate vehicle for accommodating central banks and other institutions seeking to diversify out of the dollar and therefore off-market facilities must be established. Such off-market facilities might be unnecessary, it is argued, if the foreign exchange market were efficient, but the market's liquidity has been reduced by the extent of German, Japanese, and Swiss government efforts to prevent the development of assets in which short-term holdings appropriate for monetary reserves could be held. This imperfection in the market has been met, although not necessarily fully, by the growth of Euromark and Euroyen markets.

The problem of reserve diversification out of a smaller reserve currency back into the dollar may create even graver problems than the original diversification out of the dollar. As the German central bank noted in late 1979, "Since the summer of 1978 . . . , over periods of five months at a time, foreign exchange in amounts of up to DM 20 billion (or almost 4% of the simultaneous gross national product) flowed in, flowed out, and then flowed in again."[92] A flow of about $100 billion would have been required to make a similar impact, as a percentage of gross national product, on the United States. Thus, outflows from a secondary reserve center may create relatively larger problems for that center than did the original outflow for the United States because they bulk relatively larger in the secondary reserve center's smaller economy.

Assuming, however, that the evolution toward a multiple reserve currency system continues, it is likely that an entirely new set of concerns about the

90. *World Financial Markets*, December 1979, p. 9.
91. See ibid. pp. 10–13 for discussion of this proposal. See also Geoffrey Bell, "Easing the Strain on the Dollar," *Times* (London), 10 December 1979.
92. Bundesbank, "The Deutsche Mark," p. 33.

rules of such a system may emerge. So far as reserve assets are concerned, it is not easy to see how the goal of making the SDR the principal reserve asset is compatible with a system based on, say, the dollar, mark and yen. As for the exchange rate regime, attempts to peg the dollar-mark-yen rates might eventually occur. Such an evolution might lead the system to a state of affairs not too far different from the "key currency" approach discussed during World War II as an alternative to the White and Keynes plans.[93] On the other hand, some countries and perhaps the Fund may try to resist any evolution toward a multiple reserve currency system even if the new reserve centers abandon their hostility to a reserve status for their currencies.

IV. THE REGULATION OF INTERNATIONAL FINANCIAL MARKETS

An important change in discussions of exchange rate and balance-of-payments problems has been a greater emphasis on international financial markets than that which characterized such discussions either in the C-20 or under the Bretton Woods system. In part, this change is simply a reaction to the increased role of commercial bank financing in the provision of liquidity and to the massive growth in the Eurocurrency market. But it also represents greater attention to underlying economic transactions and events than to formal institutions. This is a healthy development because it recognizes the fragility of formal rules and institutions that run counter to strong evolutionary forces.

Much of the focus, however, has necessarily been on what are perceived as problems in the international financial system. Three kinds of problems have been singled out. First, the international financial system may, it is said, create too much liquidity, with potentially disastrous inflationary consequences. Second, the international financial system may be used by domestic banks and business firms to avoid efforts by central banks to run stringent monetary policies; in short, the international financial system may undercut domestic monetary policy. And third, commercial banks, especially offshore banks, may engage in unduly expansionary lending, in too large volume and on too easy terms, with several undesirable consequences—delay of necessary adjustment action in borrowing countries, undesirable risk of losses from overconcentration of loans to particular countries ("country risk") and, with such losses, the possibility of failure of large commercial banks, perhaps triggering an international financial panic.[94]

93. See discussion p. 73.
94. See the categorization of these various potential problems in *IMF Annual Report* 1979, pp. 52–54; *Bundesbank Annual Report 1979*, pp. 49–50. On loan concentration, see Lipson, pp. 21–22; see also a series of articles in the *Institutional Investor*, July 1979, pp. 47–67; and

The Eurocurrency Market

Much of the popular discussion of these issues is based on a view of the Eurocurrency market as a massive money-making machine beyond the regulation of any government and essentially out of control. Perhaps the appellation "stateless money" best captures this view of the Eurocurrency market. It is not surprising, therefore, that most proposals for dealing with international financial markets involve means of subjecting Eurocurrency transactions to national regulation.

Before the various proposals are discussed, it is worth explaining why many criticisms of the Eurocurrency market are based on unduly alarmist misunderstandings of what is involved. The total size of the market, for example, strikes some observers as shockingly large, especially since both the external claims and the external liabilities of banks passed one trillion dollars in 1979. However, these figures did not represent Euromarket transactions only, and they were inflated by double-counting of interbank deposits, which are excluded from measures of domestic money and are therefore suspect in measures of the Eurocurrency market. Excluding this double counting, the Bank for International Settlements estimated that the total of credit outstanding at the end of 1979 in the Eurocurrency markets was $475 billion, as against $300 billion at the end of 1977.[95]

Eurocurrency market deposits are not money in the narrow sense.[96] Rather, at least under present practices, they are time deposits and therefore cannot be used directly as means of payment. Although some 20 percent of the time deposits have a maturity of less than eight days, and indeed some are overnight deposits, they still must be reduced to demand deposits before pay-

---

Jonathan David Aronson, "Financial Institutions in the International Monetary System," *Case Western Reserve Journal of International Law* 12(1980):344–55.

95. *BIS 50th Report* 1980, pp. 119, 126–27. BIS figures "do not cover all international bank lending" but refer to its defined reporting area. External claims include claims in domestic currency and hence do not refer exclusively to Eurocurrency transactions. After deducting $446 billion, due to double-counting, from the initial total of $1,111 billion of external claims, the BIS total for external claims was $665 billion. Ibid. pp. 106–7. By June 1980 total gross external claims had risen to over $1,200 billion; after deducting $471 billion for double-counting, the total for external claims was $735 billion. *IMF Survey* 10(1981):2–3. See also Jay Sterling, "How Big is the International Lending Market?" *The Banker* 130(January 1980):77–87; "Money and Finance," *The Economist*, 29 November 1980; IMF, *International Capital Markets*, pp. 33–34, 51, table 28. For an explanation of differences in estimates of Euromarket size, deriving from differing bases of calculation, see M. S. Mendelsohn, *Money on the Move* (1980), pp. 92–94.

96. See Ralph C. Bryant, *Money and Monetary Policy in Interdependent Nations* (1980), pp. 99–102. For a general review of the issue which has attracted the most academic commentary—namely, whether "money" is "created" through the Eurocurrency markets, see Robert Z. Aliber, "The Integration of the Offshore and Domestic Banking System," *Journal of Monetary Economics* 6(1980):509–26; Ronald I. McKinnon, *The Eurocurrency Market*, Princeton Essays in International Finance no. 125 (1977); and Helmut Mayer, *Credit and Liquidity Creation in the International Banking Sector*, BIS Economic Papers no. 1 (1979).

ments can be made. Moreover, at least half have a maturity of more than thirty days.[97]

The notion that Eurocurrency banks operate beyond the reach of any government is patently incorrect, even though it may be true that governments have preferred to avert their eyes, even in some cases from Eurocurrency transactions wholly within their borders. All of the banks with any significant share of the Eurocurrency market are large international banks that also play major domestic roles in their home countries; in fact, a bank that failed to meet this description would be unlikely to enjoy the confidence necessary to attract Eurocurrency deposits in sufficient volume to compete in that market. Moreover, estimates are as high as 40 percent for the share of Eurocurrency operations carried out by bank offices located in the United Kingdom,[98] where the British government not only is fully aware of their transactions but actively encourages the expansion of their business. The countries in which the head offices are located have it within their power to regulate the lending activities of foreign branches and subsidiaries in the same way that they treat those activities at the head office.

Indeed, a large proportion of all Eurocurrency transactions would be carried out at the head office of the Euromarket banks if it were not for the existence of other kinds of national regulation that make booking the business at the home office economically unattractive and competitively infeasible. For example, the greatest incentive to the creation of the Eurodollar market was the capital controls imposed by the United States in the 1960s. Those controls limited increases in foreign lending from U.S. sites and, at the same time, mandated foreign borrowings by U.S. corporations to finance foreign business growth.

Today the most important regulations encouraging offshore operations are the reserve requirements and capital-to-assets ratios that are imposed in some countries on domestic banking. In the United States, for example, the reserve requirement system involves a mandatory deposit of a certain percentage of deposits with the Federal Reserve system; since such deposits do not draw interest, the reserve requirement system acts as a tax on all business, domestic and foreign, done by the home offices of U.S. banks, a tax that they do not have to pay on business transacted by offshore branches. Even if the banks

97. Edward J. Frydl, "The Debate over Regulating the Eurocurrency Markets," *Federal Reserve Bank of New York Quarterly Review* 4(1979–80):11–12, 14–15. About 40 percent of Eurobank liabilities in London are of one month maturity or less, of which half are eight days or less. Average maturity of total liabilities in London is estimated at between three and four months. Ibid. p. 15; *Bank of England Quarterly Bulletin* (March 1980), table 13.1. See also Henry C. Wallich, "Why the Euromarket Needs Restraint," *Columbia Journal of World Business* 14(Fall 1979):17–18.

98. EMB [Edward M. Bernstein] (Ltd.), "The Eurocurrency Market and International Monetary Problems," 23 August 1979 (mimeo), p. 4.

maintain equivalent reserves out of prudential motives in their offshore business, they can hold those reserves in interest-bearing form. An offshore branch of a U.S. bank continues to have a substantial financial advantage, with regard to its purely offshore operations, over a home office subject to reserve requirements, even after passage of the 1980 act which imposed reserve requirements on some limited types of offshore transactions and also reduced restrictions on payment of interest on short-term deposits.[99] Some foreign governments accomplish the same regulatory control by capital-to-asset ratios that restrain the expansion of credit but without the tax involved in mandatory non-interest-paying reserves.

Approaches to Regulation

Although the regulatory differential has been diminished by recent reductions in domestic regulation in the United States, political considerations appear to limit the effectiveness of this solution.[100] Therefore, it is not surprising that some proposals for reform of the international financing system call for extension of domestic regulation, especially to offshore banking. Such an extension could occur in two ways, by either a "domiciliary" or a "territorial" approach.[101] To take reserve requirements as an illustration, the domiciliary approach would require the country in which the head office of the bank was domiciled to impose reserve requirements on all deposits, including those of offshore branches and subsidiaries of the bank. Under the territorial approach, in contrast, the country in which a deposit was made would impose reserve requirements not only on domestic banks but also on local branches and subsidiaries of foreign banks.

In central bank discussions within the framework of the Bank for International Settlements, the United States proposed that each participating

99. *World Financial Markets*, December 1980, p. 4; *Federal Reserve Bulletin* 66(1980):901. All U.S. banks are subject to reserve requirements, and not just Federal Reserve members, under the provisions of the Depository Institutions Deregulation and Monetary Control Act of 1980, Public Law 96-221, § 103(b)(2), (5). This law continues to exempt "deposits payable only outside" the United States from reserve requirements, but applies to all transactions in which there is both American and foreign participation. The U.S. Federal Reserve has sometimes imposed reserve requirements on liabilities of U.S. banks to foreign branches but not on the liabilities of foreign branches.

100. The Federal Reserve Board issued proposals in 1980 which would modify application of U.S. regulations to "international banking facilities" so that "an IBF at a U.S. banking office would be able to conduct a banking business with foreign residents on nearly the same basis as an offshore shell branch." Federal Reserve Board, Notice of Proposed Rulemaking, International Banking Facilities, p. 1 (Docket No. R-0214, 16 December 1980) (mimeo).

101. A more graphic term for the territorial approach is the "real estate" approach, proposed by Robert Aliber. See his testimony in *The Eurocurrency Market Control Act of 1979*, Hearings before the House Subcommittees on Domestic Monetary Policy and on International Trade, Investment and Monetary Policy, 96th Cong., 1st Sess. (1979), p. 83 (hereafter cited Hearings, *Eurocurrency Market Control*).

country impose reserve requirements on a domiciliary basis.[102] This proposal was subject to two grave defects. First, the United States and Germany were alone among the Group of Ten countries in using the interest-free minimum reserve requirement system.[103] More common is the capital asset ratio method of regulating bank credit. Adoption of the U.S. approach would have required, in order to avoid the possibility that the banks of certain domiciles might be favored over those of other domiciles, either that the United States and Germany abandon reserve requirements in favor of a capital asset ratio regulation or that other countries adopt reserve requirements in place of their existing method.

Second, the U.S. approach could only work if all major countries whose banks play an important role in international financial markets were to adopt it. If the United States, for instance, were to impose reserve requirements on all operations of offshore branches and subsidiaries of banks headquartered in the United States, those offshore offices would suffer a severe competitive disadvantage. Britain and Switzerland, both of whom benefit significantly from the activities of offshore banks within their borders and therefore have an interest in keeping offshore banking free of regulation, expressed strong opposition to the U.S. proposal. Since both of these opposing countries are headquarters for a number of the large international banking firms, their opposition has effectively killed adoption of the U.S. proposal.[104]

Nor could a territorial system work effectively in view of the opposition of these two countries. Since Britain alone accounts for about one-quarter of gross international claims,[105] that country might rapidly become the center for the greater part of all offshore banking if all other countries were to adopt a territorial regulatory system. Indeed, as the first country to encourage offshore banking by exempting it from domestic regulation,[106] Britain pioneered the Eurodollar market. A further problem with a territorial system would be that it would be possible for the large international banks to establish new branches in regulation-free zones established by obliging mini-states. Already a substantial amount of Eurocurrency business, though generated from New York, is booked in "banking havens" like the Bahamas and the

102. *Bundesbank Annual Report 1979*, pp. 49–50; Harvey D. Shapiro, "The U.S.: Taking the Lead," *Institutional Investor*, July 1979, p. 51. For details for such a scheme, see Wallich, "Euromarket Restraint," pp. 22–23.
103. David Marsh, "U.S. Move on Euromarkets Stands Little Chance," *Financial Times*, 7 June 1979.
104. For a statement of U.S. views, see "A Discussion Paper Concerning Reserve Requirements on Euro-Currency Deposits" (25 April 1979), in testimony of Henry C. Wallich, Hearings, *Eurocurrency Market Control*, pp. 206–22.
105. *IMF Survey* 9(1980):89. See p. 322, above, for an estimate of 40 percent as the share in Eurocurrency operations conducted by bank offices in the United Kingdom.
106. McKinnon, *Eurocurrency Market*, pp. 5–10.

Cayman Islands, and New York bank branches conduct offshore business on a large scale in Hong Kong and Singapore.[107]

To be sure, a somewhat analogous flight from regulation could occur even under a domiciliary system because mini-states could also attempt to establish regulation-free havens for banks domiciled locally. But since all major international banks have their head offices within large developed countries, it is unlikely, if all those countries agreed to supervise their banks' worldwide business, that local banks in the banking havens could attract the deposits necessary to compete with their more regulated brethren, at least for some years. Because of the risk of bank failure, a bank's "name" appears to be a crucial factor in attracting deposits.[108]

Since neither the domiciliary nor the territorial approach appears to be workable, at least in the absence of a change of policy by Britain and Switzerland, attention has focused on prudential concerns involving overconcentration of loans to particular countries. Agreement was announced in April 1980 by the Bank for International Settlements central banks that commercial banks headquartered within their territories would be required to consolidate their worldwide accounts, including all offshore assets and liabilities. Such consolidation would permit bank examiners to regulate offshore branches and subsidiaries on the same basis as domestic offices. The regulation could concentrate on country risk and on "maturity transformation," which refers to the additional risk undertaken by banks through borrowing at shorter maturities than they lend.[109] U.S. bank regulators had already undertaken such regulation, including on-site review of the books of offshore offices, but some central banks apparently did not yet have statutory authority to do

---

107. See discussion of offshore banks outside the Group of Ten countries in *IMF Survey* 6(1977):180; Ian McCarthy, "Offshore Banking Centers: Benefits and Costs," *Finance and Development* 16(December 1979):45; *International Debt, the Banks, and U.S. Foreign Policy*, A Staff Report Prepared for the Use of the Subcommittee on Foreign Economic Policy of the Senate Committee on Foreign Relations (August 1977), pp. 18–20 (hereafter cited *Report on International Debt*).

108. See testimony of Robert Aliber, Hearings, *Eurocurrency Market Control*, p. 95; see also André Jacquemont, *L'Émission des emprunts euro-obligatoires, pouvoir bancaire et souverainetés étatiques* (1976), pp. 9, 52–53, 57–58.

109. BIS communiqué, *IMF Survey* 9(1980):113, 118. The central bank governors favored strengthening of "regular and systematic monitoring of international banking developments" and establishment of a Standing Committee on Euromarkets to report at least twice a year. Recognizing the increased risks facing the international banking system, they reaffirmed support for actions already taken "with regard to the supervision of banks' international business on a consolidated basis, improved assessment of country risk exposure, and the development of more comprehensive and consistent data for monitoring the extent of banks' maturity transformation." Ibid. p. 118; IMF, *International Capital Markets*, pp. 13–15. See also Peter Gutmann, "Assessing Country Risk," *National Westminster Bank Quarterly Review*, May 1980, pp. 58–67.

so.[110] On the basis of these national reviews of consolidated balance sheets, a standing BIS committee on Euromarkets will conduct a safety review of international bank lending twice annually.

This regulation will be national, with each BIS country remaining free to apply whatever substantive limits it chooses on the rate of growth of credit extension by its banks. The agreement thus does not address the question of control of liquidity at all. Two earlier agreements, however, do indirectly serve to slow the growth of the Eurocurrency market. One was the 1971 agreement of the Group of Ten countries not to deposit reserves in the Euromarket.[111] The purpose was apparently to prevent such reserves from providing the base for any multiple expansion of credit, at least beyond that resulting from the deposit of reserve currency holdings in banks in the reserve country. The second was the agreed assumption of lender-of-last-resort responsibility by central banks. In 1974 the Group of Ten central bankers issued a general statement of responsibility, to which the United States, Japan, and almost thirty other countries subscribed.[112] Britain later forced an agreement on countries whose banks maintain banking offices in London to assume a lender-of-last-resort responsibility for the solvency of such banks. The motivation, beyond reducing the possibility of an international banking panic, appears to have been to induce the various national banking regulatory agencies to pay more attention to the activities of their offshore offices in London.[113] Those earlier agreements not only do not restrict liquidity creation directly, but they also do not deal with the possible role of offshore banking in subverting domestic monetary policy.

Even this brief review of issues in international financial regulation reveals three primary points at which they intersect with international monetary issues. First, as noted earlier, commercial banks are a vastly more important

110. On U.S. regulation, see "A New Supervisory Approach to Foreign Lending," *Federal Reserve Bank of New York Quarterly Review* 3(Spring 1978):1. The Bank of England, for example, did not begin to review consolidated accounts until 1980. See "Bank of England Begins Study of Banks' Foreign Exposure," *Financial Times*, 25 January 1980. On legal impediments to consolidated balance sheet supervision in Germany, where banking regulation reaches offshore branches but not offshore subsidiaries, see *Bundesbank Annual Report 1979*, p. 50.

111. *IMF Annual Report 1972*, p. 16.

112. The central bankers' statement, issued at Basle on 9 September 1974, read: "The Governors . . . had an exchange of views on the problem of the lender of last resort in the Euro-markets. They recognized that it would not be practical to lay down in advance detailed rules and procedures for the provision of temporary liquidity. But they were satisfied that means are available for that purpose and will be used if and when necessary." Quoted by Henry C. Wallich in his statement before the Senate Permanent Subcommittee on Investigations, Committee on Government Operations, 16 October 1974. Printed in *Federal Reserve Bulletin*, 1974, p. 760. See also *Report on International Debt*, pp. 26–27.

113. *BIS 45th Report 1975*, pp. 133–34. See also J. Carter Murphy, *The International Monetary System* (1979), pp. 217–18; Patrick Heininger, "Liability of U.S. Banks for Deposits Placed in their Foreign Branches," *Law and Policy in International Business* 11(1979):1024; IMF, *International Capital Markets*, pp. 4, 13.

source of balance-of-payments financing than the Fund. Second, the hesitation of the Group of Ten governments to interfere significantly with the growth of Eurocurrency lending reflects an unspoken revolution in attitudes toward capital flows. Official opinion in most developed countries has shifted from a preference for controlling capital flows to a reluctance to do anything to interfere with the free movement of capital. The time when Keynes assumed that all countries would maintain capital controls gave way to the 1958–71 period, when private capital flows were widely viewed as the principal threat to the international monetary system, and then to the present, when the Eurocurrency market is viewed (primarily as a result of its efficient recycling of the OPEC surpluses after the 1973–74 oil price increases) as the primary means of providing balance-of-payments financing and thereby avoiding exchange controls. This acceptance of the Eurocurrency market as desirable represents a considerable shift in attitudes since the Committee of Twenty refused to accept U.S. proposals for changing the Fund's rules on capital controls and emphasized the need to cooperate to limit "disequilibrating capital flows."[114]

The third point of intersection between the financial regulation and international monetary issues is international liquidity. Not only has the fear of inadequate liquidity that characterized the 1960s and the creation of the SDR evaporated, but the concern with excessive liquidity that was pervasive in the early and mid-1970s has also been pushed into the background. Although strong theoretical arguments can be made against viewing liquidity as a problem and although the means by which excessive liquidity can generate inflation is a subject of considerable controversy in economics,[115] the dominant reason for the retreat from official concern is probably the growing realization that as a practical matter nothing can be done in the present economic and political circumstances to curb the overall growth of the Eurocurrency market. IMF Managing Director H. Johannes Witteveen campaigned in the mid-1970s for an international effort to control liquidity, not merely international bank lending to countries but also "offshore private liquidity." The Fund under his successor, Jacques de Larosière, has taken a more pragmatic line in which it has continued to emphasize questions con-

---

114. See pp. 247–49.
115. Compare Gottfried Haberler, "How Important Is Control Over Resources?" in *The New International Monetary System*, ed. Robert A. Mundell and Jacques J. Polak (1977), pp. 111–32; H. Robert Heller, "International Reserves and World-Wide Inflation," *IMF Staff Papers* 23(1976):61–87; Robert Triffin, *Gold and the Dollar Crisis: Yesterday and Tomorrow*, Princeton Essays in International Finance no. 132 (1978), pp. 11–12; and Thomas D. Willett, *International Liquidity Issues* (1980). On worldwide inflation in the 1970s, see Harry G. Johnson, *Money, Balance-of-Payments Theory, and the International Monetary Problem*, Princeton Essays in International Finance no. 124 (1977); David I. Meiselman and Arthur B. Laffer, eds., *The Phenomenon of Worldwide Inflation* (1975).

cerning the "adequacy" of reserves in preference to the question whether liquidity may be excessive.[116]

V. THE UNIVERSALITY OF THE FUND:
THE EUROPEAN MONETARY SYSTEM (EMS)

Just as the rapid growth of commercial bank lending has thrust the Fund off the center of the liquidity-provision stage, so too the Fund faces threats to its position as the universal world organization concerned with international monetary affairs. This time the threat is not from the Bank for International Settlements or the Group of Ten, both of which have played relatively modest roles since the 1960s in international monetary affairs. Rather, as was the case with the European Payments Union in the first decades of the Fund's existence, the threat is from regionalism. Now, as then, the question whether the significant "action" on monetary affairs will occur in a worldwide forum or in a series of regional forums, is posed squarely by the emergence of a European monetary institution.[117] Although regional monetary bodies grandly appear and then recede into relative insignificance from time to time, the European Monetary System (EMS) is both ambitious in scope and, at least at its present if not necessarily at its planned scale, a viable institution.[118]

The EMS is of interest in any study of international rules for several reasons in addition to its implicit challenge to the IMF's role. Because it constitutes a regional par value system, it is a possible model for any future worldwide par value system. The EMS is not only "very much an attempt to achieve [a] system of 'fixed but adjustable' parities,"[119] but it is also an effort to put into use the concept of objective indicators, studied at length in the Committee of Twenty.[120] Moreover, the C-20 concepts of symmetry between surplus and deficit countries and of multicurrency intervention also play a prominent role.[121] Finally, the EMS may also turn out to be a first step toward rehabilitating gold as an integral part of the international monetary system.

116. For the Witteveen approach, see *IMF Survey* 4(1975):316; "The International Monetary Fund and Euro-liquidity," *International Currency Review* 10, no. 5 (1978):19–20. The Fund under de Larosière adopted its pragmatic approach even before the OPEC oil price increases of 1979 and 1980. See, for example, *IMF Annual Report* 1978, pp. 43–50; see also IMF, *International Capital Markets*, p. 15.
117. See discussion of the European Payments Union and predecessors pp. 170–71.
118. On other regional monetary arrangements, see the section on Regional Arrangements in part one of the *IMF Annual Report on Exchange Arrangements and Exchange Restrictions* for relevant years.
119. Samuel Brittan, "EMS: a Compromise That Could be Worse Than Either Extreme," *World Economy* 2(1979):22.
120. See discussion of objective indicators, pp. 222–29.
121. See the discussion of symmetry and of multicurrency intervention pp. 239–43.

From Snake to EMS

The EMS is a descendant of the earlier European snake.[122] The snake had proved to be a failure on its original terms, and so it might appear contradictory that the EMS is considerably more ambitious than the snake. The contradiction can be reconciled in several ways.

The snake failed primarily in the sense that certain key members were not able to adhere to fixed rates, even with occasional discrete devaluations against the strongest currency, the German mark. They consequently elected to float. France, for example, dropped out twice, once from January 1974 to July 1975 and then again in 1976. Italy dropped out once and for all in 1973. The United Kingdom, and with it Ireland, adhered to the scheme for less than two months—from 1 May to 23 June 1972. The snake was thus a failure as an instrument of European integration.[123] The "first and cardinal feature" of the EMS is thus "the return of France, Italy and Ireland to a snake-type adjustable-peg system."[124]

The snake was more successful in its role as a regional currency area. But it was a German mark area, not a European Community area. The snake came to consist of "a 'hegemonial' currency and three EC satellites: the Benelux currencies and the Danish krone, with two non-EC monies—the Norwegian and Swedish kroner—in an associated status."[125] The relative resistance of the currencies in the resulting mark area to the inflation that engulfed the rest of the world, plus the strong felt need in Europe to arrive at a common policy against the dollar, led to an attempt to create a more broadly based and institutionally-improved snake in order to achieve "a zone of monetary stability in Europe."[126] Although the EMS was simultaneously envisaged as a major initiative in relaunching the process of European integration, Britain chose to stay aloof, despite special provisions allowing it and Italy to maintain 6 percent rather than 2¼ percent margins.[127]

122. See discussion of the snake pp. 193–94. For a summary of major differences between the snake and the EMS, see Gold, *Fourth Survey*, pp. 63–64.
123. Roland Vaubel, *Choice in European Monetary Union*, Institute of Economic Affairs Occasional Paper 55 (1979), p. 9. See chronology in Niels Thygesen, "The Emerging European Monetary System: Precursors, First Steps and Policy Options," in *EMS: The Emerging European Monetary System*, ed. Robert Triffin, offprint from the *Bulletin of the National Bank of Belgium* (1979), pp. 91–92, 125.
124. Vaubel, *Choice in EMS*, p. 16.
125. Thygesen, "Emerging European Monetary System," p. 92.
126. Resolution of the European Council on the establishment of the European Monetary System (EMS) and related matters (Brussels, 5 December 1978), part A, para. 1.1, European Communities Monetary Committee, *Compendium of Community Monetary Texts* (1979), p. 40.
127. "EC countries with presently floating currencies may opt for wider margins up to ±6% at the outset of the EMS; these margins should be gradually reduced as soon as economic conditions permit." Resolution of 5 December 1978, part A, para. 3.1, *Compendium*, p. 41. Britain did participate in the EMS in more limited ways. See Peter Coffey, "The European Monetary System—Six Months Later," *Three Banks Review*, no. 124 (December 1979), pp. 75–76.

The EMS, like the IMF, has a number of different facets. For the present discussion, the three most important are the provisions on exchange rates and intervention, on reserve assets, and on balance-of-payments financing.

Exchange Rates and EMS Intervention

In determining when a member had a duty to intervene, the snake arrangements relied upon what became later known as a "parity grid" in which each currency is measured against each other currency. The band of permissible fluctuation of one currency against another was 2¼ percent under the snake. When one currency (say a weak currency) reached the edge of this band of fluctuation, at least one other currency (a strong currency) was automatically at the other edge. Hence, both the weak and strong currencies were under an obligation to intervene.[128] The snake did not, however, constitute a full-fledged multicurrency intervention system; intervention tended to be in U.S. dollars, with strong currency countries buying dollars and weak currency countries selling them, often simultaneously, because the bilateral intrasnake exchange markets were usually not sufficiently liquid to support central bank intervention.[129] The EMS was to operate on the principle that intervention would normally be in EMS currencies rather than the dollar[130] with the specific objective of avoiding "simultaneous reverse interventions."[131]

In the negotiations leading to the EMS, the nonsnake countries, especially France, objected to the parity grid approach because they expected to have relatively weak currencies. They believed that even where the strong- rather than the weak-currency country actually intervened, the weak-currency country would have to bear the economic burden because of the settlement requirements. Under those requirements the weak-currency country had to buy back any of its own currency purchased by the intervening strong-currency country even though the need for intervention might stem from, say, an inflow of U.S. dollars into the strong-currency country (which at that time was usually Germany).[132] France therefore proposed to substitute for the parity grid system what became known as the "ECU basket system."

Under the French proposal the European Currency Unit (ECU) would become the numeraire. The ECU for this purpose would be strictly a unit

128. Resolution of the Council and of the Representatives of the Governments of the Member States of 21 March, 1972, para. III:1, *Compendium*, p. 31. See *Monetary Organization of the Community, Bulletin of the European Communities*, Supplement 12/73 (1973), p. 4.

129. On the consequences for the rate of the dollar vis-à-vis particular snake currencies, see Joanne Salop, "Dollar Intervention within the Snake," *IMF Staff Papers* 24(1977):64–76. On the lack of liquidity in inter-European exchange markets, see comments by Wolfgang Rieke, director of the Deutsche Bundesbank, in Triffin, *EMS*, p. 176.

130. Annex to the Conclusions of the Presidency of the European Council (Bremen, 6 and 7 July 1978), para. 3, *Compendium*, p. 39 (hereafter cited Bremen Annex); Resolution of 5 December 1978, para. 3.3, ibid. p. 41.

131. Bremen Annex, para. 3, ibid. p. 39.

132. See "The European Monetary System," *European Economy*, no. 3 (July 1979), p. 71.

of account, valued by a basket of all of the EMS currencies and using essentially the same weighted average approach used by the IMF to value the SDR.[133] Under the proposal each member's currency would have a central value defined in terms of the ECU. Margins would be imposed on either side of the ECU. The duty of intervention would fall on that country whose currency's market value diverged most from its defined value in ECUs. Moreover, the duty of buying back one's own currency acquired in intervention would be postponed until such time as the two currencies' relative exchange rate position was reversed.[134]

Germany objected strongly to the French proposal. Since the mark was usually the strong currency, Germany expected to bear the economic burden of intervention, especially under the settlement provisions advanced by the French. The result, Germany argued, would inevitably be inflationary because German purchases of weak currencies for marks would increase the German money supply, and the weak currencies would have less incentive to pursue noninflationary economic policies.[135]

The resulting German-French stand-off was thus a conflict concerning the degree of symmetry in the EMS system and was analytically similar to the debate over symmetry in the C-20 discussions. A Belgian compromise proposal, combining the parity grid with the ECU basket method, resulted in the present EMS intervention and settlement system. The essence of the compromise was that the parity grid would define the intervention obligations, but would be supplemented by an objective indicator, based on the ECU basket approach, to signal when any particular country should undertake adjustment measures.[136]

The objective indicator constitutes perhaps the most original aspect of the EMS. It takes the form of a "divergence indicator," which creates for each currency a "threshold of divergence" at 75 percent of its maximum deviation under the parity grid. When a currency crosses its threshold of divergence, a "presumption" is created that it should adjust by such measures as "diversified intervention," "measures of domestic monetary policy," "changes in central rates," and "other measures of economic policy."[137] The divergence indicator is, of course, no more than a measure to test how far an exchange rate has diverged. It is not an objective indicator of how large a policy change

133. For ways in which the ECU differs from the SDR, see Gold, *Fourth Survey*, pp. 48–50. See discussion of the SDR basket pp. 201–7 and 310–12, above.
134. *European Economy*, p. 71.
135. Ibid.; Thygesen, "Emerging European Monetary System," p. 110; Tom de Vries, *On the Meaning and Future of the European Monetary System*, Princeton Essays in International Finance, no. 138 (1980), pp. 19–20.
136. Gold, *Fourth Survey*, pp. 51–54. On the duty of intervention under the parity grid, see Resolution of 5 December 1978, part A, para. 3.1, *Compendium*, p. 41; *European Economy*, p. 73.
137. Resolution of 5 December 1978, part A, para. 3.6, *Compendium*, p. 41.

may be required to reduce the divergence or how great a parity change might be required to reestablish equilibrium.

The divergence indicator worked poorly in practice in the first year of the EMS. The Belgian compromise produced a structure of such bewildering complexity that Samuel Brittan, the British economic journalist, was moved to recall that "Bismarck, who fought a war over the [Schleswig-Holstein] issue, declared there were three people only who had understood it: an old clergyman, who had lost his reason; Palmerston, who had died; and Bismarck himself, who had forgotten all about it."[138] The complexity arises from three principal sources. First, each currency's central rate is defined in terms of the ECU, which is itself valued in terms of the market values of a basket composed of a specified number of units of each of the EMS currencies. This ECU valuation principle causes each currency's market movement to affect the value of the ECU (the extent depending upon that currency's weight in the ECU basket), and every currency's ECU value is therefore in turn affected. Second, there is a certain lack of coherence between the workings of the bilateral parity grid and that of the divergence indicator. Third, a layer of special rules is necessitated by the 6 percent margin for lira and the fact that sterling plays a role in the definition of the ECU even though Britain does not participate in the intervention system.[139] For the purposes of illustrating the difficulties likely to befall reform initiatives, and particularly technocratic solutions to economic problems that are negotiated through multilateral diplomacy, it suffices merely to note what apparently few, other than technicians, anticipated before it began to happen, namely, that EMS members would frequently reach the limits of their bilateral parity grid without ever having crossed the divergence threshold.[140]

The ECU as Reserve Asset

Like the SDR, the ECU was intended to be more than a unit of account. It was to be a "means of settlement between monetary authorities of the European Community"[141]—in short, a reserve asset. Therefore, a central institution had to "create" ECUs and the monetary authorities of EMS members had to hold them.

The transaction used to accomplish this objective was quite different from the SDR allocation system. Each EMS member was required at the outset

138. Brittan, "EMS," pp. 25–26.
139. For a technical analysis of the EMS intervention system, see Thygesen, "Emerging European Monetary System," pp. 109–15; and *European Economy*, pp. 72–80, 85–91. More general discussions, eliding most of the complexities, are to be found in *BIS 49th Report* 1979, pp. 144–48, and "The European Monetary System," *Bundesbank Monthly Report* 31(March 1979):11–18.
140. For an explanation of the circumstances in which this anomalous result is possible, see *European Economy*, pp. 85–88. See also Thygesen, "Emerging European Monetary System," pp. 113–14.
141. Resolution of 5 December 1978, part A, para. 2.2(d), *Compendium*, p. 40.

to swap 20 percent of its gold and 20 percent of its gross dollar reserves against a credit for a corresponding number of ECUs on the books of the European Monetary Cooperation Fund (EMCF).[142] These swaps are renewable each three months, and adjustments in the amounts are to be made at the beginning of each quarter to maintain the 20 percent ratio and to take account of changes in gold price and dollar exchange rate.[143]

The creation of ECUs differs in a number of respects from the creation of SDRs. ECUs, unlike SDRs, are backed by something else—namely, gold and dollars. ECUs are allocated on the basis of reserves, not quotas, with the result that a deficit country losing gold and dollar reserves also loses ECUs each quarter. As a special case of this principle, a depreciation of the dollar against gold (or vice versa) will have a differential impact on members' ECU holdings, depending upon their relative holdings of gold and dollars. SDRs, in contrast, are the numeraire for the IMF system, and a country losing dollar reserves, say by dollar depreciation, does not also lose SDRs.

The close link between ECUs and gold has the effect of mobilizing members' gold reserves, which in recent years have seldom been used at least by EMS members, and thereby making gold indirectly available in the settlement of payments imbalances. Moreover, gold is valued at the London free market price, thereby giving market price changes their full impact on international liquidity.[144]

The principal use envisaged for ECUs is in settlement of bilateral debts arising out of the EMS credit facilities established to finance exchange market intervention.[145] Thus, unlike the case of the SDR, it is not envisaged that ECUs will be used directly to obtain member currencies, except by agreement. Moreover, even in the settlement of debts, the legal tender character of ECUs is limited by the provision that a creditor central bank "shall not be obliged to accept settlement by means of ECUs of an amount more than 50% of its claim which is being settled."[146] Finally, the practical utility of ECUs is even more sharply limited by the three months duration of the underlying member-EMCF swap. In effect, ECUs are subject to a 100 percent reconstitution requirement each three months.

142. Ibid. para. 3.8, p. 41; Agreement of 13 March 1979 between the central banks of the Member States of the European Economic Community laying down the operating procedures for the European Monetary System, Article 17, *Compendium*, p. 60 (hereafter cited EMS Central Bank Agreement).
143. Ibid. Article 17.6. See Gold, *Fourth Survey*, pp. 57–58, on the implications of this method of "creating" ECUs.
144. EMS Central Bank Agreement, Article 17.4; de Vries, *Meaning of EMS*, p. 25. See David Marsh, "An Autumn of Discontent," *Financial Times*, 5 August 1980, on anxiety over resulting "inflation of international liquidity."
145. EMS Central Bank Agreement, Article 18.1. Interest is payable from net users to net acquirers of ECUs. Ibid. Article 19.1. ECUs can also be used to acquire dollars in order to meet a decline in a member's dollar reserves. Ibid. Article 18.2.
146. Ibid. Article 16.1.

These limitations on the ECU may be eliminated or reduced after the transitional phase, scheduled to last two years. It is not impossible that the ECU might be made fully as usable as the SDR. In view of the absence of an underlying ECU-link issue within the European Economic Community (EEC), comparable to the ever-present possibility that SDR allocation will come to be a means for a concessionary transfer to less-developed countries within the IMF system, there should be relatively less concern by creditor countries about the wealth distribution aspects of the ECU than has been the case for the SDR. Because of the relative wealth and solvency of the EMS members, nonmember countries might be interested in acquiring ECUs if the legal infrastructure provided for such a possibility. Similarly, and especially because the ECU is "backed" by gold and dollars, private sector firms might also want to acquire ECUs.

As in the case of the SDR, the effective yield on ECUs will be crucial to an expanded role for the ECU.[147] With the right characteristics, the ECU might become a serious competitor of the SDR even outside Europe. But such a possible development of the ECU as a store of value and means of payment lies in the future. At the time of this writing, it is by no means clear that, at the end of the two-year transitional period, the EMS members will be able to agree on the envisioned creation of a European Monetary Fund and "full utilization of the ECU as a reserve asset and a means of settlement."[148]

Balance-of-Payments Financing

The EMS financing arrangements are an outgrowth of prior snake facilities. They are of three kinds—very short-term financing, short-term monetary support, and medium-term financial assistance—with further special provision for "measures designed to strengthen the economies of the less prosperous member states."[149] In view of their complexity, attention to these financing facilities must here be limited to their size. But their size is crucial: putting aside the very short-term facility, which is in theory of unlimited amount, the initial short- and medium-term facilities totaled 25 billion ECU. It has been argued that, as a consequence, a member's access to EMS medium-term financial assistance would be at least twice as great as its quota in the Fund.[150] Comparisons on such a basis are necessarily inexact, especially as

147. *European Economy*, p. 80.
148. Resolution of 5 December 1978, part A, para. 1.4, *Compendium*, p. 40.
149. Ibid. part A, para. 4, and part B (Title), pp. 42–43. See *European Economy*, pp. 76–78.
150. See Jacques J. Polak, "The EMF: External Relations," *Banca Nazionale del Lavoro Quarterly Review*, no. 134 (September 1980), p. 364; de Vries, *Meaning of EMS*, pp. 22–24. In the first quarter of 1979 (when the EMS came into operation) the average value of one ECU was U.S. $1.35 and SDR 1.05. As the ECU is based on a basket of currencies its value varies according to the market movement of each component. *European Economy*, pp. 24–25; Samuel Brittan, "How EMS Will Work," *Financial Times*, 4 January 1979.

they do not take into account all possible sources of Fund financing, but the general point remains that the existence of the EMS financing facilities will tend to lessen an EMS member's reliance on the Fund.

Compatibility of the EMS with the IMF System

The basic resolution establishing the EMS states that the "EMS is and will remain fully compatible with the relevant articles of the IMF Agreement."[151] No doubt this pious declaration is correct and well intentioned. But with the ECU as a rival of the SDR, potentially even outside the EEC boundaries, and with the large financing facilities available within the EMS framework,[152] the political and economic compatibility of the EMS and IMF systems is less clear. The EMS is surely a greater potential threat to the IMF than the European Payments Union ever was.

The prospects for the EMS depend on two prime questions. The first concerns the shape of the EMS when and if the transition from the initial period is successfully completed. The second concerns the prospects for growth of the German mark as a reserve currency. These two questions are related. Just as the snake became a mark zone, so too the EMS might evolve into a currency bloc centered on the mark, with the mark in turn related to the dollar and yen as principal reserve currencies. Moreover, political and prestige considerations may lead European statesmen in the direction of attempting to find a role for the ECU transcending the EMS.[153] If, for example, the United States and Japan should come to hold ECUs as reserve assets, then the IMF would be driven even more surely into the role of a financing institution primarily for the benefit of less-developed countries.

The EMS mechanisms may constitute important precedents for another possible line of development—a return to par values or at least to pegged rates among the world's leading currencies under a key currency approach. The divergence indicator provides, as previously suggested, important experience with the concept of objective indicators. Already EMS proponents have argued that the experience of the EMS with small parity realignments has important lessons.[154] Strains within the EMS led to minor adjustments on two occasions during the first year, when adjustments to central rates

151. Resolution of 5 December 1978, part A, para. 5.3, *Compendium*, p. 42.
152. Polak, "EMF: External Relations," p. 364. It has been suggested, however, that the SDR has a competitive advantage over the ECU in offering more satisfactory diversification, in that it is not purely European-based. Thygesen, "Private Use of ECU," p. 24.
153. See the brief comments of a key Bank of England official suggesting such a role for the ECU in Christopher McMahon, "The Long-Run Implications of the European Monetary System," in *The European Monetary System; Its Promise and Prospects*, ed. Philip H. Trezise (1979), p. 89 (hereafter cited Trezise, *EMS*).
154. See *European Economy*, pp. 78–79; Jacques van Ypersele de Strihou, "Operating Principles and Procedures of the European Monetary System," in Trezise, *EMS*, p. 9. Cf. Roland Vaubel, "Why the EMS May Have To Be Dismantled," *Euromoney* 12(January 1980):78, 86. For the system's effectiveness in stabilizing intracommunity exchange rates in its first year, see Peter

reflected changes in fundamental conditions that could not be adequately offset by interest rate differentials.[155]

One interpretation of these small parity changes is that the EMS has informally adopted a crawling peg system. A Belgian official has argued that small enough parity changes, especially if made early enough and not controlled by a formula or other specific criteria, can avoid the so-called disequilibrating capital flow problem that beset the Bretton Woods system:

> Often one hears that speculation cannot but gain from a system of stable and adjustable exchange rates. That is not right. To the extent that changes in central rates are smaller than twice the width of the margin of fluctuation it is not at all sure that speculation will gain. If before the change of the central rate a currency is at the floor rate, and after the change is at the ceiling, speculation will not have gained, provided the change in the central rate is smaller than twice the margin.[156]

More experience with this variant of a crawling peg will be required to test this proposition. Certainly it can only be correct so long as required parity changes are not large. The EMS can provide the necessary experience.

VI. The Future of Gold

Any discussion of issues concerning gold in the 1980s should make a sharp distinction between the role of gold in the international monetary system and the steps that might be taken with respect to the Fund's holdings of gold. The latter is likely to be on the agenda even if, and perhaps especially if, gold is somehow actually phased out of the international monetary system.

The Fund's 100 odd million ounces of gold represent an enormous body of assets, especially at the gold prices experienced in recent years. At $500 per ounce, the Fund's gold is worth $50 billion, some three times the gross financial assistance provided by the Fund in the peak year of 1977.[157] The fertile minds of Fund and national officials do not fail to consider ways of using those assets to remedy the limitations of the Fund and of other reserve assets. The Trust Fund worked once, and could be revived to provide added

Riddell, "Bright spot in Community Scene: European Monetary System," World Banking Survey III, *Financial Times*, 19 May 1980.

155. The adjustments occurred on 23 September and 30 November 1979. *Bundesbank Annual Report 1979*, p. 59. See also *BIS 50th Report* 1980, pp. 137, 142–43; Pardee, p. 52.

156. Van Ypersele, "Operating Principles," p. 10.

157. *IMF Annual Report* 1980, p. 76, chart 15. The figure of $500 per ounce represents a conservative mid-1980 estimate of the market price of gold. When gold sales ended in May 1980, the IMF had reduced its gold holdings by one-third to approximately 100 million ounces. *IMF Survey* 9(1980):145.

resources for lending to less-developed countries.[158] Gold could be used to provide the resources for a subsidy account. It could serve as collateral, explicit or implicit, for Fund borrowing. It could be used to bridge financial gaps in other schemes, as it nearly did in the 1979–80 negotiations over a substitution account.[159]

Reform initiatives of one kind or another are thus likely to be successful in harnessing the financial power embodied in the Fund's gold. Whether the role of gold in the international monetary system will yield to such reform initiatives is a different question. Certainly U.S. and IMF officials seeking "to phase gold out of the system" found that incantation accomplished little, even when the Articles of Agreement were amended to replace gold formally with the SDR.[160] As the manager of the Bank for International Settlements observed in 1980, "Gold may have no official status in the monetary system. But it is not unloved."[161]

Indeed, it is far from clear what objective indicators could be established to tell an observer whether, at any particular time, gold was becoming more or less important in the international monetary system. It is not even possible to say with any conviction whether gold was a more or less important factor at the end of the 1970s than it was, say, at the time generalized floating began in 1973. Although the Fund Articles of Agreement accorded it a less important role, its greatly increased price made it, when valued at market prices, a much larger portion of world reserves. The free market price of gold rose for the first time above $250 per ounce in 1979, reaching a peak of more than $800 an ounce in early 1980, and then returned to the $400–$700 range.[162] The effect on market price valuation of gold reserves was dramatic. By the end of 1979 official world gold reserves increased in market value to $485 billion, whereas nongold reserves totaled only $355 billion. Just three years earlier, at the end of 1976, the comparable figures had been $136 billion and $216 billion respectively. As a result, it has been argued that by 1979 gold had "re-established its role as the principal reserve asset."[163]

158. See discussion pp. 272–73. The Fund provided for termination of the Trust Fund in 1981 and transfer of SDR 750 million of its resources to the Subsidy Account. "Instrument Establishing the Supplementary Financing Facility Subsidy Account," Section 4, *IMF Survey* 10(1981):10.

159. See discussion pp. 313–14.

160. The Report to Board of Governors by Committee of Twenty, 14 June 1974, declared that "the SDR should become the principal reserve asset, with the role of gold and of reserve currencies being reduced." IMF, *International Monetary Reform: Documents of the Committee of Twenty* (1974), p. 5.

161. René Larre, quoted in David Marsh, "Gold Suppliers Get Wise to a Surge in Demand," *Financial Times*, 7 July 1980.

162. *BIS 49th Report* 1979, p. 152; *BIS 50th Report* 1980, pp. 147–48; Michael G. Martin, "The Changing Gold Market, 1978–80," *Finance and Development* 17(December 1980):40–43.

163. John Makinson, "Concealed Buffer for Central Banks," *Financial Times*, 30 July 1980, supplement on gold (hereafter cited Makinson). See also *IMF Annual Report* 1980, p. 59, table 14; gold accounted for 57 percent of the total value of world reserves in May 1980. See also *BIS*

The higher price was increasingly recognized in countries' calculation of their own reserves, as more and more countries adopted some market-related method of calculating the value of gold reserves and abandoned the use of the old official price.[164] The allocation of ECUs against gold, with gold valued at the London market price, provided a means of realizing on the higher price of gold without actually selling it. One of the questions about the significance of the higher price of gold is whether it could be sustained if monetary authorities actually supplied gold freely to the market in the same way they supplied dollars in times of payments deficits. Despite the resilience of the gold market in the face of Trust Fund sales, U.S. Treasury sales and sales by other monetary authorities, gold has remained "at the bottom of the pile" for most governments.[165] The EMS issuance of ECUs against gold valued at the market price is, in this light, a potentially important way of remonetizing gold without disturbing its market price.[166] The contribution of the EMS to a revitalized role for gold may in fact turn out to be one of its principal long-term effects.

A Return to the Gold Standard?

A possible return to the gold standard is a subject that attracts many popular writers on monetary affairs and some economists as well. Interest in such a return rises when inflation seems most serious because the gold standard represents financial probity and price stability. But few advocates spell out exactly what they mean by "the" gold standard, apparently assuming that everyone understands by that term the perfectly automatic system that operated before World War I.[167] The increasing popularity of proposals for a return to the gold standard represents more an expression of lack of confidence in money and in the economic policies of contemporary governments than any concrete plan for a radical reform of the international monetary system.[168]

Any specific proposal by a government for a return to the pre–World War I gold standard would be met by a host of practical objections. Proponents of a gold standard rarely make clear how, in democracies, voters and interest groups can be persuaded to abandon the insistence on government action— responsibility for employment, interest rate policy, social welfare transfers, and all of the other policy objectives that led to the abandonment of the

50th Report 1980, p. 151. The BIS points out the difficulty of establishing "the actual increase in the effective value of gold reserves." Ibid. p. 150.

164. Gold, *Floating Currencies* (1977), pp. 52–54; Gold, *Third Survey*, pp. 33–34; Makinson surveys national gold pricing practices as of July 1980.

165. Canada sold gold in 1980. *Bundesbank Annual Report* 1979, p. 58; "Canada To Sell More Gold from Reserves," *Financial Times*, 6 August 1980.

166. See discussion pp. 332–33. On the effect of the use of gold market valuation of ECUs, see *IMF Annual Report* 1980, p. 60.

167. This view represents the mythical version of the gold standard, discussed pp. 15–17.

168. See, however, the proposals in Arthur B. Laffer, *Reinstatement of the Dollar: The Blueprint*, Economic Study, A. B. Laffer Associates (29 February 1980), pp. 3–5.

interwar version of the gold standard in the 1930s. Political innocence about government spending and monetary policy was lost, and it is difficult to see how it can be reestablished.

Opponents of a gold standard proposal would surely point to the great volatility of the gold price in recent years as making gold a singularly inappropriate anchor to which to tie not only a new international monetary system but also the fate of each national economy. To meet this point it is often proposed that the principal central banks peg the price of gold.

The difficulties faced by commodity stabilization and buffer stock plans suggest the difficulties that any gold-pegging plan might encounter. Such proposals confront two kinds of problems. The first is the economic problem of how to make such a pegging operation successful. Much of course would turn on the initial price chosen.[169] Although the recent volatility of the gold price makes a correct choice difficult, the difficulties can be exaggerated. The price was successfully pegged throughout the Bretton Woods period. Governments have, in principle, an unlimited amount of their own currency available to support the price of gold, though they may have to pay inflationary consequences if they in effect print money to do so. Many have vast stocks of gold available for sale to prevent the gold price from rising. The Fund's gold might be used in support of such an agreement. A product in which reserve stocks are roughly forty times as large as annual production is obviously different from commodities like tin or coffee.

The second problem involved in pegging the gold price arises from the legal and institutional arrangements for sharing the burden of doing so. The United States unilaterally undertook that burden at Bretton Woods, even though it did not stand ready to buy and sell at the $35 per ounce price except in transactions with official institutions. Only later did burden sharing arise, and that was because the private market price was pegged. The Gold Pool of 1961 was the device through which this sharing was accomplished, though it broke down in 1968 when the two-tier system was adopted.[170]

The largest problem connected with burden sharing, and hence with any policy of gold price pegging, is the underlying exchange rate scheme. The greater the reliance on exchange rate changes and particularly on floating, the more complicated must be the arrangements for allocation of the responsibility for intervention and for risk of loss. Moreover, each exchange rate change becomes a gold price change in at least one country. Hence, the greater the volatility of exchange rates, the greater the opportunities for speculation in gold markets and the more often the resolve of the pegging central banks is likely to be tested.

169. For one approach to choosing the pegging price, see ibid. pp. 4–5.
170. See discussion of the Gold Pool, pp. 137–38.

The pegging of the gold price, however successful, would not constitute a return to the gold standard. Accomplishment of the goals of many gold standard proponents would require some more direct link between national currencies and gold. A system in which countries can escape the discipline envisaged by gold standard advocates through repeated devaluations offers few advantages. Indeed, it would merely put the world back in the same position that all countries other than the United States were in during the Bretton Woods period. The pre-1914 gold standard involved redemption of currency in gold at the instance of private parties and the circulation of gold coin as well. And it also involved a direct link between the money supply, or at least the supply of currency, and the quantity of gold in the coffers of the monetary authorities. As Edward M. Bernstein has noted, "The significant characteristic of the classical gold standard was not that the currency was defined in terms of gold or even that it was redeemable (convertible) in gold, but that the expansion of the money supply was limited by the gold reserves."[171] It takes a considerable stretch of imagination to conceive of modern governments agreeing to accept any such constraints on their economic policies, and an even greater leap of faith to expect any such agreement to gain the credibility that would be necessary for long-run success. Who would believe that modern governments would continue to tie their hands with these gold standard obligations in the face of popular dissatisfaction and electoral opposition?

For these reasons it is unlikely that a return to a gold standard could be accomplished through technocratic reform, and especially through multilateral diplomatic negotiations. But a return by national action in one or two key countries is not inconceivable. It might become possible if unprecedentedly high rates of inflation were destroying the fabric of political life and creating a social revolution in even advanced industrialized countries. The conditions might then be created in which the government and the people would be willing to forego the luxury of flexibility in fiscal and monetary policies and submit themselves to the external control of an arbitrary and unyielding external standard like gold for the sake of economic and social stability. The runaway German inflation of 1923 was brought to a halt in part through the device of purportedly backing the currency with land; that it might not work or was at base legerdemain did not matter to the populace, which was ready to accept anything that might bring the juggernaut of inflation to a halt. Surely a gold standard is a more plausible and rational economic mechanism than the German rentenmark scheme.[172]

171. Edward M. Bernstein, "The History of the International Monetary Fund, 1966–71," *Finance and Development* 14(December 1977):17.
172. On the rentenmark scheme, see Leland B. Yeager, *International Monetary Relations: Theory, History and Policy*, 2d ed. (1976), p. 315; William Adams Brown, Jr., *The International Gold Standard Reinterpreted, 1914–1934* (1940), 1:362–65.

The fact that the gold standard developed at the national level and became an international system only through the interaction of separate national systems rather than through any international agreement lends some plausibility to the notion of a gold standard starting in one country and then, having proved itself there, spreading into an international system through emulation by other countries. Yet what country would be first? Any country so racked with inflation that it would be prepared to accept the rigors of the gold standard would surely long since have lost most of its reserves, unless it had previously refused to intervene to support its exchange rate. Certainly the United States would find it difficult to move to a gold standard in the pre-1914 sense since its reserves, measured net of external liabilities, are negative, even when gold is valued at the market price.[173] Thus, even the notion of a gold standard, spreading outward from one or two successful countries, is probably only a nostalgic fairy tale.

On the other hand, the nostalgia for a gold standard might be an important factor supporting a return to a fixed-rate system. Against the background of the floating period since 1973, a fixed-rate system with several governments willing to support their currencies through gold sales in addition to foreign exchange market intervention could be presented under the gold standard banner. But it would be far from the pre-1914 model. Indeed, it is hard to imagine any prompt return to immutably fixed rates as opposed to an adjustable peg of the late 1960s variety or a crawling peg of the EMS variety.

VII. REFORM AND EVOLUTION: THE ROLE OF RULES

Radical solutions like the gold standard or a comprehensive reconstruction of the international monetary system along the lines of the U.S. proposal to the Committee of Twenty are thus unlikely outcomes for the 1980s. The more probable lines of development lie along two competing paths. Those are, now as often in the past, reform and evolution. Down the reform path lie further legal and institutional efforts to promote the SDR and to bring the IMF back to the center of the international monetary system by expanding its borrowing and lending power and perhaps its regulatory power. Down the evolutionary path lies a movement toward a multiple reserve currency system.

Public choice, even within a single system, rarely takes the form of clearly opting for one alternative rather than another. Public choice normally involves

173. IMF, *International Financial Statistics* 33(July 1980):402–3. In the first quarter of 1978 (the most recent period for which *IFS* carries a figure for U.S. external liabilities) gross U.S. reserves (including gold valued at the official rate) were $19.2 billion; external liabilities were $207.2 billion. Even after valuing the gold component at a later market price figure of $500 per ounce, gross reserves amounted to no more than $146.2 billion, still less than external liabilities.

a compromise between alternatives—a welding of elements of different solutions. Reform and evolution, regulated and organic growth, remain strands
in the world's monetary development which are less competitive than mutually dependent and mutually sustaining. Although reform and evolution
may conceptually offer competing rather than complementary alternatives,
it is probable that the 1980s will involve both. The SDR is likely to be
promoted through one or more international schemes, and the Fund's lending
power is likely to be expanded. Meanwhile, evolution toward a multiple
reserve currency system is likely to continue or even accelerate.

The question is thus not whether reform or evolution will be chosen but
rather where the balance will lie. This author's hunch is that reform will
turn out to have less economic substance than evolution. But the crucial point
is that progress along either path is likely to involve new levels of complexity
in legal rules. Surely new and more complex rules would be required to
enhance the role of the SDR and to bring the IMF back to a more central
position in the system. But new rules are also likely to play some role in
what appear inevitable efforts to channel the operations of an evolving multiple reserve currency system.

The period since 1945 has shown that an international system of rules
such as that formulated at Bretton Woods requires pragmatic, evolutionary
interpretation as well as occasional constitutional reform. Some of the changes
merely gave shape and meaning to existing rules, but others were of such
originality that no one at the Bretton Woods negotiating table could have
foreseen them. Attempts to adapt the system to changing circumstances and
to incorporate the contributions of institutions and organizations legally external to it produced unprecedented and successful innovations such as the
General Arrangements to Borrow and, for a time, the Gold Pool. Attempts
at root-and-branch reform produced a new international financial instrument,
the SDR. Neither evolution nor reform could prevent the breakdown of the
Bretton Woods system in the early 1970s, but the arrival of the "floating
world" was accompanied by the intensive reform negotiations in the C-20
and by development of an alternative European "system." The changes and
crises of the late 1970s and early 1980s have produced a host of proposals
for new rules. These proposals include expansion of the role of the SDR
through formal schemes such as the substitution account as well as increased
and adapted use of existing recycling mechanisms, extension of activities of
international bodies other than the Fund, and increased regulation of international banking.

Rules thus have an inescapable and important role in the international
monetary system. This is obviously the case where the international community attempts to legislate. Reform can normally only be brought about
through the use of new rules. But experience with the international monetary

system also shows that even when change is basically evolutionary, rules can be expected to increase in detail and complexity.

The ultimate importance of rules that serve to institutionalize or to resist evolutionary change can be debated. An undue emphasis on formal rules may obscure more of the operation of the international monetary system than it exposes. Nevertheless, the role of rules in the development of the international monetary system must be recognized not merely by those who concern themselves day by day with the workings of the system but also by those who would gain a better appreciation of the system in practice.

REFERENCES

DOCUMENTS AND OFFICIAL PUBLICATIONS

Bank for International Settlements (BIS)

Bank for International Settlements, Annual Report, 1931–.
The Gold Exchange Standard. Monetary and Economic Department, C.B. 60. Basle, 1932. Mimeo.
The Sterling Area. Basle, 1953.

European Economic Community (EEC)

Compendium of Community Monetary Texts. Brussels-Luxembourg, 1979.
European Economy, No. 3 (July 1979). Luxembourg, 1979.
Monetary Organization of the Community. Bulletin of the European Communities, Supplement 12/73. Luxembourg, 1973.

France

Ministère des Affaires Étrangères. Commission de Publication des Documents Relatifs aux Origines de la Guerre 1939–1945. *Documents diplomatiques français 1932–1939.* 1st series, 1932–1935, vol. 3. Paris, 1967.

Germany

Monthly Report of the Deutsche Bundesbank, 1949–.
Report of the Deutsche Bundesbank [annual], 1957–.

Group of Ten

Communiqué of Ministers and Governors and Report of Deputies. [Frankfurt], 1966.
Report of the Study Group on the Creation of Reserve Assets. Washington, D.C., 1965 (Ossola report).
Statement by Ministers of the Group of Ten and Annex prepared by their Deputies. London, 1964.

International Monetary Fund (IMF)

Official Documents and Reports

Annual Report of the Executive Directors, 1946–.
Annual Report on Exchange Restrictions, 1950–.
Articles of Agreement of the International Monetary Fund. 1944.
———. *First Amendment* (1968).
———. *Second Amendment* (1976).
By-Laws, Rules and Regulations, 1947–.
International Financial Statistics, 1948–.
Selected Decisions of the Executive Directors, 1962– (title varies).
Summary Proceedings of the . . . Annual Meeting of the Board of Governors, 1946–.

Histories

Horsefield, J. Keith, and others. *The International Monetary Fund 1945–1965: Twenty Years of International Monetary Cooperation.* 3 vols. Washington, D.C., 1969.
De Vries, Margaret Garritsen. *The International Monetary Fund 1966–1971: The System Under Stress.* 2 vols. Washington, D.C., 1976.

Other Publications

IMF Staff Papers, 1950–.
IMF Survey, 1972–.
International Capital Markets: Recent Developments and Short-Term Prospects. Occasional Paper 1. Washington, D.C., 1980.
International Financial News Survey, 1948–1972.
International Monetary Reform: Documents of the Committee of Twenty. Washington, D.C., 1974.
International Reserves and Liquidity: A Study by the Staff of the International Monetary Fund. Washington, D.C., 1958.
International Reserves: Needs and Availability. Papers and Proceedings. Seminar at the International Monetary Fund, 1–3 June 1970. Washington, D.C., 1970.
Proposed Second Amendment to the Articles of Agreement of the International Monetary Fund: A Report by the Executive Directors to the Board of Governors. Washington, D.C., 1976.
Reform of the International Monetary System: A Report by the Executive Directors to the Board of Governors. Washington, D.C., 1972.
The Role of Exchange Rates in the Adjustment of International Payments: A Report by the Executive Directors. Washington, D.C., 1970.

League of Nations

The Course and Control of Inflation: A Review of Monetary Experience in Europe after World War I. II.A.6. Geneva, 1946.

International Currency Experience: Lessons of the Inter-war Period. II.A.4. Geneva, 1944.

The League of Nations Reconstruction Schemes in the Inter-war Period. Economic, Financial and Transit Department. II.A.C.59.M.59. Geneva, 1945.

Report on Exchange Control Submitted by a Committee composed of Members of the Economic and the Financial Committees (II. Economic and Financial). II.A.10. Geneva, 1938.

Second Interim Report of the Gold Delegation of the Financial Committee (II. Economic and Financial). II.A.2. Geneva, 1931.

United Kingdom

Bank of England Quarterly Bulletin, 1960–.

Parliament, Parliamentary Papers:

The Basle Facility and the Sterling Area. October 1968. Cmnd. 3787. London, 1968.

Committee on Finance & Industry Report. June 1931. Cmd. 3897. London, 1931. (Macmillan committee.)

Committee on National Expenditure Report. July 1931. Cmd. 3920. London, 1931. (May committee.)

Committee on the Working of the Monetary System: Principal Memoranda of Evidence. Vol. 1. London, 1960. (Radcliffe committee.)

First Interim Report of the Committee on Currency and Foreign Exchanges after the War. [Cd. 9182.] 1918. (Cunliffe committee.)

Report of the Committee on the Currency and Bank of England Note Issues. Cmd. 2393. London, 1925. (Bradbury committee.)

Report of the Royal Commission on Indian Currency and Finance. Vol. 2, Appendices. Cmd. 2687. London, 1926.

Reserves and Liabilities 1931 to 1945. September 1951. Cmd. 8354. London, 1951.

United States

Broadbent v. Organization of American States., 628 F. 2d 27 (D.C. Cir. 1980).

Congress. House. Committee on Banking and Currency. *Bretton Woods Agreements Act,* Hearings on H.R. 2211, 79th Cong., 1st sess., Vol. 2. Washington, D.C., 1945.

Congress. House. Committee on Banking and Currency. National Advisory Council on International Monetary and Financial Problems. *Special Report to the President and to the Congress on Special Borrowing Arrangements of the International Monetary Fund, January 1962.* 87th Cong., 2d sess. Washington, D.C., 1962.

Congress. House. Committee on Banking and Currency. Subcommittee on International Finance. *The International Monetary Fund's Special Drawing Rights Proposal and the Current International Financial Situation.* Hearing, 90th Cong., 2d sess. Washington, D.C., 1968.

Congress. House. Committee on Banking, Currency and Housing. National Advisory Council on International Monetary and Financial Policies. *Special Report to the President and to the Congress on Amendment of the Articles of Agreement of the International*

Monetary Fund and on an Increase in Quotas in the International Monetary Fund, April 1976. 94th Cong., 2d sess. Washington, D.C., 1976.

Congress. House. Committee on Banking, Currency and Housing. Subcommittee on International Trade, Investment and Monetary Policy. *To Provide for Amendment of the Bretton Woods Agreements Act.* Hearings on H.R. 13955, 94th Cong., 2d sess. Washington, D.C., 1976.

Congress. House. Committee on Banking, Finance and Urban Affairs. Subcommittee on Financial Institutions Supervision, Regulation and Insurance. *International Banking Operations.* Hearings, 95th Cong., 1st sess. Washington, D.C., 1977.

Congress. House. Committee on Banking, Finance and Urban Affairs. Subcommittee on International Trade, Investment and Monetary Policy. *To Amend the Bretton Woods Agreements Act to Authorize Consent to an Increase in the United States Quota in the International Monetary Fund.* Hearings on H.R. 5970, 96th Cong., 2d sess. Washington, D.C., 1980.

Congress. House. Committee on Banking, Finance and Urban Affairs. Subcommittees on Domestic Monetary Policy and on International Trade, Investment and Monetary Policy. *The Eurocurrency Market Control Act of 1979.* Hearings on H.R. 3962. Washington, D.C., 1979.

Congress. Senate. Committee on Banking and Currency. *Bretton Woods Agreements Act.* Hearings on H.R. 3314, 79th Cong., 1st sess. Washington, D.C., 1945.

Congress. Senate. Committee on Foreign Relations. *Special Drawing Rights in the International Monetary Fund.* Hearing on S.3423 and H.R. 16911, 90th Cong., 2d sess. Washington, D.C., 1968.

Congress. Senate. Committee on Foreign Relations. Subcommittee on Foreign Economic Policy. *International Debt, the Banks, and U.S. Foreign Policy.* Staff Report, 95th Cong., 1st sess. Washington, D.C., 1977.

Congress. Joint Economic Committee. Subcommittee on International Economics. *The IMF Gold Agreement.* Hearing, 94th Cong., 1st sess. Washington, D.C., 1976.

Department of State. *Postwar Foreign Policy Preparation 1939–1945.* General Foreign Policy Series 15; Publication 3580. Washington, D.C., 1949.

———. *Proceedings and Documents of the United Nations Monetary and Financial Conference, Bretton Woods, New Hampshire, July 1–22, 1944.* 2 vols. Washington, D.C., 1948.

Economic Report of the President Transmitted to the Congress February 1970. Washington, D.C., 1970.

Economic Report of the President Transmitted to the Congress January 1980. Washington, D.C., 1980.

Federal Reserve Bulletin, 1913–.

Federal Reserve System, Board of Governors. *Annual Report,* 1915–.

———. *Banking and Monetary Statistics.* Washington, D.C., 1943.

———. *Banking and Monetary Statistics 1941–1970.* Washington, D.C., 1976.

———. Notice of Proposed Rulemaking, International Banking Facilities. Docket No. R-0214. December 1980. Mimeo.

The Public Papers and Addresses of Franklin D. Roosevelt. 1933, 1934. Vols. 2 and 3. New York, 1938.

Public Papers of the Presidents of the United States. Richard Nixon. Containing the Public Messages, Speeches, and Statements of the President. 1971. Washington, D.C., 1972.

Treasury. *Annual Report of the Secretary of the Treasury . . . for the fiscal year ended June 30, 1973.* Washington, D.C., 1973.
———. *Statistical Appendix to Annual Report of the Secretary of the Treasury . . . for the fiscal year ended June 30, 1975.* Washington, D.C., 1976.

Other

Archives de Droit International et de Législation Comparée. Vol. 1. 1874.
The Consolidated Treaty Series. Edited by Clive Parry. Dobbs Ferry, N.Y.
World Bank. *Articles of Agreement of the International Bank for Reconstruction and Development.*

BOOKS AND ARTICLES

Acheson, A. L. K., J. F. Chant, and M. F. J. Prachowny, eds. *Bretton Woods Revisited.* Toronto, 1972.
Aliber, Robert Z. "Gresham's Law, Asset Preferences, and the Demand for International Reserves." *Quarterly Journal of Economics* 81(1967):628–38.
———. "The Integration of the Offshore and Domestic Banking System." *Journal of Monetary Economics* 6(1980):509–26.
———. *The International Money Game.* 3d ed. New York, 1979.
———. "Speculation in the Flexible Exchange Revisited." *Kyklos* 23(1970):303–12.
———. "Speculation in the Foreign Exchanges: The European Experience, 1919–1926." *Yale Economic Essays* 2(1962):171–245.
Altman, Oscar L. "Quotas in the International Monetary Fund." *IMF Staff Papers* 5(1956):129–50.
Amuzegar, Jahangir. "The North-South Dialogue: From Conflict to Compromise." *Foreign Affairs* 54(1976):547–62.
Anderson, Benjamin M. *Economics and the Public Welfare.* Princeton, 1949.
Aronson, Jonathan David, ed. *Debt and the Less Developed Countries.* Boulder, 1979.
———. "Financial Institutions in the International Monetary System." *Case Western Reserve Journal of International Law* 12(1980):341–61.
———. *Money and Power: Banks and the World Monetary System.* Sage Library of Social Research, vol. 66. Beverly Hills and London, 1977.
Artus, Jacques R., and Andrew D. Crockett. *Floating Exchange Rates and the Need for Surveillance.* Princeton Essays in International Finance, no. 127. Princeton, 1978.
———. "National Sovereignty and International Cooperation over Exchange Arrangements." *Case Western Reserve Journal of International Law* 12(1980):327–39.
Auboin, Roger. *The Bank for International Settlements, 1930–1955.* Princeton Essays in International Finance, no. 22. Princeton, 1955.
Aufricht, Hans. "Exchange Restrictions under the Fund Agreement." *Journal of World Trade Law* 2(1968):296–321.
Bagshaw, J. F. G. *Practical Banking.* London, 1920.
Balogh, T. "Britain's External Problem." *The Banker* 72(1944):7–15.
Bareau, Paul. "The Belgian, Dutch and Swiss Exchange Funds." *The Banker* 48(1938):33–40.
———. "The Sterling Area—Its Use and Abuse." *The Banker* 73(1945):131–36.

Bassett, R. *Nineteen Thirty-One: Political Crisis.* London, 1955.

Bauer, Peter. "Inflation, SDRs and Aid." *Lloyds Bank Review,* no. 109 (July 1973), pp. 31–34.

———. "The SDR Link Scheme—A Comment." *Lloyds Bank Review,* no. 111 (January 1974), pp. 42–43.

Bell, Geoffrey. "Easing the Strain on the Dollar." *Times* (London), 10 December 1979.

[Bernstein, Edward M.] EMB (Ltd.). "The Eurocurrency Market and International Monetary Problems." 23 August 1979. Mimeo.

Bernstein, Edward M. "The History of the International Monetary Fund 1966–1971." *Finance and Development* 14(December 1977):15–17.

———. "Scarce Currencies and the International Monetary Fund." *Journal of Political Economy* 53(1945):1–14.

Bernstein, Edward M., and others. *Reflections on Jamaica.* Princeton Essays in International Finance, no. 115. Princeton, 1976.

Birkenhead, Earl of. *The Prof in Two Worlds.* London, 1961.

Black, Cyril E., and Richard A. Falk, eds. *The Future of the International Legal Order.* Vol. 4: *The Structure of the International Environment.* Princeton, 1972.

Blanc, Jacques, and François Rigaux. *Droit Économique II.* Paris, 1979.

Bloomfield, Arthur I. *Monetary Policy under the International Gold Standard, 1880–1914.* New York, 1959.

———. "Operations of the American Exchange Stabilization Fund." *Review of Economics and Statistics* 26(1944):69–87.

———. *Short-Term Capital Movements under the Pre-1914 Gold Standard.* Princeton Studies in International Finance, no. 11. Princeton, 1963.

Blum, John Morton. *From the Morgenthau Diaries: Years of War, 1941–1945.* Vol. 3. Boston, 1967.

"British Banking 1966: A Survey by the Economist." *The Economist,* 18 June 1966, pp. i–xl.

Brittan, Samuel. "EMS: A Compromise That Could Be Worse Than Either Extreme." *The World Economy* 2(1979):1–30.

———. "How EMS Will Work." *Financial Times,* 4 January 1979.

———. "Oil Restores Sterling's Reserve Role." *Financial Times,* 11 December 1980.

———. *Steering the Economy: The Role of the Treasury.* Rev. ed. Harmondsworth, England, 1971.

Broches, Aron. "International Legal Aspects of the Operations of the World Bank." *Académie de Droit International, Recueil des Cours 1959* 98(1960), vol. 3, pp. 301–408.

Brown, Weir M. *World Afloat: National Policies Ruling the Waves.* Princeton Essays in International Finance, no. 116. Princeton, 1976.

Brown, William Adams, Jr. "Gold: Master or Servant?" *Foreign Affairs* 19(1941):828–41.

———. *The International Gold Standard Reinterpreted, 1914–1934.* 2 vols. New York, 1940.

Brunner, Karl. "Reflections on the State of International Monetary Policy." *Banca Nazionale del Lavoro Quarterly Review,* no. 131 (December 1979), pp. 361–75.

Bryant, Ralph C. *Money and Monetary Policy in Interdependent Nations.* Washington, D.C., 1980.

Cairncross, A. K. *Factors in Economic Development.* London, 1962.

Carli, Guido. "Perspectives on the Evolution of the International Monetary System." *Journal of Monetary Economics* 4(1978):405–14.

Carr, Jonathan. "Bonn: The Uncertain Stride of a New Political Giant." *Financial Times*, 11 April 1980.

Cassel, Gustav. *The Downfall of the Gold Standard.* London, 1936.

Chandler, Lester V. *American Monetary Policy 1928–1941.* New York, 1971.

————. *Benjamin Strong, Central Banker.* Washington, D.C., 1958.

Clapham, John. *The Bank of England: A History.* Vol. 2: *1797–1914.* Cambridge, 1945.

Clare, George. *A Money-Market Primer, and Key to the Exchanges.* 2d ed. London, 1903.

Clarke, Stephen V. O. *Central Bank Cooperation, 1924–31.* New York, 1967.

————. *Exchange-Rate Stabilization in the Mid-1930's: Negotiating the Tripartite Agreement.* Princeton Studies in International Finance, no. 41. Princeton, 1977.

————. *The Reconstruction of the International Monetary System: The Attempts of 1922 and 1933.* Princeton Studies in International Finance, no. 33. Princeton, 1973.

Clarke, W. M. *The City in the World Economy.* London, 1965.

Clay, Henry. *Lord Norman.* London, 1957.

[Clayton, Will]. *Selected Papers of Will Clayton.* Edited by Fredrick J. Dobney. Baltimore, 1971.

Coffey, Peter. "The European Monetary System—Six Months Later." *Three Banks Review*, no. 124 (December 1979), pp. 66–77.

Coffey, Peter, and John R. Presley. *European Monetary Integration.* London, 1971.

Cohen, Benjamin J. *The Future of Sterling as an International Currency.* London, 1971.

Cohen, Stephen D. *International Monetary Reform, 1964–69.* New York, 1970.

Columbia University School of Law. *Public International Development Financing in Chile.* Public International Development Financing. A Research Project, Report no. 8. 1964.

Coombs, Charles A. *The Arena of International Finance.* New York, 1976.

Cooper, Richard N. "Eurodollars, Reserve Dollars, and Asymmetries in the International Monetary System." *Journal of International Economics* 2(1972):325–44.

————. "Monetary Theory and Policy in an Open Economy." *Scandinavian Journal of Economics* 78(1976):146–63.

————. "Prolegomena to the Choice of an International Monetary System," *International Organization* 29(1975):63–97.

Craig, John. *The Mint: A History of the London Mint from A.D. 287 to 1948.* Cambridge, 1953.

Crockett, Andrew. *International Money: Issues and Analysis.* New York, 1977.

Cross, Colin. *Philip Snowden.* London, 1966.

Cutler, David S. "The Liquidity of the International Monetary Fund." *Finance and Development* 16(June 1979):36–39.

Daane, J. Dewey, and others. "The Evolving International Monetary Mechanism: The Report of the Group of Ten." *American Economic Review, Papers and Proceedings* 55(1965):150–88.

Dam, Kenneth W. *The GATT: Law and International Economic Organization.* Chicago, 1970.

————. *See also* Shultz, George P.

Dehem, Roger. *De l'étalon-sterling à l'étalon-dollar.* Paris, 1972.

De Onis, Juan. "Peru Unable to Pay Its Creditors . . . ." *New York Times*, 17 December 1977.

Despres, Emile, Charles P. Kindleberger, and Walter S. Salant. "The Dollar and World Liquidity." *The Economist*, 5 February 1966, pp. 526–29.

"The Deutsche Mark as an International Investment Currency." *Monthly Report of the Deutsche Bundesbank* 31(November 1979):26–34.

De Vries, Tom. "Jamaica, or the Non-Reform of the International Monetary System." *Foreign Affairs* 54(1976):577–605.

———. *On the Meaning and Future of the European Monetary System.* Princeton Essays · in International Finance, no. 138. Princeton, 1980.

Diebold, William, Jr. *Trade and Payments in Western Europe.* New York, 1952.

Dodwell, David. "The IMF Gives Pakistan a Fighting Chance." *Financial Times*, 5 December 1980.

Dornbusch, Rudiger. "The Theory of Flexible Exchange Rate Regimes and Macroeconomic Policy." *Scandinavian Journal of Economics* 78(1976):255–75.

Dreyer, Jacob S., Gottfried Haberler, and Thomas D. Willett, eds. *Exchange Rate Flexibility.* Washington, D.C., 1978.

Drummond, Ian M. *London, Washington, and the Management of the Franc, 1936–39.* Princeton Studies in International Finance, no. 45. Princeton, 1979.

Dulles, Eleanor Lansing. *The Bank for International Settlements at Work.* New York, 1932.

———. *The French Franc, 1914–1928.* New York, 1929.

Edwards, Richard W., Jr. "The Currency Exchange Rate Provisions of the Proposed Amended Articles of Agreement of the International Monetary Fund." *American Journal of International Law* 70(1976):722–62.

———. "The European Exchange Rate Arrangement Called the 'Snake.' " *University of Toledo Law Review* 10(1978):47–72.

Einzig, Paul. *Bankers, Statesmen and Economists.* London, 1935.

———. *A Dynamic Theory of Forward Exchange.* 2d ed. London, 1967.

———. *The World Economic Crisis 1929–1931.* 2d ed. London, 1932.

———. *World Finance 1935–1937.* New York, 1937.

Ellis, H. S., and L. A. Metzler, eds. *Readings in the Theory of International Trade.* Homewood, Ill., 1950.

Emminger, Otmar. *On the Way to a New International Monetary Order.* Washington, D.C., 1976.

Ethier, Wilfred, and A. I. Bloomfield. *Managing the Managed Float.* Princeton Essays in International Finance, no. 112. Princeton, 1975.

———. "The Reference Rate Proposal and Recent Experience." *Banca Nazionale del Lavoro Quarterly Review*, no. 26 (September 1978), pp. 211–32.

"The European Monetary System." *European Economy*, no. 3 (July 1979), pp. 63–111.

"The European Monetary System: Structure and Operation." *Monthly Report of the Deutsche Bundesbank* 31(March 1979):11–18.

"The European System of Narrower Exchange Rate Margins." *Monthly Report of the Deutsche Bundesbank* 28(January 1976):22–29.

Ezekiel, Hannan. "The Present System of Reserve Creation in the Fund." *IMF Staff Papers* 13(1966):398–418.

Feavearyear, Albert. *The Pound Sterling.* 2d ed. Oxford, 1963.

Federal Reserve Bank of Boston. *Managed Exchange-rate Flexibility: The Recent Experience.* Conference Series no. 20. Boston, 1978.

Feis, Herbert. "Keynes in Retrospect." *Foreign Affairs* 29(1950–51):564–77.

Field, Peter. "The IMF Now: De Larosière's troubled institution." *Euromoney* 10(October 1978):14–29.

Fleming, J. Marcus. "Dual Exchange Markets and Other Remedies for Disruptive Capital Flows." *IMF Staff Papers* 21(1974):1–27.

———. *Reflections on the International Monetary Reform.* Princeton Essays in International Finance, no. 107. Princeton, 1974.

Ford, A. G. *The Gold Standard 1880–1914: Britain and Argentina.* Oxford, 1962.

Fraser, H. F. *Great Britain and the Gold Standard.* London, 1933.

Fraser, Leon. "Reconstructing World Money." *Proceedings of the Academy of Political Science* 20(1944):371–74.

Frenkel, Jacob A. "A Monetary Approach to the Exchange Rate: Doctrinal Aspects and Empirical Evidence." *Scandinavian Journal of Economics* 78(1976):200–24.

Frenkel, Jacob A., and Harry G. Johnson, eds. *The Monetary Approach to the Balance of Payments.* Toronto, 1976.

Friedman, Milton. *Essays in Positive Economics.* Chicago, 1953.

———. "Money." In *Encyclopaedia Britannica*, 15th ed., Macropaedia, 12:349–56, Chicago, 1975.

———. "Real and Pseudo Gold Standards." *Journal of Law and Economics* 4(1961):66–79.

Friedman, Milton, and Robert V. Roosa. *The Balance of Payments: Free versus Fixed Exchange Rates.* Washington, D.C., 1967.

Friedman, Milton, and Anna J. Schwartz. *A Monetary History of the United States, 1867–1960.* Princeton, 1963.

Frydl, Edward J. "The Debate over Regulating the Eurocurrency Markets." *Federal Reserve Bank of New York Quarterly Review* 4(Winter 1979–80):11–19.

Galbraith, John Kenneth. *Money, Whence It Came, Where It Went.* Boston, 1975.

Gardner, Richard N. *Sterling-Dollar Diplomacy.* 2d ed. New York, 1969.

Ghiles, Francis. " 'Carter Bond' Issue Attracts DM 4.6bn." *Financial Times*, 25 January 1980.

Gilbert, Milton. *Quest for World Monetary Order: The Gold-Dollar System and Its Aftermath.* New York, 1980.

Gold, Joseph. See Joseph Gold: A Select Bibliography, p. 362, below.

Goodhart, C. A. E. *The Business of Banking, 1891–1914.* London, 1972.

Goreux, Louis M. *Compensatory Financing Facility.* IMF Pamphlet Series, no. 34. 1980.

Graham, Frank D., and Charles R. Whittlesey. *Golden Avalanche.* Princeton, 1939.

Grigg, P. J. *Prejudice and Judgment.* London, 1948.

Group of Thirty. *The Foreign Exchange Markets under Floating Rates.* New York, 1980.

———. *Towards a Less Unstable International Monetary System: Reserve Assets and a Substitution Account.* New York, 1980.

Grubel, Herbert T., ed. *World Monetary Reform: Plans and Issues.* Stanford, 1963.

Guillebaud, C. W. "Hawtrey, R. G." In *International Encyclopedia of the Social Sciences* 6:328–29. New York, 1968.

Guindey, Guillaume. *Mythes et réalités de la crise monétaire internationale.* Paris, 1973.

Guitián, Manuel. "Fund Conditionality and the International Adjustment Process: The Early Period, 1950–70." *Finance and Development* 17(December 1980):23–27.

Gupta, Dhruba. "The Operation of the Trust Fund." *Finance and Development* 15(September 1978):37–40.

Gutmann, Peter. "Assessing Country Risk." *National Westminster Bank Quarterly Review* (May 1980), pp. 58–68.

Haberler, Gottfried. *The World Economy, Money, and the Great Depression, 1919–1939.* Washington, D.C., 1976.

Habermeier, Walter. *Operations and Transactions in SDRs: The First Basic Period.* IMF Pamphlet Series, no. 17. 1973.

Hall, N. F. *The Exchange Equalisation Account.* London, 1935.

Harris, S. E. *Monetary Problems of the British Empire.* New York, 1931.

Harrod, R. F. *The Life of John Maynard Keynes.* New York, 1951.

———. *Reforming the World's Money.* London, 1965.

Hawtrey, R. G. "The Genoa Resolutions on Currency." *Economic Journal* 32(1922):290–304.

———. *The Gold Standard in Theory and Practice.* 5th ed. London, 1947.

Heaton, Herbert. *Economic History of Europe.* Rev. ed. New York, 1948.

Heininger, Patrick. "Liability of U.S. Banks for Deposits Placed in Their Foreign Branches." *Law and Policy in International Business* 11(1979):903–1034.

Heller, H. Robert. "Choosing an Exchange Rate System." *Finance and Development* 14(June 1977):23–27.

———. "International Reserves and World-Wide Inflation." *IMF Staff Papers* 23(1976):61–87.

Hepburn, A. Barton. *A History of Currency in the United States.* Rev. ed. New York, 1924.

Hill, Martin. *The Economic and Financial Organization of the League of Nations.* Washington, D.C., 1946.

Hirsch, Fred. *Money International.* Rev. ed. Harmondsworth, England, 1969.

Horsefield, J. Keith. "Proposals for Using Objective Indicators as a Guide to Exchange Rate Changes: A Historical Comment." *IMF Staff Papers* 20(1973):832–37.

Høst-Madsen, Poul. "Gold Outflows from the United States, 1958–63." *IMF Staff Papers* 11(1964):248–61.

Howson, Susan. *Sterling's Managed Float: The Operations of the Exchange Equalisation Account, 1932–39.* Princeton Studies in International Finance, no. 46. Princeton, 1980.

"The International Monetary Fund and Euro-liquidity." *International Currency Review* 10, no. 5 (1978):18–29.

Jack, D. T. *The Restoration of European Currencies.* London, 1927.

Jacobsson, Erin E. *A Life for Sound Money: Per Jacobsson, His Biography.* Oxford, 1979.

Jacquemont, André. *L'Émission des emprunts euro-obligatoires, pouvoir bancaire et souverainetés étatiques.* Paris, 1976.

Janssen, Albert E. *Les Conventions monétaires.* Paris, 1911.

Jastram, Roy W. *The Golden Constant: The English and American Experience, 1560–1976.* New York, 1977.

Johnson, Harry G. "The International Monetary Crisis of 1971." *Journal of Business* 46(1973):11–23.

———. "The International Monetary System and the Rule of Law." *Journal of Law and Economics* 15(1972):277–92.

———. "The Link That Chains." *Foreign Policy*, no. 8 (Fall 1972), pp. 113–20.

———. *Money, Balance-of-Payments Theory, and the International Monetary Problem.* Princeton Essays in International Finance, no. 124. Princeton, 1977.

———. "The Sterling Crisis of 1967 and the Gold Rush of 1968." *Nebraska Journal of Economics and Business* 7(Autumn 1968):3–17.

———. "World Inflation and the International Monetary System." *The Three Banks Review*, no. 107 (1975), pp. 3–22.

Jones, Edgar. "The Fund and the GATT." *Finance and Development* 9(September 1972):30–33.

Kafka, Alexandre. *The IMF: The Second Coming?* Princeton Essays in International Finance, no. 94. Princeton, 1972.

———. "The International Monetary System in Transition—Parts I and II." *Virginia Journal of International Law* 13(1972):135–57, 539–52.

Kahn, Richard. "SDRs and Aid." *Lloyds Bank Review*, no. 110 (October 1973), pp. 1–18.

Kemp, Donald S. "The U.S. Dollar in International Markets: Mid-1970 to Mid-1976." *Federal Reserve Bank of St. Louis Review* 58(August 1976):7–14.

Keynes, John Maynard. "The Balance of Payments of the United States." *Economic Journal* 56(1946):172–87.

———. *The Collected Writings of John Maynard Keynes.* Vol. 25: *Activities 1940–1944; Shaping the Post-War World: The Clearing Union;* vol. 26: *Activities 1941–1946; Shaping the Post-War World: Bretton Woods and Reparations.* Edited by Donald Moggridge. Royal Economic Society. London, 1980.

———. "The Committee on the Currency." *Economic Journal* 35(1925):299–304.

———. *The Economic Consequences of the Peace.* New York, 1920.

———. *Essays in Persuasion.* New York, 1932.

———. *The General Theory of Employment, Interest and Money.* New York, 1936.

———. *Indian Currency and Finance.* London, 1913.

———. "Reflections on the Sterling Exchange." *Lloyds Bank Limited Monthly Review* n.s. 3 (1932):143–60.

———. *A Treatise on Money.* 2 vols. New York, 1930.

Kindleberger, Charles P. *The World in Depression, 1929–1939.* Berkeley, 1973.

Kissinger, Henry. *White House Years.* Boston, 1979.

Krause, Lawrence B., and Walter S. Salant, eds. *European Monetary Unification and Its Meaning for the United States.* Washington, D.C., 1973.

Kuhn, Thomas S. *The Structure of Scientific Revolutions.* Chicago, 1962.

Laffer, Arthur B. *Reinstatement of the Dollar: The Blueprint.* Economic Study, A. B. Laffer Associates. Rolling Hills Estates, Cal., 29 February 1980.

Laughlin, J. Laurence. *The History of Bimetallism in the United States.* New York, 1886.

Leith-Ross, Frederick. *Money Talks: Fifty Years of International Finance.* London, 1968.

Lindert, Peter H. *Key Currencies and Gold, 1900–1913.* Princeton Studies in International Finance, no. 24. Princeton, 1969.

Lipson, Charles. "The International Organization of Third World Debt." Paper prepared for delivery at the 1980 American Political Science Association, Washington, D.C. Mimeo.

"The London Gold Market." *Bank of England Quarterly Bulletin* 4(1964):16–21.

Lowenfeld, Andreas F. *The International Monetary System.* Vol. 4 of *International Economic Law.* New York, 1977.

McCarthy, Ian. "Offshore Banking Centers: Benefits and Costs." *Finance and Development* 16(December 1979):45–48.

McKinnon, Ronald I. *The Eurocurrency Market.* Princeton Essays in International Finance, no. 125. Princeton, 1977.

Machlup, Fritz. "The Cloakroom Rule of International Reserves: Reserve Creation and Resources Transfer." *Quarterly Journal of Economics* 79(1965):337–55.

———. *International Payments, Debts, and Gold.* New York, 1964.

———. *Remaking the International Monetary System: The Rio Agreement and Beyond.* Baltimore, 1968.

Makinson, John. "Gold. V: Concealed Buffer for Central Banks." *Financial Times* (supplement on gold), 30 July 1980.

Marjolin, Robert. "The French Exchange Fund." *The Banker* 48(1938):25–32.

Marmorstein, Victoria E. "Responding to the Call for Order in International Finance: Cooperation between the International Monetary Fund and the Commercial Banks." *Virginia Journal of International Law* 18(1978):445–83.

Marsh, David. "An Autumn of Discontent." *Financial Times,* 5 August 1980.

———. "Gold Suppliers Get Wise to a Surge in Demand." *Financial Times,* 7 July 1980.

———. "The Move Away from the Dollar." *Financial Times,* 7 March 1979.

———. "OPEC Piles Up Sterling." *Financial Times,* 15 August 1980.

———. "U.S. Move on Euromarkets Stands Little Chance." *Financial Times,* 7 June 1979.

Martin, Michael G. "The Changing Gold Market, 1978–80." *Finance and Development* 17(December 1980):40–43.

Mason, Edward S., and Robert E. Asher. *The World Bank since Bretton Woods.* Washington, D.C., 1973.

Mayer, Helmut. *Credit and Liquidity Creation in the International Banking Sector.* BIS Economic Papers no. 1. 1979.

Mayer, Martin. *The Fate of the Dollar.* New York, 1980.

Meier, Gerald M. *Problems of a World Monetary Order.* New York, 1974.

Meiselman, David I., and Arthur B. Laffer, eds. *The Phenomenon of Worldwide Inflation.* Washington, D.C., 1975.

Mendelsohn, M. S. *Money on the Move.* New York, 1980.

Merillat, H. C. L., ed. *Legal Advisers and International Organizations.* Dobbs Ferry, N.Y., 1966.

Mertens, Jacques E. *La Naissance et le développement de l'Étalon-or, 1696–1922.* Louvain, 1944.

Meyer, Richard Hemmig. *Bankers' Diplomacy: Monetary Stabilization in the Twenties.* New York, 1970.

Mikesell, Raymond F. *The Economics of Foreign Aid.* Chicago, 1968.

———. *The Emerging Pattern of International Payments.* Princeton Essays in International Finance, no. 18. Princeton, 1954.

———. *Foreign Exchange in the Post-War World.* New York, 1954.

Mikesell, Raymond F., and Henry N. Goldstein. *Rules for a Floating-Rate Regime.* Princeton Essays in International Finance, no. 109. Princeton, 1975.

Mitchell, Wesley C. *Gold, Prices, and Wages under the Greenback Standard.* Berkeley, 1908.

———. *A History of the Greenbacks.* Chicago, 1903.

Moggridge, D. E. *British Monetary Policy, 1924–1931.* Cambridge, 1972.

———. "From War to Peace—How Much Overseas Assistance?" *The Banker* 122(1972):1163–68.

———. "From War to Peace—The Sterling Balances." *The Banker* 122(1972):1032–35.

———. "New Light on Post-War Plans." *The Banker* 122(1972):337–42.

———. *The Return to Gold, 1925.* Cambridge, 1969.

Montagnon, Peter. "The New, Improved SDR." *Financial Times,* 8 January 1981.

Moreau, Émile. *Souvenirs d'un gouverneur de la Banque de France: Histoire de la stabilisation du franc (1926–1928).* Paris, 1954.

Morgan, E. Victor. *Studies in British Financial Policy, 1914–25.* London, 1952.

Morgan, Theodore. *Introduction to Economics.* New York, 1950.

Morgenthau, Henry, Jr. "Bretton Woods and International Coöperation." *Foreign Affairs* 23(1945):182–94.

Mundell, R. A. "The International Monetary Fund." *Journal of World Trade Law,* 3(1969):455–97.

———. "The Monetary Consequences of Jacques Rueff: Review Article." *Journal of Business* 46(1973):384–95.

Mundell, R. A., and Alexander K. Swoboda. *Monetary Problems of the International Economy.* Chicago, 1969.

Mundell, Robert A., and Jacques J. Polak, eds. *The New International Monetary System.* New York, 1977.

Murphy, J. Carter. *The International Monetary System: Beyond the First Stage of Reform.* Washington, D.C., 1979.

Mussa, Michael. "The Exchange Rate, the Balance of Payments and Monetary and Fiscal Policy under a Regime of Controlled Floating." *Scandinavian Journal of Economics* 78(1976):229–48.

"A New Supervisory Approach to Foreign Lending." *Federal Reserve Bank of New York Quarterly Review* 3(Spring 1978):1–6.

Nielsen, Axel. "Monetary Unions." In *Encyclopaedia of the Social Sciences,* 10:595–601. New York, 1933.

Nossiter, Bernard D. "New Pragmatism at the I.M.F." *New York Times,* 5 February 1980.

Nussbaum, Arthur. *A History of the Dollar.* New York, 1957.

———. *Money in the Law.* Chicago, 1939.

Oppenheimer, P. M. *International Monetary Arrangements: The Limits to Planning.* Bank of England, Papers presented to the Panel of Academic Consultants, no. 8, July 1979. London, 1979.

Pardee, Scott E. "Treasury and Federal Reserve Foreign Exchange Operations." *Federal Reserve Bank of New York Quarterly Review* 5(Spring 1980):36–54.

———. "Treasury and Federal Reserve Foreign Exchange Operations: Interim Report." *Federal Reserve Bulletin,* 1980, pp. 953–55.

Paris, James Daniel. *Monetary Policies of the United States, 1932–1938.* New York, 1938.

Patterson, Gardner. *Discrimination in International Trade: The Policy Issues, 1945–1965.* Princeton, 1966.

Penrose, E. F. *Economic Planning for the Peace.* Princeton, 1953.

Pigou, A. C., ed. *Memorials of Alfred Marshall.* London, 1925.

Plumptre, A. F. W. *Three Decades of Decision: Canada and the World Monetary System, 1944–75.* Toronto, 1977.

Polak, Jacques J. "The EMF: External Relations." *Banca Nazionale del Lavoro Quarterly Review,* no. 134 (September 1980), pp. 359–72.

————. "The Fund after Jamaica." *Finance and Development* 13(June 1976):7–11.

————. "The SDR as a Basket of Currencies." *IMF Staff Papers* 26(1979):627–53.

————. *Some Reflections on the Nature of Special Drawing Rights.* IMF Pamphlet Series, no. 16. 1971.

————. *Thoughts on an International Monetary Fund Based Fully on the SDR.* IMF Pamphlet Series, no. 28. 1979.

————. *Valuation and Rate of Interest of the SDR.* IMF Pamphlet Series, no. 18. 1974.

Polk, Judd. *Sterling: Its Meaning in World Finance.* New York, 1956.

Pressnell, L. S. "The End of the Sterling Area." *The Three Banks Review,* no. 121 (March 1979), pp. 3–20.

————, ed. *Studies in the Industrial Revolution, Presented to T. S. Ashton . . . .* London, 1960.

Rees, David. *Harry Dexter White.* New York, 1973.

Res, Z., and G. Zis. "The Basle Agreement: An Exercise in Monetary Mismanagement." *The Banker* 125(1975):1268–71.

"Reserve Diversification and the IMF Substitution Account." *World Financial Markets,* September 1979, pp. 5–14.

Riddell, Peter. "Bright Spot in Community Scene: European Monetary System." *Financial Times* (World Banking Survey III), 19 May 1980.

Robbins, Lionel. *Autobiography of an Economist.* London, 1971.

Robertson, D. H. "The Post-War Monetary Plans." *Economic Journal* 53(1943):352–60.

Robinson, Joan. "The International Currency Proposals." *Economic Journal* 53(1943):161–75.

Roessler, Frieder. "The Gatt Declaration on Trade Measures Taken for Balance-of-Payments Purposes: A Commentary." *Case Western Reserve Journal of International Law* 12(1980):383–403.

Royal Institute of International Affairs. *Survey of International Affairs 1961.* Edited by D.C. Watt. London, 1965.

Sacchetti, Ugo. "The SDR: Ten Years of Experience." *Banca Nazionale del Lavoro Quarterly Review,* no. 131 (December 1979), pp. 391–405.

Salop, Joanne. "Dollar Intervention within the Snake." *IMF Staff Papers* 24(1977):64–76.

Samuelson, Paul. *Economics.* 8th ed. New York, 1970.

Sayers, R. S. *Bank of England Operations, 1890–1914.* London, 1936.

————. *The Bank of England, 1891–1944.* 3 vols. Cambridge, 1976.

————. *Financial Policy, 1939–1945.* History of the Second World War. United Kingdom Civil Series. London, 1956.

————. *Modern Banking.* Corrected ed. Oxford, 1939.

Schloss, Henry H. *The Bank for International Settlements.* Amsterdam, 1958.

Schweitzer, Pierre-Paul. "Political Aspects of Managing the International Monetary System." *International Affairs* 52(1976):208–18.

Shapiro, Harvey D. "The U.S.: Taking the Lead." *Institutional Investor*, July 1979, pp. 51–52.

Shultz, George P., and Kenneth W. Dam. *Economic Policy Beyond the Headlines*. Stanford, 1977; New York, 1978.

Sichel, Werner, ed. *Economic Advice and Executive Policy*. New York, 1978.

Silard, Stephen A. "Carriage of the SDR by Sea: The Unit of Account of the Hamburg Rules." *Journal of Maritime Law and Commerce* 10(1978):13–38.

———. "The General Standard of International Value in Public International Law." American Society of International Law, *Proceedings of the 73rd Annual Meeting*, pp. 15–24. Washington, D.C., 1979.

———. "Money and Foreign Exchange." In *International Encyclopedia of Comparative Law*, vol. 17, *State and Economy*, chap. 20. The Hague, 1975.

Snowden, Philip. *An Autobiography*. 2 vols. London, 1934.

Sobol, Dorothy Meadow. "A Substitution Account: Precedents and Issues." *Federal Reserve Bank of New York Quarterly Review* 4(Summer 1979):40–48.

Solomon, Robert. *The International Monetary System, 1945–1976*. New York, 1977.

"Some Observations on Floating." *World Financial Markets*, October 1973, pp. 4–9.

Sterling, Jay. "How Big is the International Lending Market?" *The Banker* 130(January 1980):77–87.

"The Sterling Pool." *Lloyds Bank Limited Monthly Review*, n.s. 3 (1932):64–67.

Strange, Susan. *International Monetary Relations*. Vol. 2 of *International Economic Relations of the Western World 1959–1971*, edited by Andrew Shonfield. London, 1976.

———. *Sterling and British Policy*. London, 1971.

Studenski, Paul, and Herman E. Krooss. *Financial History of the United States*. New York, 1952.

Sturc, Ernest. "The Trust Fund." *Finance and Development* 13(December 1976):30–31.

Tether, C. Gordon. "Sth. African Gold—Fund's Embarrassing Position." *Financial Times*, 18 June 1968.

Thirlwall, A. P., ed. *Keynes and International Monetary Relations*. London, 1976.

Tonge, David. "IMF Debating How to Borrow." *Financial Times*, 26 November 1980.

Tosini, Paula A. *Leaning against the Wind: A Standard for Managed Floating*. Princeton Essays in International Finance, no. 126. Princeton, 1977.

"Treasury and Federal Reserve Foreign Exchange Operations" (March 1961–August 1962). *Federal Reserve Bulletin*, 1962, pp. 1138–53.

"Treasury and Federal Reserve Foreign Exchange Operations" (February–July 1978). *Federal Reserve Bank of New York Quarterly Review* 3(Autumn 1978):47–64.

Treverton, Gregory F. *The Dollar Drain and American Forces in Germany*. Athens, Ohio, 1978.

Trezise, Philip H., ed. *The European Monetary System: Its Promise and Prospects*. Washington, D.C., 1979.

Triffin, Robert, ed. *EMS: The Emerging European Monetary System*. Reprinted from the *Bulletin of the National Bank of Belgium*. Louvain-la-neuve, 1979.

———. *Europe and the Money Muddle: From Bilateralism to Near-Convertibility, 1947–1956*. New Haven, 1957.

———. "The Future of the International Monetary System." *Banca Nazionale del Lavoro Quarterly Review*, no. 132 (March 1980), pp. 29–55.

———. *Gold and the Dollar Crisis*. Rev. ed. New Haven, 1961.

———. *Gold and the Dollar Crisis: Yesterday and Tomorrow.* Princeton Essays in International Finance, no. 132. Princeton, 1978.

Tsiang, S. C. "Fluctuating Exchange Rates in Countries with Relatively Stable Economies." *IMF Staff Papers* 7(1959):244–73.

"The U.K. Exchange Control: A Short History." *Bank of England Quarterly Bulletin* 7(1967):245–60.

Underwood, Trevor G. "Analysis of Proposals for Using Objective Indicators as a Guide to Exchange Rate Changes." *IMF Staff Papers* 20(1973):100–117.

Van Dormael, Armand. *Bretton Woods: Birth of a Monetary System.* London, 1978.

Vaubel, Roland. *Choice in European Monetary Union.* Institute of Economic Affairs Occasional Paper 55. London, 1979.

———. "Why the EMS May Have To Be Dismantled." *Euromoney*, January 1980, pp. 78–86.

Viner, Jacob. "Two Plans for International Monetary Stabilization." *Yale Review* 33(1943–44):77–107.

Volcker, Paul A. "The Political Economy of the Dollar." *Federal Reserve Bank of New York Quarterly Review* 3(Winter 1978–79):1–12.

Von Mises, Ludwig. "The Foreign Exchange Policy of the Austro-Hungarian Bank." *Economic Journal* 19(1909):201–11.

Waight, Leonard. *The History and Mechanism of the Exchange Equalisation Account.* Cambridge, 1939.

Wallich, Henry C. "International Monetary Evolution." Remarks at Columbia University, New York, 20 February 1980. Mimeo.

———. "Why the Euromarket Needs Restraint." *Columbia Journal of World Business* 14(Fall 1979):17–24.

———. "The World Monetary System after Postponement of the Substitution Account." Address to the HWWA-Institut für Wirtschaftsforschung, Hamburg, Germany, 12 June 1980. Mimeo.

Wallich, Henry C., C. J. Morse, and I. G. Patel. *The Monetary Crisis of 1971–The Lessons To Be Learned.* Per Jacobsson Foundation. Washington, D.C., 1972.

Wheeler-Bennett, John W., ed. *Documents on International Affairs, 1933.* London, 1934.

Whitaker, J. K., and Maxwell W. Hudgins. "The Floating Pound Sterling of the Nineteen Thirties: An Econometric Study." *Southern Economic Journal* 43(1977):1478–85.

White, Harry D. *The French International Accounts, 1880–1913.* Harvard Economic Studies, 40. Cambridge, Mass., 1933.

———. "The Monetary Fund: Some Criticisms Examined." *Foreign Affairs* 23(1945):195–210.

White, Horace. *Money and Banking, Illustrated by American History.* 5th ed. Boston [1914].

Whitman, Marina v. N. *Reflections of Interdependence.* Pittsburgh, 1979.

Whittlesey, C. R., and J. S. G. Wilson, eds. *Essays in Money and Banking in Honour of R. S. Sayers.* Oxford, 1968.

Willett, Thomas D. *International Liquidity Issues.* Washington, D.C., 1980.

Williams, David. "The Gold Markets, 1968–72." *Finance and Development* 9(December 1972):9–16.

————. "Increasing the Resources of the Fund: Borrowing." *Finance and Development* 13(September 1976):19–23.

————. "London and the 1931 Financial Crisis." *Economic History Review*, n.s. 15 (1963):513–28.

Williams, John H. *Postwar Monetary Plans and Other Essays.* 3d ed. New York, 1947.

Williamson, John. *The Failure of World Monetary Reform, 1971–74.* New York, 1977.

————. "Surveys in Applied Economics: International Liquidity." *Economic Journal* 83(1973):685–746.

Willis, Henry Parker. *A History of the Latin Monetary Union: A Study of International Monetary Action.* Chicago, 1901.

Winch, Donald. *Economics and Policy: A Historical Study.* New York, 1969.

Witteveen, H. Johannes. "The Emerging International Monetary System." *IMF Survey* 5(1976):177–82.

Wittich, Günter, and Masaki Shiratori. "The Snake in the Tunnel." *Finance and Development* 10(June 1973):9–13, 38.

Wolfe, Martin. *The French Franc between the Wars, 1919–1939.* New York, 1951.

Wright, E. Peter. "World Bank Lending for Structural Adjustment." *Finance and Development* 17(September 1980):20–23.

Yeager, Leland B. *International Monetary Relations: Theory, History, and Policy.* 2d ed. New York, 1976.

Young, John H. "Surveillance over Exchange Rate Policies." *Finance and Development* 14(September 1977):17–19.

Young, John Parke. "Developing Plans for an International Monetary Fund and a World Bank." *Department of State Bulletin* 23(1950):778–90.

JOSEPH GOLD:
A SELECT BIBLIOGRAPHY

The following bibliography lists only the works of Sir Joseph Gold cited in the text of this book.

"A Comparison of Special Drawing Rights and Gold as Reserve Assets." *Law and Policy in International Business* 2(1970):326–51.
Conditionality. IMF Pamphlet Series, no. 31. 1979.
"Constitutional Development and Change." Part 5 of J. Keith Horsefield and others, *The International Monetary Fund, 1945–1965*, vol. 2. Washington, D.C., 1969.
"Exchange Arrangements and International Law in an Age of Floating Currencies." American Society of International Law, *Proceedings of the 73rd Annual Meeting*, pp. 1–15. Washington, D.C., 1979.
Financial Assistance by the International Monetary Fund: Law and Practice. IMF Pamphlet Series, no. 27. 1979.
Floating Currencies, Gold, and SDRs: Some Recent Legal Developments. IMF Pamphlet Series, no. 19. 1976.
Floating Currencies, SDRs, and Gold: Further Legal Developments. IMF Pamphlet Series, no. 22. 1977.
Fourth Survey. See *SDRs, Currencies, and Gold.*
"The Fund Agreement in the Courts—XIII." *IMF Staff Papers* 25(1978):343–67.
The Fund's Concepts of Convertibility. IMF Pamphlet Series, no. 14. 1971.
"The Fund's Interim Committee—An Assessment." *Finance and Development* 16(September 1979):32–35.
Interpretation by the Fund. IMF Pamphlet Series, no. 11. 1968.
Legal and Institutional Aspects of the International Monetary System: Selected Essays. Edited by Jane B. Evensen and Jai Keun Oh. Washington, D.C., 1979.

The Legal Character of the Fund's Stand-by Arrangements and Why It Matters. IMF Pamphlet Series, no. 35. 1980.

Maintenance of the Gold Value of the Fund's Assets. IMF Pamphlet Series, no. 6. 1965.

Membership and Nonmembership in the International Monetary Fund. Washington, D.C., 1974.

"New Directions in the Financial Activities of the International Monetary Fund." *International Lawyer* 14(1980):449–70.

The Reform of the Fund. IMF Pamphlet Series, no. 12. 1969.

"A Report on Certain Recent Legal Developments in the International Monetary Fund." *Vanderbilt Journal of Transnational Law* 9(1976):223–45.

The Rule of Law in the International Monetary Fund. IMF Pamphlet Series, no. 32. 1980.

SDRs, Currencies, and Gold: Fourth Survey of New Legal Developments. IMF Pamphlet Series, no. 33. 1980.

SDRs, Gold, and Currencies: Third Survey of New Legal Developments. IMF Pamphlet Series, no. 26. 1979.

SDRs: Role of Language. See *Special Drawing Rights.*

The Second Amendment of the Fund's Articles of Agreement. IMF Pamphlet Series, no. 25. 1978. Revised version of "The Second Amendment of the Fund's Articles of Agreement: A General View," I and II, and "Some First Effects of the Second Amendment," *Finance and Development* 15(March 1978):10–13; (June 1978):15–18; (September 1978):24–29.

A Second Report on some Recent Legal Developments in the International Monetary Fund. World Association of Lawyers. Washington, D.C., 1977.

Selected Essays. See *Legal and Institutional Aspects.*

Special Drawing Rights. Character and Use. IMF Pamphlet Series, no. 13. 2d ed. 1970.

Special Drawing Rights: The Role of Language. IMF Pamphlet Series, no. 15. 1971.

The Stand-By Arrangements of the International Monetary Fund. Washington, D.C., 1970.

"The Structure of the Fund." *Finance and Development* 16(June 1979):11–15.

"Substitution in the International Monetary System." *Case Western Reserve Journal of International Law* 12(1980):265–326.

"Symmetry as a Legal Objective of the International Monetary System." *New York University Journal of International Law and Politics* 12(1980):423–77.

A Third Report on Some Recent Legal Developments in the International Monetary Fund. World Association of Lawyers. Washington, D.C., 1978.

Third Survey. See *SDRs, Gold, and Currencies.*

"Trust Funds in International Law: The Contribution of the International Monetary Fund to a Code of Principles." *American Journal of International Law* 72(1978):856–66.

"Unauthorized Changes of Par Value and Fluctuating Exchange Rates in the Bretton Woods System." *American Journal of International Law* 65(1971):113–28.

Use, Conversion, and Exchange of Currency under the Second Amendment of the Fund's Articles. IMF Pamphlet Series, no. 23. 1978.

Voting and Decisions in the International Monetary Fund. Washington, D.C., 1972.

INDEX

Pardee, Scott E., 318n
Paris, 36
Paris, James Daniel, 49n
parity, 11–12, 93, 158, 214–15; cross
parity, 240; "sliding parities," 214
Parliament. *See* Great Britain
Parry, Clive, 21n
par value(s): 11, 93, 191, 267–68, 269;
changes, 176–77; common
denominator, 268n; and dollar, 86,
191–92; and gold, 86; obligations,
215; regime, 92; return to, 335; and
SDR valuation, 201–2; system, 128,
196, 243
Par Value Modification Act, 1972
(U.S.), 191n
Patel, I. G., 222n
Patterson, Gardner, 181n
Peel's Act of 1819 (U.K.), 24
pegged rate system, 191; pegging in
multicurrency intervention system,
241–42
Penrose, E. F., 75n, 78n, 83–84nn
performance clauses, criteria, 124–26
Peru, 129, 285n, 300, 300n
Pigou, A. C., 20n
Plumptre, H. F. W., 73n, 112n, 129n,
178n
Poincaré, Raymond, 45
Polak, Jacques, xviii, 152n, 154n, 160,
161n, 164n, 168n, 198n, 202–6nn,
210n, 256n, 262n, 288n, 310–11,
327n, 334–35nn
Poland, 48
Polk, Judd, 181n
Pompidou, Georges, 190
Portugal: escudo, 132
Prachowny, M. F. J., 72n
premium sales (of gold), 135–37
Presley, John R., 171n
Pressnell, L. S., 44n, 184
pressures: 232–35; activation of, 233;
graduated, 227, 232–33; and the
IMF, 234–35; trade restrictions, 233
principle of uniformity, 86–87, 95, 127
"proportion." *See* Bank of England
Prout, Christopher, 127n

quotas: 101–2; and borrowing, 303–5;
and compensatory financing facility,
128; and credit tranche policies, 121;
enlargements of, 168; and gold

tranche policy, 118–19; and IMF
access, 303–5; in Keynes and White
plans, 83, 83n; increases, 146–48,
251, 280; and subscription formula,
102–3

Rambouillet declaration, 197
Rasminsky, Louis, 76n, 88n
reconstitution, 163–64
redemption of U.S. notes, 28n
Rees, David, 74n
Rees-Mogg, William, xix
reform: and amendment, 268n, 289–90;
and Bretton Woods system, 211–13;
and evolution, 2–3, 221; in
international monetary system,
215–16, 341–43; initiatives, 221–22;
negotiations, 196, 213, 216;
negotiations in C-20, 211–52 *passim;*
reformed system, 235–36, 254;
studies, before C-20, 213–16
regionalism, 328
Reichsbank. *See* Germany
remuneration, 160n, 205n, 281n
repurchase: period, 108, 304;
requirements, 107–8
Res, Z., 185n
reserve assets, 9–13, 64–65, 269–81
reserve centers, 64–65, 68
reserve currency, 9, 64–66, 314–20;
dollar as, 185–87; multiple reserve
currency system, 9, 316–20; reserve
currency mechanism, 141; sterling as,
178–85
reserve currency countries, 178–79
reserve holdings: composition of, and
asset settlement, 237; and foreign
exchange, 56–57, 229
reserve indicators, 222–29; basic
balance indicator, 230; reserve
indicator proposal, 236
reserves, 9; calculation of, 229–31;
composition of, 144–45; conditional,
143; creation, and SDR link, 249;
excess, 232–34; in Euromarket, 326;
measurement of, 229–31
reserve tranche, 284, 312
Reuss, Henry S., 263n, 274n
Riddell, Peter, 335–36nn
Rieke, Wolfgang, 330n
Rigaux, François, 260n
Robbins, Lord, 76–78nn